Practice-Oriented Research in Psychotherapy

The wide gap between science and practice in psychotherapy is due in part to the one-way direction that has mostly defined the connection between researchers and clinicians, with researchers generating empirical knowledge with the hope that practitioners will implement it in their working environments. This traditional approach has not been optimal in addressing the day-to-day concerns of clinicians or in providing easily generalizable practice guidelines in clinical routines.

This book offers an alternative approach to psychotherapy research, based on a partnership between clinicians and researchers in different aspects of the decision, design, implementation, and dissemination of studies conducted in day-to-day practice. More specifically, it describes how to conduct practice-oriented research (POR) by presenting studies and lessons learned (in terms of obstacles faced, strategies used to overcome problems, benefits earned, and general recommendations) by eleven groups who have been involved in POR in different settings around the world. This book provides tools to help clinicians be active participants in conducting clinically relevant studies and set the agenda for future research. It seeks to foster collaboration between researchers and practitioners, generating knowledge that can improve our understanding of the process of change and the impact of psychotherapy. This book was originally published as a special issue of *Psychotherapy Research*.

Louis G. Castonguay is Professor of Psychology at Penn State University, State College, PA, USA. His work focuses on the process, outcome, and training of psychotherapy, as well as on the development of practice-research networks. He has co-edited seven books on psychotherapy integration, psychotherapy research and practice, principles of therapeutic change, insight and corrective experience in psychotherapy, and psychopathology.

J. Christopher Muran is Associate Dean and Professor in the Derner Institute, Adelphi University, Garden City, NY, USA. He is also the Director of the Psychotherapy Research Program at Mount Sinai Beth Israel, a New York City hospital. His research has concentrated on alliance ruptures and resolution processes, and has resulted in seven book collaborations, including *Negotiating the Therapeutic Alliance* (2000), *Self-Relations in the Psychotherapy Process* (2001), *Dialogues on Difference* (2007), and *The Therapeutic Alliance* (2010).

Practice-Oriented Research in Psychotherapy

Building partnerships between clinicians and researchers

Edited by
Louis G. Castonguay and J. Christopher Muran

LONDON AND NEW YORK

First published 2016 by Routledge

2 Park Square, Milton Park, Abingdon, Oxfordshire OX14 4RN
711 Third Avenue, New York, NY 10017

Routledge is an imprint of the Taylor & Francis Group, an informa business

First issued in paperback 2017

British Library Cataloguing in Publication Data
A catalogue record for this book is available from the British Library

ISBN 13: 978-1-138-18574-6 (hbk)
ISBN 13: 978-1-138-50243-7 (pbk)

Typeset in Plantin
by RefineCatch Limited, Bungay, Suffolk

Publisher's Note
The publisher accepts responsibility for any inconsistencies that may have
arisen during the conversion of this book from journal articles to book chapters,
namely the possible inclusion of journal terminology.

Disclaimer
Every effort has been made to contact copyright holders for their permission to
reprint material in this book. The publishers would be grateful to hear from any
copyright holder who is not here acknowledged and will undertake to rectify
any errors or omissions in future editions of this book.

Contents

CONTENTS

Citation Information

The chapters in this book were originally published in *Psychotherapy Research*, volume 25, issue 1 (January 2015). When citing this material, please use the original page numbering for each article, as follows:

Introduction
Fostering collaboration between researchers and clinicians through building practice-oriented research: An introduction
Louis G. Castonguay and J. Christopher Muran
Psychotherapy Research, volume 25, issue 1 (January 2015) pp. 1–5

Chapter 1
Implementing routine outcome monitoring in clinical practice: Benefits, challenges, and solutions
James F. Boswell, David R. Kraus, Scott D. Miller, and Michael J. Lambert
Psychotherapy Research, volume 25, issue 1 (January 2015) pp. 6–19

Chapter 2
Developing practice-based evidence: Benefits, challenges, and tensions
Rolf Holmqvist, Björn Philips, and Michael Barkham
Psychotherapy Research, volume 25, issue 1 (January 2015) pp. 20–31

Chapter 3
Benefits and challenges in practice-oriented psychotherapy research in Germany: The TK and the QS-PSY-BAY projects of quality assurance in outpatient psychotherapy
Bernhard Michael Strauss, Wolfgang Lutz, Andres Steffanowski, Werner W. Wittmann, Jan R. Boehnke, Julian Rubel, Carl E. Scheidt, Franz Caspar, Heiner Vogel, Uwe Altmann, Rolf Steyer, Anna Zimmermann, Ellen Bruckmayer, Friedrich von Heymann, Dietmar Kramer, and Helmut Kirchmann
Psychotherapy Research, volume 25, issue 1 (January 2015) pp. 32–51

Chapter 4
Practice research network in a psychology training clinic: Building an infrastructure to foster early attachment to the scientific-practitioner model
Louis G. Castonguay, Aaron L. Pincus, and Andrew A. McAleavey
Psychotherapy Research, volume 25, issue 1 (January 2015) pp. 52–66

Chapter 5
Practice-oriented research: What it takes to do collaborative research in private practice
Kelly Koerner and Louis G. Castonguay
Psychotherapy Research, volume 25, issue 1 (January 2015) pp. 67–83

Chapter 6
Bridging the gap between research and practice in a clinical and training network: Aigle's Program
Héctor Fernández-Alvarez, Beatriz Gómez, and Fernando García
Psychotherapy Research, volume 25, issue 1 (January 2015) pp. 84–94

For any permission-related enquiries please visit:
http://www.tandfonline.com/page/help/permissions

Notes on Contributors

Robert W. Adelman is a Doctor of Psychology at Sundown Ranch, TX, USA.

Uwe Altmann is a Doctor of Psychology at the Institute of Psychosocial Medicine and Psychotherapy, University Hospital of Jena, Germany.

Jacques P. Barber is Dean and Professor of Psychology at the Derner Institute of Advanced Psychological Studies, Adelphi University, Garden City, NY, USA.

Michael Barkham is a Professor of Psychology at the University of Sheffield, UK.

Jan R. Boehnke is a Doctor of Psychology at the University of Trier, Germany.

James F. Boswell is an Assistant Professor of Psychology at the University at Albany, State University of New York, Albany, NY, USA

Lauren Brookman-Frazee is an Associate Professor of Psychiatry and the Associate Director of the Child and Adolescent Services Research Center at the University of California, San Diego, CA, USA.

Ellen Bruckmayer is a psychotherapist in private practice and member of the Initiating Group, QS-PSY-BAY project, Munich, Germany.

Franz Caspar is a Professor of Psychology at the University of Bern, Switzerland.

Louis G. Castonguay is a Professor of Psychology at Penn State University, University Park, PA, USA.

Lisa Countis is a research associate at the American Psychiatric Institute for Research and Education, Arlington, VA, USA.

Johnathan H. Duff is a graduate student of Counseling Psychology and a graduate assistant in the Department of Public Health Sciences at the University of Miami, FL, USA.

Farifteh F. Duffy is a Doctor of Philosophy and the Director of Quality of Care Research at the American Psychiatric Institute for Research and Education, Arlington, VA, USA.

Héctor Fernández-Alvarez is a Doctor of Psychology at the Aiglé Foundation, Buenos Aires, Argentina.

Fernando García is a Doctor of Psychology at the Aiglé Foundation, Buenos Aires, Argentina.

Ann F. Garland is Professor and Chair in Counseling & Marital and Family Therapy at the University of San Diego, CA, USA.

Beatriz Gómez is a Doctor of Psychology at the Aiglé Foundation, Buenos Aires, Argentina.

Jeffrey A. Hayes is a Professor of Psychology and Education at Penn State University, University Park, PA, USA.

C. Hendricks Brown is Professor of Psychiatry and Behavioral Sciences at Northwestern University, Chicago, IL, USA.

Rolf Holmqvist is a Professor of Psychology at Linkoping University, Linkoping, Sweden.

Helmut Kirchmann is a Doctor of Psychology at the Institute of Psychosocial Medicine and Psychotherapy, University Hospital Jena, Germany.

Kelly Koerner is a Doctor of Psychology and CEO of the Evidence-Based Practice Institute, Seattle, WA, USA.

Dietmar Kramer is a member of the Association of Statutory Health Insurance Physicians Bavaria, Munich, Germany.

David R. Kraus is President and Chief Scientific Officer at Outcome Referrals Inc, Framingham, MA, USA.

Michael J. Lambert is a Professor of Psychology at Brigham Young University, Provo, UT, USA.

Allison J. Lockard is a Doctoral Intern in Professional Psychology at Penn State University Center for Counseling and Psychological Services, University Park, PA, USA.

Benjamin D. Locke is Associate Director, Clinical Services, at Penn State University Center for Counseling and Psychological Services, University Park, PA, USA.

Wolfgang Lutz is a Professor of Psychology and Head of Clinical Psychology and Psychotherapy at the University of Trier, Germany. He is also editor-in-chief of *Psychotherapy Research*.

Andrew A. McAleavey is a Doctor of Psychology and Postdoctoral Associate, Department of Psychology in Psychiatry, at Weill Cornell Medical College, New York, NY, USA.

Scott D. Miller is the founder of the International Institute for Clinical Excellence, Chicago, IL, USA.

Eve K. Mościcki holds a Doctor of Science Degree and is the Director of the American Psychiatric Institute for Research and Education Practice Research Network, Arlington, VA, USA.

Joan A. Muir is a Doctor of Psychology and Associate Director of the Brief Strategic Family Therapy Institute at the University of Miami Miller School of Medicine, Miami, FL, USA.

J. Christopher Muran is a Professor of Psychology and Associate Dean at Adelphi University, Garden City, NY, USA.

William E. Narrow is Associate Director of the Division of Research at the American Psychiatric Institute for Research and Education, Arlington, VA, USA.

Björn Philips is an Associate Professor of Psychology at Linkoping University, Linkoping, Sweden.

Aaron L. Pincus is a Professor of Psychology at Pennsylvania State University, University Park, PA, USA.

Darrel A. Regier is a Psychiatrist and Executive Director of the American Psychiatric Institute for Research and Education, Arlington, VA, USA.

Julian Rubel is a graduate student of Psychology at the University of Trier, Germany.

Carl E. Scheidt is a Professor of Psychosomatic Medicine at the University Hospital, Freiburg, Germany.

Seth J. Schwartz is a Doctor of Psychology and Professor of Public Health Sciences at the University of Miami Miller School of Medicine, Miami, FL, USA.

Andres Steffanowski is a Professor of Psychology at SRH Hochschule Heidelberg, Heidelberg, Germany.

Rolf Steyer is a Professor of Psychology at the University of Jena, Germany.

Bernhard Michael Strauss is a Professor of Psychology at the Institute of Psychosocial Medicine and Psychotherapy, University Hospital of Jena, Germany.

José Szapocznik is a Doctor of Psychology, Professor & Chair of the Department of Public Health Sciences, and Director of the Brief Strategic Family Therapy Institute at the University of Miami Miller School of Medicine, Miami, FL, USA.

Heiner Vogel is a Doctor of Psychology at the University of Würzburg, Germany.

Friedrich von Heymann is a member of the Initiating Group, QS-PSY-BAY project, Munich, Germany.

Joshua E. Wilk is a Doctor of Psychology at the Walter Reed Army Institute of Research, Silver Spring, MD, USA.

Werner W. Wittmann is a Professor of Psychology at the Otto-Selz-Institute for Applied Psychology, Mannheim, Germany.

Joyce C. West is a Doctor of Philosophy at the Johns Hopkins University Bloomberg School of Public Health, Department of Mental Health (adjunct), and the Policy Research Director at the American Psychiatric Institute for Research and Education, Arlington, VA, USA.

Henry Xiao is a graduate student of Psychology at Penn State University, University Park, PA, USA.

Soo Jeong Youn is a graduate student of Psychology at Stanford University Medical Center, Department of Psychiatry, Stanford, CA, USA.

Sanno E. Zack is a Doctor of Psychology at Stanford University Medical Center, Department of Psychiatry, Stanford, CA, USA.

Anna Zimmermann is a doctoral student of Psychology at the Institute of Psychosocial Medicine and Psychotherapy, University Hospital Jena, Germany.

Fostering collaboration between researchers and clinicians through building practice-oriented research: An introduction

LOUIS G. CASTONGUAY[1] & J. CHRISTOPHER MURAN[2]

[1]Department of Psychology, Penn State University, University Park, PA, USA & [2]Derner Institute of Advanced Psychological Studies, Adelphi University, Garden City, NY, USA

Abstract
This paper is an introduction to a special series that attempts to foster collaboration between clinicians and researchers by presenting the experiences of 11 groups of contributors who have conducted practice-oriented research (POR) in various countries and naturalistic settings. Each of these groups was asked to describe the context in which their collaborative initiatives took place, as well as some of the studies conducted, obstacles faced, strategies employed to address these challenges, and benefits earned. Authors were also invited to provide general recommendations to facilitate future POR. In order to integrate the lessons learned so far, as well as to consolidate suggestions for future collaboration of clinicians, researchers, and other stakeholders in the field of mental health, the series ends with a conclusion paper that identifies convergences and particular characteristics that cut across the partnerships featured.

It is well known that the connection between the science and practice of psychotherapy is a tenuous one, at best. Clinicians are not substantially or primarily guided by empirical findings in their clinical practice (Morrow-Bradley & Elliott, 1986; Safran, Abreu, Ogilvie, & DeMaria, 2011; Stewart & Chambless, 2007). At the same time, they increasingly face pressure to implement "evidence-based practice." Not surprisingly, research is viewed by many of them as being both irrelevant and alien to their work (Castonguay, Locke, and Hayes, 2011). Yet, many clinicians have chosen to go into mental health graduate programs (e.g., clinical or counseling psychology) in part because they were interested in doing research that could contribute to a better understanding, if not an improvement of psychosocial treatments. Sometime during or after graduate school, the interest in and/or opportunity to conduct research has, for many of them, all but faded away.

It has been argued that one way for clinicians to reconnect with their early interest and training in scientific investigations is by establishing an active collaboration with researchers in conducting clinically relevant research (Borkovec, Echemendia, Ragusea, & Ruiz, 2001). Fortunately, different forms of partnerships have now emerged allowing clinicians to be involved, in various degrees, in the design and implementation of research within their own clinical routine. This type of research, called "practice-oriented research" (POR), can be viewed as complementary to the more traditional psychotherapy studies, which are frequently conducted in controlled settings and primarily guided by the interests and expertise of academicians. As recently reviewed, POR has led to a wide variety of empirical investigations addressing numerous aspects of the delivery, process, and impact of psychotherapy (Castonguay, Barkham, Lutz, & McAleavey, 2013). It is also clear, however, that the number of practice-oriented studies pales in comparison with the more traditional, or what could be referred to as "evidence-based" investigations. In order to provide a broad and robust empirical base of knowledge, both types of research should be encouraged and recognized by trainers, practitioners, researchers, and policy-makers (Barkham & Margison, 2007; Barkham, Stiles, Lambert, & Mellon-Clark, 2010).

The goal of this special issue in *Psychotherapy Research* is to help foster POR by presenting lessons learned from existing clinicians and researchers partnerships. While the aforementioned review describes what has been done so far, the aim of this series of papers is to offer guidelines about what to do next and, more importantly, how to develop and optimize future collaborations between researchers and clinicians in conducting empirical investigations in clinical practice. To achieve this aim, we invited clinicians and/or researchers who have conducted and published POR in a diversity of naturalistic settings, and asked them to write a paper addressing the following points:

- The context or goals of their research program in which they have developed a clinician–researcher partnership;
- A brief description of some of the studies conducted within this research program;
- The obstacles, challenges, difficulties, frustrations encountered in developing and implementing these studies;
- The strategies, successful and not, that they have come up with to deal with challenges and obstacles faced;
- The benefits (for researchers, clinicians, clients, administrators, the field of mental health, and society) that came along with the partnership they have built and the studies that emerged from it; and
- Their recommendations for future studies involving collaboration between clinicians and researchers.

In addition to the present introduction, the series includes 11 main papers and a conclusion. The first paper addresses what is clearly a foundational issue in the conduct and use of research in practice: the implementation of outcome monitoring within routine clinical care. Integrating empirical findings from three distinct instruments, Boswell, Kraus, Miller, and Lambert (in press), highlight the difficulties and advantages of collecting data on change, as well as on strategies (i.e., giving feedback about client's progress and providing clinical tools to therapists) to reduce deterioration in psychotherapy. In doing so, the authors directly address "elephants in the room"—factors that have been mostly ignored but that have interfered with the collection and use of research findings in clinical practice. Interestingly, the authors also draw from non-psychotherapy literatures to derive innovative recommendations for the implementation of outcome monitoring. Also based on the use of outcome measurements in day-to-day practice, the next two papers focus on research programs that have been conducted within national health services. The first of these (Holmqvist, Philips, & Barkham, in press) has emerged from a wide body of practice-oriented studies conducted in Sweden and the UK; all of which were based on a shared standardized measure of treatment outcome. The second derives from the collaborative experience of researchers, therapists, and administrators in the design and implementation of two major naturalistic studies conducted in the German health system (Strauss et al., in press). Focusing on highly relevant clinical issues (such as the effectiveness of theoretical orientations, services, feedback procedures, and individual therapists; therapy process; patterns and prediction of client change; and health-related costs of psychotherapy), these two papers provide guidelines for different stakeholders (researchers, practitioners, health insurance companies, health services institutions, and governmental agencies) who might want to work together in establishing a large research program anchored in clinical care.

The next three papers are based on partnerships that have been developed within more narrow settings, which may nevertheless represent clinical milieus that are familiar to a large number of practitioners. With the goal of providing a context where, optimally, the seamless integration of science and practice should begin, Castonguay, Pincus, and McAleavey (in press) describe the transformation of a graduate training clinic into a practice research network (PRN). Based on the collaboration of students, faculty members, clinic staff and administrators, and private practitioners, the authors describe an infrastructure that permits students to simultaneously meet the clinical and empirical requirements of their graduate degree—while advancing knowledge that is directly related to their academic courses, supervision, and the research program they are pursuing in their particular laboratories. Koerner and Castonguay (in press) then present two distinct partnerships that have been built both within the context of private practice: One that is led by a clinical researcher orchestrating several studies with separate groups of clinicians, and the other that is based on an active collaboration between researchers and clinicians in all aspects of the selection, design, implementation, and dissemination of studies conducted in outpatient clinical care.

Combining the clinical realities reflected in the previous two papers, Fernández-Álvarez, Gómez, and García (in press) depict how an extensive research program can be generated from a private organization that provides both clinical services and training. Although anchored in one center in Buenos Aires, Argentina, the development of this research program has involved the collaboration of clinicians, clinical agencies, universities, researchers, and reputed scholars across Argentina, as well as in many countries in Latin America and around the world. As a whole, these three collaborative initiatives have led to studies that address interest and concerns of clinicians in day-to-day practice, such as patterns of change of highly severe clients; the use and/or impact of specific interventions, treatments and principles of change; the training of therapists in using outcome monitoring and conducting single-case experimental designs in their clinical routine; the integration of different theoretical approaches; helpful and hindering events; as well as the therapist's personal style.

The following four papers of this series share a focus on the treatment of youth populations (children, adolescents, and young adults). Garland and Brookman-Frazee (in press) describe a partnership between researchers and practitioners in community centers, aimed at measuring the use of evidence-based interventions in routine care, as well as developing supervision tools to facilitate the implementation of these techniques with children with disruptive behavioral problems and their families. Based on literature from organizational management and public health, the authors also present a conceptual model that has guided the building and functioning of their partnership, which can provide a road map for others interested in developing a similar collaboration. Within the context of a residential program for juvenile substance abusers, the next paper provides a window on the experience of a clinician who, in collaboration with the practitioners and administrators of his center, first implemented an outcome monitoring system to assess the clinical needs of patients, and then organized the implementation (and measurement) of a treatment specifically attuned to the unexpected needs identified (Adelman, Castonguay, Kraus, & Zack, in press). In a candid and open way, the paper also describes the collaboration with academicians that was established to further develop this clinically anchored research program, with the goal of identifying barriers to change (i.e., client's history of poor attachment) and potential factors to address them (i.e., corrective experiences provided by a good therapeutic alliance). The next paper by Szapocznik, Muir, Duff,

Schwartz, and Brown (in press) exemplifies how the scientific-practitioner model can have a major impact on the mental health system when it is based on a full partnership between individuals with various expertise and resources. It describes a major research program on the efficacy, effectiveness, and process of change of a brief form of family therapy for adolescents of diverse ethnic backgrounds with substance abuse and delinquency problems. Guided by an implementation model that they developed from their systemic theoretical framework, the authors illustrate how the collaboration with different stakeholders (clinical scientists, clinicians, supervisors, members of treatment agencies, funders, and referral sources) can facilitate the adoption, fidelity, and sustainability of an empirically supported treatment in community-based settings, as well as the promotion of interventions that may have important social impact (such as decrease of incarceration and hospitalization). Another example of a partnership that cuts across diverse worlds of stakeholders, including clinical, administrative, academic, software engineering, and funding agencies, is the Center for Collegiate Mental Health (CCMH). As presented in McAleavey, Lockard, Castonguay, Hayes, and Locke's (in press) paper, CCMH is a PRN infrastructure that involves more than 200 university counseling centers. Based on the aggregation of several thousands of clients who fill out the same measures of symptoms and demographics yearly, this infrastructure has been built to collect data as part of clinical routine and for the sake of describing, informing, and improving day-to-day practice. Allowing each center to contribute to a centralized repository of data (used, for example, in studies of minority and underserved populations, services utilization, and therapeutic change), as well as to monitor outcome and gather information particular to their own site, CCMH embodies a principle that has been promoted for the future of POR: work locally and collaborate globally (Castonguay et al., 2013).

The last main paper of this series focuses on what appears to be the first PRN devoted to mental health, the American Psychiatric Institute of Research and Education (West et al., in press). For over two decades, this partnership of researchers and practicing psychiatrists has investigated a wide range of patient variables, therapist activities, and treatment characteristics in routine practice (conducted in a variety of public and private settings). With an attention to a variety of clinical populations (such as schizophrenia, depression, post-traumatic stress disorders, substance abuse, and clients of diverse ethnic backgrounds), studies were also conducted on the assessment and monitoring of symptoms, measurement of treatment fidelity, and evaluation of quality of care with a primary focus on conformity of routine practice along evidence-based practice guidelines. Established by the American Psychiatric Association, this PRN provides a model for researchers attached to professional organizations (such as the Society for Psychotherapy Research) who are interested in building a partnership with clinicians, other scientific organizations, academic settings, governmental agencies, advocacy groups, and health services systems—as well as in learning how to increase the impact of research findings in terms of clinical practice and health care policy.

Taken together, these 11 papers represent a breadth of POR that spans over several countries in three continents, various types of natural settings, a diversity of clinical populations and treatment approaches, and a myriad of research methodologies (including descriptive, qualitative, correlational, and experimental investigations). While many of the research programs have been led by full-time researchers, others have been carried on primarily by practitioners. A number of studies have also emerged from a full and equal collaboration between academicians and clinicians, and several of them have involved the participation of administrators, third-party payers, as well as governmental and private funding. As an attempt to integrate the wealth of lessons learned by these collaborative initiatives, the concluding paper of this series identifies convergences in terms of topics investigated, challenges faced, coping strategies used, benefits earned, and recommendations offered (Castonguay, Youn, Xiao, Muran, & Barber, in press). The concluding paper also highlights issues that have been found in only a few of the particular partnerships featured. Considering the variety of infrastructures and experiences it reflects, we hope that this issue of *Psychotherapy Research* will offer a wide range of lessons to design and implement scientifically rigorous and clinically relevant studies in different naturalistic settings and, more importantly, to foster active collaborations between researchers and clinicians in their shared ambition to better understand and improve mental health care.

References

Adelman, R. W., Castonguay, L. G., Kraus, D. R., & Zack, S. (in press). Conducting research and collaborating with researchers: The experience of clinicians in a residential treatment center. *Psychotherapy Research*. doi:10.1080/1050330 7.2014.935520

Barkham, M., & Margison, F. (2007). Practice-based evidence as a complement to evidence-based practice: From dichotomy to chiasmus. In C. Freeman & M. Power (Eds.), *Handbook of evidence-based psychotherapies: A guide for research and practice* (pp. 443–476). Chichester: Wiley.

Barkham, M., Stiles, W. B., Lambert, M. J., & Mellor-Clark, J. (2010). Building a rigorous and relevant knowledge-base for the psychological therapies. In M. Barkham, G. E. Hardy, & J. Mellor-Clark (Eds.), *Developing and delivering practice-based evidence: A guide for the psychological therapies* (pp. 21–61). Chichester: Wiley.

Borkovec, T. D., Echemendia, R. J., Ragusea, S. A., & Ruiz, M. (2001). The Pennsylvania practice research network and future possibilities for clinically meaningful and scientifically rigorous psychotherapy research. *Clinical Psychology: Science and Practice, 8*, 155–167. doi:10.1093/clipsy.8.2.155

Boswell, J. F., Kraus, D. R., Miller, S. D., & Lambert, M. J. (in press). Implementing routine outcome monitoring in clinical practice: Benefits, challenges, and solutions. *Psychotherapy Research*. doi:10.1080/10503307.2013.817696

Castonguay, L. G., Barkham, M., Lutz, W., & McAleavey, A. A. (2013). Practice-oriented research: Approaches and application. In M. J. Lambert (Eds.), *Bergin and Garfield's handbook of psychotherapy and behavior change* (6th ed.; pp. 85–133). New York, NY: Wiley.

Castonguay, L. G., Locke, B. D., & Hayes, J. A. (2011). The center for collegiate mental health: An example of a practice-research network in university counseling centers. *Journal of College Student Psychotherapy, 25*(2), 105–119. doi:10.1080/ 87568225.2011.556929

Castonguay, L. G., Pincus, A. L., & McAleavey, A. A. (in press). Practice research network in a psychology training clinic: Building an infrastructure to foster early attachment to the scientific-practitioner model. *Psychotherapy Research*. doi:10.1080/1050330 7.2013.856045

Castonguay, L. G., Youn, S., Xiao, H., Muran, J. C., & Barber, J. P. (in press). Building clinicians-researchers partnership: Lessons from diverse natural settings and practice-oriented initiatives. *Psychotherapy Research, 24*.

Fernández-Álvarez, H., Gómez, B., & García, F. (in press). Bridging the gap between research and practice in a clinical and training network: Aigle's program. *Psychotherapy Research*. doi:10.1080/ 10503307.2013.856047

Garland, A. F., & Brookman-Frazee, L. (in press). Therapists and researchers: Advancing collaboration. *Psychotherapy Research*. doi:10.1080/10503307.2013.838655

Holmqvist, R., Philips, B., & Barkham, M. (in press). Developing practice-based evidence: Benefits, challenges, and tensions. *Psychotherapy Research*. doi:10.1080/10503307.2013.861093

Koerner, K., & Castonguay, L. G. (in press). Practice-oriented research: What it takes to do collaborative research in private practice. *Psychotherapy Research*. doi:10.1080/10503307.2014. 939119

McAleavey, A. A., Lockard, A. J., Castonguay, L. G., Hayes, J. A., & Locke, B. D. (in press). Building a practice research network: Obstacles faced and lessons learned at the Center for Collegiate Mental Health. *Psychotherapy Research*. doi:10.1080/ 10503307.2014.883652

Morrow-Bradley, C., & Elliott, R. (1986). The utilization of psychotherapy research by practicing psychotherapists. *American Psychologist, Special Issue: Psychotherapy Research, 41*, 188–197.

Safran, J. D., Abreu, I., Ogilvie, J., & DeMaria, A. (2011). Does psychotherapy research influence the clinical practice of researchers-clinicians? *Clinical Psychology: Science and Practice, 18*, 357– 371. doi:10.1111/j.1468-2850.2011.01267.x

Stewart, R. E., & Chambless, D. L. (2007). Does psychotherapy research inform treatment decisions in private practice? *Journal of Clinical Psychology, 63*, 267– 281. doi:10.1002/jclp.20347

Strauss, B., Lutz, W., Steffanowski, A., Wittmann, W. W., Böehnke, J. R., Rubel, J., ... Kirchmann, H. (in press). Benefits and challenges in practice-oriented psychotherapy research in Germany: The TK and the QS-PSY-BAY projects of quality assurance in outpatient psychotherapy. *Psychotherapy Research*. doi:10.1080/10503307.2013.856046

Szapocznik, J., Muir, J. A., Duff, J. H., Schwartz, S. J., & Brown, H. (in press). Brief strategic family therapy: Implementing evidence-based models in community settings. *Psychotherapy Research*. doi:10.1080/10503307.2013.856044

West, J. C., Moscicki, E. K., Duffy, F. F., Wilk, J. E., Countis, L., Narrow, W. E., & Regier, D. A. (in press). APIRE practice research network: Accomplishments, challenges, and lessons learned. *Psychotherapy Research*. doi:10.1080/10503307.2013.868948

Implementing routine outcome monitoring in clinical practice: Benefits, challenges, and solutions

JAMES F. BOSWELL[1], DAVID R. KRAUS[2], SCOTT D. MILLER[3], & MICHAEL J. LAMBERT[4]

[1]Department of Psychology, University at Albany, State University of New York, Albany, NY, USA; [2]Outcome Referrals, Framingham, MA, USA; [3]ISTC, Chicago, IL, USA & [4]Department of Psychology, Brigham Young University, Provo, UT, USA

Abstract

This article reviews the benefits, obstacles, and challenges that can hinder (and have hindered) implementation of routine outcome monitoring in clinical practice. Recommendations for future routine outcome assessment efforts are also provided. Spanning three generations, as well as multiple developed tools and approaches, the four authors of this article have spent much of their careers working to address these issues and attempt to consolidate this learning and experience briefly here. Potential "elephants in the room" are brought into the discussion wherever relevant, rather than leaving them to obstruct silently the field's efforts. Some of these topics have been largely ignored, yet must be addressed if we are to fulfill our promise of integrating science and practice. This article is an attempt to identify these important issues and start an honest and open dialogue.

"Ideas are a dime a dozen. People who implement them are priceless."

Mary Kay Ash

In 1662, the Flemish medicinal chemist Jan Baptist van Helmont proposed what is considered the first randomized clinical trial (RCT) in history. He challenged conventional wisdom held as fact by practitioners of his day. Venesection, better known as bloodletting, was a major therapeutic tool. The procedure, believed effective for the remedy of a variety of pathologic conditions, was bolstered by an elaborate rationale, system of differential diagnosis, and specific tools and techniques. Confident that science would prevail over tradition, he offered a wager of 300 Florins—approximately 60,000 modern US dollars—to any of his contemporaries willing to test their methods against his:

Let us take out of the Hospitals, out of the Camps, or from elsewhere, 200, or 500 poor People, that have Fevers, Pleurisies, etc. Let us divide them in Halfes, let us cast lots, that one half of them may

fall to my share and the other to yours; I will cure them without bloodletting...but you do as ye know...we shall see how many funerals both of us shall have." (Harford, 2011, p. 121).

No record exists of anyone accepting van Helmont's bet. What is known is that he was arrested, interrogated, condemned, and confined by authorities of the day. Bloodletting continued for another 200 years. Even if his contemporaries had agreed to put their practices to the test and been proven wrong, it would be a mistake to assume rapid acceptance and adoption of the data. Then as now, implementation significantly lags behind discovery (McHugh & Barlow, 2012). Despite a culture favorable to the scientific method, a literate population, and the ability to transmit information at speeds unimaginable in van Helmont's age, available evidence indicates that as much as two decades can pass before discoveries are integrated into clinical practice (Brownson, Kreuter, Arrington, & True, 2006).

The purpose of this paper is, in part, to identify the barriers to implementation—important factors that when ignored silently impede progress. In particular, we focus on the implementation of routine outcome monitoring (ROM). Following a brief introduction and making a case for the impact of ROM, we identify philosophical and practical barriers to such monitoring. Finally, we offer some potential solutions to impediments encountered by front-line clinicians and healthcare systems when putting ROM into practice.

Outcome Monitoring

In 1996, Howard, Moras, Brill, Martinovich, and Lutz first suggested using session-to-session measures of client progress to evaluate and improve treatment outcome. Their approach differed from traditional efficacy and effectiveness research, which focuses on the average response of participants in either experimental or naturalistic settings. As a complement to traditional nomothetic approaches, these researchers proposed directing increased attention to a more idiographic approach, asking, "Is this treatment, however constructed, delivered by this particular provider, helpful to this client at this point in time?"

Since Howard et al.'s (1996) pioneering work, over a dozen RCTs and several meta-analyses have been published (e.g., Shimokawa, Lambert, & Smart, 2010). These studies provide strong empirical support for ROM. When implemented, the risk of patient deterioration is significantly decreased. At the same time, effect sizes are enhanced, and in some extreme cases tripled (Anker, Duncan, & Sparks, 2009; Kraus, Castonguay, Boswell, Nordberg, & Hayes, 2011). Moreover, technological advances now enable practitioners to quickly and efficiently administer reliable and valid measures, track progress, and receive individualized feedback for their clients in real time (Barkham, Mellor-Clark, Connell, & Cahill, 2006; Kraus, Wolf, & Castonguay, 2006; Lambert, 2012; Miller, Duncan, Sorrell, & Brown, 2005). As can be seen in the companion papers of this series, ROM has been the focus of practice-oriented research in diverse naturalistic settings (Castonguay, Pincus, & McAleavey, in press; Fernández-Álvarez, Gómez & García, in press; Holmqvist, Philips, & Barkham, in press; McAleavey, Lockard, Castonguay, Hayes, & Locke, in press; Strauss et al., in press; West et al. in press).

If adoption and implementation were a simple matter of combining evidence with a practicable methodology, then ROM would not only be known and accepted, but widely used. This is not consistently the case (Miller, Hubble, Chow, & Seidel, 2013). Surveys spanning different countries indicate that few clinicians actually employ ROM in their day-to-day work (Gilbody, House, & Sheldon, 2002; Hatfield & Ogles, 2004; Zimmerman & McGlinchey,

2008). Furthermore, although the collection of routine data has received more attention from service organizations and provider groups in recent years, there is considerable variability in the implementation, sustainability, and subsequent use of routine outcome data. Despite indications of low utilization, Bickman (2000) found that a large percentage of therapists held interest in receiving regular reports of client progress. Subsequently, Hatfield and Ogles (2004) conducted a survey with a national sample of licensed psychologists to investigate this discontinuity. As before, clinicians expressed interest in having reliable outcome information. Among the reasons given by those choosing not to use outcome measures, the top were "practical (e.g., cost and time) and philosophical (e.g., relevance) barriers" (p. 485).

Outcome Monitoring Systems

Drapeau (2012) identified 10 measures/systems for tracking mental health changes in routine care and had the authors of each system describe their purposes and implementation procedures. Obviously, there are many unique ways to monitor patients' mental health functioning over the course of treatment. In order to maximize the discussion of lessons learned about implementing ROM in clinical care, discussion will be limited to the following systems, several of which some of the present authors have developed: PCOMS ICCE, TOP, CORE, and OQ Systems.

The *Partners for Change Outcome Management System: International Center for Clinical Excellence* (PCOMS ICCE) includes measures of progress and the therapeutic alliance. Scales are available for adults, youth, and children and have been translated into 25 different languages. The brevity of these measures makes them ideal for use at every session. Following an independent review, PCOMS ICCE was recently listed on the National Registry of Evidence-based Programs and Practices. Based on three RCTs included in a recent meta-analysis, Lambert and Shimokawa (2011) found an effect size of $g = .53$ for the treatment-as-usual vs. feedback groups, with an odds ratio indicating that the feedback groups were 3.5-times more likely to achieve *reliable change*.

Another ROM and feedback measurement system is the *Treatment Outcome Package* (TOP; Kraus, Seligman, & Jordan, 2005), with different versions for adults, adolescents, and children. The TOP system was built on the recommendations of the Core Battery Conference (Strupp, Horowitz, & Lambert, 1997), and is unique in its multidimensional focus (Kraus, Boswell, Wright, Castonguay, & Pincus, 2010). The TOP factor structure allows clinicians to track change across 12 different dimensions of behavior, symptoms, quality of life and functioning. The adult version of the instrument assesses dimensions that include substance abuse, depression, panic, psychosis, mania, suicide, violence, sleep, quality of life, and social, work and sexual functioning. Recent research using the TOP has focused on identifying clinicians' relative strengths and weaknesses in specific problem domains and with particular types of clients (Kraus et al., 2011), including the examination of outcomes for clients with complex comorbidity (Nordberg et al., 2010).

A third system, used extensively in the United Kingdom, is the *Clinical Outcomes in Routine Evaluation* (CORE) system developed by Barkham and colleagues (2001, 2006). Similar to the TOP, the CORE has been used not only to track client progress but to benchmark patient outcomes for use at clinic and system levels. Thus, administrators in conjunction with clinicians can identify underperforming units and track improvements following modification to routine care. At relatively little cost, therapists can formally measure, monitor, and track patient self-reported well-being, and predict as well as improve final treatment response, especially with clients who worsen during the course of treatment (for a detailed description of the CORE, see Holmqvist et al., in press).

The final group of measures considered is the *Outcome Questionnaire System* (OQ System). Much of the pioneering research on the subject of ROM was done using the scales developed by Lambert and colleagues (Lambert et al., 1996). The OQ system offers different outcome measures for adults, children, adolescents, and clients considered seriously mentally ill. Additional features of the OQ and supporting research are discussed in the section that follows.

Each of the above-named systems has similarities and differences, as well as strengths and weaknesses (Youn, Kraus, & Castonguay, 2012), and adequate empirical support. PCOMS is the briefest of the group, thereby potentially facilitating greater acceptance by practitioners. Similarly, the CORE is widely used in Europe and has two abbreviated versions for use in routine clinical practice. The TOP and OQ systems are both relatively longer, and the OQ is the most researched tool of the lot. Involving the greatest number of items and multidimensional feedback, the TOP was recently tested by the Annie E. Casey Foundation with users in Ohio. The range of administration times was 3 to 5 minutes. The TOP has also been a data linchpin for innovative and productive community practice research networks (PRNs; e.g., Castonguay et al., 2010) and data-driven treatment initiatives (see Adelman, 2005). That said, choosing the right tool for a particular setting involves working to strike a balance between the competing demands of validity, reliability, and feasibility as well as meeting individual clinician or agency preferences and needs (Miller, Duncan, & Hubble, 2004). Following this introduction, we now briefly make the case for ROM before discussing philosophical and practical barriers to such monitoring, as well as offering some solutions to impediments encountered by front line clinicians and healthcare systems when putting ROM into practice.

Why Do We Need Outcome Monitoring?

In a recent article, Youn, Kraus, and Castonguay (2012) identified several benefits to ROM. For example, the detection of even slight improvements can reassure skeptical clients that they are making recognizable progress in treatment and further improve the therapeutic alliance. Furthermore, ROM can provide therapists with "off track" alerts indicating that the current course of treatment may be ineffective or even harmful. Even in controlled treatment settings, rates of deterioration and nonresponse are not insignificant. Hansen, Lambert, and Forman (2002) examined a representative sample of randomized clinical trial outcomes based on 89 treatment comparisons (mostly CBT) and reported an average of 57% to 67% recovered or improved after receiving an average of 13 sessions of treatment. These outcomes were contrasted with those found in over 6,000 clients who participated in routine care that lasted an average of four sessions with patients ranging from those treated in community mental health centers to those being seen in outpatient clinics. Rates of improvement/recovery averaged 35% and deterioration varied from a low of 3.2% to a high of 14%, with an average rate of 8%. As Hansen et al. (2002), point out, even when an EST is offered to individuals who have the same disorder and see therapists who have been carefully selected, monitored, and supervised, 30% to 50% of patients fail to respond to treatment.

The situation for child and adolescent outcome in routine care is also sobering. In a comparison of children being treated in community mental health ($N = 936$) or through managed care ($N = 3,075$), estimates of deterioration were 24% and 14%, respectively (Warren, Nelson, Mondragon, Baldwin, & Burlingame, 2010). This means that even if there were a right treatment or "best practice" for an individual, we would need to identify patients who are failing to respond to this treatment before they left our care. Furthermore, increased attention to deterioration in treatment may be warranted given the high rates of treatment dropout observed in clinical practice. It is estimated that 40–60% of children and adolescents discontinue treatment prematurely (Kazdin, 1996; Wierzbicki & Pekarik,

1993); many of these dropouts are probably due to perceived lack of benefit from treatment. With regard to measuring treatment response in child and adolescent psychotherapy, Kazdin (2005) noted that "such information would be enormously helpful if used to monitor and evaluate treatment in clinical practice" (p. 555).

Unfortunately, clinicians' view of their own clients' outcome is much more positive. Walfish, McAlister, O'Donnell, and Lambert's (2012) survey of clinicians suggests that clinicians estimate that about 85% of their clients improve or recover. In addition, they have the common impression that they are unusually successful, with 90% rating themselves in the upper quartile and none seeing themselves as below average in relation to their peers. Another serious problem in practice is that doubt exists regarding the ability of clinicians to identify clients during the course of therapy who ultimately deteriorate and to note worsening during treatment as a warning sign of deterioration and treatment failure (Hannan et al. 2005; Hatfield, McCullough, Plucinski, & Krieger, 2010). Clinicians could benefit from using tracking systems because of their likely overly optimistic estimates of their clients' outcome and their inability to predict treatment failure, specifically, reliable negative change.

Predicting Negative Change

One core element of some feedback systems is their proven ability to predict treatment failure, risk of hospitalization, or other negative outcomes. In order to improve outcomes of clients who are responding poorly to treatment, such clients must be identified before termination, and ideally as early as possible in the course of treatment. Systems employ a variety of methods to predict treatment failure, e.g., the OQ system plots a statistically generated expected recovery curve for differing levels of pre-treatment distress and uses this as a basis for identifying clients who are not making expected treatment gains and are at risk of having a poor outcome (not-on-track cases). The accuracy of this signal-alarm system has been evaluated in a number of empirical investigations (e.g., Ellsworth, Lambert, & Johnson, 2006; Lambert, Whipple, Bishop, et al., 2002) that suggest 85% to 100% of those who eventually deteriorate can be identified before they leave treatment. This rate of recognition far exceeds clinical judgment alone (Hannan et al., 2005).

The Benefits of Routine Outcome Monitoring: Beyond Prediction

In the most recent meta-analytic review of one ROM system, Shimokawa and colleagues (2010)

re-analyzed the combined dataset ($N = 6151$) from six OQ-45 feedback studies published to that date (Harmon et al., 2007; Hawkins, Lambert, Vermeersch, Slade, & Tuttle, 2004; Lambert et al., 2001; Lambert, Whipple, Vermeersch, et al., 2002; Slade, Lambert, Harmon, Smart, & Bailey, 2008; Whipple et al., 2003). Each of the studies evaluated the effects of providing feedback about each client's improvement through the use of progress graphs and warnings about clients who were not demonstrating expected treatment responses. The six studies shared many design and methodological features: (a) consecutive cases seen in routine care regardless of client diagnosis or co-morbid conditions (rather than being disorder specific); (b) random assignment of clients to experimental conditions (various feedback interventions) and treatment as usual (TAU) conditions (no feedback) was made in four of the six studies, while reasonable measures were taken in two studies to ensure equivalence in experimental and control conditions at pre-treatment; (c) psychotherapists provided a variety of theoretically guided treatments, with most adhering to cognitive behavioral and eclectic orientations and fewer representing psychodynamic and experiential orientations; (d) a variety of therapist experience— post-graduate therapists and graduate students each accounted for about 50% of clients seen; (e) *therapists saw both experimental (feedback) and no feedback cases*, thus limiting the likelihood that outcome differences between conditions could be due to therapist effects; (f) the outcome measure as well as the methodology rules/standards for identifying signal-alarm clients (failing cases) remained constant; (g) the length of therapy (dosage) was determined by client and therapist rather than by research design or arbitrary insurance limits.

The meta-analysis (Shimokawa et al., 2010) involved both intent-to-treat (ITT) and efficacy analyses on the effects of various feedback interventions in relation to TAU (treatment without feedback) on clients who were predicted to have a negative outcome. When the not-on-track feedback group was compared to the not-on-track TAU group, the effect size for post-treatment OQ score difference averaged a $g = .53$. These results suggest that the average at risk client whose therapist received feedback was better off than approximately 70% of at risk clients in the no feedback condition. In terms of the clinical significance at termination, 9% of those receiving feedback deteriorated while 38% achieved clinically significant improvement. In contrast, among at risk clients whose therapists did not receive feedback, 20% deteriorated while 22% clinically significantly improved. When the odds of deterioration and clinically significant improvement were compared, results indicated those in the feedback group had less than half the odds of experiencing deterioration while having approximately 2.6-times higher odds of experiencing reliable improvement.

The OQ feedback system went beyond progress feedback by asking clients who were predicted to deteriorate to complete a 40-item measure of the therapeutic alliance, motivation, social supports, and recent life events. Therapists were provided with feedback on these domains, a problem-solving decision tree, and intervention suggestions to assist them in resolving issues that may be causing clients to have a negative treatment response. Together this intervention was referred to as a *Clinical Support Tool*. When the outcome of clients whose therapist received the Clinical Support Tool feedback were compared to the treatment-as-usual clients, the effect size for the difference in mean post-treatment OQ scores was $g = 0.70$. These results indicate that the average clients in the Clinical Support Tool feedback group, who stay in treatment to experience the benefit of this intervention, are better off than 76% of clients in treatment-as-usual. The rates of deterioration and clinically significant improvement among those receiving Clinical Support Tools were 6% and 53%, respectively. The results suggest that clients whose therapists used Clinical Support Tools with off-track cases have less than a fourth the odds of deterioration, while having approximately 3.9-times higher odds of achieving clinically significant improvement.

The applications of not-on-track predictive modeling are potentially far-reaching. For example, TOP outcome data have been tied to prospective health-plan claims data to build and test algorithms that predict near-future psychiatric and substance abuse hospitalizations. These predictive models allow resources to be diverted to prevent costly and potentially life-threatening incidents (McAleavey, Nordberg, Kraus, & Castonguay, 2012). Additional advantages of some outcome monitoring approaches include the general documentation of change for accountability purposes, assistance in formulating treatment plans with built-in evaluations of success, as well as improved communication between therapist and client, especially as it pertains to the discontinuation and prolonging of treatment (Youn et al., 2012).

The preceding information suggests an answer to the question posed: Why would clinicians want to formally monitor client treatment response? Because the research evidence strongly supports the conclusion that it is in clients' (and, thus, therapists') best interests to do so. However, there are many obstacles to the implementation of ROM in routine treatment settings. Examples of such obstacles, and a few strategies that have been used to overcome them, are discussed in the next section.

Obstacles and Challenges to Routine Data Collection

While we view ROM and feedback as having clear benefits for clients, therapists, and healthcare, there are many obstacles and challenges to routine data collection, spanning individual and systems levels. Furthermore, some obstacles and challenges may be unique to the healthcare systems of specific countries. It is clear that researchers would like access to real-world outcome data and that clinicians hold access rights to these data. Cooperation is obviously required, and it is imperative that researchers understand the needs of clinicians, who often need help with answers and solutions to time-critical, sometimes life-threatening, problems. Understanding the clinician's challenges and context is vital. Using some of the primary reasons for non-ROM use reported by Hatfield and Ogles (2004) as broad categories ("practical" and "philosophical"), we now briefly review several obstacles and challenges to data collection that we have encountered.

Practical Obstacles

Financial burden. At the systems level, we believe that there is a financial "elephant in the room." In most healthcare settings, when the industry decides that a type of laboratory data (e.g., an X-ray) is important for delivering quality care, it is billable and reimbursed (either by a third-party payer or by the national health system). Physicians do not pay out of pocket for X-rays. If an orthopedist purchases an X-ray machine for her office, she bills the insurance company each time it is used. This type of reimbursement does not occur with the collection and reporting of outcome data (through a diagnostic or testing code), despite the fact that it clearly improves clients' lives. Importantly, the National Business Group on Health recommended that patient monitoring as a lab test be reimbursed (Finch & Phillips, 2005); however, the insurance industry failed to act on this recommendation. We presume that if the industry had followed this recommendation, many more behavioral health providers would begin routinely collecting data on their clients. If routine monitoring were reimbursed at $25/month, the process would not be a financial burden to providers. We can find no articles that bemoan the fact that physicians have to pay for non-reimbursable tests for their patients. Furthermore, we can think of no parallel medical example where physicians are expected to pull out their wallets and pay for a routine procedure that has been demonstrated in clinical trials (as reviewed above) to improve health and outcomes.

Time burden. Time is everything to a busy behavioral health provider, and providers are often overscheduled. Many providers have reported feeling pressured to see clients even though they are probably too tired, distracted, or sick to give their clients their full effort (see Pope, Tabachnick, & Keith-Spiegel, 1987). Similarly, if providers had more time to make phone calls to collaborating providers, as well as request and read previous medical records that relate not only to previous behavioral health treatments but to interrelating co-morbid medical conditions, routine treatment would likely result in better outcomes. In our experience, it often seems that simply having the time to reflect on a case and integrate ideas learned from continuing education or recent journal articles is a luxury that most providers do not have.

Routine data collection must be placed within this context; otherwise clinicians may rightly feel dismissed. Depending on the method or system of measurement, potential time burdens include: administering questionnaires (providing and collecting); scoring and interpretation of results; creating a report and providing feedback to the client; establishing a tracking and reminder system that reliably prompts when follow-up assessments should be conducted (if not collected at every session). Some systems also require time for aggregate reporting, benchmarking, risk adjusting, quality improvement integration, and report interpretation aids. To most agencies, and certainly clinicians in private practice, these challenges can be daunting. The development of software systems can alleviate some of these burdens, yet the time commitment is real.

It is also important to remember that the time burden can affect creativity and self-learning. The average clinician may not have time to research different outcome monitoring systems (e.g., how does one pick the "right" measure) or how to integrate an outcome monitoring and feedback system into his or her practice. Additionally, even if a clinician already is routinely collecting data, he or she may not have much time to reflect on its use or impact. Each of the present authors has had experiences where previously "resistant" clinicians apologized for initially assuming that outcome monitoring would be a distraction rather than an aid to treatment; literally calling to apologize and to relate a story of some unexpected clinical utility. However, these calls are more the exception rather than the rule—likely due to the diminished opportunity to reflect.

Multiple stakeholders with different needs. It is difficult enough to develop an outcome monitoring and feedback system that meets the needs of just one key stakeholder, and we cannot forget that clients will always be the principal stakeholder. Clients want the highest quality of care, but they also want relatively brief scales with a high degree of face validity. Clinicians need actionable data that informs treatment planning and warns of off-track or emergent problems, as well as data that helps to foster and support the development of a stronger therapeutic alliance. Administrators also need actionable data, yet with minimal disruption and cost. In the United States, health plans have a contractual obligation to manage the care secured by the purchasers of healthcare (e.g., employers), yet need to abide by privacy and security laws. A poorly designed system that does not meet the needs of all stakeholders is sure to be short lived (Fixsen, Naoom, Blase, Friedman, & Wallace, 2005).

Turnover. For provider agencies that have already begun to implement ROM, the departure of the right clinical or administrative ("local") champion can cause years of data collection and integration to unravel within weeks. For example, the new CEO might ask, "Why are we spending this money handing out questionnaires? Are we required to do this?" After this, it does not take long for routine data collection and feedback efforts to be jettisoned. In addition, clinical staff turns over in many locations at an increasingly rapid pace, causing the need for ongoing training, education, and seemingly never-ending "buy-in" discussions. As such, turnover not only effects motivation, but also greatly impacts the sustained implementation of routine data collection procedures.

Philosophical Obstacles

Perception that outcome assessment is different from other assessment. As much as we may try, psychologists will likely never be able to create the "perfect" assessment tool: Perfect in the sense that it is perfectly reliable, valid, appropriate and sufficient (i.e., relevant) for each individual client. Because behavioral health providers see a wide range of individuals presenting with diverse and comorbid problems, clinicians are often skeptical about the relevance and utility of outcome measures, despite very solid empirical support for the reliability and validity of many different measures. Despite the accuracy of actuarial prediction, all assessment tools must be interpreted within a context and while taking into consideration multiple sources of information (McAleavey et al., 2012). A psychologist would (hopefully) never diagnose a child with attention-deficit hyperactivity disorder (ADHD) on the basis of a single self-report scale. However, this is not because the self-report scale is necessarily faulty or provides no incremental validity. Simply put, outcome assessment is assessment, and should be approached as such. One manifestation of this issue emerges when a client may believe it is in his or her best interest to understate (or overstate) their problems and produce inaccurate ratings on feedback systems. These systems and their usefulness in treatment are predicated on accurate self-reporting of levels of disturbance and corresponding changes. Some clinicians may falsely interpret this as a problem with the measure or feedback system. However, this may actually provide an opportunity for the clinician to take other information into consideration and discuss the discrepancy openly with the client. Such moments can provide glimpses into the unique world-view of the patient and the window through which the therapist and patient can look together (Youn et al., 2012).

Additionally, Youn et al. (2012) note that therapists may resist integrating routine outcome assessments due to concerns that clients will refuse to cooperate and that the process of outcome assessment will interfere with forming a therapeutic alliance. We are aware of no studies (single-case or otherwise) that support this proposition. On the contrary, Youn et al. note that well-introduced outcome procedures may actually improve the therapeutic alliance and clients often welcome the opportunity to track their progress in treatment.

Fear and mistrust. Most formal monitoring of patient mental health is being imposed on clinicians by systems of care that have come to realize that such practices can enhance patient outcomes or because they believe that the data can be used to increase the quality of care offered to patients through accountability measures. This development provides clinicians with further reasons to resist monitoring—we do not like external control and management. Clinicians don't like "big brother" and perhaps with good reason. What will happen with the data? Who will have access to the data? Will it be used to cut reimbursement? Will the insurance companies use it to deny other care? These concerns extend to clinicians and employers. For example, how will the hospital or community mental health center use data as it relates to performance reviews, supervision, and raises? In addition, most clinicians are not used to anything intruding on the therapy hour, including

the prying eyes of assessments that will be potentially seen by someone else. Nor do they like having their patients' outcomes compared to those of other therapists (Okiishi et al., 2006). Clinicians may fear that the results of outcome monitoring will reveal them as incompetent (Youn et al., 2012). Obviously, this can raise anxieties and most clinicians will need time to find the process worthy of their trust.

Privacy and ethics. Confidentiality is an absolutely crucial element of psychotherapy, and anything perceived to potentially breach confidentiality can and should be met with skepticism. Ethics charges have been levied against programs that are not perceived to ensure confidentiality (Koocher & Keith-Spiegel, 2008) and the American Psychological Association (APA) has set forth some basic recommendations that health plans are encouraged to follow (APA, 2009). For example, if an outcome system tracks an individual with an identifiable field, such as a name or social security number, simply complying with HIPAA requirements may not be enough unless the outcome/data collection organization has contractual business associate agreements with providers, health plans and any other covered entity involved in the program.

Attempts to Overcome Obstacles

The present authors are keenly aware of the practical and philosophical obstacles described above because we have directly faced and continue to wrestle with them. Through these experiences, we have attempted several strategies to address these difficulties, which have resulted in some success. For example, in order to address potential concerns about the reliability and validity of outcome measures, research is continually being conducted to improve our measurement and feedback systems and provide additional support for psychometric properties and clinical utility. As more data are collected, our predictive analytics will continue to improve.

We have also noted that the perceived time and energy burden is a frequently expressed concern. In order to reduce this time burden and make outcome assessment more user-friendly, each of us has been involved in building software applications that help to ameliorate time burdens. Systems have been built to take over the reminder and administrative burdens by "pushing" questionnaires to consenting patients at required intervals, a process that can eliminate the need for paper or computer solutions in waiting rooms.

The issues of trust and confidentiality are complex and multifaceted. In our experience, clinician trust is enhanced when there is a high degree of transparency and everything is spelled out in writing. We have also learned that researchers' attempts to impart the "wisdom of routine outcome monitoring" are far less effective than the wisdom imparted by fellow clinicians who have used the particular outcome monitoring system of interest. It is through direct clinical experience and by sharing these experiences (e.g., through vignettes) that other clinicians begin to seriously entertain the potential benefits. We envision a book or online repository of these clinician-driven case vignettes, which can be mined by other clinicians and administrators who feel as if they are "herding cats."

Furthermore, in our experience, agencies that have successfully solved the turnover challenge (and loss of a "local champion") have done two things. First, outcome data and monitoring become a routine agenda item of every board meeting so that a new executive will learn from their board why the data are invaluable. Second, the champion filling the role of "outcomes project manager" (usually a clinical or quality director) has created a new clinician initial training protocol that introduces staff to the requirements, expectations and benefits of outcome management.

Recommendations for Future Efforts

Despite considerable evidence that psychotherapists are not alert to treatment failure (e.g., Hannan et al., 2005; Hatfield, et al, 2010), and strong evidence that clinical judgments are usually inferior to actuarial methods (Garb, 2005), therapists' confidence in their clinical judgment alone stands as a barrier to implementation of monitoring and feedback systems. We advocate the employment of real-time client feedback procedures to compensate for therapists' limited ability to accurately detect client worsening in psychotherapy. Clients are best served when standardized procedures are used by clinicians to monitor clients' response to psychotherapy and satisfaction with the therapy relationship. Such feedback improves psychotherapy outcomes and certainly does so for clients at risk of deterioration or dropout. Based on our experience developing and implementing routine outcome assessment tools and systems (our successes and failures), we offer the following specific recommendations for future efforts in this crucial area. These recommendations intentionally span practical and conceptual issues related to adoption, implementation, and sustainability, in order to be applicable to a wider range of current and potential ROM adopters.

Consider Additional Incentives

Theories of motivation indicate that goals are more likely to be pursued and achieved when there is frequent, objective feedback that is tied to specific behaviors, and when those specific behaviors (or one's performance) is clearly tied to an outcome that is perceived to be worthwhile (Kluger & DeNisi, 1996; Koestner, 2008). The feedback research reviewed above underscores the value of ROM and clearly demonstrates the direct benefits to both clinicians and their clients. The results are robust and clinically meaningful—at the level of the individual client. However, Hatfield and Ogles (2007) found that clinicians were more likely to report using outcome measures when this practice was linked to payer factors. In the context of healthcare reform, calls have been made to link reimbursement rates with use of evidence-based practices and so-called "proof of" or likelihood of "benefit" (Diamond & Kaul, 2009; Rosenthal, 2008). One method for enhancing the adoption of outcome monitoring and feedback systems may be to incentivize such routine outcome data collection. The obvious incentives would be monetary; however, other potentially useful incentives could be utilized. For example, client referrals could be made based on whether or not a clinician routinely monitors client outcomes or has a track record of helping clients with similar profiles; or clinicians could obtain CEUs through their involvement in data collection and feedback-seeking. Importantly, starting in 2015, the Medicare Physician Quality Reporting System (PQRS) will begin *penalizing* providers with reduced reimbursement rates if data are not reported on designated service measures.

Data Collection Process Must be Simple and Minimally Disruptive

The ROM process must be made as simple as possible and minimally disruptive to clinicians' routine practice. This includes minimal disruption to the clinician *as well as the client* (Slade, Thornicroft, & Glover, 1999). Completion of relevant self-report measures typically consumes no more than 5 minutes of a client's time, which we believe meets the spirit of minimal disruption. Even when the implementation of an outcome monitoring system is relatively straightforward, clinicians' needs must be considered. For example, will implementing this procedure necessitate any formal training, which might also include a tutorial on how to interpret and make use of specific feedback (e.g., Clinical Support Tools)? Clinicians should know how to speak with their clients about the importance of outcome monitoring because certain clients feel it may be in their interest to understate (or overstate) their problems and produce inaccurate ratings on feedback systems. Generally speaking, we advocate using electronic versions of feedback systems that expedite and ease practical difficulties. Fortunately, the software for the OQ and TOP, for example, can provide instantaneous feedback to clinicians. If the client completes these measures immediately prior to the scheduled psychotherapy session, electronic feedback is available within seconds to the therapist prior to beginning that session.

Increased Flexibility

Depending on the individual clinician and practice setting, interests, needs, and resources are likely to vary. For example, sophisticated electronic/online outcome assessment, tracking and feedback systems exist; however, many clinicians may be unwilling or able to use such a system (e.g., due to lack of a computer in their office, concerns about confidentiality). In such cases, alternative methods of data collection and scoring may be preferred. For example, a clinician who primarily works with older adults might have concerns about the use of technology, making a paper-pencil option more preferable in some instances. Although different assessment methods may theoretically introduce another source of error variance, studies comparing paper and computer or internet scale administration have found high correspondence between the two assessment methods (Cook et al., 2007; Merten & Ruch, 1996; Ogles, France, Lunnen, Bell, & Goldfarb, 1998; Peterson, Johannsson & Carlsson, 1996). Maintaining flexibility is also consistent with Bohanske and Franczak's (2010) recommendation to think "evolution" when implementing an innovation, rather than "revolution." At the same time, however, failing to take advantage of modern information technology cannot be excused by lack of familiarity or discomfort if progress is to be made.

Transparent and Non-Hierarchical Approach

Outcome monitoring and feedback is an evidence-based practice, and can be treated as such (McHugh & Barlow, 2012). In fact, the effect sizes reported in experiments comparing feedback with treatment as usual exceed those typically reported in comparative outcome studies that justify the use of evidence-based therapies and other evidence-based practices that are widely advocated (Lambert, 2013). With regard to evidence-based practices, skepticism and "top-down" approaches to dissemination and implementation are significant contributors to the science-practice "chasm"

(Castonguay, Barkham, Lutz, & McAleavey, 2013). Clinician mistrust can be attenuated by increased transparency regarding the nature, goals, costs, and benefits of monitoring client outcomes. Although we view the costs as very minimal in comparison to the clear benefits outlined above, dissemination and implementation models and research indicate that changing clinician behavior (or anyone's behavior for that matter) is a difficult process, particularly in the beginning (see McHugh & Barlow, 2012; Riemer, Rosof-Williams, & Bickman, 2005; Rogers, 2003), and the ROM implementation process can span several years (Fixsen et al., 2005).

There are many different approaches to changing human systems (Chin & Benne, 1969). The so-called empirical-rational approach assumes that individuals are rational and will follow the data if it makes sense and seems to suit their self-interests; "If we publish enough studies with large effect sizes, then clinicians will start monitoring outcomes." The power-coercive approach assumes that change is facilitated through external leverage where power is the primary factor (e.g., economic pressures, sanctions); "Clinicians will start monitoring outcomes because we will mandate that they do so or refuse to reimburse for services." Alternatively, the normative-educative approach is more a systems approach, where the individual is seen as actively searching to satisfy needs and interests. In contrast with the inherent passivity in a power-coercive approach, the individual takes specific action to advance interests and goals—change is seen as a development of new habits and a realization of values; "If we together discuss why this would be important for clinicians self-interests and the interests of their clients, then we can begin working together to devise a plan." This approach is more participatory, less hierarchical (top-down), and involves clinicians in the planning, which is likely to increase motivation (Koestner, 2008; Latham & Locke, 2006; Locke & Latham, 2006). This also improves transparency.

In line with this, concerns about confidentiality, who will have access to the data collected (during and after a specified collection period) and how, specifically, the data are to be used should be addressed and made clear from the outset. For example, clinicians should be made aware that in addition to tracking (and, therefore, improving) outcomes, they can objectively assess their effectiveness with particular groups of clients once enough data have been collected. Administrators should be made aware that outcomes data can be used as a needs assessment to direct future training initiatives at their mental health center. Additionally, although individual clinician "buy in" is paramount, the context of care delivery is typically much more complex. Many initiatives, particularly those at the organizational level (e.g., introducing an electronic records system that integrates ROM), will need to involve administrators, supervisors, non-direct service staff (e.g., receptionists), and in some cases, third-party payers or referral sources.

Identify a Local Champion and Ensure this Role is Always Filled

One of the most consistently reported factors in the successful adoption (Greenhalgh, Robert, Macfarlane, Bate, & Kyriakidou, 2004) and implementation of evidence-based practices, including ROM, is the presence of a "local champion" (Aarons, 2005; Marty, Rapp, McHugo, & Whitley, 2007; Trauer, Gill, Pedwell, & Slattery, 2006). A local champion is a prominent and well-respected individual (or set of individuals) within a setting, organization, or culture who has had positive experiences with a process or intervention and who takes enthusiastic responsibility for assisting in the adoption, implementation, and sustainability of a specific program or intervention. For example, a well-liked and respected veteran clinician or administrator at a clinic who has had positive experiences with routine outcome monitoring and feedback might function as a local champion. This person is not only important for her or his technical and procedural expertise (e.g., can assist in the day-to-day training or troubleshooting when a question or problem arises), but because this individual can engender a more open or positive attitude toward adoption and implementation.

While this problem is likely endemic, anecdotally, each of the present authors has been directly involved in an initiative that eventually lost momentum or failed due to the absence or loss of a local champion. Consequently, we advocate identifying several potential local champions, if possible, rather than a single local champion, at least one of whom holds an administrative position (where applicable). Many clinics and community mental health centers, particularly those specializing in substance abuse, have a high staff turnover rate (Eby, Burk, & Maher, 2010). Once a local champion leaves a setting, particularly if the attitudes of other clinicians are equivocal and the monitoring system is relatively new, sustainability will likely be undermined (Rogers, 2003).

Supplement Outcome Feedback with Clinical Support Tools

Although feedback alarm-signals alone have been shown to be effective in decreasing deterioration and increasing response rates, clinicians are likely to benefit from additional information or decision-support tools

in their attempts to help clients who are at risk. Consequently, we recommend that outcome monitoring be supplemented with clinical support tools. As suggested by the general literature on feedback and the evidence presented here, problem-solving and decision-enhancement tools prove helpful to clinicians and, most importantly, clients whose treatment response is in doubt.

Use of Benchmarking and Risk-Adjustment

In order to maximize the validity and "informational payload" of data collected through routine outcome monitoring, benchmarks at the inter- and intraindividual levels should be established and, when possible, data should be risk-adjusted. Statistical benchmarking enhances the utility and interpretability of a measure or indicator (Tremblay, Hevner, & Berndt, 2012), and allows for the identification of types of patients with whom a clinician is particularly effective (or ineffective) as well as those clinicians who generally evidence better outcomes (e.g., outcomes achieved by the top 10% of clinicians; Weissman et al., 1999). There is some evidence that outcomes are enhanced when individuals receive feedback that compares their performance with a statistically derived benchmark, rather than feedback on individual performance (e.g., Kiefe et al., 2001). Risk-adjustment algorithms are important for increasing the comparability of collected data because they adjust for patient characteristics (i.e., case-mix variables, or case-mix adjustment) that could account for differences between clinicians or mental health centers (data collected at centers that serve individuals with differing levels of baseline severity or functional impairment). Of course, the relevance of risk-adjustment likely depends on the aim and scope of the project. For example, if a large mental health provider organization was interested in identifying which of its satellite clinics was achieving particularly good outcomes and which was achieving particularly poor outcomes, risk-adjustment would be important for increasing the fairness and validity of comparisons. Once identified using a valid, data-driven approach, more resources can be allocated to the satellite center that may be struggling, or clinicians from the satellite clinic that is performing particularly well can offer insights into what seems to be working for them.

Conduct More Basic Research on Adoption and Implementation

Basic research on ROM and feedback is essential. Although some attention has been paid to general models of dissemination and implementation (e.g.,

Fixsen et al., 2005; Rogers, 2003), more needs to be learned about the adoption, implementation, and sustained use of outcome monitoring and feedback systems, as this information may enhance future adoption and compliance, and, therefore, further improve outcomes. For example, more research is needed to empirically test implementation models, such as the one proposed by Fixsen et al. (2005) involving the following stages: *exploration, installation, initial implementation, full implementation,* and *sustainability.* More basic research is also sorely needed on the factors (e.g., participant factors, organizational factors, training factors) that facilitate or inhibit the adoption, implementation, and sustainability of ROM (see De Jong, van Sluis, Nugter, Heiser, & Spinhoven 2012 for an example of such research).

Foster the Scientist-Practitioner Professional Identity

Narrowly defining the scientist-practitioner as a clinician who delivers empirically supported treatments (ESTs) may unintentionally weaken clinicians' identification with this model in a manner that is specifically relevant to valuing outcome monitoring and feedback-seeking. That is, in line with the notion of the local clinical scientist (see Stricker & Trierweiler, 1995), a scientist-practitioner is always an active participant (rather than an observer or mode of delivery) in all relevant domains and sees each clinical encounter as an opportunity to gather "local data" that will not only be relevant with this client, but with future clients. Consequently, training programs should instill the value of collecting routine data, on both process and outcome, and using this information to inform case conceptualization and treatment planning (Castonguay, Boswell, Constantino, Goldfried, & Hill, 2010). In addition, training faculty would do well to encourage an openness to receiving progress feedback (Boswell & Castonguay, 2007), as well as encourage the use of outcomes data to answer clinically relevant research questions early on in training (Castonguay et al., in press).

Conclusion

Movement toward evidence-based and outcome-driven healthcare decision making and resource allocation is an inevitability. Despite the obstacles and challenges outlined above, we believe that most clinicians would agree with the spirit of routine outcome monitoring given that the ultimate goal is reducing suffering and improving individuals' quality of life. How this is precisely achieved and its success will be dependent on the active and open collaboration of researchers and clinicians. Although Jan Baptist van Helmont's challenge was apparently unmet, more attention and resources are being directed toward the rigorous testing of patient-centered approaches to treatment decision making and care, such as the Association for Health Care Research and Quality (AHRQ) and the Patient-Centered Outcome Research Institute (PCORI). We are all excited about the potential improvements in care and the benefits to the individual client and therapist.

References

Aarons, G. A. (2005). Measuring provider attitudes toward evidence-based practice: Consideration of organizational context and individual differences. *Child and Adolescent Psychiatric Clinics of North America, 14,* 255–271. http://dx.doi.org/10.1016/j.chc.2004.04.008

Adelman, R. (2005). Reducing adolescent clients' anger in a residential substance abuse treatment facility. *Journal on Quality and Patient Safety, 31,* 325–327.

American Psychological Association. (2009). Criteria for the Evaluation of Quality Improvement Programs and the Use of Quality Improvement Data. *American Psychologist, 64,* 551–557. doi:10.1037/a0016744

Anker, M. G., Duncan, B. L., & Sparks, J.A. (2009). Using client feedback to improve couple therapy outcomes: a randomized clinical trial in a naturalistic setting. *Journal of Consulting & Clinical Psychology, 77,* 693–704. doi:10.1037/a0016062

Barkham, M., Margison, F., Leach, C., Lucock, M., Mellor-Clark, J., Evans, C., … McGrath, G. (2001). Service profiling and outcomes benchmarking using the CORE-OM: Towards practice-based evidence in the psychological therapies. *Journal of Consulting and Clinical Psychology, 69,* 184–196. doi:10.1037/0022-006X.69.2.184

Barkham, M., Mellor-Clark, J., Connell, J., & Cahill, J. (2006). A core approach to practice-based evidence: A brief history of the origins and applications of the CORE-OM and CORE System. *Counselling & Psychotherapy Research, 6,* 3–15. doi:10.1080/14733140600581218

Bickman, L. (2000). Summing up program theory. *New Directions for Evaluation,* 103–112. doi:10.1002/ev.1186

Bohanske, R. T., & Franczak, M. (2010). Transforming public behavioral health care: A case example of consumer-directed services, recovery, and the common factors. In B.L. Duncan, S.D. Miller, B.E. Wampold, & M.A. Hubble (Eds.), *The heart and soul of change: Doing what works in therapy* (2nd ed., pp. 299–322). Washington DC: American Psychological Association.

Boswell, J. F., & Castonguay, L. G. (2007). Psychotherapy training: Suggestions for core ingredients and future research. *Psychotherapy: Theory, Research, Practice, Training, 44,* 378–383. doi:10.1037/0033-3204.44.4.378

Brownson, R. C., Kreuter, M. W., Arrington, B. A., & True, W. R. (2006). Translating scientific discoveries into public health action: How can schools of public health move us forward? *Public Health Reports, 121,* 97–103.

Castonguay, L. G., Barkham, M., Lutz, W., & McAleavey, A. A. (2013). Practice-oriented research: Approaches and applications. In M.J. Lambert (Ed.), *Bergin and Garfield's handbook of therapeutic change* (6th ed.). New York: Wiley & Sons.

Castonguay, L. G., Boswell, J. F., Constantino, M. J., Goldfried, M.R., & Hill, C.E. (2010). Training implications of harmful effects of psychological treatments. *American Psychologist, 65,* 34–49. doi:10.1037/a0017330

Castonguay, L. G., Boswell, J. F., Zack, S. E., Baker, S., Boutselis, M. A., Chiswick, N. R.... Grosse Holtforth, M. (2010). Helpful and hindering events in psychotherapy: A practice research network study. *Psychotherapy: Theory, Research, Practice, Training, 47,* 327–344. doi:10.1037/a0021164

Castonguay, L. G., Pincus, A. L., & McAleavey, A. A. (in press). Practice-research networks in training clinics. *Psychotherapy Research.*

Chin, R., & Benne, K. D. (1969). General strategies for effecting changes in human systems. In W.G. Bennis, K.D. Benne, & R. Chin (Eds.), *The planning of change* (pp. 32–59). New York: Holt, Rinehart & Winston.

Cook, I. A., Balasubramani, G. K., Eng, H., Friedman, E., Young, E. A., Martin, J., ... Wisniewski, S. R. (2007). Electronic source materials in clinical research: Acceptability and validity of symptom self-rating in major depressive disorder. *Journal of Psychiatry Research, 41,* 737–743. doi:10.1016/j.jpsychires.2006.07.015

De Jong, K., van Sluis, P., Nugter, M. A., Heiser, W. J., & Spinhoven, P. (2012). Understanding the differential impact of outcome monitoring: Therapist variables that moderate feedback effects in a randomized clinical trial. *Psychotherapy Research, 22,* 464–474. doi:10.1080/10503307.2012.673023

Diamond, G. A., & Kaul, S. (2009). Evidence-based financial incentives for healthcare reform: Putting it together. *Circulation: Cardiovascular quality and outcomes, 2,* 134–140. doi:10.1161/CIRCOUTCOMES.108.825695

Drapeau, M. (2012). The value of tracking in psychotherapy. *Integrating Science & Practice, 2,* 2–6.

Eby, L. T., Burk, H., & Maher, C. P. (2010). How serious of a problem is staff turnover in substance abuse treatment? A longitudinal study of actual turnover. *Journal of Substance Abuse Treatment, 39,* 264–271. doi:10.1016/j.jsat.2010.06.009

Ellsworth, J. R., Lambert, M. J., & Johnson, J. (2006). A comparison of the Outcome Questionnaire-45 and Outcome Questionnaire-30 in classification and prediction of treatment outcome. *Clinical Psychology & Psychotherapy, 13,* 380–391. doi:10.1002/cpp.503

Fernández-Álvarez, H., Gómez, B., & García, F. (in press). Bridging the gap between research and practice in a clinical and training network. *Psychotherapy Research*

Finch, R. A., & Phillips, K. (2005). Center for Prevention and Health Services. *An employer's guide to behavioral health services: A roadmap and recommendations for evaluating, designing, and implementing behavioral health services.* Washington DC: National Business Group on Health.

Fixsen, D. L., Naoom, S. F., Blase, K. A., Friedman, R. M., & Wallace, F. (2005). Implementation research: A synthesis of the literature. Tampa, FL: University of South Florida, Louis de la Parte Florida Mental Health Institute, The National Implementation Research Network (FMHI Publication #231).

Garb, H. N. (2005). Clinical judgment and decision making. *Annual Review of Clinical Psychology, 1,* 67–89. doi:10.1146/annurev.clinpsy.1.102803.143810

Gilbody, S., House, A., & Sheldon, T. (2002). Psychiatrists in the United Kingdom do not use outcomes measures. *British Journal of Psychiatry, 180,* 101–103. doi:10.1192/bjp.180.2.101

Greenhalgh, T., Robert, G., Macfarlane, F., Bate, P., & Kyriakidou, O. (2004). Diffusion of innovations in service organizations: Systematic review and recommendations. *Milbank Quarterly, 82,* 581–629. doi:10.1111/j.0887-378X.2004.00325.x

Hannan, C., Lambert, M. J., Harmon, C., Nielsen, S. L., Smart, D. W., Shimokawa, K., & Sutton, S. W. (2005). A lab test and algorithms for identifying clients at risk for treatment failure.

Journal of Clinical Psychology: In Session, 61, 155–163. doi:10.1002/jclp.20108

Hansen, N. B., Lambert, M. J., & Forman, E. V. (2002). The psychotherapy dose-response effect and its implications for treatment delivery services. *Clinical Psychology: Science and Practice, 9,* 329–343. doi:10.1093/clipsy.9.3.329

Harford, T. (2011). *Adapt: Why success always starts with failure.* London: Macmillan.

Harmon, S. C., Lambert, M. J., Smart, D. W., Hawkins, E. J., Nielsen, S. L., Slade, K., & Lutz, W. (2007). Enhancing outcome for potential treatment failures: Therapist/client feedback and clinical support tools. *Psychotherapy Research, 17,* 379–392. doi:10.1080/10503300600702331

Hatfield, D., McCullough, L., Plucinski, A., & Krieger, K. (2010). Do we know when our clients get worse? An investigation of therapists' ability to detect negative client change. *Clinical Psychology & Psychotherapy, 17,* 25–32.

Hatfield, D. R., & Ogles, B. M. (2004). The current climate of outcome measures use in clinical practice. *Professional Psychology: Research and Practice, 35,* 485–491. doi:10.1037/0735-7028.35.5.485

Hatfield, D. R., & Ogles, B. M. (2007). Why some clinicians use outcome measures and others do not. *Administrative Policy Mental Health and Mental Health Services Research, 34,* 283–291. doi:10.1007/s10488-006-0110-y

Hawkins, E. J., Lambert, M. J., Vermeersch, D. A., Slade, K., & Tuttle, K. (2004). The effects of providing patient progress information to therapists and patients. *Psychotherapy Research, 14,* 308–327. doi:10.1093/ptr/kph027

Holmqvist, R., Philips, B., & Barkham, M. (in press). Developing and delivering practice-based evidence: Observations, tensions, and challenges. *Psychotherapy Research.*

Howard, K. I., Moras, K., Brill, P. L., Martinovich, Z., & Lutz, W. (1996). Evaluation of psychotherapy. *American Psychologist, 51,* 1059–1064. doi:10.1037/0003-066X.51.10.1059

Kazdin, A. E. (1996). Dropping out of child therapy. Issues for research and implications for practice. *Clinical Child Psychology and Psychiatry, 1,* 133–156. doi:10.1177/1359104596011012

Kazdin, A. E. (2005). Evidence-based assessment for children and adolescents: Issues in measurement development and clinical application. *Journal of Clinical Child & Adolescent Psychology, 34,* 548–558. doi:10.1207/s15374424jccp3403_10

Kiefe, C. I., Allison, J. J., Williams, O. D., Person, S. D., Weaver, M. T., & Weissman, N. W. (2001). Improving quality improvement using achievable benchmarks for physician feedback: a randomized controlled trial. *JAMA, 285,* 2871–2879. doi:10.1001/jama.285.22.2871

Kluger, A. N., & DeNisi, A. (1996). The effects of feedback interventions on performance: A historical review, a meta-analysis, and a preliminary feedback intervention theory. *Psychological Bulletin, 119,* 254–284. doi:10.1037/0033-2909.119.2.254

Koestner, R. (2008). Reaching one's personal goals: A motivational perspective focused on autonomy. *Canadian Psychology, 49,* 60–67. doi:10.1037/0708-5591.49.1.60

Koocher, G. P., & Keith-Spiegel, P. (2008). *Ethics in psychology and the mental health professions: Standards and cases.* New York: Oxford University Press.

Kraus, D. R., Boswell, J. F., Wright, A. G. C., Castonguay, L. G., & Pincus, A. L. (2010). Factor structure of the treatment outcome package for children. *Journal of Clinical Psychology, 66,* 627–640.

Kraus, D. R., Castonguay, L. G., Boswell, J. F., Nordberg, S. S., & Hayes, J. A. (2011). Therapist effectiveness: Implications for accountability and patient care. *Psychotherapy Research, 21,* 267–276. doi:10.1080/10503307.2011.563249

Kraus, D. R., Seligman, D., & Jordan, J. R. (2005). Validation of a behavioral health treatment outcome and assessment tool designed for naturalistic settings: The Treatment Outcome Package. *Journal of Clinical Psychology, 61,* 285–314. doi:10.1002/jclp.20084

Kraus, D. R., Wolf, A., & Castonguay, L. (2006). A kinder philosophy to the management of outcomes. *Psychotherapy Bulletin, 41,* 23–31.

Lambert, M. J. (2010). *Prevention of treatment failure: The use of measuring, monitoring, and feedback in clinical practice.* Washington DC: American Psychological Association Press.

Lambert, M. J. (2012). Helping clinicians to use and learn from research-based systems: The OQ-Analyst. *Psychotherapy, 49,* 109–114. doi:10.1037/a0027110

Lambert, M. J. (2013). The efficacy and effectiveness of psychotherapy. In M. J. Lambert (Ed.) *Bergin & Garfield's Handbook of psychotherapy & behavior change* (6th ed.). New York: Wiley.

Lambert, M. J., Burlingame, G. M., Umphress, V., Hansen, N. B., Vermeersch, D. A., Clouse, G. C., & Yanchar, S. C. (1996). The reliability and validity of the outcome questionnaire. *Clinical Psychology & Psychotherapy, 3,* 249–258. doi:10.1002/(SICI)1099-0879(199612)3:4<249::AID-CPP106>3.0.CO;2-S

Lambert, M. J. & Shimokawa, K. (2011). Collecting client feedback. In J.C. Norcross (Ed.), *Psychotherapy relationships that work* (2nd ed., pp. 203–223). New York: Oxford University Press.

Lambert, M. J., Whipple, J. L., Bishop, M. J., Vermeersch, D. A., Gray, G. V., & Finch, A. E. (2002). Comparison of empirically derived and rationally derived methods for identifying clients at risk for treatment failure. *Clinical Psychology and Psychotherapy, 9,* 149–164. doi:10.1002/cpp.333

Lambert, M. J., Whipple, J. L., Smart, D. W., Vermeersch, D. A., Nielsen, S.L., & Hawkins, E.J. (2001). The effects of providing therapists with feedback on client progress during psychotherapy: Are outcomes enhanced? *Psychotherapy Research, 11,* 49–68. doi:10.1080/713663852

Lambert, M. J., Whipple, J. L., Vermeersch, D. A., Smart, D. W., Hawkins, E. J., Nielsen, S. L., & Goates, M. K. (2002). Enhancing psychotherapy outcomes via providing feedback on client progress: A replication. *Clinical Psychology and Psychotherapy, 9,* 91–103. doi:10.1002/cpp.324

Latham, G. P., & Locke, E. A. (2006). Enhancing the benefits and overcoming the pitfalls of goal setting. *Organizational Dynamics, 35,* 332–340. doi:10.1016/j.orgdyn.2006.08.008

Locke, E. A., & Latham, G. P. (2006). New directions in goal-setting theory. *Current Directions in Psychological Science, 15,* 265–268. doi:10.1111/j.1467-8721.2006.00449.x

Marty, D., Rapp, C. A., McHugo, G. J., & Whitley, R. (2007). Factors influencing consumer outcome monitoring in implementation of evidence-based practices: Results from the National EBP Implementation Project. *Administration and Policy in Mental Health, 35,* 204–211. doi:10.1007/s10488-007-0157-4

McAleavey, A. A., Lockard, A. J., Castonguay, L. G., Hayes, J. A., & Locke, B.D. (in press). Research by, with, and for clinicians: Lessons from a large-scale PRN for University and College Counseling Centers. *Psychotherapy Research.*

McAleavey, A. A., Nordberg, S. S., Kraus, D. R., & Castonguay, L.G. (2012). Errors in treatment outcome monitoring: Implications of multidimensional and general measurements for real-world psychotherapy. *Canadian Psychology, 53,* 105–114. doi:10.1037/a0027833

McHugh, R. K., & Barlow, D. H. (2012). *Dissemination and implementation of evidence-based psychological interventions.* New York: Oxford University Press.

Merten, T., & Ruch, W. (1996). A comparison of computerized and conventional administration of the German versions of the Eysenck Personality Questionnaire and the Carroll Rating Scale

for Depression. *Personality and Individual Differences, 20,* 281–291. http://dx.doi.org/10.1016/0191-8869(95)00185-9

Miller, S. D., Duncan, B. L., & Hubble, M. A. (2004). Beyond integration: The triumph of outcome over process in clinical practice. *Psychotherapy in Australia, 10,* 32–43.

Miller, S. D., Duncan, B. L., Sorrell, R., & Brown, G. S. (2005). The Partners for Change Outcome Management System. *Journal of Clinical Psychology: In-Session, 61,* 199–208. doi:10.1002/jclp.20111

Miller, S. D., Hubble, M. A., Chow, D. L., & Seidel, J. A. (2013). The outcome of psychotherapy: Yesterday, today, and tomorrow. *Psychotherapy, 50,* 88–97. doi:10.1037/a0031097

Nordberg, S. S., Boswell, J. F., Kraus, D. R., Castonguay, L. G., Hayes, J., & Wampold, B. (2010, June). *Therapist effectiveness treating depression with and without co-morbid substance abuse.* Paper presented at the Society for Psychotherapy Research Conference, Asilomar, CA.

Ogles, B. M., France, C. R., Lunnen, K. M., Bell, M. T., & Goldfarb, M. (1998). Computerized depression screening and awareness. *Community Mental Health Journal, 34,* 27–38. doi:10.1023/A:1018760128239

Okiishi, J., Lambert, M. J., Eggett, D., Nielsen, S. L., Dayton, D.D., & Vermeersch, D.A. (2006). An analysis of therapist treatment effects: Toward providing feedback to individual therapists on their clients' psychotherapy outcome; *Journal of Clinical Psychology, 62,* 1157–1172. doi:10.1002/jclp.20272

Peterson, L., Johannsson, V., & Carlsson, S. (1996). Computerized testing in a hospital setting: Psychometric and psychological effects. *Computers in Human Behavior, 12,* 339–350. http://dx.doi.org/10.1016/0747-5632(96)00012-X

Pope, K. S., Tabachnick, B. G., & Keith-Spiegel, P. (1987). Ethics of practice: The beliefs and behaviors of psychologists as therapists. *American Psychologist, 42,* 993–1006. doi:10.1037/0003-066X.42.11.993

Riemer, M., Rosof-Williams, J., & Bickman, L. (2005). Theories related to changing clinician practice. *Child and Adolescent Psychiatric Clinics of North America, 14,* 241–254. doi:10.1016/j.chc.2004.05.002

Rogers, E. (2003). *The diffusion of innovation* (5th ed.). New York: The Free Press.

Rosenthal, M. B. (2008). Beyond pay for performance—emerging models of provider-payment reform. *New England Journal of Medicine, 359,* 1197–1200. doi:10.1056/NEJMp0804658

Shimokawa, K., Lambert, M. J., & Smart, D. (2010). Enhancing treatment outcome of patients at risk of treatment failure: Meta-analytic and mega-analytic review of a psychotherapy quality assurance system. *Journal of Consulting & Clinical Psychology, 78,* 298–311. doi:10.1037/a0019247

Slade, K., Lambert, M. J., Harmon, S. C., Smart, D. W., & Bailey, R. (2008). Improving psychotherapy outcome: The use of immediate electronic feedback and revised clinical support tools. *Clinical Psychology & Psychotherapy, 15,* 287–303. doi:10.1002/cpp.594

Slade, M., Thornicroft, G., & Glover, G.S.O. (1999). The feasibility of routine outcome measures in mental health. *Social Psychiatry and Epidemiology, 34,* 243–249. doi:10.1007/s001270050139

Strauss, B., Lutz, W., Steffanowski, A., Wittmann, W., Böhnke, J.R., Rubel, J., … Kirchmann, H. (in press). Benefits and challenges in practice-oriented psychotherapy research in Germany: The TK and the QS-PSY-BAY projects of quality assurance in outpatient psychotherapy. *Psychotherapy Research.*

Stricker, G., & Trierweiler, S. J. (1995). The local clinical scientist: A bridge between science and practice. *American Psychologist, 50,* 995–1002. doi:10.1037/0003-066X.50.12.995

Strupp, H. H., Horowitz, L. M., & Lambert, M. J. (1997). *Measuring patient changes in mood, anxiety, and personality disorders: Toward a core battery.* Washington DC: American Psychological Association Press.

Trauer, T., Gill, L., Pedwell, G., & Slattery, P. (2006). Routine outcome measurement in public mental health—what do clinicians think? *Australian Health Review, 30,* 144–147. doi:10.1071/AH060144

Tremblay, M. C., Hevner, A. R., & Berndt, D. J. (2012). Design of an information volatility measure for health care decision making. *Decision Support Systems, 52,* 331–341. doi:10.1016/j.dss.2011.08.009

Walfish, S., McAlister, B., O'Donnell, P., & Lambert, M. J. (2012). An investigation of self-assessment bias in mental health providers. *Psychological Reports, 110,* 639–644. doi:10.2466/02.07.17

Warren, J. S., Nelson, P. L., Mondragon, S. A., Baldwin, S. A., & Burlingame, G.M. (2010). Youth psychotherapy change trajectories & outcome in usual care: Community mental health versus managed care. *Journal of Clinical & Consulting Psychology, 78,* 144–155. doi:10.1037/a0018544

Weissman, N. W., Allison, J. J., Kiefe, C. I., Farmer, R., Weaver, M.T., Williams, O.D., ... Baker, S. (1999). Achievable benchmarks of care: The ABCs of benchmarking. *Journal of Evaluation in Clinical Practice, 5,* 269–281. doi:10.1046/j.1365-2753.1999.00203.x

West, J. C., Mościcki, E. K., Duffy, F. F., Wilk, J.E., Countis, L., Narrow, W.E., & Regier, D.A. (in press). APIRE Practice Research Network: Accomplishments, challenges, and lessons learned. *Psychotherapy Research.*

Whipple, J. L., Lambert, M. J., Vermeersch, D. A., Smart, D. W., Nielsen, S.L., & Hawkins, E.J. (2003). Improving the effects of psychotherapy: The use of early identification of treatment failure and problem solving strategies in routine practice. *Journal of Counseling Psychology, 58,* 59–68. doi:10.1037/0022-0167.50.1.59

Wierzbicki, M. & Pekarik, G. (1993). A meta-analysis of psychotherapy dropout. *Professional Psychology: Research and Practice, 24,* 190–195. doi:10.1037/0735-7028.24.2.190

Youn, S.J., Kraus, D. R., & Castonguay, L.G. (2012). The Treatment Outcome Package: Facilitating practice and clinically relevant research. *Psychotherapy, 49,* 115–122. doi:10.1037/a0027932

Zimmerman, M., & McGlinchey, J. B. (2008). Why don't psychiatrists use scales to measure outcome when treating depressed patients? *Journal of Clinical Psychiatry, 69,* 1916–1919.

METHOD PAPER

Developing practice-based evidence: Benefits, challenges, and tensions

ROLF HOLMQVIST[1], BJÖRN PHILIPS[1], & MICHAEL BARKHAM[2]

[1]Department of Behavioural Sciences and Learning, Linköping University, Linköping, Sweden & [2]Centre for Psychological Services Research, University of Sheffield, Sheffield, UK

Abstract

Attempts to regulate service delivery in line with results from randomized trials have been vigorously debated. In this paper, results from practice-based studies using the CORE System illustrate the potential to enrich knowledge about the actual outcome of psychological therapy in routine care. These studies also provide data for important questions in psychotherapy research, like orientation differences, the importance of the therapist factor, number of sessions needed for clinical effect, and the alliance–outcome question. Obstacles and challenges in making such studies are illustrated. In conclusion, arguments are put forward for introducing a common measurement system that strikes a balance between clinicians' questions and the need for comparable data, and that encompasses the complexities of patients' reasons for seeking psychological help.

Introduction

Recent decades have seen an immense increase in developing and delivering improvements in accessing quality psychological healthcare for people in need. Efforts to enhance the effectiveness of psychological treatments have tended to follow one of two possible tracks. One track has involved developing psychological treatment methods "in the lab," testing their efficacy in well-controlled trials, and then disseminating them to routine care (Hunsley & Lee, 2007). This paradigm is often termed *evidence-based practice* (McHugh & Barlow, 2012). Considerable effort and money in the UK and in Sweden have been invested in disseminating such treatments to service providers and education programs. By contrast, the other track has been to study the effects of psychological treatments as they are delivered in routine clinical practice, a paradigm termed *practice-based evidence*[1] (Barkham, Hardy, & Mellor-Clark, 2010; Barkham & Margison, 2007). In such studies, allowance is made for variation in patient symptoms and comorbidity, therapist competence, and treatment

contexts. These components can be investigated within the naturally occurring hierarchical nature of large-scale practice-based datasets, which allows for the use of sophisticated multilevel modeling techniques. And then findings from practice-based studies can later be tested in systematic treatment trials that, in turn, lead to further practice-based studies, thereby resulting in a naturally occurring cycle of research activity (Barkham & Mellor-Clark, 2003).

These two tracks are sometimes—mistakenly—viewed as competing with each other. However, they are in fact complementary paradigms, as both are needed in order to build a robust and rigorous science of the psychological therapies (Barkham, Stiles, Lambert, & Mellor-Clark, 2010). The purpose of the present article is to set out both the common and contrasting obstacles and tensions experienced in two countries—Sweden and the UK—in pursuit of redressing the balance between evidence-based practice and practice-based evidence.

At the health political level, there are clear similarities between the UK and Sweden. The government and state authorities have large influence on the health service in both countries. Treatment of psychiatric disorders and psychological problems is to a large extent delivered by publicly financed service units (e.g., primary care centers and psychiatric outpatient clinics). The governments in both countries have taken strong initiatives to promote evidence-based treatments in these treatment services, requiring that only therapists with knowledge of evidence-based methods should provide treatment.

There are at present also some unifying components between Sweden and UK with regard to psychotherapy research and practice. In ongoing programs of practice-based studies in both countries, predominantly, although not exclusively, the same measurement system is being used. In both countries, there is also a dominance of the paradigm of evidence-based practice, best exemplified by the randomized controlled trial.

Accordingly, in this article, first we set out the origins and philosophy of our common measurement system. Second, we focus on the role of such a measurement system in underpinning the paradigm of practice-based evidence and the need for studies in this paradigm. And third, we draw out benefits, challenges, and tensions relating to implementing practice-based studies in Sweden and the UK together with the generic issues associated with developing a common outcome measure for practitioners.

The CORE Measures and System: Origins and Philosophy

The CORE program is a fluid and organic portfolio of work that began in the mid-1990s with the aim of developing a free-to-use, pantheoretical outcome measure which tapped the core components that practitioners considered as central when evaluating patient change: subjective wellbeing, problems, functioning, and risk. Accordingly, the measure—and much of the subsequent work—has been premised on meeting practitioners' needs and building an evidence base that speaks to local service requirements but that also can be the basis for building a cumulative evidence base to complement trials-based evidence.

The CORE initiative arose in response to the SPR-initiated symposium revisiting the concept of a core outcome battery (Strupp, Horowitz, & Lambert, 1997), which had its own origins in a seminal symposium held in 1970 focusing on the measurement of change (Waskow & Parloff, 1975). These two symposia provided the impetus for an initiative in the UK whereby a UK charity—the Mental Health Foundation—funded two successive pieces of research focusing first on the acceptability and feasibility of developing a core outcome battery and then on the development of a core outcome

measure. This work yielded the Clinical Outcomes in Routine Evaluation-Outcome Measure (CORE-OM; Barkham et al., 2001; Evans et al., 2002). A further and final grant supported the implementation of the CORE-OM (i.e., a roll out to services), which also comprised a wider CORE system incorporating the collection of contextual information within which patient outcomes could be placed (for details, see Mellor-Clark & Barkham, 2012). These data—outcomes and contextual—were supported initially by a personal computer version of the CORE system (PC-CORE) and more recently by a web-based support—CORE Net. This information technology (IT) platform provides services with the facility for managing their data using multiple options and filters that determine the level of complexity in data reporting required by a service.

The original CORE-OM became the parent version for a family of CORE measures that derived from the original items (although with some adaptations), which yielded the following variants (see Barkham, Mellor-Clark, et al., 2010, for summary details): (i) two parallel shorter versions for intensive research (CORE-Short Form, A and B), (ii) a 10-item version (CORE-10), (iii) a five-item monitoring version (CORE-5), as well as versions for (iv) the general population (GP-CORE), (v) young people (YP-CORE), and (vi) people experiencing learning difficulties (CORE-LD). In addition, subsequent research has yielded the identification of six items from the CORE-OM to determine health utility status (CORE-6D; Mavranezouli, Brazier, Rowan, & Barkham, 2013; Mavranezouli, Brazier, Young, & Barkham, 2011), Most importantly, and crucial to the potential of building collaboration with practitioners, there has been an ongoing program of securing standardized translations of the CORE-OM and its variants into more than 25 languages, including a Swedish version (Elfström et al., 2013).[2]

The development of a comprehensive option of measures based on the CORE-OM together with the contextual information relating to patients' presenting problems and service provision provides a *measurement system*—as opposed to a simple outcome measure—that provides the core component for delivering on the agenda of practice-based evidence. In turn, practice-based evidence provides the overarching framework for collaborating with practitioners with the aim of both improving practice and building an evidence base to complement trials methodology.

Practice-Based Evidence in the UK and Sweden

Although a bona fide measurement system is the key component for practice-based evidence, other components are also required. These include a commitment to the philosophy of practice-based evidence, an infrastructure to support the research activities, and a willingness (and technical ability) to share data. Perhaps a key axiom to the philosophy underpinning practice-based evidence is that practitioners have a genuine sense of local ownership regarding the measurement system and the data it yields, be it in relation to an individual practitioner or at the level of psychological services. Accordingly, in this paradigm, the accumulation of evidence assumes a *bottom-up model* whereby routine data are used at an individual level and locally within the service but then also accumulated across services and used to generate a higher-order evidence base.

However, such a paradigm runs counter to the dominant model of evidence espoused in many countries. For example, practice-based studies carried out in Sweden and the UK have been implemented in national contexts that place the primary value on research methods (and interventions arising from such studies) endorsed by national bodies such as the National Institute for Health and Clinical Excellence (NICE) in the UK and the Socialstyrelsen (the National Board for Health and Welfare) and the Swedish Council on Technology Assessment (SBU) in Sweden. These national bodies place a central value on a *top-down model* in which evidence from randomized trials is then espoused in routine practice via clinical guidelines. Adherence to these guidelines at the level of individual services can then be evaluated by national audit—in the UK this has been achieved through the National Audit of Psychological Therapies involving feedback to services in the form of benchmarking their compliance against overall standards (Royal College of Psychiatrists, 2011). Similarly in Sweden, governmental authorities (e.g., the Ministry of Health and Social Affairs) base resource allocation to health services that provide specified evidence-based treatments.

Set against the dominant model of evidence-based practice, research programs utilizing routine outcome data have been carried forward. In the UK, this program of work has considered a range of issues including the benchmarking of services (Barkham et al., 2001; Evans, Connell, Barkham, Marshall, & Mellor-Clark, 2003), the comparative effectiveness of different models of therapies (Stiles, Barkham, Mellor-Clark, & Connell, 2008; Stiles, Barkham, Twigg, Mellor-Clark, & Cooper, 2006), and enhancing our understanding of dose-effect relations and the role of the good-enough model in providing an account of the dose-effect curve (Barkham et al., 2006). More recently attention has focused on the area of therapist variability (Saxon & Barkham, 2012). Research has also focused on

patient change via work addressing the phenomenon of sudden gains (Stiles et al., 2003), responsiveness (Stiles, Barkham, Connell, & Mellor-Clark, 2008), as well as the prediction of patient change (Lutz et al., 2005; Stulz, Lutz, Leach, Lucock, & Barkham, 2007).

In Sweden, a research program comprising data from psychological treatment in primary care and psychiatric clinics has recently started. To date, analyses have been carried out on treatment outcome with different treatment methods (Holmqvist, Ström, & Foldemo, 2013), on different aspects of the relationship between treatment alliance and outcome (Falkenström, Granström & Holmqvist, 2013a, 2013b; Larsson, Andersson & Holmqvist, 2013; Sinclair & Holmqvist, 2013), and on the significance of congruence between patient and therapist in the perception of symptoms (Holmqvist, Philips, & Mellor-Clark, 2013). Collectively, these research activities illustrate how the practice-based paradigm focuses on factors such as patient resources, therapist and relationship qualities, and setting variables.

A key advantage of the practice-based paradigm is that it provides possibilities to test treatment methods that clinical experience has supported and to understand patient and treatment moderating factors that influence results in clinical practice (Cahill, Barkham, & Stiles, 2010). An apparent advantage with practice-based studies is that they may elucidate the significance of contextual factors for the results. It is important to analyze what conditions may determine or influence outcome results in routine practice. Recent examinations have found large variations in outcome scores depending on which subsample of patients is studied and what outcome measures are used, with effect sizes ranging from .60 to 1.95 (Barkham, Stiles, Connell, & Mellor-Clark, 2012).

Benefits of Practice-Based Studies

Although the twin framing of evidence-based practice and practice-based evidence is appealing as an overarching model for broadening our knowledge base about the psychological therapies, it is important to have evidence of the added value—the additional benefits—of the latter approach. Two benefits of practice-based evidence are (i) local ownership by practitioners and services, and (ii) cumulatively enhancing evidence in areas in which trial designs are not appropriate. Here we provide examples of these two yields.

Local Ownership

In contrast to the adoption of outcome measures via government mandate, a practice-based approach would aim for a service to select a measure, from a battery of bona fide measures, that best suited their purpose. Exercising choice in selecting a validated measure would greatly facilitate a sense of ownership of the resulting data. Two UK examples where services have adopted CORE and provided accounts of its implementation are the Women's Counselling and Therapy Service (Leeds; womenstherapyleeds. org.uk/wp-content/.../What-Happened-Next.pdf) and My Sister's Place (Middlesbrough; www.coreims.co. uk/site_downloads/MSP_study_of_excellence.pdf). Both services have been set up for women, the former to provide long-term therapy and the latter as a response to domestic violence. Both adopted CORE around 2004–2005 and have integrated it into their service, and both have been recipients of awards from the British Association for Counselling and Psychotherapy in recognition of their work: the Women's Counselling and Therapy Service received the award for Outstanding Research Project (2011) while My Sister's Place received the award for Excellence in Counselling and Psychotherapy (2011).

In recounting the adoption of CORE, My Sister's Place have reported that, given the main goal was to improve service quality for clients, CORE "was enthusiastically embraced by all members of the counselling team." Adopting CORE was facilitated by therapists being given as much support as necessary to ensure they were using the system effectively, including one-to-one training sessions. And for practitioners, CORE is presented as a means for them to reflect on their practice and develop as skilled practitioners rather than being used as a means of assessing their performance. The impact of adopting CORE included the following: Improved assessment procedures; development of a domestic violence-specific therapeutic model; support of additional therapeutic provision: alerting to an increase in the number of clients presenting with more complex trauma; building working partnerships with external referral sources and promoting the service to other referrers; and demographic data have been used to improve therapeutic provision to more marginal groups (e.g., a Disabled Outreach Therapy Service has been established, which offers therapy for disabled clients in their homes). Overall, it enabled the service to adapt to the changing needs of the clients, to expand the service, and to increase service provision and provide an evidence base to support funding applications for the service.

Enhancing Evidence

One of the central issues within the field of psychotherapy research that can best be addressed with the broad collection of data that practice-based studies make possible is the phenomenon of natural variability in aspects of human performance and service delivery. By definition, trials place constraints on a range of features in order to test a candidate intervention. By contrast, practice-based studies have the potential for understanding natural variability when not constrained by strict treatment protocol. Two examples of this would be therapist *drift* (e.g., Waller, 2009) and therapist *effects* (e.g., Baldwin & Imel, 2013). The former arises from therapists in routine practice not implementing proven techniques in keeping with the theoretical model of therapy delivered, and the latter captures the phenomenon that not all therapists are equally effective—that is, some yield consistently better outcomes. Both these examples place a focus on the practitioner rather than the intervention per se and both are features of routine practice.

In relation to therapist effects, a recent review of this field analyzed 46 studies that used random effects (Baldwin & Imel, 2013). While the overall effect was 5%, there was a significant difference in the extent of therapist effects between efficacy (trials) and effectiveness (naturalistic) studies, with a mean therapist effect for trials of 3% while for naturalistic studies it was 7%. Hence, while the overall (average) effect is in the region of 5%—similar to that of the therapeutic alliance—practice-based studies reveal the effect to be larger. One conclusion that the authors arrive at is "Advancement in our understanding of therapist effects will likely only come from larger studies of therapist effects .... Researchers will likely need to collaborate and pool resources to obtain sufficient amounts of data. It is a challenge but a challenge we must face if we are to move this literature forward." (p. 280).

One example of this collaboration in aid of yielding larger studies is a report published subsequent to the above review and using CORE-OM data derived from 22 services and comprising one of the largest studies of therapist effects, in which 119 therapists each saw a minimum of 30 patients (Saxon & Barkham, 2012). After adjusting for case-mix, the therapist effect was 6.6%. However, of particular note was the finding that when considering the CORE scores (but excluding the Risk component), a low score yielded a therapist effect in the region of 1–2%. However, as patient intake scores increased, the therapist effect rose upwards to 10%. That is, the higher the patient initial severity score, the more it matters whom the patient sees. This makes clinical sense but is a finding that is unlikely to have arisen from an RCT. Although practice-based studies provide a context within which to investigate these effects, we need to be able to combine process and qualitative research components in order to be able to unpack therapist effects.

More generally, in comparison with the strict inclusion criteria in efficacy studies, the results from practice-based studies underline the satisfactory results of routine psychotherapy treatment. They emphasize the importance of testing routine treatments in order to understand their effectiveness. But practice-based studies not only contribute to a better understanding of treatment results in routine care, they also open up for analyses issues that often cannot be properly handled in randomized studies considering their restriction of range in key variables.

Key Foci in Practice-Based Studies

In this section, we set out briefly some of the arguments for practice-based studies, focusing on the key areas relating to patients, therapists, and services providing psychological therapies.

Patients. Patients have complex combinations of psychiatric, relational, and social problems that the treatment must handle. Stirman, DeRubeis, Crits-Christoph, and Brody (2003) found that results from RCTs performed in research settings may be less useful in clinical practice as the patients have heterogeneous psychopathology. More than half of community outpatients had primary diagnoses that were not represented in the existing psychotherapy outcome literature.

Therapists. Therapists often have heterogeneous therapeutic competencies. Many therapists are trained in several treatment methods, and it is common for therapists to describe themselves as integrative (Larsson, Kaldo, & Broberg, 2009). It is probable that therapists often combine treatment approaches according to their clinical sensibility and experience (Street, Niederehe, & Lebowitz, 2000). It is also probable that services vary in the extent of existing competencies among their staff and in their encouragement of developing diverse competencies.

Treatment length. Treatment length varies depending on symptom reduction rate and extraneous factors and not according to a manual (Baldwin, Berkeljon, Atkins, Olsen, & Nielsen, 2009). Findings from randomized studies with manualized treatments do not usually give information about number of sessions needed for symptom improvement, as guidelines usually prescribe treatment length. However, in actual practice treatment duration may differ considerably from the manuals' recommendations. Previous studies have suggested a general asymptotic dose-response rate for improvement (Howard, Kopta, Krause, & Orlinsky, 1986), but a linear "good-enough" model has recently been proposed (Baldwin et al., 2009; Barkham et al., 2006), implying that the individual symptom reduction trajectory determines when the therapy will terminate.

Under-represented treatments. Some treatments are rarely or never studied in systematic trials although they represent a large part of actual therapeutic work in routine psychiatry (Pingitore, Scheffler, Schwalm, Zarin, &. West, 2001; Tanielian, Marcus, Suarez, A. P, & Pincus, 2001). In contrast to manual-based methods, some of which have been repeatedly studied in efficacy trials, these treatments have hardly ever been studied except as comparison treatments, often under disadvantageous conditions. Several studies have indicated that the effects of treatment methods do not differ in practice studies (Stiles, Barkham, Connell et al., 2008; Holmqvist, Ström et al., 2013) but more studies on frequently used methods are needed. This question includes the issue of interaction between service unit and treatment method. Knowledge about this apart from clinical lore is virtually non-existent. An example is supportive treatment, which has hardly ever been tried in an RCT as a treatment purported to be effective (Budge, Baardseth, Wampold, & Fluckiger, 2010). Although supportive therapy has been described in several handbooks (Novalis, Rojcewicz, & Peele, 1993; Pinsker, 1997; Winston, Rosenthal, & Pinsker, 2012), it is often described in pejorative terms (Hellerstein & Markowitz, 2008).

Therapist effects and training. As noted above, particularly interesting is the possibility of detecting therapist effects. Although the size of therapist effects has been debated (e.g., Elkin, Falconnier, Martino-vitch, & Mahoney, 2006; Kim, Wampold, & Bolt, 2006), which factors contribute to them is not well understood (Crits-Christoph et al., 1991; Luborsky, McLellan, Diguer, Woody, & Seligman, 1997; Wampold & Brown, 2005). It is also important to understand the potential interaction between therapist and treatment method. One question is: What is the level and extent of therapist training that contributes to outcome? This issue has been vigorously debated but has delivered meager results (O'Donovan, Bain, & Dyck, 2005). The few studies that have been done often suggest that training has limited importance. This issue is too often evaded in research. In contrast to RCTs in controlled settings, practice-based studies include staff with various training levels and make it possible to assess the importance of psychotherapy training and experience.

Patient-treatment matching. In a natural clinical setting, efforts are often made to match each patient to a suitable treatment, unlike the randomization procedure used in clinical trials. Both formal assessment procedures might be used or more informal clinical judgments. Hence, the ordinary routine in a clinic often includes assigning patients with different types of problems and different treatment goals to the therapy methods available at the clinic (Philips, 2009). A naturalistic study design appears to be the best way to measure therapy process and outcome under such clinical conditions.

Dropouts. Outcome in treatment studies is usually measured as symptom reduction. A large problem arises, however, in the guise of dropouts from treatment (Baekeland & Lundwall, 1975; Clarkin, Levy, Lenzenweger, & Kernberg, 2004; Klein, Stone, Hicks, & Pritchard, 2003; Reis & Brown, 2006; Wierzbicki & Pekarik, 1993; Young, Grusky, Jordan, & Belin, 2000). It is striking that figures on treatment dropout vary widely between studies (Barrett, Chua, Crits-Christoph, Gibbons, & Thompson, 2008; Chiesa, Wright, & Neeld, 2003; Hoffman, 1985; Kazdin & Mazurick, 1994; McMuran, Huband, & Overton, 2010). The overall mean for dropout from treatment in routine practice seems to be around 50%. This is, of course, a large problem both for the individual, for the service, and for society at large. It is therefore also important to measure outcome as the proportion of patients completing the treatment course.

Service effects. Differences in patient outcome between delivery services have been noted in some studies (Brown, Dreis & Nace, 1999; O'Brien, Fahmy, & Singh, 2009). In randomized studies, attempts are made to reduce systematic variation in all variables except between the treatments—the independent variable. Results are considered to be generalizable to all services, across cities or regions or even countries. In practice-based studies, allowance is made for and interest is focused on differences in the treatment deliverance context. In practice, it is hard to imagine a randomized study where patients are randomized to different treatment services. It is, however, quite conceivable that services differ in the quality and extent of delivery of treatment (Bickman, 2008; Bickman, Kelley, Breda, Vides de Andrade, & Riemer, 2011), and it is important to understand better the factors that contribute to such potential differences, which may be due to different treatment models but also to differences in organizational structures. The significance of organizational factors for patient outcome has only received limited research interest.

Benefits for Clinicians

Practice-based studies require close cooperation with the participating clinicians. The question of "What's in it for me" must be taken seriously. As an example, an ongoing study in both the UK and Sweden explores clinicians' thoughts about what kind of feedback they want. Using a randomized design, the influence of different therapist attitudes to sessional feedback on the factual use of feedback and on outcome is explored.

Challenges in Practice-Based Studies

As an example of challenges that have to be met in practice-based data collection, we offer here some experiences from an ongoing project in Sweden. This study was initiated at the request of therapists in primary care who feared losing their jobs as a consequence of organizational changes. They were strongly motivated to participate and to engage patients, and data from about 1200 patients were obtained. The design was essentially an outcome study with measurements at each session, using the CORE-OM and the Working Alliance Inventory (Hatcher & Gillaspy, 2006). Psychiatric clinics in the same region decided to use the same design in order to make comparisons with the primary care data possible. At this stage, more hurdles and problems occurred. Although service management was positive, the therapists were more ambivalent. Common reasons for hesitancy were that the administration and completion of questionnaires took too much time, that patients were referred to neuropsychiatric examinations rather than to psychotherapy and thus not possible to include, and that many patient contacts could not really be considered as therapies. Still another reason may have been that therapists were not certain about what kind of feedback they would obtain.

Patient participation does not, however, seem to be a problem. Although some patients decline to participate, most of them accept and a few express appreciation about the study. Data attrition from patients is low. At present, the percentage of delivered CORE-OM forms, in relation to the number of sessions that the therapists have reported that patients have attended, is about 97%.

At present, two strategies are used in order to engage therapists. The first is to accept that not all therapists at a specific service participate with their patients. At these services, information about service performance will not be available unless more therapists choose to participate. The other strategy, adopted by some clinic managements, is to mandate that participation by all therapists is compulsory.

Nine agencies have contributed data to the study so far and shortly another 15 agencies will join the study. Some preliminary analyses have been made. One study found that supportive treatment, the most frequently used treatment orientation, compared well with more systematic treatments when adequate control for relevant factors such as patient age and treatment length was made (Holmqvist, Ström et al., 2013) Other studies have found that treatment alliance predicts outcome from the first session onwards, both from session to session and for the whole treatment, even when outcome for each session has been controlled (Falkenström et al., 2013a, 2013b), and that sessions where the alliance has a rupture-resolution pattern have better outcomes than "stable" sessions (Larsson, Andersson, & Holmqvist, 2013). In still another analysis of the data, it was found that congruence between patient and therapist in the perception of the patient's level of depression and anxiety did not influence either treatment alliance or treatment outcome (Holmqvist, Philips et al., 2013).

Feedback is a central part of practice-based studies. In this study, feedback has, up to now, been given to those therapists with a substantial number of patients in the form of mean CORE-OM scores for the whole scale and subscales at the start of therapy, and as mean change scores for patients who have completed the treatment. Therapists are also informed about mean scores on the WAI ratings, on several social and psychiatric characteristics of the patients, and about treatment process variables.

As a part of this project, a special study of the effects of session-wise feedback, using CORE Net, is being carried out at two outpatient psychiatric clinics. The aim of this study is primarily to capture the reactions of therapists to the possibility of getting immediate information about a patient's symptoms and problems. It is not self-evident that immediate feedback, when offered, is always wanted or regularly used. Data suggest that it is primarily when the patient's condition worsens without the therapist being aware of it that session-wise feedback substantially increases outcome (Lambert, 2010).

An interesting aspect of studies collecting large data sets at different services is that such designs may allow for meaningful comparisons between units. In Sweden, this is a very timely issue, as a radical change in the provision of medical and psychiatric care has occurred during the last 15 years. From a system that almost entirely relied on public provision of health care, Sweden now has opened for private, even profit-driven, providers. But still, the main part of the care is paid from taxes. Thus, the state, counties, or cities allow public and private agencies and companies to compete for the right to deliver care. This competitive situation has come about rapidly, and authorities often have an underdeveloped ability to negotiate contracts. Input variables, like opening hours and number of posts, are often used in the contract negotiations instead of outcome figures. Recently, researchers and agency representatives have started discussing better ways of handling the competitive situation. The CORE project might give important knowledge for the further development of good care for less money. Several authors (e.g., Lambert, 2010) have noted the surprising fact that both researchers and care providers have been content "to use informal judgments instead of patient outcome data to evaluate therapists" (p. 175). The same verdict pertains to the service level.

Other Challenges

Evaluations of treatment results at therapist or service level have a value for society at large. But there is a risk that both public agencies and private companies may want to present more positive figures of treatment outcome than the data really warrant. An important challenge in studies at the service level is to publish figures with caution, always analyzing therapist and service effects with a caseload perspective and putting results within the frame of the socio-economic context.

Tensions

In this final section, we focus on methodological issues pertaining to measurement within practice-based evidence and the associated tensions. Our rationale is that a key axiom of practice-based evidence is the rigor, robustness, and relevance of the measurement system that lies at the heart of research efforts. This is a major foundation for enabling practitioners to adopt and receive appropriate acknowledgement as a contribution to the knowledge base for the psychological therapies.

Outcome Measures: Being Fit for Purpose and Fitting the Political Space

A major tension at the level of measure development is to devise a measure that is informed and/or endorsed by practitioners and service users—that is, ensuring measures are fit for purpose and appropriate for specific populations—whilst at the same time delivering to a *national agenda* in an increasingly outcome-oriented and politicized health delivery system—that is, meeting the requirement of the current political space. The dominant focus on diagnosis has resulted in an over-valuing of symptom-specific (i.e., unifocal) outcome measures. This situation is exemplified in the UK, where the PHQ-9 (Kroenke, Spitzer, & Williams, 2001) and GAD-7 (Spitzer, Kroenke, Williams, & Löwe, 2006) have been mandated for use in the Improving Access to Psychological Therapies (IAPT) initiative and, accordingly, have become dominant. These two measures are derived directly from the DSM-IV criteria for depression and anxiety respectively. In contrast to these symptom-specific measures, the dimensions comprising the CORE-OM were based on surveying practitioners' views as to what domains of change were important for their patients (Barkham et al., 2001).

An intrinsic strength of the CORE-OM is its coverage of a broad scope of symptoms as well as well-being and aspects of social and general functioning (including close relationships) together with a robust coverage of risk (to self and to others). Although the IAPT initiative also uses a short measure of functioning—the Work and Social Adjustment Scale (Mundt, Marks, Shear, & Greist, 2002)—definitions of *moving to recovery* are made using only the PHQ-9 and GAD-7. Hence, functioning does not contribute to the definition of recovery, which is operationalized as a patient's score on both PHQ-9 and GAD-7 measures falling below measure-specific cut-off scores.

While the language of symptoms and diagnoses is a good fit within trials methodology, the language of functioning is probably a fairly dominant index for everyday life. It may be that future measure development will focus more on the multiple aspects of functioning and such instruments may become better indicators of meaningful patient change. Until then, a conceptual problem remains in assuming that combining independent symptom-based measures represents an integrated clinical sense of recovery for a patient and that what matters most to a patient is achieving a specific score on wholly symptom-based measures. Indeed, a subsequent independent evaluation by service users of 24 commonly used outcome measures rated the CORE-OM more positively than the PHQ-9 (Crawford et al., 2011). Interestingly, the measure rated most highly by service users was the Warwick-Edinburgh Wellbeing Scale, perhaps because all the items were framed positively (Tennant et al., 2009). Certainly, any future measure development needs to ensure it is informed by the views and aspirations of service users.

A recent development within the CORE methodology is the ability to derive a health utility state from the CORE-OM via the CORE-6D (Mavranezouli et al., 2011 Mavranezouli et al., 2011, 2013), a facet that is not available with current symptom-based measures and in which the EQ-5D (EuroQol Group, 1990) has been prominent. However, the ability of a generic measure that has shorter versions for repeated administration together with the ability to generate a health utility state is a potentially rich measurement source.

Outcome Measures: Empirical and Conceptual Mapping

Notwithstanding the strengths of the CORE measure, future research effort needs to progress the *conceptual and empirical mapping* between outcome measures—sometimes referred to as the *walk across*—whereby practitioners have choices from a selection of bona fide measures but with each measure being able to be mapped onto a uniform or standard benchmark denoting valued change. For example, earlier work produced walk-across tables for use by researcher and practitioners between the CORE-OM and BDI-I (Leach et al., 2006) and subsequent work compared the PHQ-9 with the CORE-OM (Gilbody, Richards, & Barkham, 2007).

Thus, although we have described advantages with the CORE system, it is important to realize the tension arising from any specific measure having dominance, as it may freeze the scientific field and reduce practitioner and—by implication—patient/service user choice. Simple logic would suggest that no outcome measure is immune to future measure development. Hence, service delivery systems and national government polices need to be able to adapt and adopt a range of bona fide measures that meet a given set of required criteria in order that practitioners can select the measure that best suits their needs and that the empirical relationship between these measures is known. Moreover, collaboration with practitioners is best achieved if the measurement system operates at a holistic level akin to the practitioner working with the whole person of the patient rather than with fragmented parts determined by diagnosis and dominated by symptom-specific measures.

A key process that needs to be achieved in practice-based evidence is to ensure a sense of local ownership by practitioners in the data they collect. Part of this equation is that the measure itself is consistent with the theoretical models used by practitioners and acceptable to patients. Addressing this first step is one move towards responding to the *colander effect* in which data collected every day across clinical services are lost (i.e., slip through the holes of the colander) through lack of infrastructure and coordinated effort (Kazdin, 2008).

Some Concluding Words

Practice-based studies of psychological treatment in routine care offer potentially rich sources of knowledge that complement the knowledge gained from randomized trials. The variability in patients, therapists, and settings mirrors the forms of treatment that patients in routine care are offered. At this stage in the development of practice-based evidence, the challenge is to consider and decide, on a common basis both within and between countries, as to the kind of information that should be collected that will enrich and stimulate treatment providers, therapists, patients, and therapy researchers. The day may have come for decisions on common measurement methods that were initiated several decades ago.

Acknowledgments

The CORE initiative in the UK has been a collaborative venture and reflects the ideas and efforts of many practitioners and patients as well as the CORE System Trustees (MB, Chris Evans, Richard Evans, & Frank Margison) and CORE Information Management Systems (John Mellor-Clark & Alex Curtis Jenkins). The recently launched CORE-based practice network in Sweden is growing due to the collaborative effort of researchers, patients, therapists, and service managers. We want particularly to thank Tommy Skjulsvik and Ylva Gidhagen Söderberg.

Notes

[1] This paradigm has also been termed *practice-oriented research* (Castonguay, Barkham, Lutz, & McAleavy, 2013).

[2] This research program has been led by Professor Chris Evans and enquiries should be directed to chris@psyctc.org. Translations are available in the following languages: British Sign Language (BSL), Brazilian, Portuguese, Argentinian, Spanish, Romanian, Bulgarian, Arabic, French, Czech, Bangla/Bengali/-Sylheti, isiXhosa, Catalan, Farsi, Kurdish, Kannada, Hindi, Urdu, Tamil, Sámi, Scottish Gaelic, Irish (Irish Gaelic), Swedish, Danish, Norwegian, Mandarin (and other Chinese languages), and Japanese.

References

Baekeland, F., & Lundwall, L. (1975). Dropping out of treatment: A critical review. *Psychological Bulletin, 82*, 738–783. doi: doi:10.1037/h0077132

Baldwin, S. A., Berkeljon, A., Atkins, D. C., Olsen, J. A., & Nielsen, S. L. (2009). Rates of change in naturalistic psychotherapy: Contrasting dose-effect and good-enough level models of change. *Journal of Consulting and Clinical Psychology, 77*, 203–211. doi:10.1037/a0015235

Baldwin, S. A., & Imel, Z. E. (2013). Therapist effects: Findings and methods. In M. J. Lambert (Ed.), *Bergin & Garfield's handbook of psychotherapy and behavior change* (6th ed., pp. 258–297). Hoboken, NJ: Wiley.

Barkham, M., Connell, J., Stiles, W. B., Miles, J. N. V., Margison, J., Evans, C., & Mellor-Clark, J. (2006). Dose-effect relations and responsive regulation of treatment duration: The good enough level. *Journal of Consulting and Clinical Psychology, 74*, 160–167. doi:10.1037/0022-006X.74.1.160

Barkham, M., Hardy, G. E., & Mellor-Clark, J. (2010a). *Developing and delivering practice-based evidence: A guide for the psychological therapies*. Oxford: Wiley-Blackwell.

Barkham, M., & Margison, F. (2007). Practice-based evidence as a complement to evidence-based practice: From dichotomy to chiasmus. In C. Freeman & M. Power (Eds.), *Handbook of evidence-based psychotherapies: A guide for research and practice* (pp. 443–476). Chichester: Wiley.

Barkham, M., Margison, F., Leach, C., Lucock, M., Mellor-Clark, J., Evans, C., ... & McGrath, G. (2001). Service profiling and outcomes benchmarking using the CORE-OM: Towards practice-based evidence in the psychological therapies. *Journal of Consulting and Clinical Psychology, 69*, 184–196. doi:10.1037/0022-006X.69.2.184

Barkham, M., & Mellor-Clark, J. (2003). Bridging evidence-based practice and practice-based evidence: Developing a rigorous and relevant knowledge for the psychological therapies. *Clinical Psychology & Psychotherapy, 10*, 319–327. doi:10.1002/cpp.379

Barkham, M., Mellor-Clark, J., Connell, J., Evans, R., Evans, C., & Margison, F. (2010b). The CORE measures & CORE system: Measuring, monitoring, and managing quality evaluation in the psychological therapies. In M. Barkham, G. E. Hardy, & J. Mellor-Clark (Eds.), *Developing and delivering practice-based evidence: A guide for the psychological therapies* (pp. 175–219). Chichester: Wiley.

Barkham, M., Stiles, W. B., Connell, J., & Mellor-Clark, J. (2012). The meaning of treatment effectiveness in routine NHS primary care psychological therapy services. *Psychology and Psychotherapy: Theory, Research and Practice, 85*, 1–16. doi:10.1111/j.2044-8341.2011.02019.x

Barkham, M., Stiles, W. B., Lambert, M. J., & Mellor-Clark, J. (2010). Building a rigorous and relevant knowledge-base for the psychological therapies. In M. Barkham, G. E. Hardy, & J. Mellor-Clark (Eds.), *Developing and delivering practice-based evidence: A guide for the psychological therapies* (pp. 21–61). Chichester: Wiley.

Barrett, M. S., Chua, W, Crits-Christoph, P., Gibbons, M. B., & Thompson, D. (2008). Early withdrawal from mental health treatment: Implications for psychotherapy practice. *Psychotherapy Theory, Research, Practice, Training, 45*, 247–267. doi:10.1037/0033-3204.45.2.247

Bickman, L. (2008). A measurement feedback system (MFS) is necessary to improve mental health outcomes. *Journal of the American Association of Child and Adolescent Psychiatry, 47*, 1114–1119. doi:10.1097/CHI.0b013e3181825af8

Bickman, L., Kelley, S., Breda, C., Vides de Andrade, A. R., & Riemer, M. (2011). Effects of routine feedback to clinicians on youth mental health outcomes: A randomized cluster design. *Psychiatric Services, 62*, 1423–1429. doi:10.1176/appi.ps.002052011

Brown, J., Dreis, S., & Nace, D. K. (1999). What really makes a difference in psychotherapy outcome? Why does managed care want to know? In M. A. Hubble, B. L. Duncan, & S. D. Miller (Eds.), *The heart and soul of change*. Washington DC: American Psychological Association.

Budge, S., Baardseth, T. P., Wampold, B. E., & Fluckiger, C. (2010). Researcher allegiance and supportive therapy: Pernicious effects on results of randomized clinical trials. *European Journal of Psychotherapy & Counselling, 12*, 23–39. doi:10.1080/13642531003637742

Cahill, J., Barkham, M., & Stiles, W. B. (2010). Systematic review of practice-based research on psychological therapies in routine clinic settings. *British Journal of Clinical Psychology, 49*, 421–454. doi:10.1348/014466509X470789

Castonguay, L. G., Barkham, M., Lutz, W., & McAleavy, A. (2013). Practice-oriented research: Approaches and applications. In M. J. Lambert (Ed.), *Bergin & Garfield's handbook of psychotherapy and behavior change* (6th ed., pp. 85–133). Hoboken, NJ: Wiley.

Chiesa, M., Wright, M., & Neeld, R. (2003). A description of an audit cycle of early dropouts from an inpatient psychotherapy unit. *Psychoanalytic Psychotherapy, 17*, 138–149. doi:10.1080/1474973031000105294

Clarkin, J. F., Levy, K. N., Lenzenweger, M. F., & Kernberg, O. F. (2004). The Personality Disorder Institute/Borderline Personality Disorder Research Foundation randomized control trial for borderline personality disorder: Rationale, methods, and patient characteristics. *Journal of Personality Disorders, 18*, 52–72. doi:10.1521/pedi.18.1.52.32769

Crawford, M. J., Robotham, D., Thana, L., Patterson, S., Weaver, T., Barber, R., Wykes, T., & Roze, D. (2011). Selecting outcome measures in mental health: The views of service users. *Journal of Mental Health, 20*, 336–346. doi:10.3109/09638237.2011.577114

Crits-Christoph, P., Baranckie, K., Kurcias, J., Beck, A., Carroll, K., Perry, K., ... & Zitrin, C. (1991). Meta-analysis of therapist effects in psychotherapy outcome studies. *Psychotherapy Research, 1*, 81–91. doi:10.1080/10503309112331335511

Elfström, M. L., Evans, C., Lundgren, J., Johansson, B., Hakeberg, M., & Carlsson, S. G. (2013). Validation of the Swedish version of the Clinical Outcomes in Routine Evaluation Outcome Measure (CORE-OM). *Clinical Psychology & Psychotherapy, 20*, 447–455.

Elkin, I., Falconnier, L., Martinovitch, Z., & Mahoney, C. (2006). Therapist effects in the National Institute of Mental Health Treatment of Depression Collaborative Research program. *Psychotherapy Research, 16*, 144–160. doi:10.1080/10503300500268540

EuroQol Group. (1990). EuroQol - a new facility for the measurement of health-related quality of life. *Health Policy, 16*, 199–208. doi:10.1016/0168-8510(90)90421-9

Evans, C., Connell, J., Barkham, M., Margison, F., Mellor-Clark, J., McGrath, G., & Audin, K. (2002). Towards a standardised brief outcome measure: Psychometric properties and utility of the CORE-OM. *British Journal of Psychiatry, 180*, 51–60. doi:10.1192/bjp.180.1.51

Evans, C., Connell, J., Barkham, M., Marshall, C., & Mellor-Clark, J. (2003). Practice-based evidence: Benchmarking NHS primary care counselling services at national and local levels. *Clinical Psychology & Psychotherapy, 10*, 374–388. doi:10.1002/cpp.384

Falkenström, F., Granström, F., & Holmqvist, R. (2013a). Therapeutic alliance predicts symptomatic improvement session by session. *Journal of Counseling Psychology, 60*, 317–328. doi:10.1037/a0032258

Falkenström, F., Granström, F., Holmqvist, R., & Psychotherapy Research. (2013b). Working alliance predicts psychotherapy outcome even while controlling for prior symptom improvement. *Psychotherapy Research*. Online publication. doi:10.1080/10503307.2013.847985

Gilbody, S., Richards, D. A., & Barkham, M. (2007). Diagnosing depression in primary care using self-completed instruments: a UK validation of the PHQ-9 and CORE-OM. *British Journal of General Practice, 57*, 650–652.

Hatcher, R. L., & Gillaspy, J. A. (2006). Development and validation of a revised short version of the Working Alliance Inventory. *Psychotherapy Research, 16*, 12–25. doi:10.1080/10503300500352500

Hellerstein, D. J., & Markowitz, J. C. (2008). Developing supportive psychotherapy as evidence-based treatment. *American Journal of Psychiatry, 165*, 1355–1356. doi:10.1176/appi.ajp.2008.08040565

Hoffman, J. J. (1985). Client factors related to premature termination of psychotherapy. *Psychotherapy: Theory, Research, Practice, Training, 22*, 83–85. doi:10.1037/h0088530

Holmqvist, R., Philips, B., & Mellor-Clark, J. (2013). Client and therapist congruence about the client's problems, treatment alliance, and outcome. Manuscript.

Holmqvist, R., Ström, T., & Foldemo, A. (2013). The effects of psychological treatment in primary care. *Nordic Journal of Psychiatry, 64*, 1–9.

Howard, K. I., Kopta, S. M., Krause, M. S., & Orlinsky, D. E. (1986). The dose-effect relationship in psychotherapy. *American Psychologist, 41*, 159–164. doi:10.1037/0003-066X.41.2.159

Hunsley, J., & Lee, C. M. (2007). Research-informed benchmarks for psychological treatments. Efficacy studies, effectiveness studies, and beyond. *Professional Psychology: Research and Practice, 38*, 21–33. doi:10.1037/0735-7028.38.1.21

Kazdin, A. E. (2008). Evidence-based treatment and practice: New opportunities to bridge clinical research and practice, enhance the knowledge base, and improve patient care. *American Psychologist, 63*, 146–159. doi:10.1037/0003-066X.63.3.146

Kazdin, A. E., & Mazurick, J. L. (1994). Dropping out of child psychotherapy: Distinguishing early and late dropouts over the course of treatment. *Journal of Consulting and Clinical Psychology, 62*, 1069–1075. doi:10.1037/0022-006X.62.5.1069

Kim, D.-M., Wampold, B. E., & Bolt, D. M. (2006). Therapist effects in psychotherapy: A random-effects modeling of the National Institute of Mental Health Treatment of Depression Collaborative Research Program data. *Psychotherapy Research, 16*, 161–172. doi:10.1080/10503300500264911

Klein, E. B., Stone, W. N., Hicks, M. W., & Pritchard, I. L. (2003). Understanding dropouts. *Journal of Mental Health Counseling, 25*, 89–100.

Kroenke, K., Spitzer, R. L., & Williams, J. B. W. (2001). The PHQ-9: Validity of a brief depression severity measure. *Journal of General Internal Medicine, 16*, 606–613. doi:10.1046/j.1525-1497.2001.016009606.x

Lambert, M. J. (2010). *Prevention of treatment failure: The use of measuring, monitoring, and feedback in clinical practice.* Washington DC: American Psychologist Association.

Larsson, M., Andersson, G., & Holmqvist, R. (2013). Rupture-repair events in psychological treatments in primary care. Manuscript.

Larsson, B. P. M., Kaldo, V., & Broberg, A. G. (2009). Similarities and differences between practitioners of psychotherapy in Sweden: A comparison of attitudes between psychodynamic, cognitive, cognitive-behavioral, and integrative therapists. *Journal of Psychotherapy Integration, 19*, 43–66.

Larsson, M., Andersson, G., & Holmqvist, R. (2013). Rupture-repair events in psychological treatments in primary care. Manuscript.

Leach, C., Lucock, M., Barkham, M., Stiles, W. B., Noble, R., & Iveson, S. (2006). Transforming between Beck Depression Inventory and CORE-OM scores in routine clinical practice. *British Journal of Clinical Psychology, 45*, 153–166. doi:10.1348/014466505X35335

Luborsky, L., McLellan, A. T., Diguer, L., Woody, G., & Seligman, D. A. (1997). The psychotherapist matters: Comparison of outcomes across twenty-two therapists and seven patient samples. *Clinical Psychology: Science and Practice*, *4*, 53–65. doi:10.1111/j.1468-2850.1997.tb00099.x

Lutz, W., Leach, C., Barkham, M., Lucock, M., Stiles, W. B., Evans, C., ... & Iveson, S. (2005). Predicting rate and shape of change for individual clients receiving psychological therapy: Using growth curve modeling and nearest neighbor technologies. *Journal of Consulting and Clinical Psychology*, *73*, 904–913. doi:10.1037/0022-006X.73.5.904

Mavranezouli, I., Brazier, J., Rowan, D., & Barkham, M. (2013). Estimating a preference-based index from the Clinical Outcomes in Routine Evaluation—Outcome Measure (CORE-OM): valuation of CORE-6D. *Medical Decision Making*, *33*, 381–395. doi:10.1177/0272989X12464431

Mavranezouli, I., Brazier, J., Young, T., & Barkham, M. (2011). Using Rasch analysis to form plausible health states amenable to valuation: the development of CORE-6D and CORE-Utility from CORE-OM in order to elicit preferences for common mental health problems. *Quality of Life Research*, *20*, 321–333. doi:10.1007/s11136-010-9768-4

McHugh, R. K., & Barlow, D. H. (2012). *Dissemination and implementation of evidence-based psychological interventions*. New York: Oxford University Press.

McMuran, M., Huband, N., & Overton, E. (2010). Non-completion of personality disorder treatments: A systematic review of correlates, consequences, and interventions. *Clinical Psychology Review*, *30*, 277–287. doi:10.1016/j.cpr.2009.12.002

Mellor-Clark, J., & Barkham, M. (2012). Using the CORE System to support service development. In C. Feltham & I. Horton (Eds.), *Handbook of counselling and psychotherapy* (3rd ed.). London: Sage.

Mundt, J. C., Marks, I. M., Shear, M. K., & Greist, J. H. (2002). The Work and Social Adjustment Scale: A simple measure of impairment in functioning. *British Journal of Psychiatry*, *180*, 461–464. doi:10.1192/bjp.180.5.461

Novalis, P. N., Rojcewicz, S. J., & Peele, R. (1993). *Clinical manual of supportive psychotherapy*. Washington DC: American Psychiatric Publishing.

O'Brien, A., Fahmy, R., & Singh, S. P. (2009). Disengagement from mental health services: A literature review. *Journal of Social Psychiatry and Psychiatric Epidemiology*, *44*, 558–568. doi:10.1007/s00127-008-0476-0

O'Donovan, A., Bain, J. D., & Dyck, M. J. (2005). Does clinical psychology education enhance the clinical competence of practitioners? *Professional Psychology: Research and Practice*, *36*, 104–111. doi:10.1037/0735-7028.36.1.104

Philips, B. (2009). Comparing apples and oranges: How do patient characteristics and treatment goals vary between different forms of psychotherapy? *Psychology and Psychotherapy*, *82*, 323–336. doi:10.1348/147608309X431491

Pingitore, D. P., Scheffler, R. M., Schwalm, D., Zarin, D. A., &. West, J. C. (2002). Variation in routine psychiatric workload: The role of financing source, managed care participation, and mental health workforce competition. *Mental Health Services Research*, *4*, 141–150. doi:10.1023/A:1019759029241

Pinsker, H. A. (1997). *Primer of supportive therapy*. Hillside, NJ: Analytic Press.

Reis, B. F., & Brown, L. G. (2006). Preventing therapy dropout in the real world: The clinical utility of videotape preparation and client estimate of treatment duration. *Professional Psychology: Research and Practice*, *37*, 311–316. doi:10.1037/0735-7028.37.3.311

Royal College of Psychiatrists. (2011). *National Audit of Psychological Therapies for Anxiety and Depression*. National Report.

Saxon, D., & Barkham, M. (2012). Patterns of therapist variability: Therapist effects and the contribution of patient severity and risk. *Journal of Consulting and Clinical Psychology*, *80*, 535–546. doi:10.1037/a0028898

Sinclair, M., & Holmqvist, R. (2013). Congruence in the therapists' and clients' ratings of the therapeutic alliance does not predict outcome in psychological treatment. Manuscript.

Spitzer, R. L., Kroenke, K., Williams, J. B. W., & Löwe, B. (2006). A brief measure for assessing generalized anxiety disorder: The GAD-7. *Archives of Internal Medicine*, *22*, 1092–1097. doi:10.1001/archinte.166.10.1092

Stiles, W. B., Barkham, M., Connell, J., & Mellor-Clark, J. (2008). Responsive regulation of treatment duration in routine practice in United Kingdom primary care settings: Replication in a larger sample. *Journal of Consulting and Clinical Psychology*, *76*, 298–305. doi:10.1037/0022-006X.76.2.298

Stiles, W. B., Barkham, M., Mellor-Clark, J., & Connell, J. (2008). Effectiveness of cognitive-behavioural, person-centred, and psychodynamic therapies in UK primary care routine practice: Replication in a larger sample. *Psychological Medicine*, *38*, 677–688.

Stiles, W. B., Barkham, M., Twigg, E., Mellor-Clark, J., & Cooper, M. (2006). Effectiveness of cognitive-behavioural, person-centred, and psychodynamic therapies as practiced in UK National Health Service settings. *Psychological Medicine*, *36*, 555–566. doi:10.1017/S0033291706007136

Stiles, W. B., Leach, C., Barkham, M., Lucock, M., Iveson, S., Shapiro, D. A., Iveson, M., & Hardy, G. E. (2003). Early sudden gains in psychotherapy under routine clinic conditions: Practice-based evidence. *Journal of Consulting and Clinical Psychology*, *71*, 14–21. doi:10.1037/0022-006X.71.1.14

Stirman, S. W., DeRubeis, R. J., Crits-Christoph, P., & Brody, P. E. (2003). Are samples in randomized controlled trials of psychotherapy representative of community outpatients? A new methodology and initial findings. *Journal of Consulting and Clinical Psychology*, *71*, 963–972. doi:10.1037/0022-006X.71.6.963

Street, L. L., Niederehe, G., & Lebowitz, B. D. (2000). Toward greater public health relevance for psychotherapeutic intervention research: An NIMH workshop report. *Clinical Psychology: Science and Practice*, *7*, 127–137. doi:10.1093/clipsy.7.2.127

Strupp, H. H., Horowitz, L., & Lambert, M. J. (Eds.). (1997). *Measuring patient changes in mood, anxiety, and personality disorders: Toward a core battery*. Washington DC: American Psychological Association

Stulz, N., Lutz, W., Leach, C., Lucock, M., & Barkham, M. (2007). Shapes of early change in psychotherapy under routine outpatient conditions. *Journal of Consulting and Clinical Psychology*, *75*, 864–874. doi:10.1037/0022-006X.75.6.864

Tanielian, T. L., Marcus, S. C., Suarez, A. P., & Pincus, H. A. (2001). Trends in psychiatric practice. 1988–1998: II. Caseload and treatment characteristics. *Psychiatric Services*, *52*, 880. doi:10.1176/appi.ps.52.7.880

Tennant, R., Hiller, L., Fishwick, R., Platt, S., Joseph, S., Weich, S., ... & Stewart-Brown, S. (2009). The Warwick-Edinburgh Mental Well-being Scale (WEMWBS): Development and UK validation. *Health and Quality of Life Outcomes*, *5*, 63. doi:10.1186/1477-7525-5-63

Waller, G. (2009). Evidenced-based treatment and therapist drift. *Behaviour Research and Therapy*, *47*, 119–127. doi:10.1016/j.brat.2008.10.018

Wampold, B. E., & Brown, G. S. (2005). Estimating variability in outcomes attributable to therapists: A naturalistic study of outcomes in managed care. *Journal of Consulting and Clinical Psychology*, *73*, 914–923. doi:10.1037/0022-006X.73.5.914

Waskow, I. E., & Parloff, M. B. (1975). *Psychotherapy change measures*. Washington DC: US Government Printing Office.

Wierzbicki, M., & Pekarik, G. (1993). A meta-analysis of psychotherapy dropout. *Professional Psychology: Research and Practice, 24*, 190–195. doi:10.1037/0735-7028.24.2.190

Winston, A., Rosenthal, R., & Pinsker, H. (2012). *Learning supportive therapy. An illustrated guide*. Arlington, VA: American Psychiatric Association.

Young, A. S., Grusky, O., Jordan, D., & Belin, T. R. (2000). Routine outcome monitoring in a public mental health system: The impact of patients who leave care. Psychiatric Services, 51, 85–91.

EMPIRICAL PAPER

Benefits and challenges in practice-oriented psychotherapy research in Germany: The TK and the QS-PSY-BAY projects of quality assurance in outpatient psychotherapy

BERNHARD MICHAEL STRAUSS[1], WOLFGANG LUTZ[2], ANDRES STEFFANOWSKI[3], WERNER W. WITTMANN[4], JAN R. BOEHNKE[2], JULIAN RUBEL[2], CARL E. SCHEIDT[5], FRANZ CASPAR[6], HEINER VOGEL[7], UWE ALTMANN[8], ROLF STEYER[8], ANNA ZIMMERMANN[1], ELLEN BRUCKMAYER[9], FRIEDRICH VON HEYMANN[9], DIETMAR KRAMER[10], & HELMUT KIRCHMANN[1]

[1]*Institute of Psychosocial Medicine and Psychotherapy, University Hospital Jena, Jena, Germany;* [2]*Clinical Psychology and Psychotherapy, University of Trier, Trier, Germany;* [3]*SRH Hochschule Heidelberg, Germany;* [4]*Otto-Selz-Institute for Applied Psychology, Mannheim, Germany;* [5]*Psychosomatic Medicine, University Hospital, Freiburg, Germany;* [6]*Department of Psychology, University of Bern, Bern, Switzerland;* [7]*Psychotherapy and Medical Psychology, University Hospital, Würzburg, Germany;* [8]*Department of Psychology, University of Jena, Jena, Germany;* [9]*Initiating Group, QS-PSY-BAY project, Munich, Germany &* [10]*Association of Statutory Health Incurance Physicians Bavaria, Munich, Germany*

Abstract
Objective: Two patient-focused long-term research projects performed in the German outpatient psychotherapy system are focused on in this article. The TK (Techniker Krankenkasse) project is the first study to evaluate a quality assurance and feedback system with regard to its practical feasibility in German routine care. The other study ("Quality Assurance in Outpatient Psychotherapy in Bavaria"; QS-PSY-BAY) was designed to test a new approach for quality assurance in outpatient psychotherapy using electronic documentation of patient characteristics and outcome parameters. In addition this project provides the opportunity to analyze data on health-related costs for the patients undergoing outpatient psychotherapy. **Method:** Both projects and their results indicating high effect sizes are briefly described. **Results:** From the perspectives of the research teams, advisory boards and other stakeholders, the experiences with these projects are discussed focusing on obstacles, challenges, difficulties, and benefits in developing and implementing the studies. The triangle collaboration of therapists, researchers, and health insurance companies/health service institutions turned out to be fruitful in both studies. **Conclusions:** Despite some controversies between the partners the experiences indicate the importance of practiced-research collaborations to provide relevant information about the delivery of outpatient psychotherapy in the health system.

Practice-oriented research within psychotherapy has recently been differentiated into three main approaches, i.e., patient-focused research, practice-based evidence, and practice research networks (Castonguay, Barkham, Lutz, & McAleavy, 2013). Practice-oriented research evolved mainly from some doubts concerning the relevance of outcome research based on randomized controlled trials (RCTs) for clinical practice due to its limited external validity. As a consequence, practice-based research has become a strong focus of interest as an alternative to the "top down" evidence provided by traditional outcome research, and an attempt to take practitioners concerns related to research seriously.

The two projects focused on in this article can be best located in the area of patient-focused research

(Howard, Moras, Brill, Martinovich, & Lutz, 1996; Lambert, 2001; 2007; Lutz, 2002). Patient-focused research is based, as are scientist-practitioner networks, on the idea of an ongoing collaboration between practitioners and scientists. Practitioners deliver the actual treatment and collect data by assessing patients' progress repeatedly during therapy. Continuous aggregation of data allows an increasingly subtle modeling of treatment profiles, which then can be used for feedback, or to benchmark and evaluate individual cases (bottom-up evidence). The important advantage of this approach as compared to guidelines based on traditional outcome research is that it is considerably closer to the individual patient.

Practice-generated data provide researchers with a continuously growing database of patients' change information. Researchers accordingly can develop tools to support clinical decision-making for clinical practice in a real-time modus, allowing empirical progress or change information to be directly fed back to therapists and patients as soon as it is available. These tools can be based on empirical data or rational decision strategies and can help to identify negative and positive developments early in treatment (e.g., Lutz, Stulz, Martinovich, Leon, & Saunders, 2009). Feedback to practitioners allows them to track progress on an individual level and to improve treatment as delivered especially for patients with an early negative development (Lambert, 2007; Shimokawa, Lambert, & Smart, 2010). In that way, patient-focused research helps to narrow the scientist-practitioner gap and tries to establish a permanent exchange between research and practice. Furthermore, data generated in projects following a patient-focused research paradigm can be used on a systems or group level as part of an evaluation or quality assurance study.

Patient-focused research methods and quality assurance (QA) in psychotherapy have formed a close relationship, although patient-focused research and quality assurance do not have exactly the same and sometimes may even have divergent goals, especially if QA is established by legal regulations defining strategies of internal and external quality control, and if it is not based on the initiative of practitioners such as in one of the projects described in this paper. The law in Germany (German Federal Government, 2010), however, requires a cross-institutional QA, so that a minimum level of standardization is appropriate with regard to the selection of methods and contents in treatment documentation.

Based upon a brief description of the German outpatient psychotherapy system, this paper will describe and discuss two different studies performed within this system which can both serve as examples of patient-focused research. Following a summary of the available main findings, both projects will be discussed in relation to problems and benefits of their development and implementation. Although the views of these aspects are different depending on the perspective (e.g., that of the advisory boards or the research teams), the concluding recommendations are based on a consensus and might be helpful for designing future studies of that kind.

Outpatient Psychotherapy in Germany

Outpatient psychotherapy in Germany is largely provided by approved psychotherapists (psychologists/medical doctors specialized in psychiatry or psychosomatic medicine) working in private practices. The German health insurance system covers the costs of two different forms of psychotherapy, i.e., CBT and psychodynamic psychotherapy (including psychoanalytic treatment). The insurance companies usually reimburse the costs for 25 up to 45 (maximum 80) sessions for CBT and 25–50 (maximum 80–100) sessions for psychodynamic psychotherapy as well as up to 300 sessions for psychoanalytic treatments. Quality assurance in outpatient psychotherapy traditionally has been based on a peer review system. For each individual patient who plans to undergo psychotherapeutic treatment, the therapist has to write a structured case report based upon early "probatory" sessions, containing details of the case history, the diagnostic assessment and the treatment plan. Evidence has to be given (i) that the treatment is indicated, (ii) that the goals of the treatment can be achieved by the suggested intervention, either psychodynamic or CBT, and (iii) within the requested time frame. The central goal of this form of quality assessment is to ensure an appropriate use of economic resources by controlling the process of treatment selection and its prospect of success. Usually, other common strategies of quality assurance, such as patient monitoring using outcome measures, are not regularly practiced in the German health system.

The case report system has been generally well established for decades and is accepted among psychotherapists who—using this tool—allow a high amount of transparency towards the health service system. Nevertheless, the validity of the case-report-based peer review system as a central component of quality assurance has also been questioned from various perspectives. Some clinical practitioners, for example, criticized the disproportion between the time-consuming preparation of the reports, their high acceptance rates, and questions related to their effectiveness. Some people doubt that the traditional peer review system is effective in maintaining a rational resource allocation. It is assumed that the guarantee of a certain number of therapy sessions in advance, which is part of the system, might invite a too generous and perhaps even ineffective use of therapeutic sessions. This controversial discussion specifically was the starting point of the "TK project", which was intended to evaluate different forms of quality assurance in outpatient psychotherapy.

The TK and the QS-PSY-BAY Projects of Quality Assurance in Outpatient Psychotherapy

As mentioned above, this article focuses on two different studies that have recently been performed in the German outpatient psychotherapy system. In collaboration with the Techniker Krankenkasse (TK), a large German health insurance company, a quality monitoring study was conducted in outpatient psychotherapy with therapists in private practices, which included decision rules about treatment and feedback tools. The TK project is the first study to evaluate a quality assurance and feedback system with regard to its effects on treatment outcome and its practical feasibility in routine care within the German health insurance system (Lutz, Böhnke, Köck, & Bittermann, 2011; Lutz, Wittmann, Böhnke, Rubel, & Steffanowski, 2012; Wittmann et al., 2011). The main goal of the study was to test the hypothesis that a quality management strategy using patient-focused research methods and feedback procedures would be feasible and would be associated with a better clinical outcome of psychotherapeutic treatments as compared to the outcome of therapies subjected to the traditional peer review system of quality assurance as outlined above (Wittmann et al., 2011).

The increasing demand for outpatient psychotherapy brings new challenges to quality assurance and routine documentation in this field. Besides relying on traditional criteria (e.g., therapists' education, training, supervision and peer review) another strategy for QA is empirically based. The basic idea is to provide more transparency for all participants with quantifiable and comparable inter-individual quality indicators and to obtain data for psychotherapeutic care research. Accordingly, a group of psychotherapists in the state of Bavaria considered how to implement an empirically based QA that meets the statutory demands and additionally provides support for the psychotherapists' daily practice. This concern, which was shared by the Bavarian Association of Statutory Health Insurance Physicians (KVB), led to the second investigation described in this paper: The "Quality Assurance in Outpatient Psychotherapy in Bavaria" (QS-PSY-BAY) study. In this study,

a new approach to quality assurance in outpatient psychotherapy was tested, using electronic documentation of patient characteristics and outcome parameters. The individual course of therapy was compared with aggregated scores of subgroups of patients with the same principal diagnosis and results were then fed back to the therapists. Since the study was built to answer questions of health services research, as well as to address health-related costs for the patients undergoing outpatient psychotherapy, cost-related data were provided by a group of insurance companies (Verband der Ersatzkassen, vdek) as well as the KVB. To relate these data to a solid representative sample in a second part of the QS-PSY-BAY project, it additionally focuses the health costs for a large sample (see below) who also were insured by the vdek companies. Taken together, research questions addressed in this study cover the effectiveness of outpatient psychotherapy and its potential predictors, as well as monetary aspects such as cost-effectiveness.

TK Project Design, Methods and Sample

In order to test the major hypothesis that a quality management strategy using patient-focused research methods would be associated with a better clinical outcome as compared to the outcome of therapies subjected to the traditional peer review system, the TK study was designed as a cluster-randomized controlled trial involving a large sample of psychotherapists ($N = 403$) from three different regions of Germany. The participating therapists were randomly allocated to two groups: One group applied the traditional case report model of quality assurance (Quality Assurance As Usual, QAAU). The other group applied an alternative approach to quality management including the following components: (i) a standardized assessment procedure including a structured diagnostic interview (related to ICD-10 criteria; Hiller, Zaudig, & Mombour, 2004) before the commencement of treatment, (ii) psychometric testing at defined measurement points in the course of treatment and feedback of the results to the therapist, (iii) an evaluation—as in the QAAU condition—of outcome at the end of treatment, and (iv) a modified peer review system, in which the reviewers made use of the results of the psychometric testing in addition to a brief description of the course of treatment (TK model, TKM).

In the intervention group (IG), therapist ratings were obtained at intake, re-application, and termination of therapy. In the control group (CG), data were only obtained at intake and termination. Therapists in both groups provided information on the general severity of impairment (BSS, Severity of Impairment

Score; Schepank, 1995), the therapeutic alliance (HAQ - Helping Alliance Questionnaire, Luborsky et al., 1996), and on the patient's global functioning (GAF, Global Assessment of Functioning; Endicott, Spitzer, Fleiss, & Cohen, 1976). Patients provided self-reports on five measures: the general distress (BSI, Brief Symptom Inventory; Derogatis, 1975), interpersonal problems (IIP-D; Horowitz, Strauss, & Kordy, 2000), therapeutic alliance (HAQ, Helping Alliance Questionnaire; Luborsky et al., 1996), and health-related quality of life (SF-12; Ware, Kosinski, & Keller, 1996). In order to assess problems associated with the specific disorder (here: main diagnosis of the patient), one out of five disorder-specific instruments was used (for details see Lutz et al., 2011). Client self-reports were obtained at intake and termination of therapy as well as at the 1-year follow-up in both groups. In the IG, assessments were also conducted between intake and termination in order to generate feedback on therapeutic progress. The amount of sessions between these measurements depends on the type of therapy applied (see Figure 1).

After each assessment, the gathered information was fed back to the therapists in the IG within a few days.

To further support the interpretation of this information, therapists were provided with rationally derived decision rules about therapy based on an extension of clinically significant change criteria (e.g., Lutz et al., 2011). Feedback information was

used for two decisions: (i) the decision to start treatment (treatment-selection); (ii) the decision to continue or to terminate treatment (treatment continuance vs. termination of treatment). For both decisions rules were defined: A treatment was started if an ICD 10 diagnosis could be established and the total score of at least one self-report questionnaire (BSI, IIP or disorder-specific questionnaire) was in the clinical range. If this criterion failed, a peer review was initiated in order to check the validity of the algorithm-based decision.

For the decision on continuance versus termination of therapy, rules were also defined based on self-report questionnaires (BSI, IIP, and BDI). Feedback information resulted in four different clinical descriptions (derived from concepts of clinical significance; Jacobson & Truax, 1991): (i) significant decrease of symptoms; (ii) decrease of symptoms; (iii) no decrease of symptoms; (iv) increase of symptoms. These descriptions were linked to clinical recommendations. For example, if a significant decrease of symptoms was observed repeatedly then end of therapy was recommended as an option.

Feedback to the therapists was based on a patient's reports at intake and on his or her amount of change by a specific session. This information was implemented in a graphical report, which was then fed back to therapists, who had the option to discuss these results via progress charts with patients. To give feedback on initial patient status and patient progress to therapists at every assessment, the BSI,

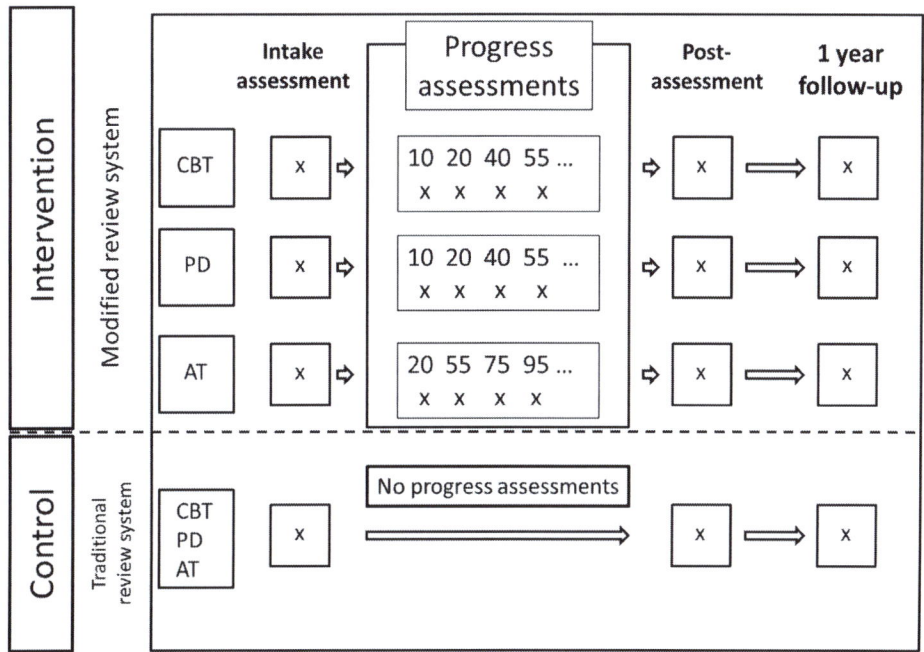

Figure 1. Schematic overview of the design and assessments in the TK study.
Note. Numbers represent the session numbers after which assessments have been routinely conducted. CBT = Cognitive Behavioral Therapy; PD = Psychodynamic Therapy; AT = Analytical Therapy.

the IIP, and a disorder-specific instrument (e.g., a patient diagnosed with a depressive disorder would complete the BDI; Beck, Ward, Mendelson, Mock, & Erbaugh, 1961) were used.

Furthermore, the therapist could also be informed on the stability of treatment progress by reporting on progress over several administrations of the measures (for further details, see Lutz, Böhnke, & Köck, 2011; Lutz et al., 2009).

Besides providing feedback about intake and change information of the patients, the following instructions were adopted in the IG (Feedback Group): (i) a detailed application report was not needed when psychometric instruments (BSI, IIP, disorder-specific) indicated high impairment in at least one psychometric dimension; (ii) at re-application for further sessions, results from the psychometric instruments had to be reported to evaluators of further funding combined with a less detailed application for further sessions, if the impairment in the psychometric instruments was still high.

In summary, the study was performed as a cluster-randomized trial in which two hypotheses were tested: (i) Quality assurance according to TKM leads to a better clinical outcome as compared to QAAU; (ii) quality assurance according to TKM is associated with a higher efficacy (a better dose-response ratio), leading to a more economic use of resources. These hypotheses were tested in a confirmatory study design. The goal of the study reported was therefore not only a feasibility study on the effects of an empirically based feedback system but a comparison study evaluating two competing strategies of quality assurance. This fact is important to note because it explains some of the challenges and obstacles which came up during the phase of realization of the project.

Four hundred and three psychotherapists were enrolled in the study and randomly assigned to the two conditions. The randomization of the therapists leads to a cluster-randomized sample of patients in the two treatment arms, implying differences between the two treatment groups (Figure 2). The flow of patients through the study is illustrated in Figure 2. Of the 403 psychotherapists who had been enrolled in the study during the recruitment period between May 2005 and June 2008, 4452 patients were eligible. Of these 1708 agreed to participate. The other 2744 patients either declined to participate for various reasons (lack of time, doubts concerning data protection or resentment towards standardized questionnaires) or participation was not offered. Of the 1708 patients who had enrolled in the study 1598 participated in the baseline measurement. For a subsample of 226 patients, therapist-reported reasons for not offering study

participation were available: The clinical status of the patient (26.1%), the continuous test completion could overstrain the patient (8.8%), participation could have negative consequences for the treatment (10.2%), the effort for the patient would be too high (4.4%), the patient had a negative attitude towards tests (6.2%), other reasons (44.2%). For a subsample of 469 patients, therapist-reported reasons for why patients refused the offered study participation were available: Patient dislikes tests (18.8%), distrusts in data security (22.0%), dislikes additional expenditure of time (33.7%), fears refusal of cost reimbursement due to the psychometrics (2.1%), has already participated in studies and is not interested now (3.2%), does not feel able to complete the questionnaire (10.7%), missing payment (0.6%), other reasons (23.7%).

At post-treatment the study sample had decreased to 597 (complete data sets across two measurement points) and at 12-month follow-up to 468 patients. Only in 300 patients were complete data sets across all three measurement points available (Figure 2).

Results of the TK-Project: A Summary

Summarizing the results of the study concerning the two main hypotheses it can be stated that no statistically significant differences emerged between the clinical outcomes in the two treatment arms. The second main hypothesis on dose-effect relationships and the economic use of resources could not be answered due to a lack of data. It was observed, however, that the average number of treatment sessions in the TKM arm outweighed that in the QAAU condition, indicating that feedback and other components of the TKM had not led to a general reduction in the number of sessions.

The feedback system used in the IG, even though having several shortcomings, was feasible in clinical routine. Also no negative effects in terms of treatment outcome (pre-post effect sizes in a multiple status indicator: $d_{IG \, vs.CG} = .06$, $p = .46$; pre-post effect sizes in the GSI of the BSI: $d_{IG \, vs.CG} = .01$, $p = .91$; BDI: $d_{IG \, vs.CG} = .18$, $p = .09$) were detected, when psychometric feedback was implemented in clinical practice in comparison to the traditional case-report peer review system (for further details see Lutz et al., 2011, 2012; Scheidt et al., 2012; Wittmann et al., 2011).

Beyond these main findings, the study provided valuable insights into psychotherapy in German private practice settings. For example, the average intake in BSI values was $M = 1.23$ ($SD = 0.67$, $N = 1577$), which is well above the clinical cut-off score of .52. Also, both groups (IG and CG) showed a high average pre to post effects size (GSI of the

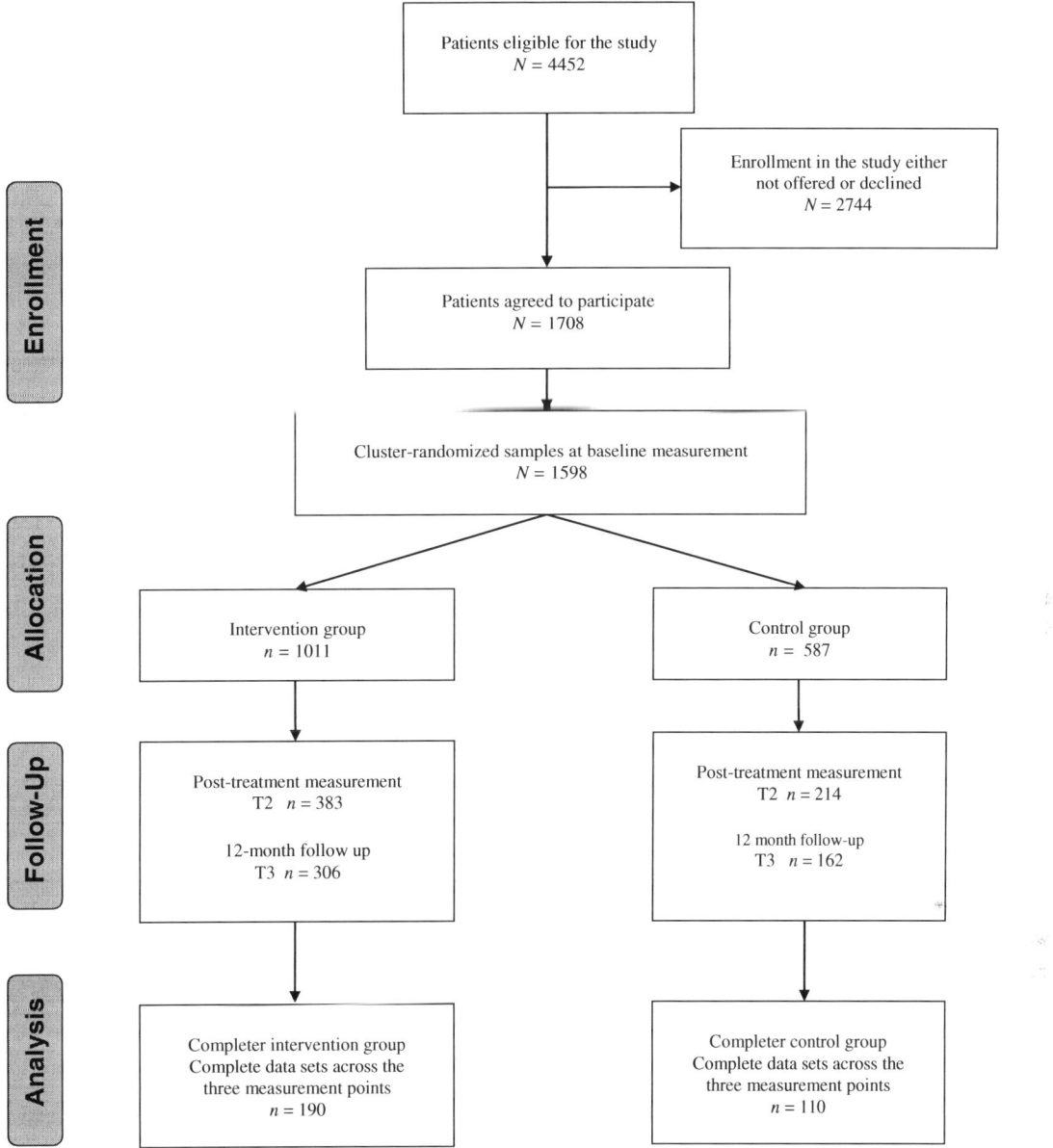

Figure 2. Consort flow chart: TK study sample.

BSI: d_{IG} = .94, d_{CG} = .95; multiple status indicator: d_{IG} = 1.23, d_{CG} = 1.16; BDI: d_{IG} = 1.35, d_{CG} = 1.17). It can be stated that outpatient psychotherapy within the German health insurance system is delivered to clearly distressed patients and reaches similar effects in this setting as with patients in more controlled settings (see also Stiles, Barkham, Mellor-Clark, & Connel, 2008).

Within the IG interesting findings related to the process were found: It was possible to group patients in the IG based on their early feedback results. Patients who were unchanged or worse off at session 10 or 20 were also worse off at termination and at the 1-year follow-up compared to patients who already showed improvement at session 10 or 20. The treatment duration of both groups was well within the range of reference data for Germany. Nevertheless, patients improving early in therapy also showed shorter treatment durations (Lutz et al., 2012). This finding is well along the lines of prior studies. These found repeatedly that feedback leads to shorter treatments for early positively changing patients and to longer ones for patients showing no or negative change early in treatment (Lambert et al., 2002). The same holds for treatment outcome. The early deterioration group did clearly improve after the first feedback was given, even though not reaching the same final outcome level as the early positively changing group. However, these changes, although very plausible since consistent with the feedback literature, cannot be clearly attributed to feedback alone given this study design. To disentangle feedback effects it would have been necessary to implement a third control group in which the instruments were administered repeatedly, but without feedback. This will be the task for future studies within that applied context.

Another result indicates the potential use of psychometric feedback in clinical practice and its perceptions of the patients: After treatment, patients in the IG were asked to evaluate their satisfaction with the project. At least for some therapists who originally were somewhat critical towards repeated psychometric assessments as an additional burden for patients, it came as a surprise that almost all patients who had remained in the study evaluated the project very positively. Most patients in the IG perceived the feedback system as an important feature of the therapy (92.9% out of 597 patients), accepted the time needed to fill out the questionnaires (97.1% out of 597 patients), and experienced it as helpful (66.3% out of 258 patients).

The QS-PSY-BAY Project: Design, Methods and Sample

As mentioned above, the QS-PSY-BAY project (see Acknowledgments) can be split up into two parts: First, questionnaire data of 1696 outpatients related to symptoms or therapeutic alliance were measured at several sampling points (for details see Steffanowski et al., 2011; the major measures comprised a standardized documentation of patient characteristics and individual treatment goals, the Patient Health Questionnaire, PHQ, and a Quality of Life Scale, SEL, as outcome measures, as well as the Helping Alliance Questionnaire, HAQ, to assess the therapeutic relationship). Second, treatment cost data of 80,726 individuals (including the outpatient sample) covering all costs related to inpatient, outpatient treatment and medication and including related information such as diagnosis, treatment, etc. over several years were received. Matching questionnaire and cost-related data will allow us to study many interesting questions such as typical treatment courses, cost-effectiveness of outpatient psychotherapy, issues related to the duration of treatment, etc. However, the resulting database was very extensive and complex so that data security, data protection, and data management became an essential issue.

The project has been initiated and developed by psychotherapists with support of a scientific advisory board consisting of three researchers either with a medical (two) or a psychological background (see Acknowledgments). Since April 2004 the Bavarian Association of Compulsory Health Insurance Physicians (KVB) has been managing this project. The KVB is responsible for organizing the statutory outpatient medical health care and medical services for over 12 million residents of Bavaria and acts as a service provider for over 24,000 contracted freelancing physicians of all disciplines and psychotherapists. Quality and efficacy of the treatments are the legal responsibilities of the KVB. The project is financed by an association of six health insurance companies (organized within the "vdek") with over 25 million insured individuals in Germany (approximately 3.2 million of them living in Bavaria). It is the legal responsibility of the health insurance companies to finance all necessary and efficient health-related treatments for their insured persons.

Criteria for selecting the questionnaires were a generic applicability for the most common psychological problems/therapeutic approaches, free access, and potentially quick completion. For assessment of patient characteristics the basic documentation "Psy-BaDo-PTM" (Heuft & Senf, 1998) served as a template. From the 10 Psy-BaDo items for detection of impairment in several problem areas, an explorative sum scale (PPB) was computed, measuring problem-based coping skills in everyday relevant areas of life. To capture symptom-related mental impairment (depression, anxiety, stress experience, somatic symptoms) the "Patient Health Questionnaire" PHQ-D (Löwe, Spitzer, Zipfel, & Herzog, 2002) was used. The health and psychosocially related quality of life was measured with the SEL-K scale (Averbeck et al., 1997). To assess a process-related variable, the "Helping Alliance Questionnaire" (HAQ, German version) (Bassler, Potratz & Krauthauser, 1995) was used.

Assessment as well as feedback of treatment characteristics and treatment success were conducted via an electronic documentation system. After each data collection, the therapist sent the current data to a data center set up especially for the project at the University of Mannheim; the transmission of the data was performed using a certified asymmetric encryption method on the Internet. In this way it was possible to set up a research database including a sample of 217 psychotherapists and 1696 patients. In response to each data delivery, an individual report for that therapist was created, encrypted and emailed back. In developing the appropriate software for the automated production of reports special attention was given to intuitive readability of images and patterns, so that the therapists could use the feedback with their patients without statistical expertise. Individualized therapy trajectories were graphically visualized in comparison to an anonymous reference group including all QS-PSY-BAY patients with the same main diagnosis (Percevic, Gallas, Arikan, Mößner, & Kordy, 2006).

Questionnaires were presented at intake (T0), at the end of the first five ("probatory") sessions (T1), at the end of therapy (T2) and at 1-year-follow up (T3). Beyond this, additional interim measures were assessed between T1 and T2 in the case of therapy extension. As part of this publication, only results for T0, T1, T2, and T3 are reported. In the assessment period covering April 2007 to June 2009 a total sample of 1696 patients gave their written consent to participate in the study and completed the documentation at intake (T0). Of these, 1449 (85.4% of 1696) completed the assessment after "probatory" sessions (T1); 1121 patients (66.1%) finished the final documentation (T2) and 884 patients (52.1%) the 1-year follow-up (T3). Of the patients 76.8% were female, and there was a tendency towards higher levels of education. The average age was 40.2 years ($s = 12.3$); 28.6% of patients were referred to the therapist by the family doctor, followed by psychiatrists, with 18.5%. Of all patients 17.7% came first to the therapist on their own initiative and a further 9.2% were former patients.

In the QS-PSY-BAY project, in addition to the usual drop-out within longitudinal studies (e.g., due to relocation or discontinuation of therapy), a specific methodological peculiarity was that at the end of the baseline survey in June 2009 many therapies had not yet been completed. Patients from these therapies nevertheless were asked to edit the final documentation T2 to gain as much data as possible. Accordingly, T2 was the "real" end of therapy for only 416 cases (37.1% of 1121), and for the same reason only 309 "real" 1-year follow-ups were available (74.3% of 416). This sub-sample will be referred to as "C" (completers with 1-year follow-up). So C is a relatively small and highly selected sub-sample, excluding any therapy dropouts and showing a tendency to include a higher proportion of short-term treatments. Since the sub-sample is not representative of all QS-PSY-BAY patients, the risk of overestimating the effect sizes must be carefully considered.

Therefore, a conservative estimate of the pre-post effect sizes for all 1696 patients in the initial sample was conducted following the intent-to-treat principle. In such analyses, all patients included in a study group must be included, regardless of what happens with them after the initial measurement (Schulgen & Schumacher, 2007). Doing this for all 1696 patients, the last existing assessment during the study period was used as a conservative estimate for the health condition after the treatment.

For the illustration of the global therapeutic success a multiple status indicator (Schmidt, Steffanowski, Nübling, Lichtenberg, & Wittmann, 2003; Steffanowski, Löschmann, Schmidt, Wittmann, & Nübling, 2007; Wittmann, Nübling, & Schmidt, 2002; Wittmann & Steffanwoski, 2011) was computed, including the four subscales of the PHQ-D, the six scales of the SEL and the PPB problem scale. For this purpose, the raw values were converted by linear transformation into a single metric from 0 (utmost bad status) to 100 (utmost good status) on each scale. Then the multiple status indicator MSI was aggregated by taking the average of these 11 linearly transformed scales, following the idea that for a comprehensive evaluation all domains of the bio-psycho-social model (Bengel & Koch, 2000) should be considered, including the symptomatic level, criteria of physical, mental and social well-being, as well as coping with everyday life. The data aggregation of the 11 scales not only led to a high reliability of the multiple status indicator (Cronbach's alpha = .92) but it also allowed us to reduce the problem of alpha-error inflation in multiple mean comparisons.

Results of the QS-PSY-BAY-Project: A Summary

Treatment Outcome

The most common psychotherapy indication of the initial sample was provided by the depressive disorders with an overall share of 48.7% in the ICD-10 principal diagnosis, followed by anxiety disorders with 18.8%. About 59.0% had at least one other secondary psychological disorder, and every second to third patient indicated a history of former somatic and psychosomatic diseases. On average, patients had already been suffering for almost 2 years from the disease. On the PHQ-D scale depression, at T0 a moderate clinical impairment ($M = 12.2$) was reported. Compared to the initial sample T0, a slightly higher proportion of moderate and severe depressive disorders and phobic disorders were observed among the completers (C).

For calculation of pre-post effect sizes the sub-sample C was used. On average, 26.4 outpatient therapy sessions ($SD = 21.8$) were documented and between first and last consultation, with an average of 12.7 months ($SD = 5.9$) was observed. Table I shows the results of the pre-post comparisons. Up to T1 a slight improvement of the health state was already observable, corresponding to a small ($d > .2$) to medium ($d > .5$) effect according to Cohen (1992). At T2, there are large effects ($d > .8$). These effects were stable in the 1-year follow-up and no statistically significant mean difference was observed between T2 and T3. In addition, a clinically relevant remission of symptoms was observed for the average patient; PHQ-D depression scores after therapy, for example, were on average 5 points, quite below the

Table I. Pre-post comparisons of psychometric scales for completed therapy.

	T0		T1		T2		T3		Effect size		
	M	SD	M	SD	M	SD	M	SD	$d_{T0/T1}$	$d_{T0/T2}$	$d_{T0/T3}$
PHQ-D Depression	11,94	5,50	8,89	4,86	5,51	4,47	5,30	4,41	0,55	1,17	1,21
PHQ-D Somatic symptoms	11,67	5,38	10,33	5,15	7,43	4,87	7,28	4,83	0,25	0,79	0,82
PHQ-D Stress experience	8,30	3,72	7,22	3,70	4,80	3,48	4,76	3,55	0,29	0,94	0,95
PHQ-D Anxiety	9,99	5,01	7,61	4,51	4,04	3,84	3,84	4,06	0,48	1,19	1,23
SEL-K Mood	2,92	0,86	3,10	0,76	3,71	0,77	3,69	0,76	0,21	0,92	0,90
SEL-K Physical complaints	3,42	0,70	3,63	0,68	4,03	0,64	4,01	0,65	0,30	0,87	0,84
SEL-K Subjective complaints	2,30	0,94	2,64	0,92	3,58	0,99	3,56	1,02	0,36	1,36	1,34
SEL-K Experience tone	2,58	0,74	2,86	0,78	3,77	0,78	3,79	0,83	0,38	1,61	1,64
SEL-K Social integration	3,34	0,88	3,59	0,84	4,17	0,80	4,20	0,77	0,28	0,94	0,98
SEL-K Attitude	2,40	0,92	2,71	0,90	3,59	0,89	3,63	0,92	0,34	1,29	1,34
PPB-P Problem loading	2,76	0,71	2,62	0,73	1,75	0,72	1,72	0,76	0,20	1,42	1,46
MSI Multiple status indicator	49,68	14,57	56,44	14,40	72,53	15,14	72,89	15,62	0,46	1,57	1,59

Note. N = 309 patients (therapy completers). T0, intake; T1, end of probatory sessions; T2, end of therapy; T3, 1-year follow-up. All mean comparisons T0/T1, T0/T2 and T0/T3 are statistically significant ($p < .001$).

clinical limit of 10 points defined by Löwe et al. (2002). The multiple status indicator on the health condition (MSI) improves on the 0 to 100 points overall scale from 50 to 73 points. This result corresponds to a large effect size of $d = 1.57$ (T0/T2) and 1.59 (T0/T3).

The effects estimated by intent-to-treat methodology are shown in Table II. As stated in the Methods section, the last available measurement was used for each patient. A total of 1696 − 1449 = 247 patients completed only the baseline assessment T0 without any consecutive assessment. For these 247 patients a zero effect ($d = .00$) was assumed. For 1449 − 1121 = 328 patients only T1 (after five sessions) was completed. For this group we considered a small effect in the calculation. For 1121 − 309 = 812 patients the end of study measurement T2 was before the regular end of therapy. As expected, the resulting effect sizes were lower than in the subsample C, but still consistently on an average ($d > .50$) or large ($d > .80$) level in terms of Cohen (1992). Effect size on the the PHQ depression scale reached $d = .78$, and on the MSI $d = .97$.

Further data analyses of the core data set of the 1696 patients were conducted, including the assessment of typical change patterns among the subsample of depressed patients using latent class models (Altmann et al., submitted). In this analysis, we found five different change patterns (Figure 3): "Responders" with medium depressive symptoms at the beginning (class 1, 54% of patient sample), those with intensive depressive symptoms (class 2, 25%), "late responders" (class 5, 9%), patients with minimal responses (class 4, 8%), and patients with recurrent symptoms (class 3, 4%). Furthermore, Altmann et al. (in press) found that outpatient psychotherapy is mainly extended for patients

with a low symptom reduction after the standard therapy duration and that therapy extension allows a symptom reduction that could not have been achieved otherwise. Additional data analyses will relate to the helping alliance, determinants of dropouts, and cost-effectiveness of the outpatient psychotherapies. The latter analyses will be the first using the health cost-related data that have been collected within the QS-PSY-BAY project, which has specific implications for future studies of that kind.

Table II. Intent-to-treat-corrected pre-post effect sizes.

	T0		X		Effect size $d_{T0/X}$
	M	SD	M	SD	
PHQ-D Depression	12,24	5,81	7,68	5,43	0,78
PHQ-D Somatic symptoms	11,80	5,51	8,93	5,33	0,52
PHQ-D Stress experience	8,75	3,85	6,43	3,93	0,60
PHQ-D Anxiety	10,28	5,28	6,31	5,06	0,75
SEL-K Mood	2,84	0,81	3,32	0,87	0,60
SEL-K Physical complaints	3,37	0,71	3,77	0,73	0,56
SEL-K Subjective complaints	2,28	0,92	3,09	1,08	0,88
SEL-K Experience tone	2,54	0,75	3,28	0,93	0,99
SEL-K Social integration	3,30	0,86	3,81	0,88	0,59
SEL-K Attitude	2,36	0,87	3,09	1,02	0,84
PPB-P Problem loading	2,81	0,74	2,20	0,86	0,83
MSI Multiple status indicator	48,52	15,01	63,14	17,80	0,97

Note. N = 1696 patients. T0, intake; T1, end of probatory sessions; T2, end of therapy; T3, 1-year follow-up; X, the last available measurement point was used as estimation for therapy outcome. All mean comparisons are statistically significant ($p < .001$).

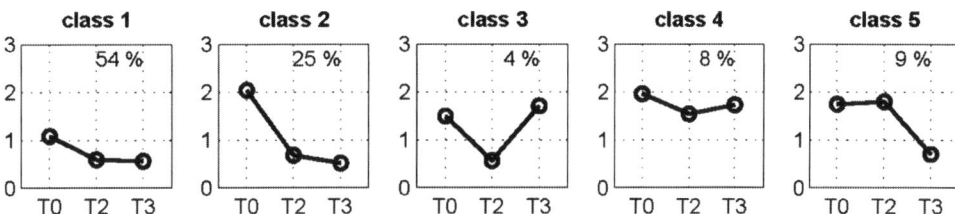

Figure 3. Change pattern of depressive symptoms found in the QS-PSY-BAY project (for details see Altmann et al., submitted).

Analysis of Cost-Related Data in the QS-PSY-BAY Project

To study the effects of psychotherapy on all aspects of medical support, the study planned to include a registry of health-related costs that will be used to (i) compare the treatment sample with other patients undergoing psychotherapy (testing representativeness) and (ii) to compare the treatment sample with other patients suffering from psychological disorders. To form such a registry, data from the KVB (including all kinds of outpatient treatments and diagnoses) and the data of the six insurance companies (including inpatient treatment, medications and work incapacity) were collected and combined with the psychotherapy data.

To produce a sample for data analysis, several selection criteria were defined (only patients of the six companies of the vdek, diagnosis according to ICD-10 F2 to F6[1] with ~50% of them receiving psychotherapy). The third quarter of the year 2008 served as a time reference to select patients corresponding to the criteria. In the end, the target population included 433,255 persons, of whom 39,334 had undergone psychotherapy (9.1%) and 393,921 had no psychotherapy (90.9%). Randomly selected, our sample includes 41,119 insured persons with an ICD-10 F-diagnosis (without organic disorders and disorders due to psychoactive drug abuse) and no psychotherapy in the third quarter of 2008, and 37,870 patients with an F-diagnosis receiving psychotherapy in this quarter; in addition

the 1696 patients from the outpatient therapy sample were included. Finally, the sample providing health-related costs included a total 80,726 persons.

Data come from eight data sources (see Figure 4). The clinical data of the 1696 outpatients and their therapists were managed separately by a group of researchers at the University of Mannheim (see Steffanowski et al., 2011) and were then sent to the University of Jena as a data file. Data related to the costs of outpatient treatments were provided by the KVB in three tranches. Health insurance companies provided the other cost-related data also in three tranches. The data were saved on a server which is specialized for fast reading and writing of large data amounts. As a database system we used MySQL, which is a free relational database management system. Besides easy and fast data handling, a MySQL database enables a high degree of data security in terms of prevention of illegal data access. Only a few users can access the database from specified computers. The database size is 42,086 MB, covering millions of entries. To analyze the data with SPSS, R, or Mplus it is necessary to reduce size and complexity. Therefore, we generated new files with definitions of person samples, data format, and variables of interest. To get a smaller and less complex database, we focus on quarterly totals of variables such as inpatient treatment costs or medication.

One of the first analyses of the cost-related data will test whether the costs related to medical

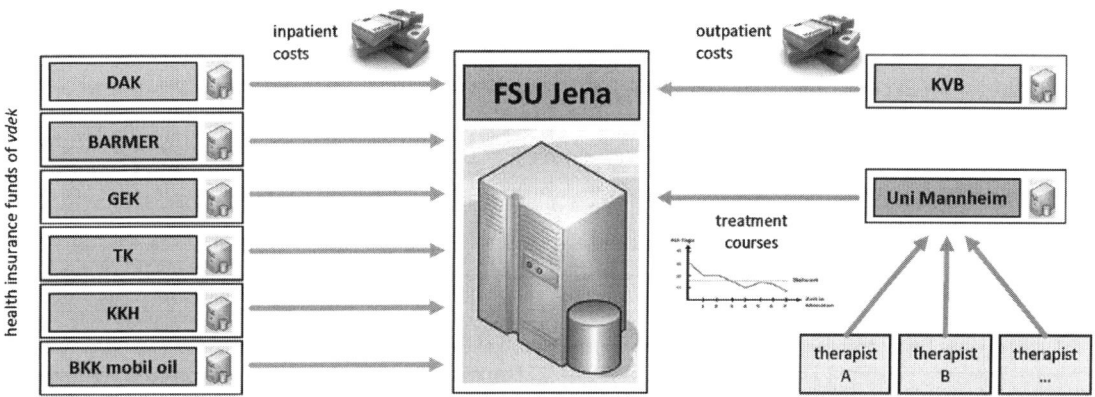

Figure 4. Data matching in the QS-PSY-BAY project.

(inpatient/outpatient) treatment and medication in the clinical sample differ between the year prior to outpatient psychotherapy and the year following psychotherapy. In a second step, these data will be compared with a matched subsample of the patients who did not receive any psychotherapy during the respective time period.

From the perspective of a research organization, the challenge of combining data sets of such a large size provides some lessons for future studies (see below).

Obstacles, Challenges, Difficulties and Benefits in Developing and Implementing the TK Study

In the following, the views from the scientific board and the research team are presented separately, since both teams had different roles and perspectives within the study and also came to somewhat different conclusions about the targets and findings of the study.

The scientific board consisted of 12 participants, six research experts, three psychotherapists, and three representatives of the medical board of the participating regions. All members, except the three representatives of the medical board, were elected by representatives of the participating psychotherapists. The main goal of the scientific board was to guarantee that the study was performed strictly according to the standards and procedures defined in the evaluation plan beforehand. The advisory board met twice per year in the beginning and once a year towards the end of the project.

The scientific evaluation of the project was done by two research teams, one from the University of Mannheim (chaired by Werner W. Wittmann) and one from the University of Berne, later (starting 2007) University of Trier, chaired by Wolfgang Lutz (see Acknowledgments). These research teams were responsible for preparing and conducting the study, which included the preparation of the assessment materials, the training of the participating therapists and negotiations with the software company (to develop a specific software system). The teams were also responsible for the data analysis and data management (not data collection, which was done by a trust center, Hogrefe Verlag) and the writing of the final report.

The View of the Scientific Board

Obstacles and challenges of the study can be attributed to two basic issues: (i) problems of the study design and method and (ii) problems of the study acceptance.

Problems of the Study Design and Method

Some problems concerning the loss of data were intrinsically linked to the study design. The study was planned for a 6 year duration. Included were therapies of long-term duration up to 3 years and longer. Taking the 12-month follow-up period into account, it was evident that an extension of the recruitment period would lead to unfinished treatments or treatments where the follow-up measurement was not yet completed. Loss of data was in part due to the limits of the study duration and therapies that were not finished.

Furthermore the project was designed to evaluate the outcome of rather different forms of psychotherapy: Brief psychotherapy of up to 25 sessions and long-term psychotherapy up to 240 sessions. In addition, interventions of different psychotherapeutic orientations were included. There were no clear operationalized definitions or criteria on which the labels of CBT or psychodynamic treatment were based. During the planning period of the project it had therefore been agreed that in the outcome analysis the kind of intervention would not be considered for comparison.

The geographic location of the participating therapists in three different areas of the country required a relatively complex system of data monitoring. This system improved in the course of the trial but still improvement was not sufficient to avoid considerable loss of data.

Finally the main hypotheses of the project were rather complex. The two strategies of quality assurance compared were multifaceted and consisted of a variety of different components such as standardized diagnostic assessment, regular psychometric measurements during treatment, feedback procedures, peer review assessment, etc. Such multi-component interventions do not allow the attribution of outcome to a specific factor. As Lutz et al. (2012) have pointed out, considering the results of the study it cannot be decided for instance whether regular measurements without feedback may have the same effects as measurement plus feedback because the study did not include a comparison group controlling for this factor.

The implementation of feedback procedures was a central component of the trial. However, there are substantial differences in the way in which these feedback procedures were used in the current project as compared to other trials. In former studies, feedback was used to inform therapeutic interventions within the psychotherapeutic process in order to improve outcome (Lambert, Whipple, Smart, Vermeersch, & Nielsen, 2001; Shimokawa et al., 2010; Whipple et al. 2003). In the current study feedback information was used to decide whether to begin, to continue or to end treatment. The filling out of self-report questionnaires in this context acquires a different meaning. The fact that the self-report of symptoms in the TK study had an impact on treatment decisions may have interfered with the objectivity of the measurement. In the TKM feedback was not addressed only to the treating psychotherapist but also to experts who—on behalf of the insurance company—had to assess the treatment selection decision (external quality assurance). The patients answering the self-report questionaires therefore may have been influenced by their preference, e.g., to begin or to continue treatment The link between internal and external quality assessment in the TK project also led to problems of acceptance of the study.

Problems of Acceptance of the Trial on the Part of Clinical Practitioners

The problems of acceptance of the project were due to several reasons:

(1) The context in which the project was launched was a discussion on the conditions of reimbursement of outpatient psychotherapy and the allocation of resources in the field. Health insurance companies expected that the implementation of a new quality assurance system in outpatient psychotherapy might contribute to a cutting down of costs. The planning of the project therefore was embedded in a controversial discussion within the health care system.

(2) Clinical practitioners questioned the validity and clinical meaningfulness of indicators such as sum scores of self-report questionnaires. In addition, those working with long-term psychotherapy felt that ceiling effects might blur the evaluation of outcome of long-term treatments.

(3) The impact of the psychometric measurements on the treatment process was a concern for some psychotherapists. It seems that in some cases eligible patients were not offered participation in the study because therapists anticipated a negative impact on the patient or the treatment process.

(4) In an early stage of the project development it was considered that the empirically based algorithms should replace clinical decisions rather than supporting them. This consideration led to substantial resentment on the side of the participating therapists and therefore was subsequently withdrawn. It was

important that the scientific research team (Lutz et al., 2012) clearly stated that psychometric assessment and feedback were to be considered as additional information supporting clinical judgement but were not supposed to replace clinical decisions.

The average number of treatment sessions in the IG outweighed that of the CG, indicating that feedback and other components of the TKM did not lead to a reduction in the number of sessions. The interpretation of this finding was subject to a debate. According to the research team (see Acknowledgments), the higher number of sessions in the TKM condition resulted from the fact that in this arm the number of sessions allocated at the beginning of therapy was higher than in the control group, which was a problem of the design, but could not have been avoided because of issues concerning the practical implementation of the study (see paragraph on the view of the research team and Lutz et al., 2012). According to the understanding of the scientific advisory board this finding was in clear disagreeement with the hypothesis that feedback and other components of the TKM would lead to a more effective (economic) use of resources (Vogel et al., 2013).

While most of the problems about the design and the method of the study might not have been preventable, a number of suggestions can be offered to reduce problems related to clinicians' acceptance of the trial: Communication in practice-oriented psychotherapy research is of central importance. Clinical practitioners and researchers by their training, their professional identity, and their basic belief systems are rooted in different cultures. The dialogue between these groups builds on three factors: (i) transparency, (iii) the continuity of the persons involved, and (iii) a platform structure, which helps to organize the discourse.

Practice-oriented psychotherapy research might be easier to conduct if the research topics investigated are not in the center of a current debate on health policy, e.g., on quality assurance and/or the resource allocation of health insurance. If it is inevitable that topics which are highly controversial in terms of health policy are addressed by research, a maximum of transparency of stakeholder interests and potentially conflicting goals is needed. It is almost trivial to highlight that personal continuity in all active boards of such a huge research project prevents repetition of questions and discussion of single problems and issues. A platform for discussion allows these perspectives to be brought in and to be reflected. Within the TK project it was attempted to establish such a platform by the scientific advisory board. Despite the controversial nature of some of the discussions, this platform structure played an important role in coping with the debates in the professional field and in helping the project to reach high scientific standards.

Benefits of the Study

The merit of the study is that it rigorously tested the effectiveness of two different forms of quality assurance in outpatient psychotherapy under natural conditions using a cluster-randomized research design. The goals of the study were ambitious since the two conditions compared were complex in themselves and the size of the study was difficult to handle. However, quality assurance in outpatient psychotherapy is an issue of central importance and it is a merit to put the controversy about different strategies of quality assurance to empirical testing instead of leaving them the topic of an ideological debate

As mentioned above, the results of the study according to the scientific advisory board did not support the conclusion that patients could profit a great deal from a larger implementation of feedback systems. In fact, the superiority of the quality assurance approach including feedback in addition to other components (TKM) as compared to the traditional case-report peer review system (QAAU) could not be demonstrated in the TK project. The potential of this negative finding lies in its challenge to analyze and understand the reasons why feedback was not as effective as hypothesized in this study. We assume that the information derived from psychometric signals with regard to complex clinical decisions still is not specific enough. Future research should address systematically selected cases of congruence/divergence between clinical reasoning and feedback in order to better relate these two forms of information and evidence. For feedback to have a significant impact, it may also be necessary to offer therapists consultations and discussions with experts on possible reasons for a suboptimal course of therapy, and action plans for improving the situation. Such a procedure had been proposed by one of the advisory board members in the very beginning of the project, but could not be realized due to expected costs.

The View of the Research Team

From a researcher's perspective, a number of challenges related to the existing differences in the German health care system between the therapeutic orientations. It was therefore essential to include interest groups from different approaches in the development of the research design. This was not an easy task, which can be seen in the fact that the project overall took about 8 years, of which 4 were needed for preparations and group discussions in the planning phase of the study. One aspect of discussion between the different stakeholders (researchers and therapists with different clinical orientations) was the evaluation of symptom changes. Some therapists had very specific ideas about the goals of a successful therapy and on how to measure treatment outcome. While some therapists saw an increase of symptoms in an early phase of the treatment as a sometimes necessary step towards a successful ultimate treatment outcome, others saw a symptom decrease as early as possible as a positive sign for a successful outcome. As a result, the feedback was chosen to be as descriptive as possible and had to cover expectancies from different treatment approaches (see also Lutz et al., 2011). Furthermore, the plan to introduce a standardized assessment procedure including a structured diagnostic interview (related to ICD-10 criteria; Hiller et al., 2004) was not positively evaluated by all participating clinicians. Moreover, due to the divergent treatment lengths it was necessary to devise different assessment schedules for each orientation. Although advanced statistical models are at hand for the analysis of this kind of complex data structure, this fact made it hard to integrate measures from different orientations. The accomplishment of the aim of having a practice-friendly study design did not come without costs. For example, it led to the fact that no further repeated measurement control group could be included in the research design, which would have enabled us to investigate the effects of feedback in more depth.

From the perspective of these practitioners, who where asked for their opinion at the beginning of the project, different concerns were relevant in the planning and implementation of the study. Continuous progress monitoring might induce fears of being controlled and evaluated. Therefore, it was important to reassure participants that the collected data were handled with complete anonymity of every participating party (research team as well as health insurance company) and without consequences for the funding of their therapies. This goal was reached by using an independent third party (the so-called "trust center"), which was responsible for the handling and anonymization of personal data. Other therapists feared a potential disempowerment concerning their clinical decisions in favor of the recommendations from the feedback reports. Taking that possible fear into account, it was important to point out (over several meetings) that therapists' clinical judgment still should be seen as most valid for treatment decisions and that the empirical feedback might just be seen as helping tool. The therapists are ultimately responsible for integrating diagnostic multidimensional, multi-source information into a coherent picture. Accordingly, even after several repeated positive changes, "stable progress" feedback should only suggest considering the end of therapy, but not automatically terminating the intervention. Ultimately, clinical decisions have to remain clinical decisions; they cannot be fully replaced by psychometric measures, but, as could be shown by this project, can be informed by psychometric measures. In that sense, clinical decisions can receive empirically supported decisions using the introduction of feedback tools.

From a different point of view, the high resistance of some psychotherapists against statistically based psychometric decision aids reminds one of the problems of lack of knowledge transfer from research into practice. One of the best-replicated results of assessment and decision-making in psychology is related to the debate about clinical versus statistical decision-making, initiated more than half a century ago by Meehl (1954) and replicated again and again (Grove & Meehl, 1996). Meehl (1986) found via several investigations that decisions based on statistical predictions were at least equal to or often better than decisions solely based on clinical judgment. If one wants to implement such a feedback system to improve decision-making, one needs the engagement of the practitioners to have a chance to convince them about the advantages. One of the caveats of our TK project analysis is that we have not intensively analyzed so far how much the feedback system was actually used, but we are in the very process of researching this topic.

Furthermore, practitioners were skeptical about the additional expenditure of time related to data input and management. This problem was faced by an easy-to-handle software system that was able to directly collect, digitalize, and store the data, and newer software versions have even more possibilities these days (some of the data drop-outs were connected to the original problems of the software system).

As feedback systems rely on repeated patient self-ratings there were also some concerns from the therapists' and researchers' perspective. They were critical about a standardized quantitative evaluation of psychological problems. Some therapists, for example, viewed this as a simplistic reduction of complex problems to trivial numbers. Another concern was the time that is needed to answer the questions for patients and therapists. As a result of these concerns, one can learn that in order to get reliable and complete information it is crucial that participating therapists see some value in empirical research for their clinical practice, that they

communicate about this with their patients, and that the any research team should continuously highlight the importance of the collaboration of research and practice for improvement of quality.

Additionally, for the purpose of keeping patient burden low, questionnaires should be well selected and short versions should be preferred. Also some easy to use hardware and software should be available for data entry and provision of feedback. To assess how far these concerns were justified from a patient's perspective, patients were asked to evaluate their satisfaction with the project after therapy. As described in the previous section, the vast majority of patients in the intervention group thought of the feedback system as an important feature of the therapy, accepted the time needed to fill out the questionnaires, and saw it as helpful.

Benefits of the Study

Given that study arms were confounded with several other variables due to controversies with the different stakeholders (e.g., differences of approved sessions, differences in diagnostic tools and assessment schedules), in the opinion of the research team a rigorous test of the feedback condition was not possible, but the feasibility of the procedure could clearly be shown.

Also given the large amount of data within a rarely studied applied setting (e.g., 751 patients with BSI pre and post scores) and the results of (i) high patient satisfaction and acceptance of feedback, (ii) the fact that a feedback effect on treatment length could be shown (under control for the number of approved sessions, we could show that patients with a negative early response to treatment, negative feedback, were provided with more sessions and patients with a positive feedback with fewer sessions), and (iii) that therapists made use of the tools in about 75% of studied cases, we came to the conclusion that the use of feedback can be effective and feasible in private practices, which might ease the path of such tools into the mental health service system.

The establishment of ongoing progress monitoring in real-world psychotherapy would have several benefits for patients, therapists, and researchers. Quality management and feedback systems are primarily aimed at the improvement and the assurance of each patient's treatment quality. Thus, patients, therapists, and researchers could profit a great deal from a larger implementation of these tools. Considering therapists' difficulties with the identification of patients at risk of treatment failure, progress monitoring could help therapists to keep an eye on changes in patient self-reports (Hatfield,

McCullough, Frantz, & Krieger, 2010). Also, patients evaluated the use of quality monitoring in psychotherapy positively. This in itself could already be a resource to build a helpful therapeutic setting.

Therapists, as was realized within the TK study, could have access to information on the development of their patients' distress and several process variables routinely (e.g., the therapeutic alliance), giving them the possibility to compare the treatment course of their current patient with other already treated patients as a benchmark. The decision rules in place could also support their evaluations of these single-case trajectories and thus their treatment planning. Furthermore, ongoing progress monitoring and feedback provide therapists with the possibility to evaluate their own strengths and weaknesses: For example, repeatedly negative feedback reports for a specific subgroup of patients could help therapists to identify further needs of training on their own.

Researchers could draw on continuously growing databases in future research. With the help of these huge amounts of data from already treated patients, researchers can, for example, derive and continuously optimize decision support rules and tools for therapists training (Lutz, Leach, Barkham, Lucock, & Stiles, 2005; Whipple et al., 2003). Furthermore, these databases could also be used for the investigation of several other research questions regarding psychotherapy processes and outcomes and therefore be an essential tool within a new area of practice-oriented research (e.g., Castonguay et al., 2013).

Similarities and Differences Between the Scientific Board and the Research Teams About the Obstacles, Challenges, Difficulties in Developing and Implementing the TK Study

Bringing the perspectives of the two teams (scientific board and research team) together, they both agree on several fundamental obstacles, challenges, and benefits that can be derived from the TK study. Both highlight the central importance of quality assurance studies in naturalistic settings and urge the need for this kind of study in the future. It could be shown that an implementation of quality monitoring tools can successfully be accomplished in German outpatient psychotherapy practice settings. Both groups highlight a culture of transparency and communication between researchers and clinicians as a pivotal precondition for a successful realization. This transparency also implies a sensitive study design that takes into account and anticipates possible fears of clinicians, especially concerning their autonomy.

Conclusions on the benefits of feedback systems in private practice psychotherapy are an issue of debate within the TK study groups. The research team sees several shortcomings in the design of the study, but the large amount of data within a rarely studied applied setting, the high degree of patient satisfaction and acceptance, and the high use of the tools by many therapists lead to the conclusion that the use of feedback can be effective and feasible in private practices.

The scientific advisory board—in contrast—questions whether, based on the results of the TK study, it could be concluded that the use of feedback systems is effective in improving outcomes in private practice psychotherapy and therefore should be recommended for wider implementation. In contrast, according to their view, the evidence of the TK study rather demonstrates that different forms of quality assurance in outpatient psychotherapy were associated with equal outcomes and that therefore further research would be necessary in order to clarify which strategy of quality assurance in what context might be more useful. As far as the overall effects in both conditions are concerned, representativeness has been questioned, as the self-selected therapists can be assumed to be particularly confident in the quality of their therapies as a condition for exposing themselves to the scrutiny of such a study.

Obstacles, Challenges, Difficulties, and Benefits in Developing and Implementing the QS-PSY-BAY Study

Basic Design of the Study

One goal of the QS-PSY-BAY project was the exploration of a QA system based upon the initiative of practitioners with a clear focus on its usefulness, both for the patients and for the therapists. The QA system should comprise the available therapeutic "schools" within the health care system but not compare these related to their differential effectiveness. Accordingly, the entire study should be "non-punitive." To reach consensus among all participating groups, it was helpful to formulate (written) study goals, but also "non-goals." The decision to avoid addressing political issues related to differential effectiveness requires adequate deliberation concerning application of basic data and dissemination of the findings and controlling the adherence to goals and "non-goals."

In addition to some of the challenges specific to this study, medical care research in general is linked to a lot of specific problems. First, as a rule, the time intervals are comparatively long (e.g., not all therapies start at the same time as a study, therapy duration may vary largely and could reach more than 1.5 years plus 1 year for a follow-up). It is difficult to find funding for such a long-term project. Second, comprehensive studies implicate many cooperation partners. In the QS-PSY-BAY project, for example, we had eight cooperating partners providing data on different aspects of medical care. If possible, one should minimize the number of partners to reduce trouble with data matching and keeping deadlines, and to limit expenses for organization, coordination, and communication.

Development of the Study and its Implementation

In planning a study such as the QS-PSY-BAY project involving many therapists with almost no experience in research, a research team is confronted with several of concerns related to the fact that (i) collecting such an amount of data might impair patients and their therapists, that (ii) the research process might disturb the psychotherapeutic process, that (iii) results might be negative or (iv) critically interpreted. Other concerns were related to the scepticism towards any feedback based upon subjective reports. To solve these problems, all participating parties were brought together very early during the process (i.e., the practicing therapists, researchers, insurance companies, professional organizations). In addition, from the beginning it was intended to parallel all measures with formal phases of outpatient psychotherapy to make the organization easier (i.e., initial contact, "probatory sessions" and intervals of treatment) and to enable clearer interpretations of the findings. Data collected at these time points also allowed the use of the results for any reapplication.

Methodological limitations of the project relate, for example, to a selection bias of motivated therapists and patients, or the lack of control group. To test aspects of internal and external validity, the research group is currently comparing the QS-PSY-BAY study sample characteristics with the large data set provided by the insurance companies to estimate how representative the study sample might be. One major goal was to reduce research costs by using measures/instruments with open access, while, on the other hand, the selection of such measures might limit comparability with other studies.

Before the project started, a pilot study testing the feasibility was performed. In total, all participating groups accepted that the project would be of long duration. Including all data handling (see below), the entire process from the first idea to the first publication of the first results (Steffanowski et al., 2011), almost covered 10 years. Since the researchers were

not the motor of the process, it was necessary to deal with all concerns of the practicing therapists, including those related to the expenditure of time that the study would take. Accordingly, the vdek insurance companies provided financial gratification for the therapists.

Data Protection

To comply with the needs of data protection, specific software had to be developed to enable patients to fill out the questionnaires on a hand-held computer in the waiting room, to transfer data, and to combine it with the therapists' ratings. The KVB provided a program to all participating institutions which generated a 40-character ID with a hash algorithm using the combined insurance/health insurance number. The resulting one-to-one identification number (ID) was then used to match individual data from various sources. No other data identifying patients were transmitted, ensuring that the insurance companies did not receive clinical information related to the psychotherapies and that any institution analyzing the data did not have any link between ID and person. This condition and the prohibition against sharing the link or any other data finally provided a maximum of privacy/anonymity in line with the strict laws of the Federal Republic of Germany.

Data Entry

The acceptance of the software solution by the therapists and the handling of the patient software appeared to be critical. A huge number of tests, several updates and continuous support, good know-how at the unit, providing all services, its service orientation, FAQ lists, newsletters, and a comprehensive project documentation as well as three workshops served to increase compliance, information exchange and motivation.

As a rule, medical care data are complex and extensive. Special hardware, software, and most important IT personnel are needed. Costs and resources for data matching, screening, and preprocessing are easily underestimated.

Data Matching

Although the entire data set from the QS-PSY-BAY project might be seen as an unusual treasure, the matching of monetary data from different sources and questionnaire data was the most critical part of the project from the researchers' perspective. To improve data handling, we would recommend maintaining a list of individuals who are included into the study. This helps to distinguish between correct and incorrect IDs. Second, one should minimize the number of data sources and keep data tranches to a minimum. In the operation phase this will save a lot of resources. A maximum of energy should be invested in matching data adequately. Make sure that you receive data that have already been checked for their quality. Accordingly, processes to maintain data quality should be continuously tested and improved. This would, of course, be facilitated if all the insurance companies could find a standard to provide data related to routine medical care.

Benefits of the Study

Undoubtedly, the major value of the study lies in the combination of treatment-related process and outcome data, and a huge number of cost-related data (inpatient and outpatient treatments, all medication) over a longer period of time. Two primary goals of the study (testing a cross-institutional electronic QA system and collecting data for health services research) could be realized. The observed therapy outcome with large effect sizes reflects a remarkable success, documenting the good performance of outpatient psychotherapy. The data collection was performed under natural conditions, which suggests a high external validity of the study, despite all methodological limitations. Based upon an initiative by established psychotherapists, a practical comprehensive and ongoing routine electronic documentation for quality assurance in outpatient psychotherapy was realized. The therapists received a benchmarking of individual courses of treatments with simultaneously collected anonymous reference values of patients with the same disorder—a gain of information that previously has not been realized in the outpatient context. In addition, QS-PSY-BAY has provided valuable data for health care research which highlight the importance and effectiveness of outpatient psychotherapy. Overall, the cooperation between practitioners and researchers as well as institutions was of value to improve knowledge about psychotherapy practice and research and to increase motivation to make use of feedback.

Recommendations for Future Studies Involving Partnership with Clinicians

As previously discussed, studies involving partnership with clinicians will be under much less pressure if the research topics and goals are not too closely linked to controversial implications for health policy. As we also mentioned above, a dialogue between researchers and clinicians should be built upon a number of factors, including transparency, continuity, and the presence of a discussion platform. In addition, research involving such partnership should meet two other conditions: (i) anonymous data collection and handling, and (ii) the autonomy of therapists in their decision-making. Given the example of the TK study, autonomy implies the free choice of therapists to make free use of the data provided by the feedback reports. Research should focus on questions which are genuinely shared by clinicians and researchers and which clearly deserve further study. These questions should be openly discussed in an early stage of the cooperation and provide the basis for the study plan. It is vital for the commitment of therapists that they are completely informed about the aims and backgrounds of the study.

The QS-PSY-BAY study confirms most issues mentioned by the TK teams. In addition to their recommendations, the QS-PSY-BAY project has also shown that careful planning related to all aspects of such a study is of crucial importance, including early planning of data analysis and data utilization (also in terms of publications). Planning also has be related to the amount of time and money needed for such a long-term study (many outpatient therapies in Germany last more than 1 year), including also data management. As with the other research group, conclusions from the QS-PSY-BAY project underline the need for a non-punitive approach that undoubtedly will increase the motivation of psychotherapists to cooperate with research institutions. On the other hand, clinicians should continuously be informed about the state of psychotherapy research and about the relative value of single results to avoid an overestimation of their own data.

Overall Conclusion

Given the specific nature of the German health services system, the triangle collaboration of therapists, researchers, and health insurance companies/health service institutions turned out to be fruitful in both studies. Effect sizes of psychotherapy in both projects demonstrate that ambulatory psychotherapy in Germany compared to international research is impressive; the conservatively estimated effects were close to $d = 1.0$ in both projects. Considerations and controversies between the collaboration partners point to the importance of research results obtained by such naturalistic studies and should not be seen as an insurmountable obstacle. Without one of these actors as well as a patient- and clinician-friendly study design, it would hardly be possible to conduct such practice-oriented research within private practices.

As Castonguay et al. (2013) have recently shown, research based on joint ventures of practitioners and researchers is still at its beginning. Accordingly, the participating groups of the two German studies described in this paper can be proud of having reached rich and relevant information about outpatient psychotherapy in the German health system, which is not common for this or other fields in the health service system.

We recommend researchers to be open to these kinds of collaborations, which ultimately could be profitable for all participants. Clinicians and patients can learn from empirical data from prior treatment(s) about future treatments on an ongoing basis. Finally, we were surprised by the positive responses of patients with respect to including psychometric information into clinical practice. Both studies showed that patients (and the therapists) are usually willing to participate and feel appreciated by patient-oriented research as long as their therapists support such endeavors. If this is the case, one potential benefit of practice-oriented research may be fostering the engagement of patients as the crucial stakeholders in mental health care, besides advancing our knowledge obout psychotherapy process and outcome.

Acknowledgments

Members of the Scientific Advisory Board were J. Brockmann, F. Caspar, G. Rudolf, C. E. Scheidt (coordinator), U. Stangier, and H. Vogel.

The TK research team (Werner W. Wittmann, Wolfgang Lutz, Andrés Steffanowski, Jan R. Böhnke, David Kriz, Julian Rubel, Manuel Völkle) would like to thank Katharina Köck, André Bittermann, Niklaus Stulz, Armita Tschitsaz-Stucki, Eva Schürch, and Sven Tholen for their collaboration on prior reports of the project and on training courses for therapists in the introductory phase of the study. Furthermore we would like to thank all participating patients, therapists and reviewers, the Techniker Krankenkasse (Dr. Ruprecht, project management TK), the participating regional associations of statutory health insurance (Hessen, Südbaden und westfalen-Lippe), the Hogrefe test system (e.g., Prof. Hänsgen and Karl-Heinz Schlawis), the scientific advisory board (especially Prof. Scheidt and Prof. Caspar), as well as Prof. Fydrich, Dr. Nagel, Prof. Schulte and Prof. Grawe[†] for their support in different forms and phases of the project.

We would like to thank the entire project team of the KVB and the "Verband der Ersatzkassen e.V. Berlin" (vdek), the initiating group of therapists (Emma Auch-Dorsch, Ellen Bruckmayer, Dr. Friedrich von Heymann, Dr. Irmgard Pfaffinger), other supporters (Prof. H. Letzel, Klemens Funk) as well as the scientific advisory board of the QS-PSY-BAY project (Prof. P. Henningsen, Prof. H. Jungnitsch, Prof. Th. Loew), the Institute for Quality Assurance in Psychosomatics (IQP) München, the Cibait-AG Saarbrücken as well as the Otto-Selz-Institute of the University of Mannheim for their cooperation and support. We also would like to thank all therapists and patients for their engagement and trust.

Notes

1. Schizophrenia, schizotypal and delusional disorders, mood (affective) disorders, neurotic, stress-related and somatoform disorders, behavioral syndromes associated with physiological disturbances and physical factors, and disorders of adult personality and behavior.

References

Altmann, U., Steyer, R., Steffanowski, A., Kramer, D., Wittmann, W. W., Bruckmayer, E.,…Strauss, B. (submitted). Verlaufsmuster depressiver Störungen bei ambulanten psychotherapeutischen Behandlungen: Ergebnisse der QS-PSY-BAY-Studie [Process patterns of depressive symptoms during outpatient psychotherapies: Results from the QS-PSY-BAY study]. *Zeitschrift für Psychosomatische Medizin und Psychotherapie.*

Altmann, U., Steffanowski, A., Wittmann, W. W., Kramer, D., Bruckmayer, E., Pfaffinger, I.,… Strauß, B. (in press). Verlängerungen ambulanter Psychotherapien: Eine Studie zu Patienten-, Therapeuten-, Behandlungs- und Verlaufsmerkmalen [Extensions of outpatient psychotherapy: A study about patients, therapists, therapy course, and treatment characteristics]. *Psychotherapie, Psychosomatik, Medizinische Psychologie.*

Averbeck, M., Leiberich, P., Grote-Kusch, M. T., Olbrich, E., Schröder, A., Brieger, M., & Schumacher, K. (1997). *Skalen zur Erfassung der Lebensqualität (SEL)*. Frankfurt: Pearson Assessment.

Bassler, M., Potratz, B., & Krauthauser, H. (1995). Der "Helping Alliance Questionnaire" (HAQ) von Luborsky. *Psychotherapeut, 40,* 1–23.

Beck, A. T., Ward, C. H., Mendelson, M., Mock, J., & Erbaugh, J. (1961). An inventory for measuring depression. *Archives of General Psychiatry, 4,* 561–571.

Bengel, J., & Koch, U. (2000). *Grundlagen der Rehabilitationswissenschaften*. Berlin: Springer.

Castonguay, L. G., Barkham, M., Lutz, W., & McAleavy, A. (2013). Practice-oriented research – approaches and applications. In M. J. Lambert (Ed.), *Bergin and Garfield's handbook of psychotherapy and behavior change* (6th ed., pp. 85–133). New York, NY: John Wiley & Sons.

Cohen, J. (1992). A power primer. *Psychological Bulletin, 112,* 155–159. doi:10.1037/0033-2909.112.1.155

Derogatis, L. R. (1975). *Brief symptom inventory*. Baltimore, MD: Clinical Psychometric Research.

German Federal Government. (2010). *SGB V Öffentliches Gesundheitswesen*. München: Beck.

Endicott, J., Spitzer, R. L., Fleiss, J. L., & Cohen, J. (1976). The global assessment scale. A procedure for measuring overall severity of psychiatric disturbance. *Archives of General Psychiatry, 33,* 766–771.

Grove, W. M., & Meehl, P. E. (1996). Comparative efficiency of informal (subjective, impressionistic) and formal (mechanical, algorithmic) prediction procedures: The clinical-statistical controversy. *Psychology, Public Policy, and Law, 2,* 293–323. doi:10.1037/1076-8971.2.2.293

Hatfield, D., McCullough, L., Frantz, S. H., & Krieger, K. (2010). Do we know when our clients get worse? An investigation of therapists' ability to detect negative client change. *Clinical Psychology & Psychotherapy, 17*, 25–32.

Heuft, G., & Senf, W. (1998). *Praxis der Qualitätssicherung in der Psychotherapie: Das Manual zur Psy-BaDo.* Stuttgart: Thieme.

Hiller, W., Zaudig, M., & Mombour, W. (2004). *IDCL – International Diagnostic Checklists for ICD-10 and DSM-IV.* Bern: Huber.

Horowitz, L., Strauss, B., & Kordy, H. (2000). *Inventar zur Erfassung interpersonaler Probleme (IIP-D). Handanweisung* (2. Aufl.) [Inventory of Interpersonal Problems – German version (IIP-D). Manual (2nd ed.)]. Weinheim: Beltz Test Gesellschaft.

Howard, K. I., Moras, K., Brill, P. L., Martinovich, Z., & Lutz, W. (1996). Evaluation of psychotherapy. Efficacy, effectiveness, and patient progress. *The American Psychologist, 51*, 1059–1064. doi:10.1037/0003-066X.51.10.1059

Jacobson, N. S., & Truax, P. (1991). Clinical significance: A statistical approach to defining meaningful change in psychotherapy research. *Journal of Consulting and Clinical Psychology, 59*, 12–19. doi:10.1037/0022-006X.59.1.12

Lambert, M. (2007). Presidential address: What we have learned from a decade of research aimed at improving psychotherapy outcome in routine care. *Psychotherapy Research, 17*, 1–14. doi:10.1080/10503300601032506

Lambert, M. J. (2001). Psychotherapy outcome and quality improvement: Introduction to the special section on patient-focused research. *Journal of Consulting and Clinical Psychology, 69*, 147–149. doi:10.1037/0022-006X.69.2.147

Lambert, M. J., Whipple, J. L., Smart, D. W., Vermeersch, D. A., & Nielsen, S. L. (2001). The effects of providing therapists with feedback on patient progress during psychotherapy: Are outcomes enhanced? *Psychotherapy Research, 11*, 49–68. doi:10.1080/713663852

Lambert, M. J., Whipple, J. L., Vermeersch, D. A., Smart, D. W., Hawkins, E. J., Nielsen, S. L., & Goates, M. (2002). Enhancing psychotherapy outcomes via providing feedback on client progress: A replication. *Clinical Psychology & Psychotherapy, 9*, 91–103. doi:10.1002/cpp.324

Löwe, B., Spitzer, R. L., Zipfel, S., & Herzog, W. (2002). *PHQ-D Gesundheitsfragebogen für Patienten. Manual Komplettversion und Kurzform. Autorisierte deutsche Version des "Prime MD Patient Health Questionnaire (PHQ)"* (2. Auflage). Heidelberg: Medizinische Universitätsklinik, Abteilung Innere Medizin II.

Luborsky, L., Barber, J., Siqueland, L., Johnson, S., Najavits, L. M., Frank, A., & Daley, D. (1996). The Revised Helping Alliance Questionnaire (HAqII) – Psychometric Properties. *Journal of Psychotherapy Practice & Research, 5*, 260–271.

Lutz, W. (2002). Patient-focused psychotherapy research and individual treatment progress as scientific groundwork for an empirically based clinical practice. *Psychotherapy Research, 12*, 251–272. doi:10.1080/713664389

Lutz, W., Böhnke, J. R., & Köck, K. (2011). Lending an ear to feedback systems: evaluation of recovery and non-response in psychotherapy in a German outpatient setting. *Community Mental Health Journal, 47*, 311–317. doi:10.1007/s10597-010-9307-3

Lutz, W., Böhnke, J. R., Köck, K., & Bittermann, A. (2011). Diagnostik und psychometrische Verlaufsrückmeldungen im Rahmen eines Modellprojektes zur Qualitätssicherung in der ambulanten Psychotherapie. *Zeitschrift für Klinische Psychologie und Psychotherapie, 40*, 283–297. doi:10.1026/1616-3443/a000125

Lutz, W., Leach, C., Barkham, M., Lucock, M., & Stiles, W. B. (2005). Predicting change for individual psychotherapy clients on the basis of their nearest neighbors. *Journal of Consulting and Clinical Psychology, 73*, 904–913. doi:10.1037/0022-006X.73.5.904

Lutz, W., Stulz, N., Martinovich, Z., Leon, S., & Saunders, S. M. (2009). Methodological background of decision rules and feedback tools for outcomes management in psychotherapy. *Psychotherapy Research, 19*, 502–510. doi:10.1080/10503300802688486

Lutz, W., Wittmann, W. W., Böhnke, J. R., Rubel, J., & Steffanowski, A. (2012). Results from the Pilot Project of the Techniker Krankenkasse (TK) "Quality Monitoring in Outpatient Psychotherapy": The evaluators' perspective. *Psychotherapie, Psychosomatik, medizinische Psychologie, 62*(11), 413–417. doi:10.1055/s-0032-1327565

Meehl, P. E. (1954). *Clinical versus statistical prediction: A theoretical analysis and a review of the evidence.* Minneapolis: University of Minnesota Press. Online resource: http://www.tc.umn.edu/~pemeehl/pubCategories.htm#cstix.

Meehl, P. E. (1986). Causes and effects of my disturbing little book. *Journal of Personality Assessment, 50*, 370–375. doi:10.1207/s15327752jpa5003_6

Percevic, R., Gallas, C., Arikan, L., Mößner, M., & Kordy, H. (2006). Internet-gestützte Qualitätssicherung und Ergebnismonitoring in Psychotherapie, Psychiatrie und psychosomatischer Medizin. *Psychotherapeut, 51*, 395–397. doi:10.1007/s00278-006-0504-z

Scheidt, C. E., Brockmann, J., Caspar, F., Rudolf, G., Stangier, U., & Vogel, H. (2012). Das Modellprojekt der Technikerkrankenkasse. Eine Kommentierung der Ergebnisse aus der Sicht des wissenschaftlichen Beirates. *Psychotherapie, Psychosomatik, Medizinische Psychologie, 62*, 405–412. doi:10.1055/s-0032-1321781

Schepank, H. (1995). *Beeinträchtigungs-Schwere-Score (BSS). Ein Instrument zur Bestimmung der Schwere einer psychogenen Erkrankung* [Impairment Intensity Score. An instrument for the determination of the intensity of a psychogenic illness]. Göttingen: Hogrefe.

Schmidt, J., Steffanowski, A., Nübling, R., Lichtenberg, S., & Wittmann, W. W. (2003). *Ergebnisqualität stationärer psychosomatischer Rehabilitation. Vergleich unterschiedlicher Evaluationsstrategien.* Regensburg: Roderer.

Schulgen, G., & Schumacher, M. (2007). Intention-to-treat analyse. In M. Schumacher & G. Schulgen (Eds.), *Methodik klinischer Studien* (pp. 161–169). Berlin: Springer.

Shimokawa, K., Lambert, M., & Smart, D. W. (2010). Enhancing treatment outcome of patients at risk of treatment failure: Meta-analytic and mega-analytic review of a psychotherapy quality assurance system. *Journal of Consulting and Clinical Psychology, 78*, 298–311. doi:10.1037/a0019247

Steffanowski, A., Löschmann, C., Schmidt, J., Wittmann, W. W., & Nübling, R. (2007). *Meta-Analyse der Effekte stationärer psychosomatischer Rehabilitation.* Bern: Huber.

Steffanowski, A., Kramer, D., Fembacher, A., Glahn, E. M., Bruckmayer, E., Heymann, F., von, et al. (2011). Praxisübergreifende Dokumentation der Ergebnisqualität ambulanter Psychotherapie in Bayern. *Zeitschrift für Klinische Psychologie und Psychotherapie, 40*, 267–282. doi:10.1026/1616-3443/a000124

Stiles, W. B., Barkham, M., Mellor-Clark, J., & Connel, J. (2008). Effectiveness of cognitive-behavioural, person-centred, and psychodynamic therapies in UK primary care routine practice: Replication with a larger sample. *Psychological Medicine, 38*, 667–688.

Vogel, H., Brockmann, J., Caspar, F., Rudolf, G., Stangier, U., & Scheidt, C. E. (2013). Versorgungsforschung im Feld ist möglich. *Deutsches Ärzteblatt, 8*, 371–373.

Ware, J., Kosinski, M., & Keller, S. D. (1996). A 12-Item Short-Form Health Survey: Construction of scales and preliminary tests of reliability and validity. *Medical Care, 34,* 220–233.

Whipple, J. L., Lambert, M. J., Vermeersch, D. A., Smart, D. W., Nielsen, S. L., & Hawkins, E. J. (2003). Improving the effects of psychotherapy: The use of early identification of treatment and problem-solving strategies in routine practice. *Journal of Counseling Psychology, 50,* 59–68. doi:10.1037/0022-0167.50.1.59

Wittmann, W. W., & Steffanowski, A. (2011). Qualitätsmonitoring in der ambulanten Psychotherapie: Ergebnisse des TK-Modellprojektes. *Psychotherapie Aktuell, 3,* 6–12.

Wittmann, W. W., Lutz, W., Steffanowski, A., Kriz, D., Glahn, E. M., Völkle, M. C., ... Ruprecht, T. (2011). *Qualitätsmonitoring in der ambulanten Psychotherapie: Modellprojekt der Techniker Krankenkasse – Abschlussbericht* [Quality monitoring in outpatient psychotherapy: Pilot project of the Techniker Krankenkasse – Final report]. Hamburg: Techniker Krankenkasse. Online resource: http://www.tk.de/centaurus/servlet/contentblob/342002/Datei/54714.

Wittmann, W. W., Nübling, R., & Schmidt, J. (2002). Evaluationsforschung und Programmevaluation im Gesundheitswesen. *Zeitschrift für Evaluation, 1,* 39–60.

METHOD PAPER

Practice research network in a psychology training clinic: Building an infrastructure to foster early attachment to the scientific-practitioner model

LOUIS G. CASTONGUAY, AARON L. PINCUS, & ANDREW A. MCALEAVEY

Department of Psychology, Penn State University, University Park, PA, USA

Abstract
Learning how to conduct clinically meaningful and actionable research while simultaneously training to be a competent clinician may be an optimal way to develop an early attachment to the scientific-practitioner model. In this paper, the transformation of a training clinic into a practice research network (PRN) is presented as a strategy to foster a seamless integration of clinical, training, and research facets of graduate training in psychology. With the hope of providing helpful guidance to trainers and trainees interested in building such an infrastructure, the authors describe the context in which they developed their training clinic PRN, its major components, and some of the studies that have been conducted in this network. Benefits earned and lessons learned (in terms of obstacles faced and strategies implemented to deal with them) are described, as well as general recommendations and future directions regarding the implementation and impact of training clinic PRNs.

Becoming a competent clinician and researcher can be quite a challenge, both professionally and personally. It is our sense that in many doctoral programs in clinical psychology (but perhaps less so in other mental health professional training programs, such as PsyD programs and Masters degree programs in counseling psychology or social work), students can come to feel like failures if they decide or are strongly encouraged to "settle for a clinical career." Warnings about this can be expressed directly. For example, having questioned, during his first class of graduate school, the superior epistemological merit of logical positivism (as the only valid method of acquiring knowledge), the first author of this paper was summoned by his esteemed professor who let him know that he was not thinking like a scientist. He further told him that there were two types of psychologists: Those who love ideas and those who don't. Those who do, he said, "go into academia," "while those who don't," he pursued, "go into

clinical practice." And so he was, from the first moment of his doctoral training, put onto notice of a clear and consequential line dividing the field. The same message can also be conveyed less explicitly, while still having a debilitating impact. Many practicing clinicians have painful memories of some members of their Masters or doctoral committees insisting on methodological procedures that may increase the internal validity of their study (and thus making it scientifically worthwhile in the eyes of these academicians), at the expense of the clinical relevance of the idea being pursued. In its extreme form, this could be viewed as an instance of idolatry of method and ignorance of substance.

Even for those who have entered graduate school primarily to become scientists in the field of mental health, doctoral programs do not always provide an optimal environment to learn how to develop into a skilled and knowledgeable *clinical* researcher (we note that the challenges discussed in this article are primarily in the North American context and that trainees in other locales may encounter different obstacles). First, it is not easy to find a research mentor who has extensive experience in clinical work. Working with a researcher who has continued to do assessment and/or psychotherapy after his/her training may well increase the probability of a graduate student conducting studies that reflect the complexity of or improve the impact of day-to-day practice. Furthermore, not all students have access to a structured setting where they can conduct studies with a substantial number of clients and therapists following standardized procedures of care. In addition, graduate students struggle with a paucity of time, which is imposed by the daunting challenge of having to become a scholar, researcher, and clinician, all within a few short years.

One way to address these problematic issues is to transform a clinic associated with a doctoral program into a practice research network (PRN) where students can simultaneously receive expert clinical training, have the opportunity to conduct scientifically valid and clinically relevant research, and work with professionals of different mental health backgrounds—many of them involved in all aspects of their graduate training (teaching, supervising, and mentoring). This type of training infrastructure is designed to foster a seamless and in vivo assimilation of the scientist-practitioner model. Based on the assumption that when students are given the chance to integrate what is learned in class and clinical supervision with what they investigate for their Masters and dissertation, they are more likely to see how research can inform their practice—and, in turn, how clinical practice can be a main source for the generation and implementation of research ideas. In this type of environment, students are less likely to have to choose between being a researcher or a clinician. They can contemporaneously learn to be both, which might be an optimal strategy to become a skilled and knowledgeable *clinical* researcher, as well as a competent evidence-based practitioner.

The goal of this paper is to describe the efforts made to establish and maintain such a clinic/research infrastructure at the psychology clinic associated with the adult clinical program of the department of psychology at Penn State University, referred to from now on as the PSU-training clinic PRN (PSU-TCPRN). We first present the context within which these efforts took place. After describing the major components of our training infrastructure, we provide a few examples of studies that have been conducted so far. We then highlight some of the benefits that we believe students (and others) have derived from accessing this type of infrastructure during their graduate career, as well as several of the challenges

we have faced and lessons we have learned. We end this paper by presenting a few general recommendations for building a training clinic PRN, and by raising issues that might be worth addressing to fully maximize the promise that such an infrastructure can offer for the future of the scientific-practitioner model.

Context

A number of factors stimulated and facilitated the transformation of our clinic, from being purely devoted to training students in the provision of clinical services into an environment where trainees could also conduct research required by their degree and/or inspired by work in their classes. First, our efforts were sparked by the development of the Pennsylvania Psychological Association Practice Research Network (PPA-PRN). Originally conceived by Tom Borkovec (a faculty member in our department) and Stephen Ragusea (a full-time clinician practicing in the local community of our University), the PPA-PRN is aimed at creating an active collaboration between experienced practitioners and researchers into the determination, design, implementation, analyses, and dissemination of clinically meaningful and scientifically rigorous studies. As briefly described in one of the papers of this series (Koerner & Castonguay, in press), the PPA-PRN has so far led to three studies investigating several aspects of the process and outcome of psychotherapy. Over the last several years, the work conducted at the PSU-Training PRN and PPA-PRN has also influenced and benefited from the establishment of a third PRN infrastructure centered at Penn State University: The Center for Collegiate Mental Health (CCMH; also described in this series; see McAleavey, Lockard, Castonguay, Hayes, & Locke, in press). Although taking place in three different settings (training clinic, private practice, and university counseling centers), these infrastructures are all aimed at understanding and improving day-to-day clinical care via the involvement and shared ownership of various stakeholders.

Our efforts have also been facilitated by the deep and diversified commitment of the faculty members to the scientific-practitioner model. This is manifested by the fact that the majority of our tenure-track faculty in the adult clinical program are involved in research on assessment and/or psychotherapy. In addition, all of them have been hired in part because of their interest and skills in clinical supervision (all of the supervision at the PSU Clinic is conducted "in house" by the clinic staff or the tenure-track faculty members, with all of the core training provided by tenure-track faculty). With many of these faculty members having continued their clinical practice since coming to Penn State, our program is composed of a group of scholars who are not only willing (for the growth of their own research program and the quality of their teaching) but also able to train and mentor *clinical* researchers—in all the expertise required by this challenging role. In addition, the faculty members represent, in non-dogmatic ways, a host of theoretical orientations (cognitive-behavioral, psychodynamic, interpersonal, humanistic, and integrative) and have collaborated on several research projects, within and across theoretical lines. In our experience, such an open-mindedness and collaborative attitude provide facilitative conditions for students to work in different labs (to learn different theoretical models, interventions, and methodology, as well as to investigate a variety of constructs and procedures), which in turn can help them to deal with the complexity of psychotherapy, clinically and empirically.[1]

The establishment and growth of the PSU-TCPRN has also been facilitated by several features of our clinical setting. Every year, the Psychology Clinic provides services to approximately 200 clients who, as a whole, experience a wide variety of psychological problems. The services are provided by more than 25 clinicians, most of them graduate students. This allows for relatively large samples of both clients and therapists for prospective and archival studies. While the majority of the students see clients as part of their clinical practica, some of them are offered clinical assistantships that involve larger caseloads. For those who are skilled enough to be selected, these assistantships not only allow them to accumulate more clinical and supervision hours (which can be very beneficial for internship applications), they also cover their stipends and tuitions—not a bad way to ease into the scientific-practitioner model! In addition, graduate students have been hired to help create or improve several aspects of the clinic's functioning that are crucial to its research infrastructure.

The clinic staff is composed of a director, two associate directors (one of them serving specific research functions), and several part- and full-time clinicians of different professional backgrounds (e.g., clinical psychologist, psychiatrist, psychiatric nurse). The same way that tenure track faculty members provide clinical supervision for all of the core practica, most of the clinic staff members (in addition to supervising clinical assistantships) are involved in teaching courses and serve as members of dissertation and Masters committees. With the goal of facilitating the integration of different sources of knowledge about psychopathology, assessment, and psychotherapy, students are trained by and work with some of the same people across their courses, clinical responsibilities, and research endeavors.

Structure

The structure of the PSU-TCPRN is composed of four major components: A core battery, standardized assessment procedures, a framework for the submission and evaluation of research projects, and an agreement with the Office of Research Protections (ORP) regarding the approval of studies by the Institutional Review Board (IRB) of our university.

Core Battery

The central assessment tool used in our clinic is the Treatment Outcome Package (TOP; Kraus, Seligman, & Jordan, 2005), which is processed by outcome referrals (OR). Briefly described in one of the papers of this series (Boswell, Kraus, Lambert, & Miller, in press), the TOP was designed for naturalistic settings and meets all of the recommendations of the Core Battery Conference (Horowitz, Lambert, & Strupp, 1997) convened by the Society for Psychotherapy Research and the American Psychological Association. We chose the TOP not only for its strong psychometric qualities (see Kraus & Castonguay, 2010, for review) but also for its clinical utility. In particular, because it includes 12 subscales measuring common symptoms of DSM psychological disorders (e.g., depression, panic, suicidal ideation, substance abuse, psychosis, and sleep difficulties) as well as important aspects of functioning (e.g., quality of life, social conflict, sexual and work functioning), the TOP allows for a broad measurement of client difficulties. Furthermore, a recent study has provided evidence for the TOP's ability to identify therapists' particular strengths and limitations (see Kraus, Castonguay, Boswell, Nordberg, & Hayes, 2011). Because it is short enough to be administered repeatedly and the results can be available immediately, it is also optimal for monitoring the client's change (in terms of both progress and deterioration). Moreover, the clinicians working with the TOP have access to a list of evidence-based practices related to each of the domains measured; resources that can be helpful for both beginning and experienced clinicians (for a detailed description of the clinical utility of the TOP see Youn, Kraus, & Castonguay, 2012). We also chose the TOP to parallel the research pursued at the PPA-PRN. As described below, the TOP has provided us with the ability to compare the therapeutic effectiveness of our trainees with that of experienced clinicians in the local community.

Also included in our core battery is a slightly modified version of the Anxiety Disorder Interview Schedule, Fourth Edition (ADIS-IV; Brown, Di Nardo, & Barlow, 1994). Based on DSM-IV symptomatology, the ADIS complements the self-report and dimensional nature of the TOP by providing a categorical and observer-rated assessment of psychopathology. This type of assessment, obviously, serves both clinical and empirical purposes: Specific diagnostics are important components of case formulations and treatment plans and can be valuable to select clients for both prospective and archival studies. The choice (and modification) of the ADIS-R was guided by the research experience of several of our tenure track faculty members and their students in various types of Axis I psychopathology.

Finally, our core assessment includes two instruments (one self-report and one interview) measuring interpersonal difficulties: the International Personality Disorders Examination (Loranger, 1995) and the Inventory of Interpersonal Problems—Short Circumplex (IIP-SC; Hopwood, Pincus, DeMoore, & Koonce, 2008; Soldz, Budman, Demby, & Merry, 1995). In addition to allowing our trainees to assess clients' problems beyond Axis I disorders, these instruments were chosen because research on personality disorders and interpersonal problems is conducted in many of our clinical labs (again across orientations). As our faculty members also teach graduate seminars and clinical practica specifically focused on these clinical issues, our training program provides yet another pathway to integrate theory, research, and practice, within the same environment of knowledge and action.

Standardized Assessment Procedures

A strategy that we use in conducting IRB-approved studies in naturalistic settings (at the PSU-TCPRN, but also at the PPA-PRN and CCMH) is to try, as much as possible, to confound research and practice into the same activities. With regard to assessment, this means that the core instruments that we use and the procedures that we follow in collecting some of our primary research data correspond exactly to what we want to assess clinically, as well as how and when we want to measure them for clinical purposes. At a basic level, *the research protocol is the clinical protocol*. This not only increases the external validity of our studies (because we are investigating practice as it is conducted) but it reduces one of the major concerns of the IRB, which is the potential effect of coercion that researchers can have on clients to provide data and/or the conflicts of interest that a trainee may experience between the needs of a client and the need to collect data. If, however, the data are collected as part of the clinical routine and for clinical reasons (as described above), then there are no possible conflicts between research and practice:

They are confounded with each other. *Research becomes not only intrinsically relevant to clinical work, it becomes clinically syntonic* (Castonguay, 2011). As described below, other data than what are gathered as part of clinical routine are also collected at the PSU-TCPRN, and for those protocols the necessary procedures that protect clients are addressed within the context of an arrangement with the IRB.

All of the clients seen at our clinic fill out the TOP and IIP-SC before intake assessment. The TOP is also completed before every session over the Internet on Clinic-owned computers, a technology that permits OR to process the data immediately. This allows therapists to be informed, as they are getting ready to greet the clients in the waiting room, not only of their client's current scores on the subscales of the TOP but also of their scores at the previous administrations. In line with one of the major goals of practice-oriented research (see Castonguay, Barkham, Lutz, and McAleavey, 2013), the data collected by and for the therapists are immediately actionable. Repeated measurement of outcome data can not only lead to investigations of the patterns of change (as described below) but provides information that can be used clinically to address the needs of individual clients.

After the administration of IIP-SC and the first TOP and before the first therapy session, all clients are assessed with the ADIS and IPDE. To increase the efficiency of the assessment procedure, each new case is distributed to a specific trainee assessor, with the mandate of conducting the diagnostic assessment. This assessment is not conducted by the trainee who will eventually be assigned (in part based on the intake assessment) to be the client's therapist, which has the research benefit of improving the independence and standardization of the diagnostic procedure. This procedure was also chosen because it has some clinical benefits, notably to increase the efficiency of diagnostic interviews, as we observed in the past that it was difficult for clients and therapists to stay focused on the task of assessment if they knew that they will be working together in therapy. This procedure was implemented at the start of the PSU-TCPRN, and is made easier by the fact that there are a large number of therapists at this center. Smaller PRNs may not be able to efficiently use such a policy.

Review Committee and Procedures

Students, post-doctoral fellows, or faculty members who want to conduct a study in our clinic are required to write a proposal to be evaluated by the clinic research committee (CRC). To ensure a full representation of all stakeholders in the PSU-TCPRN, as well as to benefit from the expertise and knowledge of full-time practitioners, the CRC is composed of (rotating) representatives of the faculty members, clinical staff members, graduate students, and a private practice clinician.

The proposal submitted to the CRC is different from an IRB application. It is short (maximum of two single-spaced pages) and focuses mainly on the potential utility and the feasibility of the study. Applicants are asked to provide a brief description of their project and answer four questions: *What is the clinical relevance of the investigation? How does the proposal reflect the essential goals/mission of doing research in the Psychology Clinic? What is the extent of invasiveness of the proposal to the business of running the Psychology Clinic? Why is the Psychology Clinic the best place to conduct this study?* Applicants are also asked to specify the sample size sought and the length of time expected to complete data collection. Proposals are accepted or given priority if they (i) address questions directly related to the understanding, assessment, and treatment of psychological problems; (ii) can lead to actionable findings (empirical results that can be used in the provision of clinical services, within and beyond our clinic); (iii) can contribute to the advancement of science regarding psychopathology and psycho-social treatments (by adding to the evidence base and/or practice-oriented research knowledge); (iv) add minimal time-consuming responsibilities to clients, staff, and therapists; and (v) can demonstrate that by being conducted at the clinic the study will foster a seamless and efficient (in terms of time and resources) integration of the training needs and requirements of our students.

Applicants are also informed of other guidelines used to evaluate proposals: (i) collaborative proposals are encouraged; the more labs, students, faculty members involved, the better; (ii) all proposals should include the involvement of at least one clinical graduate student or faculty member; (iii) the level of time involvement for clients is not a consideration; clients can presumably decide, given informed consent, whether they would like to participate in any given study; (iv) quality of the research design or human subjects issues are not directly evaluated; investigators are granted latitude to determine the appropriate research design and the IRB ensures that human subjects issues will be dealt with appropriately; (v) investigators should be judicious about the number of proposals submitted each year; if more proposals are submitted than can be implemented at any given deadline, priority will be given to those faculty and/or their graduate students who have not submitted a proposal in the prior year; (vi) priority is given to projects that are directly related to students' research requirements; (vii) part of the committee's responsibility is to avoid accepting projects that overlap; and (viii) the committee regulates the number of proposals ongoing at any given time to facilitate recruitment and avoid undue burden to clients, therapists, and clinic staff.

To increase the efficiency of our evaluation (especially considering the fact that many proposals are related to time-sensitive requirements such as Masters and dissertations), submissions are accepted the first week of every month. The review of each proposal is assigned a chair (who is a rotating member of the CRC with no conflict of interest with the proposal), who then provides the applicant with a report (typically within 3 weeks) based on the written feedback provided by each committee member.

IRB Agreement

Our pursuit of efficiency also led to us to negotiate a unique arrangement with the IRB at Penn State University. As we were encouraging our students to conduct studies at the clinic, we realized that some aspects of the IRB application for these investigations were more burdensome than for many other studies—not only for those conducted within the psychology department subject pool but also for large randomized clinical trials! Specifically, rather than simply requiring the consent of individuals targeted by a research protocol (e.g., clinic clients), studies that were conducted in the clinic, irrespective of their focus, required the investigators to list all potential assessors and therapists as project personnel (repeatedly for each new study), and obtain written consent from them, as they all could potentially be involved in the recruitment of participants and the generation of data, even if clients were the only targeted participants. Needless to say, such requirement interfered with our efforts to foster clinically actionable investigations in an accessible and naturalistic setting: "Why bother?" many students may have said. "It would be much easier to have undergraduate students filling out a questionnaire for course credits and be done with collecting data for my Masters!"

With the chair of the IRB sympathetic to our training goals, we embarked on a long process of meetings (discussing, over the course of 2 years, a wide range of ethical, legal, and organizational issues) with different IRB representatives (including one of their lawyers!) that paved the way to a legal partnership between the IRB and the CRC regarding the review, monitoring, and approval of studies to be conducted in the clinic. Specified in this partnership agreement are two types of studies, Type I and Type II. Type I studies refer to investigations that do not require significant modification to the *standard operating procedures* for clinical care followed at the Psychological Clinic. These studies involve either the use of already collected data as part of the routine assessment protocol, or the collection of new data based on the addition of new instruments within the same scheduled protocol. Thus, if a student wants to conduct analyses on data that have been archived at the clinic, or if he/she wants some or all upcoming clients to fill out a new measure at pre-treatment, he/she does not need to submit an IRB proposal. He/she only needs to submit a proposal, as described above, to the CRC. If approved, this study becomes immediately and fully covered by the general informed consent that is being given at intake to all new clients. Archival data from the core battery (for specific diagnoses or general outpatient samples) are delivered in de-identified form through a Clinic staff person who serves as an *honest broker* functioning independently of all research projects. If a new measure is approved, for all intents and purposes, it becomes part of our routine core battery and, as such, does not represent a potential conflict between research and clinical needs of clinic stakeholders (clients, trainees, staff members, and supervisors). By allowing us to use an honest broker and granting the CRC the ability to judge whether a research instrument can be part of routine clinical assessments (i.e., if it addresses the need of clients, or if it is clinically syntonic), the IRB has made research in our clinic time- and cost-effective. At most, the CRC (not the student) merely submits a brief modification of the existing agreement, adding the additional instrument to the Clinic's core battery. Once in place, responses are available to the investigator *and* to patients' therapists as part of the clinical record to facilitate treatment planning. For the students pursuing a Type I study, getting IRB approval is about as easy as if they were going to collect data from an undergraduate subject pool.

Like all research with human participants at our university, the informed consent assigned to patients at intake is reviewed on a yearly basis by the IRB. As part of the continuing review process, the IRB is informed of changes in clinical staff, which primarily involves the addition of recently accepted first-year graduate students who are soon to serve clinical functions. When the continuing review is approved (which is contingent on all the new students and staff members having successfully passed required ethical training), the clinic is provided with a renewed IRB informed consent for the next year.

The clinic informed consent, however, is not sufficient for Type II studies. These are studies that involve substantial additions to our routine assessment protocol, for either some or all clients. These include laboratory-based, field, and other studies that recruit outpatients for participation in research protocols outside the Psychological Clinic, psychotherapy process and outcome studies examining patient and therapist variables in ongoing treatments, and studies investigating specific intervention procedures. These studies not only require approval from the CRC, but also need to be approved independently by the IRB (as part of the regular process) before being conducted at the clinic.

Studies

At this point in time, more than 20 proposals have been submitted to the CRC (all but one approved). Reflecting the wide range of interest of students and faculty members in our program (as well as others, such as the counseling program in the school of education), these proposals cover a broad array of issues related to psychopathology, assessment, and treatment. For the sake of the current paper, however, only a few studies on psychotherapy will be briefly described to give the readers a sense of the treatment research conducted in the PSU-TCPRN.

As a reflection of the diversity of evidence that could inform both clinical practice and training (see Beck et al., 2013; Castonguay, 2013; Castonguay, Boswell, Constantino, Goldfried, & Hill, 2010), the psychotherapy studies conducted by our students have investigated (quantitatively and qualitatively) factors related to client and therapist characteristics, process, and outcome. Within the context of his Masters thesis, for instance, Sam Nordberg wanted to examine whether the client's level of symptomatology before treatment could predict differential patterns of change in therapy (Nordberg, Castonguay, Fisher, Boswell, & Kraus, in press). As an example of a Type 1 study, this investigation made use of the TOP scores not only before the first session, but also during the course of treatment via the repeated administration of this instrument. In an effort to shed light on conflicting findings of previous research on pre-treatment symptomatology, this study also explored whether some characteristics of clients assessed in our core battery moderated the relationship between symptom severity and therapeutic responses. As predicted, the results showed that diverse groups of clients can be differentiated in terms of their patterns of change. Also consistent with previous studies conducted in different naturalistic settings and with different instruments (e.g., Stulz, Lutz, Leach, Lucock, & Barkham, 2007), the findings demonstrated that clients with a high level of symptoms before therapy divided into two groups once in treatment: Some rapidly improved, while others maintained a high level of symptomatology. In addition to replicating previous findings, this study extended the results by revealing that diverse features of functional impairment (e.g., social conflict and suicidality) predicted the different treatment responses in clients with more severe symptoms before therapy. Such findings are not only relevant to therapists of different orientations but they also create a meaningful connection between science and practice. Both researchers and clinicians share the need to better predict (with more confidence and precision) which clients might and might not benefit from therapy, for instance in order to develop and use targeted clinical procedures that might improve the prognosis.

Studies related to two other Masters theses assessed the link between pre-treatment and process variables, as well as the relationship between process and session impact. As examples of Type 2 studies, they employed additional measures, before and during treatment. The focus of one of these two projects, completed by James Boswell, was on differences between interventions that are theoretically specific and those that cut across different orientations. In addition to providing information about their training experience and theoretical orientation, trainees agreed to fill out a 60-item questionnaire measuring therapeutic techniques (the Multitheoretical List of Therapeutic Intervention, MULTI; McCarthy & Baber, 2009) at the end of every session. Also at the end of every session, clients filled out the Session Progress Scale (SPS; Kolden, 1991), which is a four-item measure derived from the Therapy Session Report (Orlinsky & Howard, 1966) aimed at measuring the helpfulness of the session. Although neither training variables (e.g., trainees' years of in the program and their current theoretically driven practicum/supervision) nor the therapist's theoretical orientation predicted the use of techniques, Boswell and his colleagues found that "some techniques did relate to session outcome but in a complex way that involved multiple levels of analyses (therapist, patient, session) and both unique and common factors" (Boswell, Castonguay, & Wasserman, 2010, p. 720). The findings indicated, for instance, that when clients who typically received high levels of common factors techniques had sessions in which their therapist used a lot of CBT interventions, they perceived these particular sessions to be less helpful than others. The results also indicated that such potential interference with client progress was particularly stronger when CBT interventions were used by therapists who typically prefer to use relationship-enhancing (or common) interventions. These contextual and dynamic analyses serve to caution us that a haphazard combination of techniques may actually hinder the process of change. They also suggest that although CBT interventions are powerful, their implementation is not as simple as some have been led to believe ("I read the manual" or "I attended a 2-day workshop" is frequently heard to justify one's use of CBT, but this may not be sufficient to practice it competently). Needless to say, empirical evidence informing when and how to use empirically supported interventions (unique and common) is relevant for training, especially when such evidence has emerged from a training environment.

Building on work of Boswell, the data that Andrew McAleavey collected within the context of his Masters thesis have also included the MULTI (filled out by therapists after every session), trainees' current practicum/supervision and theoretical orientation, as well as impact questionnaires filled out by clients, again at the end of every session (the SPS and the Session Impacts Scale; Elliott & Wexler, 1994). So far, this research project has led to two published studies. Like Boswell's investigation, the first study (McAleavey, Castonguay, & Xiao, in press) examined the link between techniques and session quality, and also examined whether the use of particular types of technique is associated with a higher level of helpfulness if they are consistent with the students' theoretical orientation and/or if they are consistent with the trainee's current supervision. Exploring the interaction of these factors was driven by the goal of examining the effect of techniques as they are actually used (or should be used) in practice and training: We not only know that therapists do not restrict themselves to interventions associated with their preferred theoretical orientation (Thoma & Cecero, 2009), we also know that many trainees eventually receive supervision in approaches that are different than the theoretical models with which they currently identify. Interestingly, and perhaps providing support to one of the implications of Boswell et al.'s (2010) findings mentioned above, the results show that sessions high in cognitive therapy techniques were only associated with a high level of helpfulness when the theoretical orientation of both the therapist and the supervisor was cognitive.

McAleavey's multi-faceted data were also collected with the aim of better understanding how to facilitate a particular type of impact in psychotherapy: Insight, or the acquisition of a new perspective of self and others. Like many PRN projects, the study of insight represents an optimal point of juncture on the scientific-practitioner map of action and knowledge: Although clinicians of different theoretical approaches have recognized insight as a desirable effect (see Goldfried, 1980), researchers have deplored the paucity of research on insight (see

Castonguay & Hill, 2007). Surprisingly, and perhaps reflecting a lack of flexibility that has been suggested in other studies (e.g., Piper et al., 1999; Schut et al., 2005), the trainee's use of insight-oriented techniques was negatively related to insight (McAleavey & Castonguay, 2013). In contrast, the use of directive or behavioral change oriented interventions was associated with high levels of insight. Interestingly, however, the interaction effect of diverse techniques revealed a more complex picture, as the directive techniques happened to be predictive of insight only when they were used in sessions with high levels of common or relationship-enhancing interventions. By providing both surprising and complex findings, this type of study can increase our understanding of the process of change and, in turn, may expand and refine the repertoire of interventions (*what techniques, under what circumstances, and within what context*) that might be used in effective practice and could thus be emphasized in clinical training.

While McAleavey and Castonguay's study suggests that the use of CBT interventions can help achieve a therapeutic goal that is central to psychodynamic therapy (i.e., insight), Dana Nelson's dissertation has provided promising evidence that an intervention at the core of CBT may improve the efficacy of psychodynamic treatment. In another Type II study conducted in the PSU-TCPRN, Nelson explored whether therapists could be trained to systematically and seamlessly (without disruption of treatment process) integrate homework in psychodynamic treatment, and whether such an assimilation of a theoretically "foreign" technique might improve the already established impact of this form of therapy for depression (see Follette & Greenberg, 2005). Specifically, she trained three graduate students in the implementation of a well-known psychodynamic-interpersonal treatment manual developed and tested by a group of researchers based in Sheffield (Shapiro et al., 1994; Barkham, et al., 1996), as well as in another treatment manual (which she developed herself) guiding therapists in the assignment and monitoring of homework—that is, between-session activities that are consistent with the goals of psychodynamic therapy and the issues addressed in the treatment of a particular client. Although preliminary, the investigation of three cases (selected to meet the inclusion and exclusion criteria of the Sheffield studies) has provided support for the feasibility and efficacy of this integrative treatment (Nelson & Castonguay, 2012). Quantitative results indicated that homework was assigned and implemented almost every week, that homework was perceived as relevant and helpful, that homework did not interfere with the alliance, and that the integrative treatment based on the addition of homework led to larger effect sizes (in terms of depressive symptoms and interpersonal problems) than those obtained in the psychodynamic treatment tested in Sheffield-related studies. In addition, qualitative analyses of the written description of the homework revealed that they were addressing themes emphasized in the psychodynamic model of change (e.g., increased awareness of interpersonal dynamics, wishes, and fears; negative consequences of defense; engagement in new, more adaptive ways of relating to others).

Like the previously mentioned studies, this process-outcome investigation demonstrates how PRN projects can advance knowledge while serving both clinical and empirical purposes. Clinically, it suggests that clinicians might improve their interventions without drastic change in their practice, i.e., they can increase their repertoire of interventions without having to abandon their preferred theoretical orientation. Although this particular study pertains to assimilation of CBT techniques into a psychodynamic treatment, other types of interventions can be integrated in other forms of therapy (see Castonguay, 2013). Research-wise, this illustrates that in their quest to improve the efficacy of psychotherapy, clinical scientists do not have to create entirely new forms of therapy, especially when addressing disorders for which we already have a number of empirically supported treatments. As argued elsewhere (Castonguay, 2013), a particularly fruitful way to further improve mental health care is to enhance the efficacy and effectiveness of theoretically driven ESTs by incorporating the contributions of divergent conceptual approaches, process findings, and/or basic research.

Benefits

The transformation of our clinic into a PRN has led to several benefits, some of them already mentioned in or easily derived from the pages above. First, the PSU-TCPRN gives students access to a structured environment as well as a standardized assessment battery and procedures, which allows them to conduct externally valid studies with a relatively large number of clients and therapists. In addition to being guided by their own respective interests, these studies are frequently related to what they learn in class, in supervision, or in their research lab; in part because these learning experiences (and the research projects they conduct at the clinic) mainly take place within the context of the same group of individuals (faculty members, clinical staff and, of course, other trainees). Moreover, because these studies can be conducted to meet their academic requirements, at the same place (and often at the same time) in which they fulfill their clinical training requirements, the PSU-TCPRN can help students to achieve their training goals in an efficient manner. Considering the advantages provided by the IRB agreement regarding Type I studies, our infrastructure can also protect students' most rare commodity—time. A number of other benefits that have emerged from our efforts are briefly described below.

This Is Ours Too

Very much in line with the goals of practice-oriented research, and especially PRN studies (see Castonguay et al., 2013), many students have developed a strong sense of ownership with regard to the daily functioning and growth of our research/clinic infrastructure. This is illustrated by the fact that many innovations that have taken place over the last few years have been generated and orchestrated via an active collaboration between students and members of the clinical staff (such as the administration of the TOP before every session and the digitalization of video recording of sessions). This sense of ownership helps attenuate a predominant feeling that many students have in graduate school: That most of everything they have to do during 5 to 7 years is imposed by and for the needs of faculty members!

"All for One, and One for All"

There is no doubt in our minds that the high level of therapist participation that we have observed in the studies conducted at the clinic is in part due to camaraderie—a collaborative attitude that could be expressed by many statements, including: "Graduate school is hell, but we are in together and we should do what we can to help friends get their degree" (a much more eloquent and well-known statement would be "Un pour tous, tous pour un"!). Naturally, the commitment of others to one's project tends to encourage reciprocity, which is both reflected in and increases the shared sense of community.

Making Things Count Double

Freud, Rogers, Skinner, Minuchin, and most therapists influenced by them, would agree that behaviors are multi-determined. Not surprisingly, therefore, the probability of students getting involved in clinic studies will increase if they can get many things out of it. For example, in addition to helping out a peer, the students who participated in Dana Nelson's study described above received expert training in psychodynamic therapy and CBT interventions. This not only increased their repertoire of evidence-based practice, but added to their clinical experience (in terms of hours and specific training), which helped with their upcoming internship applications. Interestingly, students have reported that internship sites where they interviewed are frequently impressed by our efforts to integrate science and practice, which can be welcome news in the midst of a very stressful and competitive application process.

Benefits to Faculty and Supervisors

Even with the co-leadership and sustained engagement of many students, the creation, maintenance, and further refinement of a clinic-training PRN require a lot of work for faculty members. "Why bother?" one might say, "I have enough service work already (for the department, college, university, professional organizations, and local community) to add another thing on my plate." Fortunately, our faculty members are gaining benefits from their contributions. In addition to fostering the careers of their students, several of them have submitted studies, including some with the main purpose of collecting pilot data aimed toward grant submissions. In addition, when conducting supervision, faculty members have access to the repeated measurement of symptoms, which allow them to integrate in their clinical teaching an established component of evidence-based practice: Outcome monitoring (Lambert, 2010).

Maintaining a Two-Way Connection with the Community

Having a full-time private clinician serving on the CRC has provided both the applicants and the members of this committee with a unique perspective on the feasibility and relevance of the studies proposed. The community-based colleagues who have volunteered their time and energy to reviewing proposals have knowledge and experience that are in many ways distinct but yet complementary to the researchers and clinicians that work within the walls of a University. As argued elsewhere (Boswell & Castonguay, 2007), such expertise can be tremendously helpful in training competent clinical researchers. At the same time, our colleagues from the other side of the same walls have gained new knowledge (in terms of topics and methods of investigations) from their exposure to new and cutting-edge research. They have also derived personal gratification and validation from their participation in the advancement of science and practice. It may well be that the optimal growth of our field, like society in general, will take a "village"—or at least an active connection between the Ivory Tower and the trenches.

Lessons Learned

All the stakeholders of our community have benefited from the PSU-TCPRN infrastructure, yet we have faced several challenges in our effort to build, maintain, and foster its growth. Next we discuss some of the lessons we have learned from the challenges we encountered along the way and some of the strategies we have used to deal with them.

You Can Never Communicate Too Much

The implementation and continued operation of major aspects of our infrastructure have required multiple and various types of meetings beyond those we initially had with the IRB and university lawyers (e.g., with all the students, faculty members, and clinic directors; between members of the CRC and student representatives; or between representatives of the CRC and every clinical practicum). Communications via these meetings and emails have involved the provision of procedural guidelines and manuals, as well as feedback from students about them. To help facilitate this communication process, we have found it helpful to identify specific times and places in our curriculum (e.g., pre-practicum course, first clinical practicum, annual meeting to discuss the TOP and its uses) to introduce the purpose and rules associated with our PRN infrastructure. We have also attempted to maintain a constant line of open dialogue, by encouraging trainees to contact (directly or via student representatives) members of the CRC about minor or major issues related to the implementation of any aspects of the infrastructure.

Miscommunications Will Happen

We have learned the hard way that providing corrective feedback (about the lapses or mistakes in adherence to assessment procedures, for example) can lead to resentment when it is perceived as blaming. Not informing students of research to be conducted in the clinic (whether or not it will require work on their part) can also create a feeling of being taken for granted by faculty members (even when the studies are related to students' Masters or dissertations). "It's the alliance, stupid," one could easily conclude from these experiences. A less harsh or self-blaming recommendation that could be derived from our experience is that one should be vigilant toward preserving the bond with trainees and be prepared to repair relationship ruptures when they emerge.

Collaboration Is a Juggling Task

Many decisions need to be made regarding the standardization of clinical and research issues, and it is often easier to work with a small group of individuals when addressing them. However, we have found that restricting input about implementation, modification, and operation of infrastructure to a few student representatives can at times lead to frustration and feelings of exclusion. Needless to say, acting within a small circle can also limit the ideas that could be generated to solve problems or improve things. Figuring how many students (let alone clinical staff and faculty members) should be involved in the decision making process for particular issues, small or large, is a difficult juggling task. It is, however, something that all training clinic PRN structures are likely to face as they attempt to balance being efficient with enhancing the sense of engagement from the students.

Motivation Can Be Improved by Addressing Fears and Wishes

We have yet to meet a graduate student in our doctoral program who claimed (at least to our faces) not to be interested in getting data from their clients that can serve both clinical and research purposes. In fact, we would like to believe that the goals and structure of our PRN training infrastructure are selling points in the very competitive graduate student recruitment process that we are facing every year. Yet, we have at times been confronted with what we view as motivation problems in adhering to, or fully engaging in, different facets of the Clinic's dual mission. One of the sources of this motivational issue is fear. This was clearly expressed by a student in a group meeting who said something to the effect of: "I am just beginning to see clients and I am convinced that I have nothing to offer them, so I feel very uncomfortable when I ask them to fill out the TOP or when I tell them they would be eligible to participate in a study that is being conducted at the clinic."

Whether or not it is expressed in such a direct and explicit way, we believe that such fears, based on a very common impostor syndrome, need to be addressed. In our experience, we observed that research-based information can be helpful to normalize trainee apprehension, such as the fact that greater experience is not associated with better outcome. We have also observed that data can be more persuasive when they have been collected by novice clinicians just like them. Because the TOP is used in both our clinic and the PPA-PRN, we were able to compare the score of clients seen by our trainees and experienced clinicians (Angtuaco, Castonguay, & Kraus, 2005). Although the data indicated that experienced therapists were particularly effective in improving patients' psychosocial functioning (such as sexual functioning), our trainees demonstrated notable success in decreasing patients' suicidal ideation, violence, and mania. Perhaps reflecting a corrective experience, our trainees were pleasantly surprised to see data suggesting that full-time psychologists could learn from them about how to work with clients in crises.

We also suspected that the motivational difficulties we observed were in part due to a feeling of being burdened by the tasks involved at the clinic (such as the structured interviews included in our assessment, let alone diagnostic reliability checks derived from these interviews that we have conducted at times). We came to see the source of this problem as being our responsibility. Specifically, we realized that we failed to remind students of their wishes. Although the cohort of graduate students who were part of the program when we developed the PSU-TCPRN were fully cognizant of why we (students and faculty) developed our standardized clinical routine, the next generations were not as aware of the goals underlying the established routines, let alone of the dream of providing them opportunities for making their research clinically meaningful and scientifically rigorous. To increase their sense of ownership and, hopefully, to remind them of why they decided to come to Penn State, we have now scheduled a yearly meeting where members of the CRC and advanced grad students describe in detail the origin and purpose of our shared dream to the first-year students. This description is driven by one message: It is not for us (faculty members), and not imposed by us. It is mostly for you and it has been driven in part by previous and current students.

Too Much of a Good Thing Is to Be Expected

While lapses of motivation are to be expected, so are binges of research proposals. To avoid burdening therapists and/or overwhelming clients with too many projects going at the same time, the CRC has had to make decisions about how handle the large number of projects that could be run simultaneously. A strategy that we have adopted is to set a time limit or request a hiatus in data collection. For example, if a new project is submitted from members of a particular lab that already recruits participants for other projects, the CRC has asked the faculty member overseeing this lab to delay, cease or interrupt the data collection for one of these studies.

Anticipate Ripple Effects

To maximize the operation of the PSU-TCPRN infrastructure, as well as to foster the integration of different facets of our training program, we decided to reorganize our curriculum and some functioning rules of our clinic. For example, we modified the content of introductory practicum (a year-long supervision course required for the first-year students). Whereas in the fall semester students are introduced to the DSM, the ADIS, and the IPDE, the same students primarily conduct intake interviews in the Spring semester, with few if any therapy cases assigned to this practicum. This training reorganization provides the students with an intensive and extensive learning experience in diagnostic interviewing, while also serving two empirical goals: Increasing or maintaining inter-rater agreement on diagnoses, and avoiding potential contamination when measurements of such agreement are conducted. To reduce redundancy in our teaching, we also moved our required course on psychopathology from the Spring to the Fall semester, decreased its emphasis to phenomenology (DSM criteria—now covered in the first year practicum), and increased its focus on etiology.

It's a Marathon, not a Sprint

This metaphor, which Marv Goldfried astutely uses to describe the pace of progress in academia, neatly reflects our experience in building and maintaining our PRN training infrastructure. Faculty members, clinic staff, and students interested in creating a similar project have to be ready for the long haul. Counting the time it required to put together the different pieces of our infrastructure, it took more than 4 years for the first studies to be approved and launched. In addition, we have found that our procedures can always be improved. For example, after implementing a systematic and extensive process to assess the inter-rater agreement on the client pre-treatment diagnostics, we were dismayed to observe low reliability estimates for many of the DSM diagnostic categories recorded. This, obviously, had serious clinical and empirical implications. To remedy the situation, we changed the instrument we used to assess Axis I disorders (replacing the Structured Clinical Interview for Axis I DSM-IV disorders [SCID; First, Spitzer, Gibbon, &Williams, 1994] with the ADIS), adopted a reliable measure to assess Axis II pathology (the IPDE), and agreed on an intense and comprehensive training on these new assessment tools. Specifically, all but one faculty member in our program (including all not-yet tenured faculty) and our students met for 3 hours per week for most of one summer reviewing diagnostic criteria, watching tapes, conducting role plays, and comparing clinical judgments. Training continued for several months during the following academic year, followed by another wave of assessment of inter-rater agreement that revealed a substantial improvement for most diagnostic categories.

Other examples of improvements include the adoption of new laptop computers to ease the administration of the TOP, as well as the increased frequency of outcome monitoring to every session. It is noteworthy that both of these improvements were generated and orchestrated in close collaboration between students and members of the clinic staff. The fact that these changes, when combined, led to additional and self-imposed tasks in the assessment procedure is a reflection of the motivational forces generated by initiatives that recognize and foster a sense of ownership and expertise, and that facilitate the synergetic actualization of meaningful goals.

Conclusion

To complement some of the specific lessons that we have learned, we would like to conclude this paper by offering general recommendations and presenting what we believe are important issues that could be addressed in the future to facilitate the implementation and growth of training clinic PRNs.

General Recommendations

Some of our recommendations are in sync with those previously made for practice-oriented research in general, PRN or otherwise (Castonguay et al., 2013). In fact, the creation of a PRN in a training clinic could be viewed as an optimal strategy to address what may be the most important advice to foster and cement research by and with clinicians: Begin early. As noted elsewhere, "simultaneous, seamless, and repeated integration of science and practice activities as early as possible in a psychotherapist's career might create an intellectual and emotional (hopefully secure) attachment to principles and merits of the Boulder model" (Castonguay, 2011, p. 135). In addition, we believe that students are more likely engage in research (above and beyond the projects required for their graduation) if their studies have an impact at home and abroad. Faculty members and clinical staff should do all they can to encourage students to present their results in their respective departments and at professional meetings. Presentations and publications of clinically relevant studies, even for students not interested in academic careers, might be crucial for

the field. At one level, professional recognition might incentivize students to continue doing research in their clinical practice. At another level, practice-oriented research needs to visible if it is to count as part of a robust empirical knowledge base and to guide our practice of psychotherapy. Evidence-based practice, in other words, should not be based solely on studies conducted in controlled environments (such as RCTs) but on a wide range of empirical investigations offering various advantages in terms of internal and external validity. Because many of them will be part of the next generation of leading researchers, trainees conducting research in a naturalistic environment have the opportunity to set a research agenda that reflects the needs and expertise of practitioners (Zarin, Pincus, West, & McIntyre, 1997).

Also reflecting a recommendation for practice-oriented research in general, we believe that students, clinically and/or academically oriented, will conduct more research in training clinic PRNs if they and their advisor design studies that confound practice and research. Described as clinically syntonic (Castonguay, 2011), this type of research involves the collection of data that simultaneously serve clinical and research functions. When students were being trained in and conducted the treatment protocol designed by Dana Nelson, for example, they were not doing clinical work or research—they were doing both at the same time. When contextualized at a more general level (with respect to development of our field rather than the growth of individual students) this type of research can move the scientific-practitioner paradigm beyond the building of bridges. Specifically, "rather than trying to connect science and practice, as if they stand on different river banks, we should strive to confound the two activities to create a new, unified landscape of knowledge and action." (Castonguay et al., 2013, p. 122)

In addition to the recommendations above, our experience leads us to make two suggestions that are specific to training clinic PRNs. First, those interested in building such an infrastructure should convey to administrators (at the clinic and departmental level) the necessity of financial and organizational support. It is easy to see the merit of the mission of combining science and practice, but investment of funds and resources are necessary. It is clear in our mind that many crucial tasks for the daily functioning and growth of our PRN (such as completing reports for continuing reviews of the IRB agreement, monitoring of ethics training required by the IRB, de-identifying of clinical information by an "honest broker" for confidentiality purposes, and orchestrating technological improvements) would have imposed unreasonable burdens on both faculty and students if they had not been part of the responsibilities assigned to the assistant director of research, full- and part-time graduate assistantships, and administrative staff. In addition, the allocation of some of the profits earned by the clinic has been required for the purchase of clinic/research equipment (e.g., laptop computers). If a clinic is not large and/or profitable enough to be a (or the unique) source of such funding, faculty members, clinic staff, and students should jointly approach their department chair and/or dean to have them invest (as yet another stakeholder) in the training potential of a fully actualized scientific-practitioner model.

Our experience has also led us to conclude that it is best to share the leadership roles in building and maintaining a training clinic PRN. Our teamwork has allowed us to distribute the primary responsibilities for major building blocks of our project, as well as to collaboratively address challenges that we have faced along the way. We would thus suggest that if one individual, such as a faculty member, intends to take the lead in organizing a clinic PRN, she/he should request and obtain adequate support; this should be recognized as a major service commitment, and should be pursued within appropriate conditions (including course reductions), especially if undertaken by a faculty member who is not yet tenured.

Future Directions

Although the studies presented above (and several others not reviewed here) demonstrate that we have, in our own infrastructure, begun to harvest tangible results from our effort, we would like to point out three issues that we believe should be addressed in the future to foster the promise of training clinic PRNs. First, in order to conduct the best possible studies (in terms of providing adequate statistical power to test hypotheses and increasing generalizability of the results), large numbers of clients and therapists are needed. As noted elsewhere, however, studies conducted within one specific PRN will almost inevitably face limitations in terms of the sample of clients and therapists available (Castonguay, 2011). In line with Borkovec's (2002) dream of a large infrastructure of training clinics contributing to a common pool of data, what we need are networks of training clinic PRNs that share a basic core battery and assessment procedures. Each clinic, of course, could add to this foundational structure (in terms of measures and/or frequency of administration) in order to meet their specific treatment, training, and research needs. However, such networks of networks would allow students to mine major archival data and conduct large prospective studies across multiple sites. Put in different words, we should "work locally but collaborate globally" (Castonguay et al., 2013). Fortunately, a number of such connective networks have begun to emerged, spearheaded for example by university training clinics in Canada (e.g., McGill University, York University, Windsor University), across the USA (Penn State, Stony Brook, University of Massachusetts, Amherst), and others associated with the Association of Psychology Training Clinics Collaborative Research Network (e.g., Eastern Michigan University, Western Michigan, University of North Carolina).

As mentioned above, students (irrespective of their ultimate career plans) are more likely to conduct research above and beyond what is required for their degree if emphasis is given toward making their findings count. At a global level, practice-oriented (including PRN) investigations are likely to flourish "if there is clear evidence that the merit and impact of these studies will be fairly considered and duly recognized by scholars, researchers, and policy makers" (Castonguay et al., 2013, p. 122). At a local level, however, we believe that the best way to make training clinic PRNs count is to find ways to use them "in house": That is, in the actual training of current and future generations of students in the PRN clinic (or networks of PRN clinics) where those findings were obtained. Creative and effective strategies should be developed, above and beyond encouraging students to present their work in departmental meetings, to make the findings actionable—not only to possibly improve the process and outcome of therapy in the here and now, but also to foster a positive feedback loop between getting scientifically rigorous data from the clinic and feeding back clinically relevant information to trainees. For instance, if we take some of the studies conducted in our own infrastructure, how do we help supervisors and therapists in psychodynamic practica to systematically and skillfully use homework? How do we teach therapists who do not frequently use CBT interventions to be mindful of their potential negative impact, as well as to learn when and how to effectively implement them, especially when working with clients who typically receive (and benefit from) relational techniques? What should we do to encourage therapists and supervisors of various orientations to carefully observe how exploratory and directive interventions are used, so that they can best foster insight? What actions do we take based on reliable and pertinent data (specific to our core battery and clinical setting) showing that some particular clients with severe symptoms at pre-treatment are likely to benefit from therapy, while others are not? Although we have in our program ample theoretical and empirical expertise to guide trainees in dealing with phenomena revealed by these findings, it is still unclear how to best communicate and learn from each other about this knowledge. Should we have annual "research practice days" to share findings and discuss implications? Should we have newsletters and/or a renewable web repository of research results? Should we systematically integrate these findings in our specific courses and practica?

Another issue that might be worth addressing in the future is how we can keep research programs generated in PRN training clinics alive and expanding. Most students leave the university where they graduate and many do not end up having the time and resources to conduct follow-up studies to all the investigations they conducted in graduate school. As a field, we should be concerned about creative and valid lines of research that go extinct just because they were started at an early phase in the career of the individuals who conducted them. This is perhaps a complement to the file drawer effect (referring to studies that have not been submitted or published because of null results), which one might call the "dusty piles in the lab" effect. Again using some of the previously described studies as cases in point, who might be able to conduct qualitative studies to shed light on the negative relationship between CBT interventions and session impact found by James Boswell? What circumstances would permit the implementation of an RCT based on Dana Nelson's outcome findings, potentially allowing her integrative treatment to become a promising new EST? Of course, this extinction problem is not specific to studies conducted in graduate programs that have transformed their training clinic into a PRN. However, as much as PRN infrastructures are currently viewed as a promising strategy to solidify the scientific-practitioner model in mental health, and because such PRN initiatives are only beginning to be adopted in training settings, this might be a perfect time to think about ways to build upon the scientifically rigorous and clinically relevant studies conducted by trainees. Perhaps open and continued exchange of information and long-term collaborations within large networks of clinic PRNs, during and after graduate school (representing yet another type of alumni), may provide optimal conditions for new landscapes of knowledge and action to be created and implemented by clinical researchers throughout their careers.

Note

[1] It should be mentioned that the faculty commitment to all aspects of the scientific practitioner model comes at a high price for our graduate students. Not only are they expected to become accomplished researchers, knowledgeable scholars, and skilled teachers, they also have to demonstrate high levels of clinical competence. Students who do not excel in research are not encouraged or allowed to "settle for a clinical career," and students who do not demonstrate the clinical ability of a skilled independent practitioner do not graduate from our program. They are all required to become good *clinical* researchers.

References

Angtuaco, L. A., Castonguay, L. G., & Kraus, D. R. (2005). *The TOP: A core battery for the assessment of psychotherapy outcome.* Paper presented at the Annual Meeting of the Society for Psychotherapy Research. Montreal (June).

Barkham, M., Rees, A., Shapiro, D. A., Stiles, W. B., Agnew, R. M., Halstead, J., Culverwell, A., & Harrington, V. M. (1996). Outcomes of time-limited psychotherapy in applied settings: Replicating the Second Sheffield Psychotherapy Project. *Journal of Consulting and Clinical Psychology, 64*, 1079–1085. doi:10.1037/0022-006X.64.5.1079

Beck, J. G., Castonguay, L. G., Chronis-Tuscano, A., Klonsky, E. D., McGinn, L. K., & Youngstrom, E. A. (2013). *Principles for training in evidence based psychology: Recommendations for the graduate curricula in clinical psychology.* Manuscript submitted for publication.

Borkovec, T. D. (2002). Training clinic research and the possibility of a national training clinics practice research network. *Behavior Therapist, 25*, 98–103.

Boswell, J. F., & Castonguay, L. G. (2007). Psychotherapy training: Suggestions for core ingredients and future research. *Psychotherapy: Theory, Research, Practice, and Training, 44*, 378–383. doi:10.1037/0033-3204.44.4.378

Boswell, J. F., Castonguay, L. G., & Wasserman, R. H. (2010). Effects of psychotherapy training and intervention use on session outcome. *Journal of Consulting and Clinical Psychology, 78*, 717–723. doi:10.1037/a0020088

Boswell, J. F., Kraus, D. R., Lambert, M. J., & Miller, S. D. (in press). Implementing routine outcome monitoring in clinical practice: Benefits, challenges, and solutions. *Psychotherapy Research, 24*.

Brown, T. A., Di Nardo, P. A., & Barlow, D. H. (1994). *Anxiety Disorders Interview Schedule for DSM-IV (ADIS-IV).* San Antonio, TX: Psychological Corporation/Graywind Publications.

Castonguay, L. G. (2011). Psychotherapy, psychopathology, research and practice: Pathways of connections and integration. *Psychotherapy Research, 21*, 125–140. doi:10.1080/10503307.2011.563250

Castonguay, L. G. (2013). Psychotherapy outcome: A problem worth re-revisiting 50 years later. *Psychotherapy: Theory, Research, Practice, and Training, 50*, 52–67 doi:10.1037/a0030898

Castonguay, L. G., Barkham, M., Lutz, W., & McAleavey, A. A. (2013). Practice-oriented research: Approaches and application. In M. J. Lambert (Ed.), *Bergin and Garfield's handbook of psychotherapy and behavior change* (6th ed., pp. 85–133). New York: Wiley.

Castonguay, L. G., Boswell, J. F., Constantino, M. J., Goldfried, M. R., & Hill, C. E. (2010). Training implications of harmful effects of psychological treatments. *American Psychologist, 65*, 34–49. doi:10.1037/a0017330

Castonguay, L. G., & Hill, C. E. (Eds.). (2007). *Insight in Psychotherapy.* Washington, DC: American Psychological Association.

Elliott, R., & Wexler, M. M. (1994). Measuring the impact of sessions in process-experiential therapy of depression: The Session Impacts Scale. *Journal of Counseling Psychology, 41*, 166–174. doi:10.1037/0022-0167.41.2.166

Follette, W. C., & Greenberg, L. S. (2005). Techinque factors in treating dysphoric disorders. In L. G. Castonguay & L. E. Beutler (Eds.), *Principles of therapeutic change that work* (pp. 83–109). New York: Oxford University Press.

First, M. D., Spitzer, R. L., Gibbon, M., & Williams, J. B. W. (1994). *Structured Clinical Interview for Axis I DSM-IV disorders: Patient Edition (SCID-I/P, Version 2.0)*. New York: Biometrics Research Department, New York State Psychiatric Institute.

Goldfried, M. R. (1980). Toward the delineation of therapeutic change principles. *American Psychologist, 35*, 991–999. doi:10.1037/0003-066X.35.11.991

Hopwood, C. J., Pincus, A. L., DeMoor, R. M., & Koonce, E. A. (2008). Psychometric characteristics of the Inventory of Interpersonal Problems—Short Circumplex (IIP-SC) with college students. *Journal of Personality Assessment, 90*, 615–618. doi:10.1080/00223890802388665

Horowitz, L. M., Lambert, M. J., & Strupp, H. H. (Eds.). (1997). *Measuring patient change in mood, anxiety, and personality disorders: Toward a core battery*. Washington, DC: American Psychological Association.

Koerner, K., & Castonguay, L. G. (in press). Conducting research in private practice. *Psychotherapy Research, 24.*

Kolden, G. G. (1991). The generic model of psychotherapy: An empirical investigation of patterns of process and outcome relationships. *Psychotherapy Research, 1*, 62–73. doi:10.1080/10503309112331334071

Kraus, D., & Castonguay, L. G., (2010). Treatment Outcome Package (TOP): Development and use in naturalistic settings. In M. Barkham, G. E. Hardy, & J. Mellor-Clark (Eds.), *Developing and delivering practice-based evidence: A guide for the psychological therapies* (pp. 155–174). New York: Wiley.

Kraus, D. R., Castonguay, L. G., Boswell, J. F., Nordberg, S. S., & Hayes, J. A. (2011). Therapist effectiveness: Implications for accountability and patient care. *Psychotherapy Research, 21*, 267–276. doi:10.1080/10503307.2011.563249

Kraus, D. R., Seligman, D., & Jordan, J. R. (2005). Validation of a behavioral health treatment outcome and assessment tool designed for naturalistic settings: The Treatment Outcome Package. *Journal of Clinical Psychology, 61*, 285–314. doi:10.1002/jclp.20084

Lambert, M. J. (2010). *Prevention of treatment failure: The use of measuring, monitoring, and feedback in clinical practice*. Washington, DC: American Psychological Association.

Loranger, A. W. (1995). *International Personality Disorders Examination (IPDE)*. Geneva: World Health Organization.

McAleavey, A. A., & Castonguay, L. G. (2013). Insight as a common and specific impact of psychotherapy: Therapist-reported exploratory, directive, and common factors interventions. *Psychotherapy*. Advance online publication.

McAleavey, A. A., Castonguay, L. G., & Xiao, H. (2013). Therapist orientation, supervision match, and therapeutic interventions: Implication for session quality in a psychotherapy training practice research network. *Counseling and Psychotherapy Research.*

McAleavey, A. A., Lockard, A. J., Castonguay, L. G., Hayes, J. A., & Locke, B. F. (in press). Practice Research Network of university counseling centers. *Psychotherapy Research, 24.*

McCarthy, K. S., & Barber, J. P. (2009). The Multitheoretical List of Therapeutic Interventions (MULTI): Initial report. *Psychotherapy Research, 19*, 96–113. doi:10.1080/10503300802524343

Nelson, D. L., & Castonguay, L. G. (2012, June). *The systematic use of homework in psychodynamic-interpersonal psychotherapy for depression.* Paper presented at the Annual meeting of the Society for Psychotherapy Research, Virginia Beach, VA.

Nordberg, S. S., Castonguay, L. G., Fisher, A. J., Boswell, J. F., & Kraus, D. (in press). Trajectories of change as a function of initial severity: Analysis of client-response to psychotherapy in a training setting. *Journal of Clinical Psychology.*

Orlinsky, D. E., & Howard, K. I. (1966). *Therapy Session Report, Forms P and T*. Chicago, IL: Institute of Juvenile Research.

Piper, W. E., Joyce, A. S., Rosie, J. S., Ogrodniczuk, J. S., McCallum, M., O'Kelly, J. G., & Steinberg, P. I. (1999). Prediction of dropping out in time-limited interpretive individual psychotherapy. *Psychotherapy, 36*, 114–122. doi:10.1037/h0087787

Schut, A. J., Castonguay, L. G., Bedics, J. D., Smith, T. L., Barber, J. P., Flanagan, K. M., & Yamasaki, A. S. (2005). Therapist interpretation, patient-therapist interpersonal process, and outcome in psychodynamic psychotherapy for avoidant personality disorder. *Psychotherapy: Theory, Research, Practice, and Training. 42*, 494–511. doi:10.1037/0033-3204.42.4.494

Shapiro, D. A., Barkham, M., Rees, A., Hardy, G. E., Reynolds, S., & Startup, M. (1994). Effects of treatment duration and severity of depression on the effectiveness of cognitive-behavioral and psychodynamic-interpersonal psychotherapy. *Journal of Consulting and Clinical Psychology, 62*, 522–534. doi:10.1037/0022-006X.62.3.522

Soldz, S., Budman, S., Demby, A., & Merry, J. (1995). A short form of the Inventory of Interpersonal Problems Circumplex scales. *Assessment, 2*, 53–63. doi:10.1177/1073191195002001006

Stulz, N., Lutz, W., Leach, C., Lucock, M., & Barkham, M. (2007). Shapes of early change in psychotherapy under routine outpatient conditions. *Journal of Consulting and Clinical Psychology, 75*, 864–874. doi:10.1037/0022-006X.75.6.864

Thoma, N. C., & Cecero, J. J. (2009). Is the integrative use of techniques in psychotherapy the exception or the rule? Results of a national survey of doctoral-level practitioners. *Psychotherapy: Theory, Research, Practice, Training, 46*, 405–417. doi:10.1037/a0017900

Youn, S. J., Kraus, D. R., & Castonguay, L. G. (2012). Treatment outcome package: Facilitating practice and clinically relevant research. *Psychotherapy: Theory, Research, Practice, and Training, 49*, 115–122 doi:10.1037/a0027932

Zarin, D. A., Pincus, H. A., West, J. C., & McIntyre, J. S. (1997). Practice-based research in psychiatry. *American Journal of Psychiatry, 154*, 1199–1208.

METHOD PAPER

Practice-oriented research: What it takes to do collaborative research in private practice

KELLY KOERNER[1] & LOUIS G. CASTONGUAY[2]

[1]Evidence-Based Practice Institute, Seattle, WA, USA & [2]Department of Psychology, Pennsylvania State University, University Park, PA, USA

Abstract

The goal of this paper is to describe the authors' experience conducting research in and for private practice. Based on two distinct research programs (one guided by a scientist practitioner leading various groups of clinicians and another from a network of practitioners and researchers), a number of practice-oriented studies are presented. Lessons learned from these collaborative projects are discussed in terms of challenges and strategies to deal with them, as well as benefits that can be earned from conducting empirical studies within clinical routine. General recommendations are then offered to foster the engagement of clinicians in their own working environment and to facilitate partnerships between researchers and practitioners in developing and implementing valid, feasible, and informative clinical studies.

Practice-oriented research can be a powerful means for improving clients' clinical outcomes in psychotherapy. We use the terms "practice-oriented research" or "practice-based research" to mean not only conducting research in a routine practice setting but also "conducting research *with* a group rather than conducting research *on* a group, and *with* a community rather than simply *in* a community or *for* a community" (Westfall et al., 2009). While a specific project's needs may dictate the exact roles practitioners and professional scientists play, the spirit of practice-oriented research is one of active collaboration and shared decision-making through all phases of research (e.g., selecting the clinical problem, formulating the research question, choosing methods, and so on). At its best, this collaboration:

> aims to foster a sense of equality, shared ownership, and mutual respect between researchers and clinicians, and promoting diversity of scholarship (i.e., different ways of understanding and investigating complex phenomena). It also capitalizes on the complementary expertise, knowledge, and experiences of each stakeholder to provide unique opportunities for two-way learning in order to conduct studies that are both clinically relevant and scientifically rigorous. (Castonguay, Barkham, Lutz, & McAleavey, 2013)

Both authors of this paper have led multiple practice-oriented research projects within day-to-day outpatient practice settings, Koerner as a scientist-practitioner based in a private institute that helps therapists learn, use, and evaluate evidence-based practices, and Castonguay from the perspective of academic-community partnerships developed not only in private practice but also in clinic training and university counseling centers.

First, we each describe our work, sharing our goals and example projects that convey the types of research that we have attempted in private practice. Then, we discuss the challenges we have encountered in conducting such practice-oriented research and the strategies we have adopted to overcome these challenges. After describing some of the benefits that practice-oriented research offers, we close this paper with general recommendations to foster the growth of research in clinical practice.

Goals and Examples from Our Practice-oriented Research Programs

Practice-oriented Research at the Evidence-based Practice Institute

At the Evidence-based Practice Institute (EBPI, Koerner), we are in the early stages of building a participatory research community of practitioners, clinical leaders, trainers, and researchers who together learn, use, and evaluate how evidence-based practices impact clients' outcomes. The first author began her career straddling the science-practice gap, part-time in an academic setting, training and supervising therapists to deliver high fidelity research protocols to develop and evaluate treatment, and part-time training the same treatments with colleagues who worked in diverse private and public mental health practice settings. The research-practice gap took on extremely practical dimensions. For example, clinical leaders and practitioners faced enormous setting constraints that impeded high fidelity implementation of evidence-based practices. Shared questions arose: What modifications to accommodate setting constraints were acceptable and which diluted the protocol to the point that clinical outcomes would be compromised? How should you proceed when your staff therapists have to be generalists in their practice and treat whoever walks through the clinic door, but have never learned cognitive-behavioral basics that underpin several evidence-based protocols for eating disorders, anxiety and mood disorders, or substance abuse? How can you tell if your therapists are doing well enough to get good outcomes?

Working daily on these and other complex issues that contribute to the research-practice gap began to shape solutions that concretely foster a rapprochement between science and clinical work. Specifically, building informal social networks began to create knowledge transfer in both directions. This led to our current efforts to support and systematize a community (called PracticeGround learning community) in which research and practice are woven as whole cloth with rigorous research procedures integrated into practitioners' routine workflow. By adopting a "citizen" science model (also known as crowd sourced science), practitioner-volunteers have begun to carry out various aspects of research in collaboration with professional scientists.

We faced three immediate methodological problems as we designed our first collaborative projects. Therapists in routine practice settings needed practical ways (i) to learn evidence-based interventions, (ii) to assess fidelity to the intervention, and (iii) to collect outcome data about clients' response to the intervention.

First, to tackle the problem of training therapists in a standardized intervention, we chose interventions that match therapists' needs to serve a wide variety of patients and designed training formats to maximize ease and convenience. We also had to have a training method that could be financially self-sustaining without grant funding. Therefore, across our five studies to date, therapist training was structured as an online professional continuing education course. Participants paid a small fee and earned continuing education credits, allowing us to underwrite the costs of the trainers' time and partially pay for undergraduate and postdoc research assistants. To maximize convenience and therapists' limited learning time, we used a "flipped classroom" format (www.practiceground.org), in which an online learning community provided didactic information asynchronously to trainees via self-paced e-learning modules, interspersed with synchronous online instructor-led training focused on active learning and the deliberate practice with feedback required to develop expertise (Ericsson, 2008). Training sessions were spaced over several weeks, thereby allowing additional practice and use of the skills between sessions and combining training with ongoing case consultation. This format allowed therapists to learn new interventions with minimal impact on their productivity (online training can be completed on-the-job without having to take time away from work), while integrating training elements and ongoing case consultation shown to be most needed for skills development (Rakovshik & McManus, 2010).

In one project, we trained participants in the Functional Analytic Psychotherapy (FAP) training model, a principle-based behavioral approach to improving therapeutic relationship skills such as genuineness, empathy, positive regard, and attunement to the nuances of the therapy alliance (Kanter, Tsai, Holman, & Koerner, 2013). This 8-week training was intended to strengthen not only practitioners' alliance skills but also teach how to directly promote change through differential reinforcement of client behavior (Tsai, Kohlenberg, & Kanter, 2010). The training protocol combined a series of exercises designed to evoke and reinforce trainee target behaviors in the training session and then homework assignments aimed at promoting generalization to their clinical work.

Participants were recruited from the PracticeGround learning community as well as from emails to professional lists. The first 16 eligible therapists-trainees (7 females, 9 males) were consented online and then randomized into either an immediate or a waitlist training group. We found a significant effect for training between the immediate training group and the waitlist group, which was demonstrated on both a self-report measure of FAP competencies and a blind, reliable observer-based assessment of skill with key FAP techniques. This was then replicated when the waitlist group completed training.

In a second project that used similar recruitment and training methods, we taught four core behavioral activation skills as modular competencies: providing rationale, assessment, activity scheduling, and targeting avoidance (Puspitasari, Kanter, Murphy, Crowe, & Koerner, 2013). Eight participants completed four 90-min online training session supplemented with reading and self-paced multi-media e-learning. Participants reported increased use of behavioral activation techniques and high satisfaction with the training format. However, because of the known limitations of therapists' self-report of their own behavior, in this project, we began to explore the feasibility of asking therapists to enroll one client from their practice into the study in order to measure the impact of training on clients. We provided detailed scripts and an online consent process to make this recruitment as easy as possible. Five of the therapists were able to recruit patients to join them in the research study, whereas logistical constraints such as lack of sufficient patient flow within the timeframe of the study or clients declining to participate interfered for the other therapists. While the learning outcomes of this project were promising as with our first FAP project, the hassle for participants in recruiting patients during such a brief four-session training protocol seemed too much. We needed to find more feasible methods for assessing therapists' behavior and fidelity and client outcomes. This, as mentioned above, represented the second methodological problem that we faced in conducting practice-based research.

To tackle this problem, we continued the line of behavioral activation training research, but also designed a standardized patient role-play assessment as a way to measure the outcomes of training. Using role-play assessment as a proxy-measure of therapist competence offered many advantages (Fairburn & Cooper, 2011), chief of which are not requiring the logistical burden of requiring therapists to provide tapes of therapy sessions for expert trained raters to review and more efficiently assuring that the therapist can be prompted by the standardized patient to use specific skills during the role-play rather than the hit-or-miss nature of real therapy where the therapist must address the problem du jour.

In our third project, we again used similar recruitment and training methods, but this time each trainee interacted with a hypothetical depressed client as role-played by a trained research assistant. These standardized role-play assessments were used to assess skill use and competence before, immediately after training, and again 6 weeks after the end of training. While scheduling the role-play assessments was a challenge for busy therapists, the face valid way that this method mapped to their own learning goals made it a natural component of training, providing a useful, self-organizing challenge that focused learning so that the therapists could benchmark what they know. Findings from this study showed again high satisfaction with training, self-reported use of behavioral activation strategies in sessions, and importantly increased competence with the behavioral activation techniques as rated by blind, reliable coders of the role-plays.

While all of these previous efforts allowed us to tackle the first two methodological problems we faced in conducting our research in naturalistic settings, we were still confronted with a third one: collecting outcome data related to clients' response to the intervention. In order to successfully address this crucial issue, we realized we needed an online infrastructure. We thus sought and were awarded a grant to develop online progress tracking software that integrates collecting data directly into clinicians' usual workflow for clinical decision-making and research purposes (National Institute of Mental Health, NIMH 1R43MH093993-01). In this study, we trained therapists in how to monitor psychotherapy progress using standardized self-report measures and an early prototype of online progress tracking software (Persons et al., 2014). The scores from patient-reported questionnaires helped therapists detect lack of progress and intervene to improve client outcomes. We taught participants how to introduce patients to the use of measures, handle non-compliance, discuss lack of progress, and use the data to inform decisions about the next possible therapeutic actions (e.g., stay the course, further assess, or change the treatment plan). Therapists, therefore, learned how to monitor client progress as a method of assessing how their implementation of interventions impacts client outcomes. Such performance monitoring and feedback methods have been shown to be crucial to performance improvement across several fields (Bickman, 2008). Many have recommended wider use of these methods as a way to improve behavioral health training and practice (Castonguay, Boswell, Constantino, Goldfried, & Hill, 2010; Kazdin & Blasé, 2011; Newnham & Page, 2010), because progress tracking systems that frequently measure patients' treatment progress with standardized measures improve clinical decision-making and treatment effectiveness in mental health care (Knaup, Koesters, Schoefer, Becker, & Puschner 2009; Reese, Norsworthy, & Rowlands, 2009).

As further examples of studies we have conducted, we began to explore how single-case experimental design might work for practice-oriented research. Single-case experimental designs offer powerful methods for studying causal relationships between therapy interventions and clients' process and outcome (Barlow, Nock, & Hersen, 2008) and increase the feasibility of research because of how easily these designs integrate within practice. For example, in collaboration with Jason Luoma, Leslie Greenberg, and Ben Shahar, we used the online modular competency training approach described above to train therapists in two-chair work for self-critical splits, a set of procedures drawn from emotion-focused therapy (Greenberg & Dompierre, 1981; Greenberg & Higgins, 1980; Shahar et al., 2012). In the same way that common procedures cut across packaged treatment protocols, common problematic processes such as shame and self-criticism broadly contribute to difficulties across a wide range of psychological disorders and therefore align well with therapists' needs. In this two-part study, we first studied what methods are needed for therapists with a primarily cognitive-behavioral background to learn the complex experiential response modes essential to emotion-focused therapy. Then in the second phase, once practitioners had reached sufficient adherence to the model, they join a distributed network of research therapists who carefully follow an agreed upon research protocol in their work settings to conduct a multiple-baseline design. The research design allowed therapists to recruit any patients they viewed as appropriate into the study. To strengthen the experimental design, therapists randomized patients to varying lengths of baseline in order to detect whether expected improvements coincide with the time of intervention.

In a second single-case design project, in collaboration with the Science Practice-Research Special Interest Group of the Association for Contextual Behavior, we trained a group of practitioners in how to design single-case experimental research. Using an online practicum format, an international group of practitioners worked for 6 months to identify meaningful research questions within their practice setting and design appropriate single-case experiments to test hypotheses. Through multiple rounds of peer and expert critique, experiments were designed to test hypotheses across a wide range of clinical interventions (e.g., testing exposure therapy with anxious youth, evaluating acceptance and commitment therapy in routine adult outpatient settings, integrating exercise within a skills training

approach to help those with borderline personality disorder). This line of research begins to build a network of therapists and a library of open enrollment research designs and protocols that make it feasible to scale single case designs to make meaningful contributions to the scientific literature.

Across these studies, with more and less success, our goal was to integrate research procedures into practitioners' routine workflow with as little disruption as possible so that rigorous research methods were harnessed as a tool to improve client outcomes by meeting therapists' learning needs. Our practice-oriented research projects have focused on helping therapists (i) learn, use, and evaluate for themselves how evidence-based practices impact their clients' outcomes, with (ii) practical methods that enable a geographically dispersed network of therapists to carry out rigorous research protocols.

Goals and Examples of the Pennsylvania Psychological Association Practice Research Network

The Pennsylvanian Psychological Association Practice Research Network (PPA-PRN) was born out of a challenge that two individuals set up to resolve long-lasting arguments that they have had for years. One of them, Tom Borkovec, had been fervently holding the position that highly rigorous research, to which he had devoted most of his professional career, can and should provide guidance to clinical practice. With the same level of conviction, the other, Steve Ragusea, had been arguing that empirical knowledge, at least of the sort pursuit by academics, has little if any meaningful relevance to the work that he, and other full-time clinicians, conduct in their day-to-day practice. They agreed that the best way to settle the score, so to speak, would be to put their respective assumption to an empirical test. Specifically, they committed to work together to determine whether or not it is possible to bring clinicians and researchers to collaboratively design and conduct research—studies that would be both clinically relevant and scientifically rigorous. With the help of the Pennsylvania Psychological Association, they sent an invitation to all licensed psychologists in the state to meet in the local community near the Pennsylvania State University. This broad invitation was motivated by a desire to get as much input as possible, as well as to create the conditions for recruiting a large sample size of both therapists and clients. The meeting led to the creation of three committees (core assessment, study protocol, and ethics), as well as a general consensus about the type of empirical investigations that could and should be conducted. To be feasible, yet at least minimally meaningful at both clinical and scientific levels, such research would first have to take place within natural practice but without interfering with clinical work. It would also have to be based on psychometrically solid instruments that could (i) be easily implemented in a standardized way, and (ii) collect clinically useful information.

Psychotherapy outcome in routine practice. In the first study conducted within the PPA-PRN, more than 50 psychologists committed to implement the same outcome measure as part of their respective clinical routine (Borkovec, Echmendia, Ragusea, & Ruiz, 2001). Also included in the study protocol were a number of demographic questions, as well as a measure of interpersonal problems that could be associated with positive or negative outcome. This study provided clear support to a key aspect of the challenge that Borkovec and Ragusea set for themselves: feasibility. It demonstrated that it is possible for clinicians and researchers to fully collaborate in the delineation of mutually agreed upon research questions, as well as to share expertise and resources toward the development and implementation of a study protocol that can minimally meet the criteria mentioned above. The study has also provided interesting information, not only revealing significant pre- and post-treatment change but also uncovering interesting correlations between different aspects of therapy and its participants, such as a negative correlation between number of clients on therapist caseloads and outcome.

Ultimately, however, this first study did not settle the Borkovec and Ragusea argument, as it failed to provide a satisfactory answer to the question of whether research can truly be clinically informative, as well as scientifically rigorous. In the eyes of several members of the PPA-PRN, including the second author of this paper, a study would optimally reach this lofty goal by investigating specific questions of immediate clinical interest and concern (as they emerge in the interaction with each and all clients), uncover phenomena or test hypothesis that are unknown or not fully settled in the field of practice, lead to actionable findings, and be designed and conducted in ways that reach high levels of both external and internal validity. Clinically, such an optimal study would have to do more than confirm what clinicians know (e.g., that therapy works). Empirically, this study would not only have to be to seamlessly integrated in clinical routine of many clinicians (as a way to maximize external validity), but it would also address the ultimate scientific pursuit: the investigation of cause and effect relationships. To optimally contribute to such pursuit, again in the opinion of the second author and some of his

PRN partners, a study should go beyond measuring whether or not change took place (from pre- to post-treatment) and identifying predictors of change (what correlates with improvement), and instead should be aimed at determining what causes change (by manipulating one variable and controlling, with the highest possible internal validity, other factors that could be responsible of change observed). As argued by Borkovec and Castonguay (1998), one of the ways that a PRN or any other practice-oriented studies could achieve this goal is by using experimental methods that maximize internal validity and yet remain feasible, such as the use of additive, dismantling, or parametric designs (as mentioned above, another strategy aimed at the same goal is the use of single case experimental designs).

One of the conclusions that core members of our PRN derived from the limitations of this first study was that a complex protocol investigating more precise and useful questions would be best designed in an environment that could allow frequent and regular contact between all practitioners and researchers involved, as well as high level of control over the implementation and monitoring of the research procedures. Guided by this conclusion, it was decided that the context for the second phase of our PRN would shift from a large milieu (the state of Pennsylvania), to a much smaller community: State College, where both Borkovec and Ragusea have been working and arguing for years.

Helpful and hindering events in psychotherapy. The first meeting of the second phase of the PPA-PRN focused on one specific and straightforward question: What do we want to study together? The group of therapists and researchers became quickly enthused about the interest voiced by one member: "What I really would like to know is what my clients found helpful, or not helpful, during a session we just conducted." Consistent with several of the characteristics of an optimal study mentioned above, all members felt that this type of feedback would provide them with information not always easy or possible to get from the client otherwise, might reveal issues that they were not aware of and/ or a perspective on the therapy that was different from theirs, and might provide them with opportunities to appropriately address the need of their client. In other words, getting such feedback from their client might help them better understand the process change with each of their clients, as it immediately and progressively happens or fails to happen. In turn, this might help them to improve the impact of their therapeutic interventions.

Having decided what to study, our group then met regularly for 12 months to decide how to study it in ways that would maximize both the external and internal validity of our search. As described in Castonguay, Boswell et al. (2010b), we first decided to adopt, as part of our clinical routine, the Treatment Outcome Package (TOP; Kraus, Jordan, Seligman, 2005) to measure, at pre- and post-treatment, several dimensions of symptoms and functioning (such as depression, panic, suicide, substance abuse, quality of life, work functioning; for a detailed description of the TOP, see Boswell, Kraus, Miller, & Lambert, 2014). We also decided to address our main question by using the Helpful Aspects of Therapy (HAT; Llewelyn, 1988). This instrument not only directly assesses what we wanted to know but had been used in a previous study conducted in naturalistic setting (Llewelyn, 1988). This meant that our study, while designed with clinicians, was in part aiming at addressing one of the most important goals of science: replication. Our study was also aimed at extending the previous investigation by directly pursuing the ultimate scientific goal mentioned above: examining cause–effect relationship. In order to do so, we decided to use an additive design where all new clients (children, adolescents, adults) of each participating therapist would be asked if they want to participate in an experimental study, where they would be randomly assigned to one of the two conditions. In the experimental condition, both client and therapist would fill out the HAT at the end of every session. In the control condition, only the therapist would fill out the HAT after each session. The therapist filling out the HAT in the experimental condition would allow us to determine whether the client and therapist had the same perspective on the significant events. This would not only be important scientifically but also clinically: giving therapists opportunities to discuss with their clients, if they judge it appropriate or useful, the similarity or discrepancies between their perspectives on helpful and/or hindering events. The therapist completion of the HAT in the control condition permitted us to control for the potential beneficial impact of having the therapists giving more thought to sessions than they typically do. Thus, the use of this additive design not only allowed for relevant and actionable information to be collected during therapy but it also led to the control of variables that may interfere with internal validity. Since the two conditions were the same with the exception of one specific procedure, if a difference was to be obtained between them it could safely be inferred that the improvement was caused by the therapist receiving feedback from client during treatment. It should be mentioned that no rules, techniques, or guidelines were prescribed about what to do with the feedback. Therapists were only asked to consider the feedback before the next session (in terms of how it might help them to be most attuned to the client's need). This meant that while pertinent and actionable, the information collected during the therapy did not have to impose drastic change to clinicians work—clinicians did not have to learn new approaches, receive specialized training, or follow treatment manuals assigning specific tasks to specific helpful or hindering events. They, on their own, decided if, when, and how to modify the focus or process of treatment to better fit the needs of clients based on the clients' HAT feedback.

Clients (N = 46) agreed to participate and provided informed consent at the end of the first session of therapy (clients were not invited to participate in study if therapists judged that it would be counter-indicated for clinical reasons). Within a period of 18 months of data collection, we obtained more than 1600 helpful or hindering events, which were then coded by three students with respect to the types of events identified and their content or focus (what these events were about). Results of these process analyses (for the combined groups of adolescent and adult clients) indicated that both clients and therapists identified as particularly helpful events that reflected an increase of awareness (such as the exploration of painful events and the experience of negative feelings). Events reflecting the strengthening of the therapeutic relationship were also viewed by therapists as particularly helpful. The coding also revealed that for both therapists and clients, issues related to the therapeutic relationship were among the most frequent content referred to in the helpful events (such as the formation of a close bond). Interestingly, the therapeutic relationship was also among the most frequent content coded in the hindering events (such as the client feeling under attack and needing to withdraw). This suggests that the therapeutic relationship, in the eyes of both participants, is a powerful ingredient of therapy that can either facilitate or interfere with the process of change. We were, however, unable to answer the question of whether the provision of feedback by clients about helpful and hindering events could improve the outcome of therapy in clinical practice. Since only 31% of terminating client completed the TOP at the end of therapy, we were not able to determine whether the experimental and control groups differed in terms of therapeutic improvement.

Techniques and impact of therapy. The PPA-PRN partnership has conducted a third study. Because we are in the process of analyzing the collected data, only the goal and protocol of this investigation are briefly summarized here. Again conducted with therapists working in State College and surrounding communities, this study focused on techniques used by therapists and their potential impact on the session and therapy. As in the second study, therapists adopted the TOP as part of their clinical routine. For up to 24 months, they assigned the TOP (before the first session and at the end of therapy) to all new individual therapy clients (18-years old or older) of their private practice. To reduce the burden of this new study, however, a maximum of four clients were recruited by each therapist at any time in the study. Also based on an additive design, clients were randomly assigned to either an experimental or a control group. In the experimental group, both client and therapist were asked to fill out, at the end of each session, a measure assessing techniques used during the session (the Multitheoretical List of Therapeutic Interventions, MULTI; McCarthy & Barber, 2009), two questions aimed at identifying techniques particularly helpful or hindering, as well as a brief questionnaire on the impact of the session (the Session Progress Scale; Kolden, 1991). None of these were filled out in the control group. The clients in both groups, however, were asked to fill out the TOP after session 7. Like in the second PPA-PRN study, clients in the experimental condition were informed that therapist would read the completed questionnaires before the next session, as a way to help them provide the best possible treatment for them. As it was also the case in the previous study, we decided not to assign any instruction about how to respond to the clients' answers on the questionnaires.

Our goal with this study is to investigate what techniques are frequently used in clinical practice, which of these are viewed as particularly helpful or unhelpful, and whether getting feedback about techniques used and the quality of the session could help improve therapy outcome in clinical practice. In designing this study, we attempt to learn from our experience by keeping the positive aspects and addressing the difficulties that we observed from our previous investigation. We investigate a specific aspect of the process of change (receiving feedback) in a way that makes the data collection immediately actionable (and thus intertwining clinical and research tasks). As an effort to address the ultimate quest of science (cause–effect relationship), we also manipulated, via an experimental design that maximizes internal validity, the process variables investigated. Furthermore, the study was designed and implemented as a full and active collaboration between clinicians and researchers. We did, however, attempt to avoid previous difficulties by making the study protocol more manageable (by limiting the recruitment of client for each clinician) and by exporting strategies from controlled research to help us improve our data collection (by having

graduate students continually monitoring the expected flow of data and by providing financial incentives to clients for filling out the TOP at post-treatment). As noted in the next section, however, our attempt to learn from our previous experiences did not remove all obstacles and challenges that we faced in pursuing practice-oriented research.

The Challenges of Practice-oriented Research

Practice-oriented research poses numerous challenges from designing studies to carrying out research procedures that work within routine practice settings.

The most significant challenges to practice-oriented research arise from incompatibilities between research procedures and practitioners' workflow. High demands for clinical productivity mean that therapists face tremendous practical barriers to participating in research. Practitioners must fill each workday with as many sessions as possible. Practitioners' typical schedule leaves short windows of time between sessions to take care of professional tasks that cannot be accomplished during sessions. Any research task, such as responding to an emailed invitation to participate in research, meetings to organize research activities, or completing a research measure, competes with income-earning and patient-care activities such as returning calls, creating clinical notes, planning for the next session, and so on. Protecting time is crucial for practitioners. Unless research pays therapists for the time it takes to do research activities, participating in practice-oriented research costs therapists money. Time is also important for maintaining well-being. Some of the clinicians we have worked with reported that they at times had to choose between completing questionnaires or going to the bathroom between two consecutive sessions. Research activities that require many procedures to plan and to remember can be particularly interfering with clinical routine, especially when therapists do not have easy access to information (and/or communication with researchers) to recall details of a study protocol or to help them to deal with circumstances unforeseen by such protocol. The non-stop workflow means that therapists might literally have 5 min to give to research before being submerged for several weeks by clinical demands before resurfacing with another 5 min to devote to research. The workflow is even tighter and more unpredictable for practitioners who work with clients whose mental health problems lead to frequent crises (e.g., borderline personality disorder or substance abuse disorder).

Another example of conflicts between research procedures and clinical work is the fact that research tasks can sometime interfere with client needs. As noted in Castonguay, Nelson et al. (2010), some therapists in the PPA-PRN reported that explaining a study and seeking clients' consent in the first session of a treatment did, on occasion, take time away to evaluate the client difficulties and establish therapeutic rapport. Having to keep in mind details of a research protocol can also compete with the attention that therapists need to give their clients' concerns. Some therapists report being uncomfortable asking a client to fill out questionnaires at the end of a very intense session, as they fear that the client might not have been willing, or at a good emotional place, to fill them out. Some therapists in the PPA-PRN have also reported difficulties recruiting clients to participate in a study (e.g., due to concerns about confidentiality). Other clients appeared to experience completing research questionnaires as an inconvenience.

Aspects of a research protocol can also be experienced by therapists as "not being worth the trouble." For example, despite having been fully involved in the decision of using the MULTI after each session (in the experimental condition), several therapists participating in the third study of the PPA-PRN were critical of specific aspects of the instrument (e.g., too long, items not appropriately reflecting therapist ways of conducting specific type of therapy) and/or did not feel that it provided them with information that could help them adjust their interventions to better address their clients' needs. Incompatible with the ultimate goal of practice-oriented research, this instrument failed to be perceived by many therapists in this study as being immediately relevant and actionable.

In addition, research requires standardization of assessment and treatment in order to best draw conclusions from the experimental manipulation. But such standardization may at times be incompatible with what the practitioner views as clinically indicated for a specific patient. Any incompatibilities between standardization needed for research and flexibility needed for clinical care and routine workflow can take on added weight in practice-based research where the therapist's income and reputation depend on client satisfaction. Designing research with the right balance between standardization and flexibility can be quite difficult. For example, in one of the practice-oriented research studies conducted at EBPI, we carefully sought to minimize the burden and maximize clinical utility of assessment by selecting a single symptom measure, the Depression Anxiety and Stress Scales (DASS; Lovibond & Lovibond, 1996) for the study. The DASS is brief, free, and extremely useful in that it provides three clinically relevant and scales (depression, anxiety,

and stress) in a single measure. However, what we found was that a significant subset of therapists in our study needed a measure of activation and improved quality of life; symptom change per se was not the primary focus of their treatment. For this group of practitioners, the DASS failed to measure what was most clinically relevant. While many of them continued to use the DASS with their patients out of obligation to their research commitments, it had become a piece of burdensome paperwork rather than a useful clinical tool. Similarly, the TOP (which measures both symptomatic and non-symptomatic [including quality of life] dimensions of functioning) was not perceived as a useful assessment tool by some therapists who recruited child and adolescent clients as part of the second PPA-PRN study. Interestingly, however, one of these therapists became the most vocal supporter of the TOP during the third study, which involved only adult clients.

A final set of incompatibilities between practice-oriented research and the usual workflow in routine settings has to do with recruitment and retention of participants. First, to initiate clinical research requires that all research procedures be reviewed to ensure they are ethical and protect the rights of the research participants. Researchers based in academic settings have access to internal review boards but for researchers without an academic affiliation, obtaining review of human subjects' protocols may require allying with a professional scientist willing to submit the research protocol to his or her university's institutional review board (IRB) or paying an independent review board to review the research protocol. In fact, this barrier to practice-oriented research proved to be so onerous to one of us (Koerner) that the best solution turned out to be joining a group of like-minded colleagues to form our own non-profit IRB to review practice-oriented research (Osborne, 2011). Further, therapists in practice-oriented research face obstacles to patient recruitment. Unlike a research study in an academic setting, practitioners in practice-oriented research cannot typically rapidly ramp up a caseload solely of research patients but instead must set aside patient slots from within already full practices. Patient flow in a study, therefore, may be slow because therapists have limited space in their practices for new patients. In some cases, it may be easier to recruit research participants from current patients. But this, then, introduces variability and constrains the research questions to those that can be asked in the context of already ongoing courses of therapy. Further, there is an ethical dilemma of whether or not therapists should charge patients their usual fee for treatment when that treatment is an experimental treatment or a treatment in the context of a research evaluation.

Care must be taken to help or train practitioners about how to recruit patients so that there is no chance of coercion to participate.

In summary, the obstacles to practice-oriented research are significant, and consequently, those who self-select by surmounting the barriers to participation may be different from the general population of practitioners in important ways. These potential selection biases, consequently, must be considered when designing the research to ensure that the study's results can meaningfully generalize beyond the specific sample. The best strategy we have found in our practice-oriented research designs is to accept the constraints faced by practitioners and design research procedures that map as directly onto clinical care already provided as possible.

Professional scientists face several additional barriers to conducting practice-oriented research. Sometimes, academic researchers can be perceived with suspicion as exploitative—the researcher determines all aspects of the study, agrees with the clinical director to take advantage of the practice setting's volume of patients, and then the therapist and client participants are roped into additional work that may not align with their goals. This can be viewed as a manifestation of what has been described elsewhere as "empirical imperialism" (Castonguay, 2011), when researchers, who see very few clients, impose their views on full-time clinicians about what to study and how to study it in order to improve psychotherapy. A more useful strategy to optimize practice-oriented research is to develop a collaborative partnership that is based on the acknowledgment of and reliance on practitioners' expertise, needs, and resources. Fostering a sense of equality and mutual respect, however, requires the academic researcher to make time for conversations and coordination with practitioners who have very limited availability, which extends all aspects of the research timeline. It may be difficult for academic researchers, who are time-pressured themselves, to "walk the talk" of sharing decision-making, building consensus, and being as truly collaborative as may be optimal for successful practice-oriented research. Professional scientists may need several years to build a trusting mutually beneficial relationship with a research site or group of practitioners. Unfortunately, the slow, collaborative pace of practice-oriented research is incompatible with the pressures on academic researchers to produce rapid publishable studies. Such incompatibility has real and important implications for the successful career pathway of academicians—the first among them might be to seriously consider the risk of initiating and developing practice-oriented partnership before getting tenure. As described later in this paper,

however, such partnership can lead to meaningful benefits, both professionally and personally.

Strategies for Success in Conducting Practice-oriented Research

Over the years, both authors have gained through trial and error a number of lessons about what works and does not work in practice-oriented research. Below, we offer three themes of advice for others interested in conducting practice-oriented research.

Make Everything Easy and Clinically Relevant

As previously discussed, practitioners in routine settings have minimal time to devote to research tasks. Our most successful strategy in practice-oriented research, therefore, has been to make everything about doing research as easy as possible and to prune research protocols to only the most clinically relevant elements.

Ideally, practice-oriented research would be designed such that practitioners can do any research task with no need to break away from their workflow in order to make sense of the procedure. This idea has implications with respect to the design of the study, as well as the implementation of the research protocol. At a design level, the fusion of empirical tasks with the practitioner workflow reflects the previously mentioned concepts of "whole cloth of research and practice" and "clinically syntonic" research. As stated elsewhere, the most important recommendations for future PRNs that emerged from one of the PPA-PRN study was "to conduct studies that intrinsically confound research with practice—studies for which it is impossible to fully distinguish whether the nature of the questions investigated, tasks implemented, or the data collected are empirical or clinical" (Castonguay, Nelson et al., 2010, p. 352).

At the implementation level, our experience suggests that the likelihood of successful practice-oriented research will increase when research questions are smaller in scope, that the protocol requires minimum time for the clinicians, the measures are useful and not too complex, and when strategies are in place to help the clinicians learn, remember, and recall the procedures. The implementation of a research protocol can also be facilitated by the availability of pragmatic support, including help from administrative assistants and students, group meetings and opportunities for consultations (among clinicians and with researchers), as well as the availability of funds. Incentives such as obtaining continued education credits for participation in research meeting can also increase clinicians' motivation.

Concrete and helpful strategies to make implementation of practice-oriented research easy and clinically relevant can be found in user centered design. For example, Krug's (2006) "Don't Make Me Think" provides principles for designing information for people, like therapists, who have limited time and need to rapidly make sense of information to perform a task. Using very simple processes such as "hassle mapping" (http://www.fast company.com/1781300/hassle-maps-genesis-demand), the research team can walk potential study participants through all elements of the proposed research design and methods to identify each point at which following the research procedures will be a hassle or become less clinically relevant and then brainstorm together how to smooth out the procedures to better respect people's time and better conform to participants' work flow. For example, when we have used this process, in EBPI studies, therapists have spotted problems with inclusion and exclusion criteria, suggested more relevant and clinically useful measures, and suggested work around and routines that were incorporated into the research design. The hassle map allows the team to build a consensus on all aspects of the study's procedures, solving many problems before they arise.

This basic idea of making things easy and clinically relevant ("don't make me think") can be applied to improve any aspect of practice-oriented research procedures. For example, when sending an emailed invitation to participate in research, remember that the practitioner is likely viewing your email within a very tight window. The potential participant wants only the succinct information needed to decide if the study meets their or their patients' needs. An easy 1-2-3 list of bullet points will make it easier for the practitioner to decide if it works to join the study. Key to deciding to join a study is being able to rapidly assess whether participation will be a wise investment of time and in part the therapist seeks reassurance that the research team has credible and trustworthy track record. A personal invitation from the most well respected member of the research team can be helpful.

Another way we make things easy is to provide scripts and easy to follow "how to" instructions wherever we can for research tasks. At EBPI, for example, we provide scripts that have been reviewed and approved by our IRB to help therapists confidently and ethically invite patients to participate in research. We prepare IRB applications for participants whose own local IRB must approve study procedures prior to their participation in one of our studies. We provide brief modeling videos and

demonstrations that can be referenced as reminders about any key research procedure. Scripts have also used in the PPA-PRN to help clinicians remember and recall research protocols. At the end of the second study, practitioners made two decisions regarding the scripts for the next one: (i) three versions should be created, varying in terms of the detailed description of each of the step involved in the study, and (ii) the instructions contained in all of the three version should be "idiot-proof" (another way of saying "don't make me think").

A number of other pragmatic lessons that emerged from the second study of the PPA-PRN also guided the preparation and implementation of the third one. For examples, substantial time was spent by clinicians and researchers to mutually organize every procedural aspects of the study that could be anticipated and planned; regular meetings were held (especially frequent in the early phase of the implementation of the study), not only to solidify the sense of community and collaboration among the team but also to identify and share strategies to deal with obstacles encountered with the research protocol.

Despite applying these helpful lessons from our previous work, the primary measure that we used in our third study failed, as we mentioned above, to be perceived as helpful by several participants. This was particularly surprising since the same instrument (the MULTI) was successfully implemented in two studies conducted in another PRN (see Castonguay et al., 2014). What we derived from this experience is that, optimally, all the participant therapists should be asked to use extensively the planned measures (process or outcome) in his/her practice before the beginning of the study. Some participants (researchers and therapists) might be too optimistic about the value and applicability of an instrument and others might be overly skeptic about the use of the same measure (or any instrument). In any case, it is probably safe to assume that no degree of anticipation and preparation will likely replace a direct exposure to the problems and benefits that might results from the use of any scale in day-to-day practice.

Other pragmatic lessons that we successfully implemented in our third study had to do with external support. Whenever possible, tasks were handled by administrative assistants in private practice to help integrated aspects of the research within clinical routine. A team of research assistants (graduate and undergraduate students) was also built and supervised to systematically and continuously collect, enter, and monitor data from all therapists participants, as well as to regularly contact therapists regarding expected, missing, and problematic data (or procedural problems) for each of their recruited clients. Efforts were also made to have advanced graduate students and as well the primary researcher to be easily reachable (via phone and email) to quickly provide information or problem-solving recommendations to participating therapists.

Extra support for busy practitioners must be planned when the research procedures deviate from usual workflow. For example, in one of the EBPI studies that required therapists to keep a self-monitoring diary, we provided multiple formats for data entry, from an online electronic format, to using an excel spreadsheet, to calling and leaving a dictated phone message of the data that one of the research staff could then transfer to the appropriate form. Reminders when therapists were late in sending in their self-monitoring forms were always friendly and completely understanding of how difficult it can be to squeeze the research task into a busy day. In studies that have required therapists to record their therapy sessions, the research team provided the audio recorder, and detailed instructions and technical help as therapists learned to record and upload mpg files to a secure file-sharing site. For practice-oriented research to work requires careful design of research procedures to make them as seamlessly part of routine care as possible or provision of the extra support to reduce the hassle involved with research tasks.

While efforts can be made to help therapists implement a research protocol, our experience also suggest that therapists themselves can and will developed a number of strategies during the study to meet its challenges. In the PPA-PRN, for example, therapists reported the useful role of practice, procedures to remember protocol details, as well as the adoption the mindset of "research champion." As noted in Castonguay, Nelson et al. (2010):

> Some psychotherapists spoke about overcoming obstacles through their attitudes toward the project, such as trusting their own judgment to handle unforeseen situations when they felt unsure … keeping the goal of the project in mind to stay motivated even when they felt frustrated … and thinking of obstacles as challenges and as providing intellectual stimulation (p. 351)

Build Infrastructure

To sustain practice-oriented research, one needs to establish an infrastructure. By infrastructure we mean everything needed to support a research study from the personnel, facilities, and equipment or tools, including an ongoing funding stream to underwrite research costs. Much of the practice-oriented

research we have done, in both EBPI and PPA-PRN contexts, has relied on volunteer effort. Practitioners have donated hours as research therapists. Students have also devoted tremendous amount of their time, whether as part of commitment to their graduate training lab (in the case of Penn State students), or in exchange for research experience and a letter of recommendation (in case of students from local universities close to EBPI).

In addition to volunteer efforts, external funding can make a big difference. In the third study of the PPA-PRN, for example, we were able to secure funding from the Pennsylvania Psychological Association and the Committee for the Advancement of Professional Practice of the American Psychological Association to better address one of the major problems we encountered in conducting our second investigation: the low rate of completion of the post-treatment outcome measure. By providing financial incentives to clients ($50 if they return the TOP within 1 week after the end of their treatment; $30 after that), the rate of completion approximately doubled. However, securing external funding is extremely difficult. At EBIP, investigators have donated money earned from non-research activities (e.g., income earned from providing training, consultation, or clinical work) to underwrite the cost of research. Notably, self-funding of research costs has also happened in other clinical settings (see Fernández-Álvarez, Gómez, & García, 2014).

Working outside an academic setting means that practice-oriented researchers incur many additional infrastructure costs such as purchasing licenses for statistical analysis software and manuscript citation management, to the costs of obtaining an IRB review. The costs to any single practice-oriented researcher are high as that individual invests the time and money to accumulate the infrastructure needed to conduct researcher. For that reason, one of us with the help of funding from the NIMH (1 R43 MH093993-01A1) is building a technology platform, PracticeGround (www.practiceground.org), that makes it easy for practitioners to collect data on their interventions and patients' responses to interventions within their routine workflow. PracticeGround's tools are intended to be used to streamline and automate practice-oriented research study management, from initial recruitment and consent of participants to online collection of measures.

Because the PPA-PRN is based on a collaborative relationship with an academic setting, few of its infrastructural costs are a burden on the clinicians in PPA-PRN. Resources and equipment link to the lab of Penn State researchers have been used to covered several needs of the research. In addition, the members of the PPA-PRN have benefited from a collaboration that was established with David Kraus, the president of the company processing the TOP (Outcome Referrals). Outcome Referrals has donated and processed the TOP for free for the last two studies, including for all the clients seen by the participating clinicians during the entire period of data collection (24 months) of the third study. The technological platform of Outcome Referrals allows for a quick and user-friendly collection (via paper/fax-based systems, online systems and handheld devises), processing, and reporting of the TOP, both at the local (for each therapist) as well as the PRN levels. In addition to providing a crucial component of our research initiative, the TOP has offered several clinical benefits for our practitioners, such as the quick (via web or fax) delivery of benchmarked outcome feedback, user-friendly depiction of current and all past assessment on the 12 TOP dimensions, and the link to empirically based guidelines for treatment of each of the measured dimensions (see Youn, Kraus, & Castonguay [2012] for description of research and clinical quality of the TOP). As described in the next section, the next step foreseen for the PPA-PRN involves the collaboration with Outcome Referrals (and the use of the TOP) in the establishment of a large clinicians-researchers infrastructure across the USA.

Move toward Community Participatory Research

Our final piece of advice for those interested in conducting practice-oriented research is to move toward a community participatory research model (Minkler & Wallerstein, 2010); Wells, Miranda, Bruce, Alegria, & Wallerstein, 2004). By establishing long-term, mutually beneficial relationships with colleagues, relationships that are based on shared goals and values regarding the best care for clients, it becomes possible to mount meaningful small and large projects whose findings contribute to both the participants in the research as well as the field at large.

At EBPI, natural communities of practice—groups of individuals or organizations who already are invested in evaluating a specific approach or whose interests align closely with the researchers' question—are brought together in an online format that allows project participants to be geographically dispersed. This is very similar to the concept of "network of networks," which is expected to guide the next developmental step of the PPA-PRN. As described elsewhere (Castonguay, 2011), clinicians (even when they collaborate with researchers) who work within one single group are confronted with limitations in terms of perspectives, expertise, and

resources. Perhaps the most constraining of such restrictions has to do with the limited sample size, in terms of clients and therapists, which can be obtained within one group of collaborators. Small samples not only restrict the generalization of findings but may also preclude the conduct of analyses that are central to a project. An unfortunate example of this problem has happened with the third Phase of the PPA-PRN. With the goal of reducing the workload of clinicians (which, as described above, was a lesson learned from our second study), we decided that rather than inviting all new clients to participate, therapist would never enroll more than four of their clients in the research protocol. Even though 10 therapists were engaged for up to 24 months of data collection (and even though we substantially increased our rate of post-treatment TOP collection via financial incentives), we were not able to recruit a sufficiently large number of clients to provide a statistically fair comparison of the two groups in terms of outcome—and thus not able to answer our question of whether receiving feedback from clients in terms of technique used and session impact could improve therapy effectiveness.

From this unfortunate situation, we then concluded that a strategy for the growth of PRN and practice-oriented research in general might be to "work locally and collaborate globally" (Castonguay et al., 2013). The participatory research communities that EBPI and the PPA-PRN are developing foster the connections among individuals and groups within a large infrastructure. Research ideas and protocols developed by one group can be offered to participants within the entire infrastructure to join in the design and/or implementation of their research ideas. Practitioners self-select based on their own interests how to invest time and energy by developing a research protocol or by participating in studies developed by other groups in the infrastructure.

This strategy combines advantages of working in both small and large groups. For example, with the first study of the PPA-PRN, working with a large group of therapists allowed the recruitment of a large sample of participants (clinicians and clients). However, in the following two studies, working within a small group of therapists in the same community permitted more frequent meetings, and thus better conditions to design internally and externally valid study, develop a research protocol covering a multitude of procedural details, as well as to get and give much needed support and advice about the implementation of the protocol. Similarly, at EBPI, the details of a research protocol are vetted first with small groups of geographically dispersed therapists in pilot projects, and then offered for open enrollment to the wider network once the kinks are smoothed out. Small groups can more agilely develop rigorous, feasible protocols while large groups enable the research to reach sufficiently large sample size.

By combining infrastructure and a participatory community research orientation, we believe that large-scale clinically meaningful research can become part of the practitioners' routine. The next step planned for the PPA-PRN is to simultaneously design a study and create (with the collaboration of David Kraus and Outcome Referrals) an infrastructure of private practice practitioners using the TOP as part of their clinical routine. Once the protocol for our study will be complete, clinicians, irrespective of their geographical location, will be invited to consider joining the research study. Hopefully, therapists working within other sites (or local PRN) will also generate ideas and/or develop research protocols and then invite therapists (including, of course, those who are part of the PPA-PRN) to join their efforts. At EBPI, practitioners, trainers, and researchers co-design pilot protocols that are rigorous and feasible, and then the project becomes available for open enrollment to others' in the network. The Practice-Ground online progress tracking tools allow practitioners to monitor clients' response to treatment in ways that are clinically meaningful yet standardized for research purposes.

Interestingly, similar types of infrastructure have begun to emerge in other naturalistic settings, such as in University counseling centers (see McAleavey, Lochart, Castonguay, Hayes, & Locke, 2014) and psychology training clinics (see Castonguay, Pincus, & McAleavey, 2014). With the same goal of fostering the engagement of a large group of clinicians in conducting and participating in research (as well as to inform and learn from research), George Taska has also created a Canadian-wide inter-disciplinary partnership called the Psychotherapy Practice Research Network (www.pprnet.ca).

Benefits of Practice-oriented Research

While conducting research in private practice comes with challenges, it also brings a number of benefits. Such benefits can, and one might say should, be harvested by the various stakeholders of clinical practice research—clinicians, therapists, students, and, of course, clients.

At a general level, practice-oriented research can be very meaningful for both researchers and clinicians (be they professionals or students), as it provides them with opportunities to work toward the integration of science and practice and, in doing so, be involved in the generation of clinically useful knowledge. Clinicians who have been actively involved in the design of a study have valued the learning (e.g., in terms of research methodology), as well as the sense of professional validation they received by being engaged in a collaborative investigation of things they do in therapy. In the PPA-PRN, some therapists appear to have gained credibility in the eyes of clients by informing them of their participation in research. Further, such meaningful experience has been shared by some clients who have reported being proud of contributing to projects that might lead to a better understanding and effectiveness of psychotherapy (Castonguay, Nelson et al., 2010).

At a more concrete level, the actual implementation of a research protocol can be beneficial to practitioners if it has the potential of leading to immediately useful information. An example of such clinically actionable information is the feedback about helpful and hindering events that therapist obtained from clients at the end of each session during the second PPA-PRN study. Without imposing any drastic change in the therapist practice (e.g., retraining in a new theoretical orientation), this type of feedback may have offered opportunities for therapists to be more attuned to their clients' needs, thus seamlessly confounding research tasks and clinical goals. Similarly, at EBPI training studies support practitioners as they learn to use evidence-based treatment procedures and because clients' process and session-by-session outcomes are tracked, practitioners can see immediately the clinical impact of the new interventions.

The implementation of research in clinical routine can also be clinically beneficial to clients. Asked to identify helpful and hindering events, for example, appeared to have given clients a chance to take a distance from, and process what took place during session. For some clients, writing down significant events seemed to make it easier for them to provide honest feedback to their therapist, as compared to verbally expressing their experience during the session. Within the context of the same study, the use of the TOP was also beneficial—as it allows for some clients (and therapists) to become more aware of their improvement, and thus more appreciative of their work. At EBPI, we have found that the training research on evidence-based practices has the effect of increasing clients' access to effective treatment because many practitioners have never had an opportunity to learn or the support needed to acquire the skills of newer evidence-based therapies.

A number of other tangible benefits can be gained by clinicians out of conducting research as part of their practice. Some of these benefits may not be crucial for their professional survival but can nevertheless be highly validating and gratifying. In the

PPA-PRN, for example, all participating therapists gained authorship on two papers that resulted from the second study. In addition, a number of these therapists were invited to present at conferences and/or publish their own paper (e.g., Hemmelstein, 2012) based on their experience as a clinician/researcher. Some therapists of the PPA-PRN have also been asked to serve on a university committee aimed at evaluating the clinical relevance and feasibility of research project conducted in another PRN initiative (see Castonguay et al., 2014). If they decide to do so, clinicians involved in research may also use their own outcome data for quality control, as well as for marketing or improved reimbursement of their services (see Adelman, Castonguay, Kraus, & Zack, 2014; Koons, O'Rourke, Carter, & Erhardt, 2013).

Above and beyond the individual benefits that can be earned from engagement in clinically relevant research, practice-oriented studies (conducted with researchers or only among clinicians) can provide clinicians with rich and gratifying experiences that are frequently associated with working groups. The participation in a common project and the communication that takes place during and between meetings (with known and new colleagues) can bring support, validation, and reinforcements, as well as intellectual and professional stimulation generated by exchanges of ideas and experiences. As described by one of the full-time practitioners in the PPA-PRN (Hemmelstein, 2012), such interpersonal dividends are well worth pay-offs for the costs (in terms of time, attention, efforts, and anxiety) incurred by the participation in practice-oriented research. Referring to his own experience, he highlighted the pleasure and validation he derived from "thinking out loud" with a researcher, his students and other clinicians, as well as from witnessing the progress that was taking place as the group was building an ambitious study. Most of all, however, he emphasized the self-reinforcement of the actual PRN meetings—the laughter, learning, and affection that emerged from them. As he evocatively puts it:

> I was glad to be there not for what it would get me in the future (more knowledge regarding Practice Research, the process of therapy, my own process). I was there because it was good being there. The icing on the cake was all that knowledge I received from the study. The "cake" was in the doing. (p. 7)

The same beneficial group processes can be experienced by researchers when they are collaborating with clinicians. For both authors of this paper, it has been an absolute privilege to have the opportunity to work with smart, devoted, competent individuals interested in the same phenomena, but approaching with different perspectives and sets of expertise. For Castonguay, in addition to making him a better psychotherapy researcher (more appreciative, among other things, of the crucial emphasis that should be put on relevance and feasibility in clinical research), such opportunity also provided him with a humbling corrective experience. For many years, he had the impression that many clinicians were resistant toward research. This impression derived from signs of reluctance that he observed when he asked practitioners to complete questionnaires for his research program. Such "resistance," however, appeared to be absent when he began working collaboratively with other clinicians in designing joint research projects. Rather than trying to convince his colleagues to use questionnaires as part of their practice, he mostly had to restrain their desire to increase the number of tasks they were willing to do as part of the research protocol. As noted elsewhere, this contrasting experience led him to conclude that:

> building a strong alliance between researchers and therapists, fostering a sense of shared ownership in the project, and being sensitive to the therapists' needs are likely to ameliorate therapists' assumed resistance to research, as well as provide antidotes to any attitude of empirical imperialism. (Castonguay, Nelson et al., 2010, p. 354)

For Koerner, the inspiration and camaraderie of shared projects that make it easier for practitioners to measure process and outcome as part of routine clinical care, has transformed what could be a dreaded research process into a lively communal activity of making "warm data"—information that is digestible, trustworthy, and actionable. When practitioners, trainers, and researchers reside in the same participatory network, there is no research-practice gap.

Conclusion and Recommendations for Future Studies in Partnership with Clinicians

The goal of this paper was to share our experience in conducting research in private practice, with the hope of providing helpful guidelines for others who might be interested pursuing this type of integration of science and practice. Part of our mutual interest in writing this paper together is that we, the first and second author, have followed different roads in conducting such research, either by serving as the lead clinician in getting different groups of practitioners engaged in a large number of practice-based studies, or as an academician joining a network of researchers and clinicians designing and implementing together a smaller number of empirical projects. We initially assumed that having followed different pathways of partnerships with clinicians we would have learned different lessons, thus broadening what we could learn from each other and share in this paper. Interestingly, despite our distinctive approaches and the fairly different types of investigations we have engaged in (e.g., studies aimed at learning, using, and monitoring evidence-based treatments, single case experimental studies, process-outcome outcome studies), what we mostly discovered is how convergent and complementary our experience has been in terms of the obstacles (and ways to deal with them) and benefits that come with conducting research within clinical practice. Perhaps this is not surprising considering that our respective research efforts share some of the most important characteristics of practice-oriented research (Castonguay et al., 2013), such as allowing clinicians to actively participate in research within their own clinical routine (rather than following predetermined procedures derived from and applied in controlled settings); providing clinicians with actionable information (e.g., in terms of learning treatment manuals or using specific type of feedback); examining questions directly related to clinicians interests and concerns (rather than investigating hypotheses tied to the research program of an academicians); and permitting practitioners to contribute to, and shape the empirical base of knowledge about mental health practice (by publishing and presenting at conferences studies that they have designed and/or participated in; which, hopefully, will in turn be recognized in by academicians and policy-makers).

As a way to complement the specific lessons that we mentioned above, we would like to end this paper by offering more general recommendations that may foster research in clinical practice. First and perhaps more importantly, clinicians should not feel that they have to wait for researchers to approach them before conducting scientifically rigorous and clinically relevant research in their own work environment. This is a conclusion that one can safely derive from the work of the first author of this paper, as well as from the research that been described in other papers of this series (Adelman et al., 2014; Fernández-Álvarez et al., 2014). As previously described, while working with researchers has advantages (in terms of increasing complementary expertise, perspectives, and resources), it also comes with costs and challenges (see also Adelman et al., 2014). Practitioners interested in conducting research with academicians must therefore be careful in choosing who to collaborate with and the agreement that is reached in terms of how (task and process wise) to work together.

In order to maximize the opportunity for clinicians to take part in research, we would also recommend that different types of engagement be offered.

While the first author of this paper, as well as the clinicians involved in the PPA-PRN have been contributing to all aspects of the studies they joined in (design, implementation, analyses, and dissemination), other clinicians might decide, based on their own interest and available time, to participate only in data collection. From our standpoint, if this data collection can be integrated in their clinical routine, address some concerns of interest, and provide knowledge that can improve therapy, such participation is a great way to contribute to the advance of knowledge and the actualization of the scientific-practitioner model.

Although research in clinical practice (as any type of practice-oriented research) can and should contribute to building a robust empirical knowledge about psychotherapy, it should also be recognized that they are limitations facing this type (like any type) of research (Castonguay et al., 2013). For example, observer based and blind assessment of psychopathology (before, during, and after therapy) is not fitting, ethically and pragmatically, with the conduct of therapy within private practice. Moreover, fidelity assessments of therapist's ability to carry out a particular type of treatment or a specific set of therapeutic procedures does not always map well to therapists' workflow. While therapist (and client) reports of interventions have been used in one of the studies in the PPA-PRN mentioned above (as well as in other practice-oriented settings, see Castonguay et al., 2014), observer coding of psychotherapy sessions would be a more optimal way to verify, for instance, that a particular form of therapy was delivered as intended (Castonguay et al., 2013). Such fidelity coding is an expensive and time-consuming step within well-funded clinical trials research. Translating this research procedure to low-budget practice-oriented research involves all manner of extra hassle from creating procedures in one's practice to routinely consenting clients to recording, to figuring out how to use a video recorder and how to upload video, to overcoming one's own reticence to have work reviewed. Even highly motivated therapists may take weeks to solve the technical glitches of recording sessions given their brief windows of availability for research tasks. At EBPI, we have begun incorporating some elements of fidelity assessment into training studies so that therapists can self-assess and solicit peer assessments, but it remains to be seen how such efforts can be made most feasible and when the effort is worth the costs.

One way of considering these limitations is to recognize that the benefits of external validity in practice-oriented research can come with costs of internal validity. On the other hand, as illustrated in some of the studies described above, some features of internal validity that one might assume to be found only in controlled settings can be implemented in clinical practice. For example, procedures associated with rigorous research such as randomization of clients to treatment condition and the completion of multiple research measures at multiple time points, were adopted in studies conducted in both EBPI and PPA-PRN. Furthermore, Ann Garland and her colleagues have shown that with the necessary funding, adequate support, and an active collaboration between researchers and clinicians, videotaping and observer rating of sessions conducted in community centers is possible (see Garland & Brookman-Frazee, 2014).

To foster the growth, in terms of quantity and quality, of research in clinical practice, we would thus recommend that we, clinicians and researchers, avoid the trap of false dichotomies. It could be argued that one of the strengths of practice-oriented studies is that they tend to be high on a continuum of external validity, and that a forte of studies conducted in controlled settings is that they are built with the aim of reaching high level on a continuum of internal validity. However, it is not the case that a specific type of research, such as a randomized trial, can be done only in one particular environment, and that only one kind of research environment can provide safeguards for a specific type of validity (for flaws of internal validity of comparative outcome trials, see Borkovec & Castonguay, 1998; Castonguay, 2013). Notwithstanding the limitations of practice-oriented research, a more nuanced (and empowering) alternative to such dichotomies is that clinicians should be given the choice of how much emphasis they want to give to making their study as internally valid as possible (Castonguay in Lampropoulos et al., 2002). While increasing the internal validity of a research protocol might improve the likelihood of publishing in a high-level peer-reviewed journal, it may also add contingencies to deal with, as well as effort, time, and resources needed to implement it. Ideally, the decision of each practitioner should be a matter of cost–benefit analysis: Should I design and/or participate in a study that address all threats of validity that I can conceive, or should I sacrifice some level of scientific rigor for a more feasible and still informative project?

It may well be, however, that in conducting research in clinical practice the process is at least as important as the outcome. As noted elsewhere (Castonguay, 2013), researchers collaborating with clinicians need to remember that these colleagues do not live in the "publish or perish" world and are likely to be motivated by other incentives than the realization and publication of the best possible study.

Writing on behalf of his clinical colleagues in the PPA-PRN, Hemmelstein (2012) captured one such sources of motivation: "The returns derived from the work we have done so far pertain more to learning about HOW to do this type of research than answering the questions asked in the particular study" (p. 6). Consistent with some of the therapists' view of research obstacles as a source of intellectual stimulation, this adaptive attitude should guide those willing to partner in future naturalistic investigations. Thus, as our last recommendation, we suggest practice-oriented research, perhaps more than any other type of research, should parallel therapy not only in terms of content but also in terms of process: We should always strive to improve what we do, but as clinicians and researchers (as well as for our clients), we should never lose sight of the importance of learning.

References

Adelman, R., Castonguay, L. G., Kraus, D. R., & Zack, S. (2014). Conducting research in residential treatment centers. *Psychotherapy Research.* doi:10.1080/10503307.2014.935520

Barlow, D. H., Nock, M., & Hersen, M. (2008). *Single case research designs: Strategies for studying behavior change.* New York: Allyn and Bacon.

Bickman, L. (2008). A measurement feedback system (MFS) is necessary to improve mental health outcomes. *Journal of the American Academy of Child and Adolescent Psychiatry, 47*(10), 1114–1119.

Borkovec, T. D., & Castonguay, L. G. (1998). What is the scientific meaning of "Empirically Supported Therapy"? *Journal of Consulting and Clinical Psychology, 66*(1), 136–142. doi:10.1037/0022-006X.66.1.136

Borkovec, T. D., Echemendia, R. J., Ragusea, S. A., & Ruiz, M. (2001). The Pennsylvania practice research network and future possibilities for clinically meaningful and scientifically rigorous psychotherapy research. *Clinical Psychology: Science and Practice, 8*(2), 155–167. doi:10.1093/clipsy.8.2.155

Boswell, J. F., Kraus, D. R., Miller, S. D., & Lambert, M. J. (2014). Implementing routine outcome monitoring in clinical practice: Benefits, challenges, and solutions. *Psychotherapy Research.* doi:10.1080/10503307.2013.817696

Castonguay, L. G. (2011). Psychotherapy, psychopathology, research and practice: Pathways of connections and integration. *Psychotherapy Research, 21*(2), 125–140. doi:10.1080/1050330 7.2011.563250

Castonguay, L. G. (2013). Psychotherapy outcome: A problem worth re-revisiting 50 years later. *Psychotherapy: Theory, Research, Practice, and Training, 50,* 52–67. doi:10.1037/a0030898

Castonguay, L. G., Barkham, M., Lutz, W., & McAleavey, A. A. (2013). Practice-oriented research: Approaches and application. In M. J. Lambert (Ed.). *Bergin and Garfield's Handbook of psychotherapy and behavior change* (4th ed., pp. 85–133). New York: Wiley.

Castonguay, L. G., Boswell, J. F., Constantino, M. J., Goldfried, M. R., & Hill, C. E. (2010a). Training Implications of harmful effects of psychological treatments. *American Psychologist, 65*(1), 34–49. doi:10.1037/a0017330

Castonguay, L. G., Boswell, J. F., Zack, S., Baker, S., Boutselis, M., Chiswick, N., … Grosse Holtforth, M. (2010b). Helpful and hindering events in psychotherapy: A practice research network study. *Psychotherapy: Theory, Research, Practice, and Training, 47,* 327–344. doi:10.1037/a0021164

Castonguay, L., Nelson, D., Boutselis, M., Chiswick, N., Damer, D., Hemmelstein, N., … Borkovec, T. (2010). Clinicians and/ or researchers? A qualitative analysis of therapists' experiences in a practice research network. *Psychotherapy: Theory, Research, Practice, and Training, 47,* 345–354. doi:10.1037/a0021165

Castonguay, L. G., Pincus, A. L., & McAleavey, A. A. (2014). Practice-research networks in training clinics: Building an infrastructure to foster early attachment to the scientific-practitioner model. *Psychotherapy Research.* doi:10.1080/1050 3307.2013.856045

Ericsson, A. K. (2008). Deliberate practice and acquisition of expert performance: A general overview. *Academic Emergency Medicine, 15,* 988–994. doi:10.1111/j.1553-2712.2008.00227.x

Fairburn, C. G., & Cooper, Z. (2011). Therapist competence, therapy quality, and therapist training *Behaviour Research and Therapy, 49,* 373 378. doi:10.1016/j.brat.2011.03.005

Fernández-Álvarez, H., Gómez, B., & García, F. (2014). Bridging the gap between research and practice in a clinical and training network. *Psychotherapy Research.* doi:10.1080/10503307.2013. 856047

Garland, A. F., & Brookman-Frazee, L. (2014). Therapists and researchers: Advancing collaboration. *Psychotherapy Research.* doi:10.1080/10503307.2013.838655

Greenberg, L. S., & Dompierre, L. M. (1981). Specific effects of Gestalt two-chair dialogue on intrapsychic conflict in counseling. *Journal of Counseling Psychology, 28,* 288–294. doi:10.1037/ 0022-0167.28.4.288

Greenberg, L. S., & Higgins, H. M. (1980). Effects of two-chair dialogue and focusing on conflict resolution. *Journal of Counseling Psychology, 27,* 221–224. doi:10.1037/0022-0167.27.3.221

Hemmelstein, N. A. (2012). Scientist-practitioner networks from the practitioner's point of view. International Federation for Psychotherapy Newsletter, January 2012, 6–7.

Kanter, J. W., Tsai, M., Holman, G., & Koerner, K. (2013). Preliminary data from a randomized pilot study of web-based functional analytic psychotherapy therapist training. *Psychotherapy, 50,* 248–255. doi:10.1037/a0029814

Kazdin, A. E., & Blase, S. L. (2011). Rebooting psychotherapy research and practice to reduce the burden of mental illness. *Perspectives on Psychological Science, 6*(1), 21–37. doi:10.1177/ 1745691610393527

Knaup, C., Koesters, M., Schoefer, D., Becker, T., & Puschner, B. (2009). Effect of feedback of treatment outcome in specialist mental healthcare: Meta-analysis. *The British Journal of Psychiatry, 195*(1), 15–22. doi:10.1192/bjp.bp.108.053967

Koerner, K. (2013). What must you know and do to get good outcomes with DBT? *Behavior Therapy, 44,* 568–579. doi:10. 1016/j.beth.2013.03.005

Kolden, G. G. (1991). The generic model of psychotherapy: An empirical investigation of patterns of process and outcome relationships. *Psychotherapy Research, 1*(1), 62–73. doi:10.1080/ 10503309112331334071

Koons, C. R., O'Rourke, B., Carter, B., & Erhardt, E. B. (2013). Negotiating for improved reimbursement for dialectical behavior therapy: A successful project. *Cognitive and Behavioral Practice, 20,* 314–324. doi:10.1016/j.cbpra.2013.01.003

Kraus, D. R., Seligman, D. A., & Jordan, J. R. (2005). Validation of a behavioral health treatment outcome and assessment tool designed for naturalistic settings: The treatment outcome package. *Journal of Clinical Psychology, 61,* 285–314. doi:10. 1002/jclp.20084

Krug, S. (2006). *Don't make me think! A common sense approach to web usability* (2nd ed.). Berkeley, CA: New Riders.

Lampropoulos, G. K., Goldfried, M. R., Castonguay, L. G., Lambert, M. J., Stiles, W. B., & Nestoros, J. N. (2002). What kind of research can we realistically expect from the practitioner? *Journal of Clinical Psychology, 58,* 1241–1264. doi:10. 1002/jclp.10109

Llewelyn, S. P. (1988). Psychological therapy as viewed by clients and therapists. *British Journal of Clinical Psychology, 27,* 223–237. doi:10.1111/j.2044-8260.1988.tb00779.x

Lovibond, S. H., & Lovibond, P. F. (1995). *Manual for the depression anxiety stress scales* (2nd ed.). Sydney: Psychology Foundation of Australia.

McAleavey, A. A., Lockard, A. J., Castonguay, L. G., Hayes, J. A., & Locke, B. F. (2014). Building a practice research network: Obstacles faced and lessons learned at the Center for Collegiate Mental Health. *Psychotherapy Research.* doi:10. 1080/10503307.2014.883652

McCarthy, K. S., & Barber, J. P. (2009). The multitheoretical list of therapeutic interventions (MULTI): Initial report. *Psychotherapy Research, 19*(1), 96 113. doi:10.1080/10503300802524343

Minkler, M., & Wallerstein, N. (Eds.). (2010). Community-based participatory research for health: From process to outcomes. Wiley. com. (MULTI): Initial report. *Psychotherapy Research, 19,* 96–113.

Newnham, E. A., & Page, A. C. (2010). Bridging the gap between best evidence and best practice in mental health. *Clinical Psychology Review, 30*(1), 127–142.

Osborne, T. L. (2011, November). *Development of an institutional review board (IRB) for practice-based research.* Presentation part of a symposium entitled "Practice-based research: How to conduct meaningful research in clinical practice." Association for Behavior and Cognitive Therapies Annual Convention, Toronto, Canada.

Persons, J. B., Koerner, K., Eidelman, P., Thomas, C., Liu, H., & Netland, E. P. (2014). *We trained psychotherapists to adopt the evidence-based practice of progress monitoring 26th APS annual convention,* May 22–25, San Francisco, CA.

Puspitasari, A., Kanter, J. W., Murphy, J., Crowe, A., & Koerner, K. (2013). Developing an online, modular, active learning training program for behavioral activation. *Psychotherapy, 50,* 256–265. doi:10.1037/a0030058

Rakovshik, S. G., & McManus, F. (2010). Establishing evidence-based training in cognitive-behavioral therapy: A review of current empirical findings and theoretical guidance. *Clinical Psychology, 30,* 496–516.

Reese, R. J., Norsworthy, L. A., & Rowlands, S. R. (2009). Does a continuous feedback system improve psychotherapy outcome? *Psychotherapy: Theory, Research, Practice, Training, 46,* 418. doi:10.1037/a0017901

Shahar, B., Carlin, E. R., Engle, D. E., Hegde, J., Szepsenwol, O., & Arkowitz, H. (2012). A pilot investigation of emotion-focused two-chair dialogue intervention for self-criticism. *Clinical Psychology & Psychotherapy, 19,* 496–507. doi:10.1002/cpp.762

Tsai, M., Kohlenberg, R. J., & Kanter, J. (2010). A functional analytic psychotherapy approach to therapeutic alliance. In C. Muran & J. Barber (Eds.), *The therapeutic alliance: An evidence-based approach to practice and training* (pp. 172–190). New York, NY: Guilford Press.

Wells, K., Miranda, J., Bruce, M. L., Alegria, M., & Wallerstein, N. (2004). Bridging community intervention and mental health services research. *American Journal of Psychiatry, 161*(6), 955–963.

Westfall, J. M., Fagnan, L. J., Handley, M., Salsberg, J., McGinnis, P., Zittleman, L. K., & Macaulay, A. C. (2009). Practice-based research is community engagement. *The Journal of the American Board of Family Medicine, 22,* 423–427. doi:10.3122/jabfm.2009.04.090105

Youn, S. J., Kraus, D. R., & Castonguay, L. G. (2012). Treatment outcome package: Facilitating practice and clinically relevant research. *Psychotherapy: Theory, Research, Practice, and Training. 49,* 115–122. doi:10.1037/a0027932

METHOD PAPER

Bridging the gap between research and practice in a clinical and training network: Aigle's Program

HÉCTOR FERNÁNDEZ-ALVAREZ, BEATRIZ GÓMEZ, & FERNANDO GARCÍA

Aiglé Foundation, Buenos Aires, Argentina

Abstract

The aim of this article is to share our experience at the Aiglé Foundation in fostering research that can conducted by (or in collaboration with) clinicians within a specific type of naturalistic setting—one that not only provides psychological services but also trains psychotherapists. After presenting the structure of Aiglé and the implementation of its scientific-practitioner philosophy, we describe some of the research that has been conducted with our network of clinicians and the benefits of connecting clinical practice and academic work. We then discuss some of the obstacles that we have encountered in conducting such studies, as well as a number of strategies that we adopted in attempting to address these challenges. We end this article by briefly describing the current state of our practice-research network, and by offering some recommendations to facilitate the conduct of research by and for clinicians.

Thirty-five years ago, Argentina was living under very difficult circumstances. It was within an extremely harsh political context that the Aiglé Foundation (Aiglé meaning the everlasting flame in ancient Greek) was founded, with the purpose of working in the mental health field and creating initiatives that would promote improvement in the quality of life. It was created as a non-governmental organization (NGO) aimed at providing an environment of freedom and tolerance in order to practice and teach psychotherapy, as well as to foster the discussion of ideas. Reflecting social values of inclusiveness, acceptance, and collaboration, the organization operates as a cooperative that has progressively been built on a network of therapists throughout the entire country, as well as several other countries in Latin America and, most recently, in Europe. At this point in time, more than 1500 therapists constitute the network. Some of them work in private clinical practice whereas others work in the public arena, although not all of them provide data for research purposes. In addition, this network is complemented by a wide range of collaborations with state and private universities, as well as public and private clinics specializing in addictions, serious developmental disorders, and psychosis, as well as cancer and cardiovascular illnesses, among others.

From the beginning, professionals who join our network are made aware of and are committed to the fact that daily work involves both patient care and ongoing research projects. This dual aspect of the functioning is reflected both in the therapist training program as well as in research and development projects. There are three main reasons for the adoption of this approach:

(1) Psychotherapy is an applied discipline, a practice that fuses principles of art and science (Hofmann & Weinberger, 2007). What we look for from a therapist is that she/he be an expert in applying procedures that help improve the quality of life of the patient, rather than a refined theorist who describes and analyzes dysfunctional processes. Moreover, a good therapist is one who can operate in specific situations (construct a therapeutic alliance,

resolve critical episodes, handle unexpected phenomena), rather than describe clinical facts with the precision of an outstanding psychopathologist or explain them with the erudition of an academician.

But at the same time, clinical practice stands on solid and reliable grounds when it does not rely only on the skill of the therapist. Practice is most likely to be effective if based on a theoretical and conceptual framework. A good link between theory, research, and practice, between models and therapeutic skills, is likely to be the best approach to optimize our interventions.

(2) Psychotherapy is efficient. A substantial amount of empirical data is now available to support this assertion (Chambless & Ollendick, 2001; Lambert & Ogles, 2004; Nathan & Gorman, 2007). Various approaches and specific procedures make it possible to alleviate symptoms, resolve problems, reduce conflictual situations, and help a person live a more meaningful and purposeful life. Although we do not yet have robust data in this regard, an integrative attitude may also help improve the strength of these interventions.

Nevertheless, the efficacy and effectiveness of psychotherapy are relative. Nowadays we have clear evidence of its limitations and associated negative effects (Barlow, 2010; Dimidjian & Hollon, 2011; Lampropoulos, 2011). A significant number of patients show early dropouts, as well as relapse and recurrence of distressing symptoms. There are also numerous clients who fail to show significant change and an appreciable percent of cases in which iatrogenic effects occur. Sound psychological research may well be able to provide us with helpful guidance to improve our therapeutic interventions.

(3) Training is a fundamental tool in acquiring and enhancing the skills of therapists. This is primarily achieved through ongoing education, such as being updated about research results, increasing our knowledge of theoretical-technical contributions, and participating in activities that encourage cultural diversity. Interestingly, participating in training programs for novice therapists as well as supervising these therapists in varied clinical contexts also strengthens the skills sets of more experienced therapists. Teaching and training are the most powerful tools for remaining updated, because they demand contact with new developments and improving training methodology in the communication of knowledge.

Although the clinical benefits of joint training and research seem obvious, such combination of knowledge and action does not always occur. In fact, disconnection between clinicians and researchers is frequent and can negatively impact training programs. This dichotomy is particularly evident in the most developed countries, where resource policies encourage exclusive dedication to either research or clinical practice, creating a gap between these areas. In Latin America, therapists tend to see themselves as suffering less from such dichotomization of the field, because they are more likely to combine their clinical practice with their academic work, mainly as teachers and sometimes as researchers.

Years ago Paul Wachtel, one of the pioneers of psychotherapy integration, wrote a book entitled *Poverty of Affluence* (Wachtel, 1989), in which he discussed some of the weak points of developed societies. In counterpoint, we can mention the "Wealth of shortage" to describe the current potential of societies like ours, where the scarcity of resources for research is a strong motivation to develop friendly programs with high translational value. These principles have been adopted by the world academic community as a basic requirement of psychological research.

The development of clinically relevant research in Latin America can be seen throughout a multitude of excellent examples in Argentina, Brazil, Colombia, Chile, and Uruguay. Among the most active groups are the Psychotherapy and Change program in Santiago, Chile (coordinated by Mariane Krause) and the Research Team in Clinical Psychology in Buenos Aires (coordinated by Andrés Roussos). The work of these groups has grown significantly in recent years, giving rise to an important number of publications. One of the "raisons d'etre" of Aiglé has been to contribute to such research efforts by cultivating therapists engagement in studies that can be conducted during, as well as inform, clinical activities.

The goal of this paper is to share our experience in fostering research that can conducted by (or in collaboration with) clinicians within a specific type of naturalistic setting—one that not only provides psychological services but also trains psychotherapists. After presenting the structure of Aiglé and the implementation of its scientific-practitioner philosophy, we describe some of the research that has been conducted within, or in collaboration with, our network of clinicians. We propose the benefits that the integration of research within clinical practice has provided for our network of therapists and supervisors. We then discuss some of the obstacles that we have encountered in conducting such studies, as well as a number of strategies that we adopted in attempting to address these challenges. Finally, we end this paper by briefly depicting the current state of our practice-research network, and by offering some recommendations to facilitate the conduct of research by and for clinicians.

Structure and Functioning of Aiglé

The Aiglé Foundation is dedicated to training and research activities. It has developed both a psychotherapy program for the general population and a community program directed to low-income populations. In terms of clinical work, the institution receives requests for consultations from individuals from both Buenos Aires and the country at large. An intake process and psychological assessment are followed by a referral to professionals who are part of a network of specialists, psychologists and psychiatrists as well as others (social workers, nutritionists, etc.). These trained professionals maintain continuing education, keep clinical records, and engage in systematic supervision. Patients living in cities outside Buenos Aires may receive their treatment by travelling regularly, by Skype or by being referred to a professional in their home city who has received full training in Aiglé. An extended network of professionals covers cities in 21 of the 23 provinces of Argentina.

Annually, Aiglé trains 500 students from Argentina and abroad. Education and training are conducted jointly with public and private universities in Argentina. Training is delivered in person or by distance learning in Buenos Aires as well as in eight other cities. Local groups in these other cities are composed of younger professionals sharing the same goal of linking clinical and academic work. They represent the foundation for training purposes and faculty members of Aiglé have traveled regularly since 1998 to give classes in these cities. Four of these groups are affiliate centers of the foundation. They share the integrative model (see below) that has guided the development of our organization and participate in research projects.

The foundation is self-supported, receiving no external funding. Affiliate centers abroad, in Guatemala and Spain, are independent and self-supported as well. Professionals at these centers follow the integrative philosophy about research, training, and practice that characterizes Aiglé, as well as the integrative psychotherapy approach.

Given the nature of the institution, the incoming demand is highly diversified. An integrative model was developed to provide a common basis and at the same time a tailored treatment, to meet the needs of the particular clinical situations. This contributes to the ductility and efficiency of the applications. The integrative model examines clinical problems in the light of two main axes: A vertical (or synchronic) one involving development and personal history and a horizontal (or diachronic) one involving the individual-context interaction. It takes into account the necessary conceptual elements of the current most

relevant psychotherapy approaches, for each clinical situation (for a detailed description of this integrative model, see Fernández-Álvarez, 1992, 2008). This model not only offers a conceptual framework for clinical practice and training, it provides guidelines for research conducted by members of our networks and their collaborators. It is also constantly modified based on new findings, theoretical advances, and clinical observations.

As part of a need to be connected to the world, Aiglé established links from the very beginning with international scholars, which have given way to numerous professional relationships. Since 1981, over 100 academicians from all over the world have been invited to give seminars and make presentations in order to share developments in the field of psychotherapy. Established exchange programs for graduate students also exist with international institutions, from the USA and Spain. Psychologists and psychiatrists from Argentina, Chile, Colombia, Ecuador, Spain, the United States, Guatemala, Italy, Uruguay, and Venezuela annually engage in professional rotations and internships with Aiglé. In Ecuador, Guatemala, Panamá, Spain, and Uruguay, Aiglé is engaged in training and education programs for which faculty members of the staff of Aiglé travel regularly.

Aiglé also conducts research in collaboration with other academic centers. Research projects initiated at the foundation were developed in collaboration with universities in Argentina and Spain, and extended to collaborations with institutions in a number of countries around the world, which also receive students engaged in doctoral programs. Aiglé also takes part of multi-site research programs.

Moreover, Aiglé has been devoted to disseminating empirical findings. For 20 years now, it has edited the Revista Argentina de Clínica Psicológica. Indexed and/or abstracted in international databases, this quarterly journal publishes psychotherapy research conducted by scholars from Latin American and other parts of the world.

How Have We Implemented Our Philosophy?

Initially, we developed a clinical register system in order to create a database of patient information that would permit the analysis of treatment outcome, obtained at the end of therapy and post-treatment follow-up. We created an Admission Form whose items were based on our integrative model, and then adjusted and modified in line with the information gathered from our patients. The Admission Form is compatible with other common register systems, making it easy to convert when we participate in multicenter studies.

The system made the direct repository of sessions a priority, first with voice recordings and later through video recordings. Video tapes have been used systematically for over 10 years and are included as a regular resource in all our intake processes. In order to tape our sessions, we seek informed consent, to which 90% of our patients have responded positively. In addition, the entire sessions of brief treatments are taped and, in some cases, long-term treatments are video-recorded as well. The data use conforms to maximum security coding processes according to international ethical standards, to ensure the best scientific use and confidentiality protection. The ethical problems that may arise are duly discussed by Roussos, Braun, and Olivera (2012). This material, duly processed, is of enormous importance for the development of clinical, training, and research activities, as well as part of exchange projects for various research programs, such as the group led by Andrés Roussos.

Research Programs

Preliminary Stage

The early years were aimed at assembling a research team. At that time, research experience in our country (and the region) was very scarce and it was necessary to promote cultural development in this regard. For several years, as mentioned above, we dedicated ourselves to working on creating a records system (Admission Form), which was completed in 1987. At the same time, bearing in mind the huge importance of evaluation for both clinical decisions and research, we concentrated on studies aimed at the adaptation of psychological tests, as well as the construction of new instruments. These studies helped us develop and refine skills in research methodologies, as well as in the recruitment of participant samples and the examination of instruments properties. One of the most representative studies of this time period was the translation of the Wechsler-Bellevue intelligence scale (Fernández-Álvarez, 1988) into Spanish. This stage also included work with cross-cultural variables that led to the first graduate degree on the subject at the University of Buenos Aires (UBA).

The evaluation and creation of psychological instruments remained a consistent part of our research program for several years. Two important examples were the studies carried out on the Inventory of Interpersonal Problems in clinical settings (Maristany, 2008) and the construction of an instrument to study hypochondria. IPHA (Aiglé's Hypochondria Inventory; Belloch, Fernández-Álvarez, & Castañeiras, 2004) is an instrument designed to provide a dimensional evaluation of hypochondria on five factors: panic-fear of the disease, hypochondria awareness, exaggerated body attention and surveillance, health concerns, and mistrust of the doctor. The instrument revealed excellent psychometric properties and is available for use in both research and clinical settings, being especially useful due to the limited amount of psychological tests in that area.

Second Stage

In subsequent years, the research program developed along two complementary lines of studies: First on the operational and functional properties of psychotherapy and, second, on therapeutic interventions. The general idea behind this program was to advance in a two-fold manner, simultaneously investigating issues related to structure and applications, in order to provide evidence for and facilitate critical reflection on the global phenomenon of psychotherapy.

Research on the Operational and Functional Properties of the Psychotherapy Setting

We have pursued two lines of work in this area. The first (1987–1998) was focused on a study of the "Social Representation of Psychotherapy" (SPR). The second (1999–present), which has led to the most substantial development of our research program, is aimed at exploring the Personal Style of the Therapist (PST).

Social Representation of Psychotherapy

The project studied societal beliefs surrounding psychotherapy. As discussed by Orlinsky and Howard (1986), cultural beliefs and value orientations of the community are part of the events constituting, influencing, and influenced by psychotherapy. It was very useful for us to know the orientation and distribution of the demand in our population, in order to direct the resources according to the demand requirements. We constructed a survey composed of 21 items that showed adequate psychometric qualities in a pilot sample. The repertoire of items explored the following issues: (i) what is the nature of psychotherapy? (ii) how long does it take? (iii) how useful is it? (iv) how can its results be observed? (v) what professionals are qualified to practice it? and (vi) what is the level of psychotherapy utilized by those surveyed and their acquaintances?

Studies with this instrument were conducted under the assumption that exploring the social representation of psychotherapy in our population in general would likely provide very useful information for fine-tuning intervention designs, given the high cultural sensitivity to psychotherapy. The findings were collected in several publications, including a chapter in the first text published by the Latin American chapter of SPR (Fernández-Álvarez, Scherb, Bregman, & García, 1995). The results were consistent with the widespread opinion held in other countries that psychotherapy provides moderately high benefits and that the consumer satisfaction is very high. Nonetheless, we also found differences in our population in comparison with other studies (Olfson & Pincus, 1994) regarding the length and number of sessions (higher in our case) and that psychotherapy was identified to a greater extent as something which serves for personal development.

In a second phase of our research program, we investigated specific populations. We found that among physicians the trend was consistent with the general population, although this specific population defined psychotherapy as part of a comprehensive treatment and as a treatment for mental disorders associated with physical illnesses (Férnandez-Álvarez, 1999; García, Guzmán, & Castañeiras, 1999).

Personal Style of the Therapist

First phase. Over the last decade, we have concentrated our research efforts on the PST program. Our interest in PST research emerged from two sources. On one hand, the academic literature suggests that little attention has been given to its influence as a variable in the therapeutic process. On the other hand, observations in our network of clinical settings indicate that the style of each therapist weighs heavily on treatment, regardless of the expertise of therapeutic interventions.

PST is defined as the set of characteristics that each therapist brings to every session of psychotherapy and which shape his/her ways of being, intervening, and interacting with patients (Fernández-Álvarez & García, 1998). It defines a phenomenon that is relatively stable over time, that is susceptible to certain changes, and that is made up of various dimensions. We identified five of these dimensions: (i) expressive mode, (ii) level of involvement in the task, (iii) attentional mode, (iv) operational functionality, and (v) how to provide instructions.

A self-descriptive questionnaire (PST-Q) was constructed, involving 36 items representing the five dimensions above (Fernández-Álvarez, García, Lo Bianco, & Corbella Santomá, 2003). Exploratory studies revealed good psychometric properties. Confirmatory analysis with an abbreviated version indicated a good match-up with the model and confirmed the construct structure around two sets

of variables: (i) a technical factor (composed of the attentional and operational functions) and three relational factors (the instructional, expressive and involvement functions) (Castañeiras, Ledesma, García, & Fernández-Álvarez, 2008). These studies include a sample with therapists from a wide theoretical spectrum: Cognitive-behavioral, humanistic-existential, psychoanalytical, systemic, integrative, and others. The PST-Q was translated into English and Portuguese and used by various research teams in Brazil, Chile, Cuba, Ecuador, Germany, Guatemala, Portugal, Spain, and the United States, in addition to several working teams in Argentina.

The research program on PST has evolved into various projects. One of the most active was the BB project (Barcelona-Buenos Aires), which grew out of an agreement between Ramón Llull University and Aiglé, and which investigated, among other issues, the compatibility between PST and the personal profile of the patient (Corbella Santomá, 2002). Among the clinically interesting conclusions emerging from that study is that therapists who are most flexible in handling the instructional function achieve a better therapeutic alliance with their patients in the intermediate and final phases of psychotherapy. This line of research was extended to studies carried out at the University of Porto, Portugal (Carvalho, 2008).

The program generated numerous other investigations, including studies on:

(1) The interaction between PST dimensions and patient characteristics that affect therapeutic change (Malik et al., 2002);
(2) the PST of the therapists who work with severe patients (Rial, García, Castañeiras, Gómez, & Fernández-Álvarez, 2006);
(3) the modulating effect of experience and technical-theoretical orientation on PST (Castañeiras, García, Lo Bianco, & Fernández-Álvarez, 2006);
(4) the PST of therapists that work in neonatal intensive care (Vega, 2006).

Another line of work was to study the PST within the context of education and training. In one study, groups were evaluated on training in therapeutic skills in graduate courses in Buenos Aires and Barcelona. The courses last for 2 years and the PST-Q was given to those in training at the beginning of the course, halfway through, and at the end. PST was related to direction of interests, attachment style, self-efficacy expectations and personality dimensions (Corbella Santomá, Botella, Saúl, García, & Fernández-Álvarez, 2009; Corbella Santomá, Fernández-Álvarez, Saúl,

García, & Botella, 2008; García, Corbella, Saúl, Fernández-Álvarez, & Botella, 2008).

Results from a 4-year study on the personal style of experienced therapists showed strong stability in style, although not entirely constant. Technical functions (attentional and operative) were seen to be more stable than relational functions (Castañeiras, Rial, García, Farfallini, & Fernández-Álvarez, 2006). For a more detailed description of the entire program see Fernández-Álvarez et al., 2003; García & Fernández-Álvarez, 2007).

Second phase. A second phase, which is currently being pursued, of our research program on PST has focused on the concurrent validity of the construct. The first step involved developing a guide for observing the actions (interventions) performed by therapists in the course of a session. Consistent with a history of work published in our region along this line of research (Roussos, Etchebarne, & Waizmann, 2006; Roussos, Waizmann, & Etchebarne, 2010; Valdés, Tomicic, Pérez, & Krause, 2010), video-tapes of entire sessions were analyzed by experts who constructed a repertoire of actions that define the interventions. From this analysis three main interventions were identified: (i) questions, for example: "Can you tolerate this fear?" (ii) instructions, for example assigning homework and (iii) statements, for example: "You are reacting now just as you reacted when ...." From this study, the Aiglé Observation Guide of Therapists (GOTA) was created (Corbella Santomá, 2012; Fernández-Álvarez, Gómez, & Gómez et al., 2011).

GOTA was then tested with independent judges (trained therapists) who rated the interventions of a sample of patients seen by different therapists, finding high levels of reliability among judges. This has enabled the beginning of new research on PST working with therapists with different therapeutic approaches and different levels of experience.

Research on Therapeutic Interventions

Evaluation of Therapeutic Process

Two lines of work related to the evaluation of therapeutic process have been developed. The first of these focuses on the Systematic Treatment Selection (STS) (Beutler & Harwood, 2000), an integrative model aimed at prescribing optimal treatment based on the delineation of principles of change and the use of strategies adapted to specific characteristics of clients, such as coping styles, resistance, and functional deterioration. The project was carried out jointly with the Private Psychotherapy Center (CPP) in Buenos Aires, in order to cross-validate the adaptation of the model to our clinical population. The study demonstrated adequate reliability and validity of the system, and allowed for an exploration of the predictive capacity for change in brief interventions based on the client variables mentioned above. Assessments were made with two different versions (for the therapist and patient) at the start of the treatment and at every third session during the process. A team of therapists acting as observers evaluated the changes in relation to the following components: Level of therapist directivity, focus of the therapy, level of subjective distress, and dimensions of the therapeutic alliance. The findings indicated that the system offered a wealth of reliable information to formulate and evaluate the operation of highly complex treatment plans. A current activity of this research program involves the provision of clinical cases to test an abridged version of STS (Regner & Beutler, 2012).

Another line of work focuses on the OQ-45 (Lambert et al., 1996). Based on the Spanish adaptation of the OQ-45 (conducted in Chile by Von Bergen and de la Parra, 2002), the research project has also been conducted with CPP in order to gain access to a more heterogeneous population. Studies were conducted to establish the psychometric properties and compare the general population with clinical samples. This allowed identifying the cut-off score and the reliable change index for the argentine population (Fernández-Álvarez, Hirsch, Maristany, & Torrente, 2005). The good psychometric properties of the instrument led to its incorporation into routine evaluations and assessments of the therapeutic process. Monitoring teams and institutional advisory groups use it as part of everyday decision-making in weighing progress in therapeutic interventions. The simplicity of its use and its transfer to the clinical setting are an eloquent testimony to the important bonds between clinical practice and research.

In addition to the previously mentioned studies, a central component in research on the therapeutic process consists in exchanging sessions materials with other research teams (such as with the team led by Roussos et al. (2006).

Outcome Studies

We have conducted several studies within this line of research. For example, focusing on therapeutic interventions with children with bedwetting led to a fruitful line of research that evaluated responses of a large population of patients treated with individual and group interventions (García, 2006).

Another line of research that we have dedicated ourselves to in the last 6 years is the study of psychotherapy for patients with OCD. In this project we are collaborating with a team at the University of Valencia led by Amparo Belloch, which itself is part of the multicenter study of the Obsessive Compulsive Cognitions Working Group (OCCWG) headed by David Clark. The program is using a cognitive approach to test specific appraisals and beliefs that reinforce the obsessions, such as inadequate strategies present in OCD. It was administered in separate categories of individual and group therapy, which were then compared in terms of process and outcome, including the result of post-treatment follow-up (Belloch et al., 2011; Cabedo et al., 2009). A qualitative investigation was also conducted with one group of patients 1 year after treatment ended. The study examined how patients' change and explored the variables influencing such change. Specific changes were seen in symptom presentation and more general changes were found in how patients attributed their outcomes: Mainly to psycho-education, cognitive restructuring interventions and, in the specific case of patients who were treated with the group intervention, interpersonal experience (Castañeiras, Fraga Míguez, García, Fernández-Álvarez, & Belloch, 2009; Férnandez-Álvarez, García & Belloch, 2011; García, Castañeiras, Fraga Míguez, & Fernández-Álvarez, 2009).

Clinicians are involved as well in single case studies showing processes and outcomes of OCD treatments (Behobi, García, & Fernández-Álvarez, 2013).

Benefits

The integration of research within clinical practice has provided a number of benefits for our network of therapists and supervisors. These can be grouped in two categories: Direct-immediate and indirect-mediate.

With regard to direct benefits, our registration system, through notes, audio or video tape as well as assessment instruments, helps collect information and make decisions on outcome evaluation. Registration facilitates the detection of difficulties in the therapeutic process and provides an appropriate assessment, which can serve as a warning sign for therapists and supervisors. For example it may lead to the addition of an interpersonal or family therapy component when results are less than expected for a clinical situation, such as a depressive patient. Functionally impaired patients benefit with increased treatment intensity (Beutler & Harwood, 2000). Appropriate assessment helps early detection of suicidal risk and the need to involve the patient's support network. For OCD patients with resistant compulsions, when partial treatment results are not as expected, more intensive formats are delivered and the effects are subsequently assessed. For

example it may guide the decision to turn to home-based treatment (Rosqvist et al., 2001). In cases where the level of severity decreases during treatment (e.g., balanced diet or weight in eating disorders) it guides the decision to reduce the session frequency. When difficulties are centered on the therapeutic alliance and the supervision process helps to identify characteristics of the therapist that hinder therapeutic progress, it may lead to changing the therapist. In this way, the system operates as a quality control system and at the same time provides clinical material for training purposes.

As to indirect-mediate benefits, staff therapists are able integrate research findings, clinical assistance, and training in a practical manner. For example, trainers can help trainees identify their personal style and observe its effects on patients, rather than struggle to change it beyond possibilities. The integrative model underlying our practice and training can also be updated from these findings; for example, learning that highly resistant patients respond better to nondirective interventions.

Another indirect benefit has been that this material has been the basis for joint projects with other centers and universities both in Argentina and outside the country, which promotes resources and enriching interchanges (such as the conjoint research program of the personal style of the therapist with Ramón Llull University, Spain, or the collaborative program on OCD with the University of Valencia, Spain). Integration with other research teams fosters an attitude of openness for those involved in ongoing programs. We have also found that various sources of personal and institutional growth have served as incentives for participating in research, especially within the context of significant important organizational challenges.

Obstacles and Strategies to Address Them

Despite our therapists' awareness and commitment to data collection during clinical work, as well as the benefits of research for clinical practice and teaching, we have encountered several obstacles in the implementation of our scientific-practitioner philosophy. Some of these obstacles reflect issues of motivation (and/or apprehension), whereas others appear to be related to cognitive shifts that come along with the clinicians' agreement to "wear a researcher hat." Other challenges involve organizational and personal costs. Below are some examples of these obstacles and challenges.

As described above, daily collection of clinical data requires clinicians to write up detailed progress notes via our registration system. According to their clinical specialization and institutional level of involvement different therapists are committed to participating in one or more of the given projects. However, we have observed that therapists tend to be reluctant to provide data for a number of reasons. For example, some therapists continue to rely on their memory as a fundamental tool for the therapeutic process; a strong psychoanalytic tradition in Argentina sustains this approach to clinical practice. In addition, we found that therapists often restrain themselves from describing specific aspects of the process, especially those related to their own emotional regulation. When therapists believe that these records are not very useful to themselves or their patients, they may be reluctant to provide the data requested by research teams.

The routine activity of note-taking implies a change of attitude from the clinical stance to the research one, from attention paid exclusively to the clinical task and its results to additional attention paid to its potential to be used for research data. The research results can only be seen in the long term, which means a challenge to participants' patience in order to weigh the value of these tasks.

Joint projects with other institutions have required special work in assigning responsibilities and have presented difficulties in distributing resources, including financial issues. In addition to the organizational difficulties, research in our network of practice and training also poses personal challenges since, as noted, research is conducted mainly with personal financial resources. All members who are part of the network are invited to make a voluntary contribution.

We have, over the years, adopted a number of strategies to tackle many of the obstacles we have faced. For example, in order to foster the participation of therapists and their use of the registration systems, we have organized a network of supervisory teams that promote the inclusion of therapists in regular teams with periodic rotations. We have also found that making records available and confirming their usefulness in the supervisory process significantly increases the motivation of therapists to provide detailed records of sessions.

We have also encouraged researchers to break down the barriers between themselves and clinicians. For instance, we have substituted the tactic of information requests with a policy that explicitly invites clinicians to join research projects based on the unique and meaningful value of their contributions. The breakdown of barriers has also included the implementation of regular meetings (with therapists within our network, as well as clinicians participating in our training programs) where information is shared about the progress of the programs and the results obtained. In our experience, providing such information increase clinicians' motivation to refine their observations and provide even more precise data.

Aiglé has countered the lack of external financial resources by promoting the integration of professionals within the institution, motivating them to become identified with and involved in our network, as well as to generate initiatives to increase clinical work. As the foundation functions in a cooperative way, this engagement is aimed at both institutional and personal growth. As mentioned above, this engagement can also involve the setting aside of personal (including financial) resources for research. This is possible because the philosophy of the institution is based on participation and mutual confidence, which means that the institutional needs are oriented to meet the individual's professional development. Primary incentives are the acquisition of knowledge, learning to working as a team, forming part of an institution which offers continuous education, as well as promoting in each individual his/her capacities to best utilize their experience to reach out for grants, academic positions, participation in international organizations or other professional or academic goals. Needless to say, we have learned that creative search within a system may be an alternative route to external resources which are not immediately at hand.

Similar to our relationship with other institutions and universities, the policy we have always followed has been that of favoring the maintenance of connections under mutually beneficial conditions and working to resolve possible conflicts.

Conclusion

This article presents the benefits, obstacles, and challenges that arise from an institution dedicated to clinical work and training and which at the same time develops a research program closely linked to psychotherapy practice. This endeavor was wisely depicted by Bowly (1981) in the conflicting attitudes of the researcher and the clinician.

As a way to conclude this paper, we would like to briefly state where we are (in terms of thinking about and conducting research) and then offer a few recommendations to other researchers (especially those early in their career) in terms of future directions of research.

Where Are We?

When taking a step back from our experience, one finding stands out: The importance of pursuing a research program that includes studies on the structural and operational properties of psychotherapy, as well as studies that examine the effects of therapeutic interventions. In the first case, dedicating efforts to deepen our understanding of how the style of the therapists influences their clinical work continues to be of primary value. Interest in this topic has grown in recent years as a sign of its clinical and theoretical importance. An excellent example is the study of the influence the real person of the therapist has on patients (Gelso, 2009).

Regarding research on interventions, we believe it is necessary to combine studies on processes and outcomes. Research on processes can contribute a great deal of insight into the elements that promote change, and the evaluation of outcome is of direct relevance to the concern that patients and society have about the benefits that psychotherapy can offer. At a time when the treatment of psychopathology reveals an unfavorable trend for psychotherapy as compared to pharmacotherapy (Olfson & Marcus, 2010), collaborative psychotherapy research should be conducted to further emphasize one of its benefits over psychotropics, i.e., higher stability of results over time (Castonguay, 2013).

Consistent with the need of such collaborative psychotherapy research, we are now more than ever convinced of the usefulness of being engaged in projects that contribute to multicenter research programs; not only to increase the critical mass of data, but to favor a broader and more heterogeneous perspective, as well as to obtain more valid information on cross-cultural phenomena. Reflecting our current commitment to collaborative research, we are now working with several programs, such as the Project Dilemma, developed by Feixas (University of Barcelona) and Saúl (UNED, Spain) (Feixas, Saúl, Avila-Espada, & Sánchez, 2001), which aims to study the presence or absence of implicative dilemmas (a specific type of cognitive conflict) and its evolution in our psychotherapy model. Another example is our participation in the "Smiling is Fun" primary care program for the emotionally disturbed, developed by Botella, Jaume I Castellón University, Spain (Serrano Zárate, Baños Rivera, & Botella Arbona, 2012).

Recommendations for Future Research Directions

Early in this paper, we stated that an integration of theory, practice, and research is most likely to optimize the effectiveness of psychotherapy. To achieve such an ambitious goal, we would recommend to therapists, as early as possible in their career, not only to take part in research but also to promote the formulation of research questions that contribute to closer ties with clinical practice. We believe that it

is necessary for members of research teams to establish friendly and collaborative relationships with professionals engaged in clinical services, so that these professional colleagues become more interested in research programs, in terms of both participating in studies and using the results for decision-making in their daily practice. To build these bridges we also believe that it is essential that research programs involve studies with a high transfer to application areas. Transferring research results to health care and prevention programs is imperative in this movement toward greater collaboration between research and clinical settings.

One paragraph on the special importance of methodology: There has been much advance in research methods which has helped the field to progress in attempts to understand and improve psychotherapy. Therapists should know how to use such methods and be able to identify the conditions under which they can be helpful in addressing crucial issues about therapeutic change; but they must also be careful not to become dependent on their indications. The value of the methods must be weighed carefully to avoid the false belief that the more sophisticated systems hold power that exceeds their real value. A prime example of this is the use of meta-analysis and the doubts that have arisen concerning this methodology in recent years. In spite of the undoubted advances of this methodology, it has not been free of criticism. Early on Eysenck (1994) argued that there may be a lack of conceptual analysis of the variables. As a more recent example, Lambert, Garfield, and Bergin (2004) proposed that the promise of a "totally objective review" is an unrealistic expectation, based on the large number of decisions to be made, such as inclusions and exclusions of studies for review, which effect sizes to calculate, and how effect sizes are summed.

As a final piece of advice, we would like researchers and clinicians to embrace psychotherapy as a discipline with multiple sources of knowledge and cultivate "an open mind" not only for our field but for other disciplines, such as the neurosciences and anthropology. We also emphasize the importance of "tolerance for uncertainty" and flexibility in order to make necessary changes and adaptations in research work and clinical practice, so that psychotherapy may maintain its role in aiding individuals in improving their quality of life.

Acknowledgments

We thank Leighna Harrison and Soo Jeong Youn for their help with the English version.

References

Barlow, D. (2010). Negative effects from psychological treatments. *American Psychologist, 65*, 13–20. doi:10.1037/a0015643

Behobi, W., García, F., & Fernández-Álvarez, H. (2013). Psicoterapia cognitiva individual del TOC [Individual cognitive psychotherapy for OCD]. *Salud mental, 36*, 347–354.

Belloch, A., Cabedo, A., Carrió, C., Fernández-Álvarez, H., García, F., & Larsson, C. (2011). Group versus individual cognitive treatment for Obsessive-Compulsive Disorder: Changes in non-OCD symptoms and cognitions at posttreatment and one-year follow-up. *Psychiatry Research, 187*, 174–179. doi:10.1016/j.psychres.2010.10.015

Belloch, A., Fernández-Álvarez, H., & Castañeiras, C. (2004). Presentación de un instrumento para la detección y valoración de las preocupaciones hipocondríacas en la población general: el Inventario de Preocupaciones Hipocondríacas Aiglé – IPHA [Presentation of an instrument for the detection and appraisal of hypochondriac worries in the general population: The inventory of Hypochondriac worries Aiglé-IPHA]. *Revista Argentina de Clínica Psicológica, 13*, 183–195.

Beutler, L. E., & Harwood, T. M. (2000). *Prescriptive psychotherapy. A practical guide to systematic treatment selection.* New York, NY: Oxford.

Bowlby, J. (1981). Psychoanalysis as art and science. *Higher Education Quarterly, 35*, 395–512. doi:10.1111/j.1468-2273.1981.tb01311.x

Cabedo, E., Belloch, A., Carrió, C., Larsson, C., Fernández-Álvarez, H., & García, F. (2009). Group versus individual cognitive treatment for obsessive-compulsive disorder: changes in severity at post-treatment and one-year follow-up. *Behavioural and Cognitive Psychotherapy, 38*, 227–232. doi:10.1017/S135246580999066X

Carvalho, H. (2008). *Being a psychotherapist: Contributions of personal history on clinical practices.* Paper presented at the 39th Annual Meeting of the Society for Psychotherapy Research, Barcelona, Spain.

Castañeiras, C., Fraga Míguez, M., García, F., Fernández-Álvarez, H., & Belloch, A. (2009). Procesos de cambio en el Trastorno Obsesivo Compulsivo: Análisis cualitativo de los resultados de un tratamiento cognitivo desde la experiencia subjetiva de los pacientes [Processes of change in obsessive-compulsive disorder: Qualitative analysis of cognitive treatment results from patients' subjective perspective]. *Revista Brasileira de Terapias Cognitivas, 5*, 1–30.

Castañeiras, C., García, F., Lo Bianco, J., & Fernández-Álvarez, H. (2006). Modulating effect of experience and theorical technical orientation on the personal style of the therapist. *Psychotherapy Research, 16*, 587–593.

Castañeiras, C., Ledesma, R., García, F., & Fernández-Álvarez, H. (2008). Evaluación del Estilo Personal del Terapeuta: Presentación de una versión abreviada del EPT-C [Assessment of the personal style of the therapist: Presentation of an abridged version of PST-Q]. *Terapia Psicológica, 26*, 5–13.

Castañeiras, C., Rial, V., García, F., Farfallini, L., & Fernández-Álvarez, H. (2006). *Autopercepción de los terapeutas sobre su estilo personal: un estudio longitudinal* [Self-perception of therapists of their personal style: a longitudinal study]. 13ª. Jornadas de Investigación de la Facultad de Psicología, UBA, Buenos Aires.

Castonguay, L. G. (2013). Psychotherapy outcome: An issue worth re-revisiting 50 years later. *Psychotherapy, 50*, 52–68. doi:10.1037/a0030898

Chambless, D. L., & Ollendick, T. H. (2001). Empirically supported psychological interventions: Controversies and evidence. *Annual Review of Psychology, 52*, 685–716. doi:10.1146/annurev.psych.52.1.685

Corbella Santomá, S. (2002). *Compatibilidad entre el estilo personal del terapeuta y el perfil personal del paciente* [Compatibility between the personal style of the therapist and the personal profile of the patient]. Tesis doctoral [Doctoral Dissertation], Facultat de Psicologia, Ciències de I'Educació i de I'Esport Blanquerna, Universitat Ramon Llull, Barcelona.

Corbella Santomá, S., Botella, L., Saúl, L.A., García, F., & Fernández-Álvarez, H. (2009). *Developing the therapist's personal style.* Paper presented at the 40th Annual Meeting of the Society for Psychotherapy Research, Santiago de Chile, Chile.

Corbella Santomá, S.Fernández-Álvarez, H., Saúl, L. A., García, F., & Botella, L. (2008). Estilo personal del terapeuta y dirección de intereses [Personal style of the therapist and direction of interests]. *Apuntes de Psicología, 26*, 281–289.

Dimidjian, S., & Hollon, S. D. (2011). Introduction: What can be learned when empirically supported treatments fail? *Cognitive and Behavioral Practice, 18*, 303–305. doi:10.1016/j.cbpra.2011.02.001

Eysenck, H. J. (1994). The outcome problem in psychotherapy: what have we learned? *Behavior Research and Therapy, 32*, 477–495. doi:10.1016/0005-7967(94)90135-X

Feixas, G., Saúl, L. A., Avila-Espada, A., & Sánchez, V. (2001). Implicaciones terapéuticas de los conflictos cognitivos [Therapeutic implications of cognitive conflicts]. *Revista Argentina de Clínica Psicológica, 10*, 5–13.

Fernández-Álvarez, H. (1988). II Apéndice de esta edición en castellano. Adaptación de Buenos Aires. [Appendix of the Spanish edition. Adaptation in Buenos Aires]. In D. Wechsler (Ed.), *Test de Inteligencia para adultos (WAIS) Manual II* (pp. 139–173). Buenos Aires: Paidós.

Fernández-Álvarez, H. (1992). *Fundamentos de un modelo integrativo en psicoterapia.* Buenos Aires: Paidós. [(2001). *Fundamentals of an integrated model of psychotherapy* New York: Jason Aronson].

Fernández-Álvarez, H. (1999). *La psicoterapia vista por los médicos* [Psychotherapy as seen by physicians]. Buenos Aires: Grupo Editor Latinoamericano.

Fernández-Álvarez, H. (2008). *Integración y salud mental. El proyecto Aiglé 1977–2008.* [Integration and mental health. The Aiglé Project 1977–2008]. Bilbao: Desclée de Brouwer

Fernández-Álvarez, H., & García, F. (1998). El estilo personal del terapeuta: Inventario para su evaluación [The personal style of the therapist: Assessment Inventory]. In S. Gril, A. Ibáñez, I. Mosca, & P. L. R. Sousa (Eds.), *Investigación en psicoterapia* (pp. 76–84). Pelotas: Educat.

Fernández-Álvarez, H., García, F., & Belloch, A. (2011). Grupo terapéutico para TOC: la evaluación del proceso desde la perspectiva de los pacientes [Therapeutic group for OCD: process assessment from the patients' perspective]. En H. J. Chappa (Ed.), *Tratamiento integrativo del trastorno obsesivo compulsivo. Manual práctico* (pp. 239–251). Buenos Aires: Akadia.

Fernández-Álvarez, H., García, F., Lo Bianco, J., & Corbella Santomá, S. (2003). Assessment questionnaire on the Personal Style of the Therapist PST-Q. *Clinical Psychology and Psychotherapy, 10*, 116–125. doi:10.1002/cpp.358

Fernández-Álvarez, H., Gómez, B., & Corbella Santomá, S. (2012). *Does theoretical orientation and level of experience influence the way therapists ask questions?* Paper presented at the 43rd Annual Meeting of the Society for Psychotherapy Research, Virginia Beach, USA.

Fernández Álvarez, H., Hirsch, H., Maristany, M., & Torrente, F. (2005). *Propiedades psicométricas del OQ-45.2 en la Argentina: un estudio piloto* [Psychometric properties of the OQ-45.2 in Argentina: a pilot study]. Poster presented at the IV World Congress of Psychotherapy, Buenos Aires, Argentina.

Fernández-Álvarez, H., Scherb, E., Bregman, C., & García, F. (1995). Creencias sobre la extensión y efectividad de la Psicoterapia en la población general de la Ciudad de Buenos Aires [Beliefs about the extension and effectivity of Psychotherapy in the general population of the city of Buenos Aires]. In J. P. Jiménez, C. Buguñá, & A. Belmar (Eds.), *Investigación en psicoterapia. Procesos y resultados* (pp. 89–107). Santiago de Chile: Society for Psychotherapy Research (SPR); Corporación de promoción Universitaria (CPU).

García, F. (2006). *Enuresis nocturna. Causas y tratamiento* [Nocturnal bedwetting. Causes and treatment]. Buenos Aires: Lugar Editorial.

García, F., Fernández-Álvarez, H. (2007). Investigación empírica sobre el Estilo Personal del terapeuta: Una actualización [Empirical research on the Personal Style of the Therapist: An update]. *Revista Argentina de Clínica Psicológica, 16*, 121–128.

García, F., Castañeiras, C., Fraga Míguez, M., & Fernández-Álvarez, H. (2009). Mediadores de cambio identificados por el paciente en terapia cognitiva para el TOC [Change mediators identified by the patient in cognitive therapy for OCD]. *Acta Psiquiátrica y Psicológica de América Latina, 5*, 147–160.

García, F., Corbella, S., Saúl, L. A., Fernández-Álvarez, H., & Botella, L. (2008). *Personal style of the therapist and personality.* Paper presented at the 39th Annual Meeting of the Society for Psychotherapy Research, Barcelona, Spain.

García, F., Guzmán, G., & Castañeiras, C. (1999). ¿Es efectiva la psicoterapia? [Is psychotherapy effective?]. *Revista de la Facultad de Ciencias Humanas, UNSL, 28*, 155–174.

Gelso, C. J. (2009). The real relationship in a post-modern world: Theoretical and empirical explorations. *Psychotherapy Research, 19*, 253–265. doi:10.1080/10503300802389242

Gómez, B., Castañeiras, C., Curtarelli, A., Fraga Míguez, M., García, F., Maristany, M., & Fernández-Álvarez, H. (2011). *Personal Style of the Therapist (PST). Intra and inter therapist verbal behavior analysis. How do therapists ask questions?* Poster presented at the 42nd Annual Meeting of the Society for Psychotherapy Research, Bern, Switzerland.

Hoffmann, J., & Weinberger, S. (2007). *The art and science of psychotherapy.* New York, NY: Routledge.

Lambert, M. J., Garfield, S. L., & Bergin, A. G. (2004). Overview trends and future issues. In M. J. Lambert (Ed.), *Bergin and Garfield's handbook of psychotherapy and behavior change* (5th ed., pp. 805–821). New York, NY: Wiley.

Lambert, M. J., & Ogles, B. M. (2004). The efficacy and effectiveness of psychotherapy. In M. J. Lambert (Ed.), *Bergin and Garfield's handbook of psychotherapy and behavior change* (5th ed., pp. 139–193). New York, NY: Wiley.

Lambert, M. J., Hansen, N. B., Umpress, V., Lunnen, K., Okiishi, J., & Burlingame, G. M. (1996). *Administration and scoring manual for the OQ-45.2.* Wilmington, DE: American Professional Credentialing Services.

Lampropoulos, G. K. (2011). Failure in psychotherapy: An introduction. *Journal of Clinical Psychology, 67*, 1093–1095. doi:10.1002/jclp.20858

Malik, M. L., Fleming, J., Penela, V., Harwood, M. T., Best, S., & Beutler, L. (2002). *Which therapist for which client? The interaction of therapist variation and client characteristics in affecting rates of change: An effectiveness study.* Paper presented at the 33rd Annual Meeting of the Society for Psychotherapy Research, San Francisco, USA.

Maristany, M. (2008). Diagnóstico y evaluación de las relaciones interpersonales y sus perturbaciones [Diagnosis and assessment of interpersonal relationships and its disorders]. *Revista Argentina de Clínica Psicológica, 17*, 19–36.

Nathan, P. E., & Gorman, J. M. (2007). *A guide to treatments that work* (3rd ed.). New York, NY: Oxford University Press.

Olfson, M., & Marcus, S. C. (2010). National trends in outpatient psychotherapy. *American Journal of Psychiatry, 167*, 1456–1463. doi:10.1176/appi.ajp.2010.10040570

Olfson, M., & Pincus, H. A. (1994). Outpatient psychotherapy in the United States, I: Volume, costs, and user characteristics. *American Journal of Psychiatry, 151*, 1281–1288.

Orlinsky, D. E., & Howard, K. I. (1986). Process and outcome in psychotherapy. In S. L. Garfield & A. E. Bergin (Eds.), *Handbook of psychotherapy and behavior change* (3rd ed., pp. 311–384). New York, NY: Wiley.

Regner, E., & Beutler, L. (2012). *Exploring the psychometrics properties of Spanish (Argentine) systematic treatment selection system.* Paper presented at the 43rd Annual Meeting of the Society for Psychotherapy Research, Virginia Beach, USA.

Rial, V., García, F., Castañeiras, C., Gómez, B., & Fernández-Álvarez, H. (2006). Estilo personal de terapeutas que trabajan con pacientes severamente perturbados: Un estudio cuanti y cualitativo [Personal style of therapists who work with severely disturbed patients: A quantitative and qualitative study]. *Revista de la Asociación Española de Neuropsiquiatría, 26*, 9–26.

Rosqvist, J., Egan, D., Manzo, P., Baer, L., Jenike, M. A., Willis, B. S. (2001). Home-based behavior therapy for obsessive-compulsive disorder: a case series with data. *Journal of Anxiety Disorders, 15*, 395–400. doi:10.1016/S0887-6185(01)00071-8

Roussos, A., Braun, M., & Olivera, J. (2012). *Conductas responsables para la investigación en Psicología* [Responsible behaviors for psychology research]. Buenos Aires: FUNICS.

Roussos, A., Etchebarne, I., & Waizmann, V. (2006). Un esquema clasificatorio para las intervenciones en psicoterapia [A classificatory schema for psychotherapeutic interventions in psychoanalytic and cognitive-behavioural psychotherapy]. *Anuario de la Universidad de Buenos Aires, XIII*, 51–61.

Roussos, A., Waizmann, V., & Etchebarne, I. (2010). Common interventions in two single cases of cognitive and psychoanalytic psychotherapies. *Journal of Psychotherapy Integration, 20*, 327–346. doi:10.1037/a0020822

Serrano Zárate, B., Baños Rivera, R. M., & Botella Arbona, C. (2012). *"Sonreír es divertido": Un programa basado en TICS para el tratamiento de la depresión* ["Smiling is fun": A program based on ICT for depression treatment]. Paper presented at the IX Congreso internacional de la sociedad española para el estudio de la ansiedad y el estrés, Valencia, España.

Valdés, N., Tomicic, A., Pérez, J. C., & Krause, M. (2010). Sistema de Codificación de la Actividad Terapéutica (scat-1.0): Dimensiones y categorías de las acciones comunicacionales de pacientes y psicoterapeutas [Dimensions and categories of patients' and therapists' communicational acts]. *Revista Argentina de Clínica Psicológica, 19*, 117–130.

Vega, E. (2006). *El psicoterapeuta en neonatología, rol y estilo personal* [The psychotherapist in neonatology, role and personal style]. Buenos Aires: Lugar Editorial.

Von Bergen, A., & de la Parra, G. (2002). OQ-45.2. Cuestionario para la evaluación de resultados y evolución en Psicoterapia: adaptación, validación e indicadores para su aplicación e interpretación [Outcome questionnaire and evolution of psychotherapy: Adaptation, validation and guidelines for its implementation and interpretation]. *Terapia Psicológica, 20*, 161–176.

Wachtel, P. (1989). *The poverty of affluence: A psychological portrait of the American way of life.* New York, NY: The Free Press.

METHOD PAPER

Therapists and researchers: Advancing collaboration

ANN F. GARLAND[1] & LAUREN BROOKMAN-FRAZEE[2]

[1]*School, Family & Mental Health Professions, University of San Diego, San Diego, CA, USA &* [2]*Psychiatry, University of California, San Diego, CA, USA*

Abstract

Collaborative partnerships between community-based clinicians and academic researchers have the potential to improve the relevance, utility, and feasibility of research, as well as the effectiveness of practice. Collaborative partnership research from a variety of fields can inform the development and maintenance of effective partnerships. In this paper we present a conceptual model of research-community practice partnership derived from literature across disciplines and then illustrate application of this model to one case example. The case example is a multi-year partnership between an interdisciplinary group of community-based psychotherapists and a team of mental health researchers. This partnership was initiated to support federally funded research on community-based outpatient mental health care for children with disruptive behavior problems, but it has evolved to drive and support new intervention studies with different clinical foci. Lessons learned from this partnership process will be shared and interpreted in the context of the presented research-practice partnership model.

Broad awareness and concern about the gap between research and practice in mental health care has driven calls for more bi-directional or multi-directional knowledge exchange involving active collaboration and partnership between researchers and community providers at all stages of research and practice implementation (Addis, 2002; Beutler, Williams, Wakefield, & Entwistle, 1995; Bradshaw & Haynes, 2012; Sobell, 1996; Wells & Miranda, 2006;). The papers in this special issue contribute to a growing literature examining such partnerships and how they can advance and improve both mental health research and practice (e.g., Bradshaw & Haynes, 2012; Chorpita & Mueller, 2008; Chorpita et al., 2002; Lindamer et al., 2009; McMillen, Lenze, Hawley, & Osborne, 2009; Southam-Gerow, Hourigan, & Allin, 2009; Wells, Miranda, Bruce, Alegria, & Wallerstein, 2004). This growing literature highlights how partnerships between mental health providers (hereinafter referred to as therapists) and researchers can promote the relevance, feasibility,

and utility of research, as well as the potential effectiveness of care, but it also highlights challenges in building and sustaining these types of partnerships. More explicit study of partnership processes is needed to capitalize on all the tacit knowledge that partnership participants have gained through varied collaborative efforts and to ultimately advance collaborative practice (Bradshaw & Haynes, 2012; Kellam, 2012; Reimer, Kelley, Casey, & Haynes, 2012).

A variety of disciplines offer useful theoretical and empirical examinations of collaboration processes and factors that influence the success of collaborative partnerships. In this paper, we present a conceptual framework for research-community practice partnership (RCPP) informed primarily by the business organizational management and public health literature, as well as other collaborative partnership research and our own ongoing work (e.g., Brookman-Frazee, Stahmer, Lewis, Feder, & Reed, 2012). This framework can be used to inform decisions on the development and maintenance of partnerships in community-based psychotherapy research, as well as to interpret variable success in partnership efforts. We begin with a brief overview of the literature that influenced the development of this framework. We then use a case study to illustrate the components of the framework as it is applied specifically for community psychotherapy research. The case example is a multi-year research-practice partnership developed in one large county to support community-based research on publicly funded outpatient psychotherapy for children and families. We highlight lessons learned regarding the development, maintenance, benefits, and challenges of research-practice partnerships.

Background in Collaboration Models from Different Disciplines

Literature addressing knowledge exchange, collaboration, and partnership in disciplines outside mental health provides valuable theoretical models, practical strategies, and emerging empirical support for effective collaborative partnership processes. In particular, relevant literature from the fields of business management and public health is summarized below; this literature provides the background for the conceptual model of Research-Community Practice Partnership presented at the end of this section.

Sources of Literature on Collaboration

Business management. Two broad areas in organizational science namely, (1) collaborative management research and (2) inter-organizational relationships, are particularly applicable to RCPP in the mental health services context. Collaborative management research examines how researchers and organizations work together to increase competence of organizations and systems, and increase the relevance of research (Pasmore, Woodman, & Simmons, 2008). Research in the second area of inter-organizational relationships addresses interactions between organizations (e.g., strategic alliances, joint ventures, networks), seeking better understanding of relationship structures, functions, and consequences (Cropper, Huxham, Ebers, & Ring, 2008). Both these areas of inquiry are linked to action research which strives to develop practical knowledge through participatory processes, and to generate pragmatic solutions to practical problems (Bradbury, 2008).

Organizational learning and knowledge management. The two related areas of management science described above share a common focus on organizational and individual learning processes. Terms such as *knowledge transfer* (both unidirectional and bi-directional) and *knowledge creation* have been used to describe collaborative learning processes (Huxham & Hibbert, 2008; Muthusamy & White, 2005). Knowledge transfer is certainly very relevant to current efforts in mental health to implement evidence-based practices in community settings. Relatedly, implementation science also examines how knowledge or technology is exchanged across organizations and the extent to which this exchange results in sustainable change in the capacity or performance of the organizations involved. Qualitative research suggests that knowledge exchange in a collaborative partnership can range from strategic (and potentially selfish) acquisition of beneficial knowledge to more reciprocal sharing of knowledge and collaborative explorations of innovative solutions to specific problems (Huxham & Hibbert, 2008). The literature on learning and knowledge management has important implications for the *process* of knowledge exchange in research-community partnerships. One of the major challenges in mental health research-community practice partnerships is the extent to which the knowledge transfer is intended to be reciprocal (i.e., knowledge exchange) or unidirectional. One of the criticisms of traditional models of evidence-based practice dissemination was that it was not a reciprocal knowledge-exchange process (Garland, Hurlburt, & Hawley, 2006).

Community health partnerships. Public health also has a rich history in research-practice collaboration. In order to address key factors associated with behavioral and environmental health risk, poor health and well-being (e.g., substance abuse, teenage pregnancy, HIV, environmental pollution), and the resulting overburdened healthcare system, many communities have formed multi-sector collaborative partnerships to work on strategies to reduce risk (Alexander, Comfort, Weiner, & Bogue, 2001). Partners may include hospitals, service organizations, insurers, government agencies, community interest groups, school districts, academic institutions, and individual citizens who join together to address social issues of importance to the community (Alexander et al., 2001; Daley, Roberts, Hahn, O'Flaherty, & Reznik, 1999; Suarez-Balcazar, Harper, & Lewis, 2005). The literature on community health partnerships in public health provides case examples and empirical studies on the key characteristics of successful (i.e., sustainable with intended outcomes) collaborative partnerships (Alexander et al., 2003), and methods to evaluate the processes and impacts of partnerships (Shortell et al., 2002). The extensive theoretical, empirical, and practical literature on public health research-community partnerships (Lasker & Weiss, 2003; Lasker, Weiss, & Miller, 2001) can be applied to RCPP in mental health.

Community-based participatory research (CBPR). CBPR is a model of community health partnership that is relatively common in public health. The literature on CBPR is replete with conceptual and increasingly empirical work addressing the functions, processes, and outcomes of collaborative health partnerships. It is strongly linked to, if not often defined by, efforts to reduce health care disparities through active involvement of community members, organizations, and researchers in all aspects of the research process (Israel, Schultz, Parker, & Becker, 1998). Core principles of CBPR dictate that it: (1) is participatory and cooperative, involving a joint, equitable decision-making process; (2) is a co-learning process based on a mutually respectful partnership between researchers and community members; and (3) involves system development and local capacity building, ideally achieving a balance between research and action (Minkler, 2004; Minkler & Wallerstein, 2003). CBPR provides an important framework for research-practice partnership efforts in mental health services (Wells & Miranda, 2006). The lessons learned from CBPR can provide direction for practical considerations of developing, sustaining, and evaluating research-community partnerships. Some of the greatest challenges include equitable decision-making regarding work expectations, resource generation and allocation, as well as the challenge of balancing research and action priorities. The CBPR model has been adapted by mental health researchers and community providers to select and test psychosocial interventions in the community (Blumenthal et al., 2006).

Rationale for Collaboration

There are a number of reasons why groups or organizations may decide to partner with others. In business, organizations can achieve desired outcomes through a "collaborative advantage" process when they partner with other organizations that have complementary resources and/or expertise (Huxham, 2003; Huxham & Vangen, 2005). They can build capacity in each collaborating organization which could not be achieved working in isolation (Hardy, Phillips, & Lawrence, 2003). Partnerships can also be formed for the more explicit purpose of specific knowledge transfer, in which partners acquire new skills or technologies from one another (e.g., evidence-based practices in mental health), or for knowledge creation, in which innovation grows

out of the process of social interactions that occur in ongoing collaborations (e.g., identification of practice-based evidence) (Hardy et al., 2003). These reasons for collaborating are not mutually exclusive and, to some extent, each is often present in collaborative partnerships.

In the context of mental health research specifically, RCPPs have the potential to increase the relevance and impact of mental health services research (Wells et al., 2004) by improving the ecological validity and clinical utility of research. Further, they can improve the efficiency of community-based research by improving access to service data (McMillen et al., 2009). Lastly, RCPPs have the potential to facilitate implementation of EBPs in usual care mental health services (Garland, Plemmons, & Koontz, 2006; McMillen et al., 2009; Sobell, 1996), and bridge the gap between research and usual care practice, thus improving care.

Conceptual Framework for Research-Community Partnerships

Figure 1 outlines an RCPP framework based on the conceptual and theoretical literature as well as "lessons learned" from case studies. This framework was adapted from the research community partnership framework outlined in Brookman-Frazee, Stahmer and colleagues (2012). The framework illustrates the iterative and dynamic process of RCPP development and the potential outcomes of these efforts. It highlights the multiple dynamic phases of RCPPs and the collaborative processes which occur in the community context of the RCPP. It posits that RCPP functioning (including both interpersonal and operational functioning) can lead to partnership synergy (proximal outcome), which can then lead to a variety of potential distal outcomes, including benefits to the individuals, organizations and communities. Following the presentation of the framework, we provide a brief description of the case example RCPP and then illustrate components of the framework with examples from this RCPP.

Case Example: "Practice & Research: Advancing Collaboration" (PRAC) Project

The aims of the PRAC project were to rigorously examine the psychotherapeutic treatment processes and outcomes of community-based care for children with disruptive behavior problems and their families (Garland, Hurlburt, et al., 2006; Garland, Plemmons, et al., 2006; Garland et al. 2010). Table I provides an outline of key aspects of this project. Prior to initiating the research study, the study PI identified the largest contracted providers of publicly

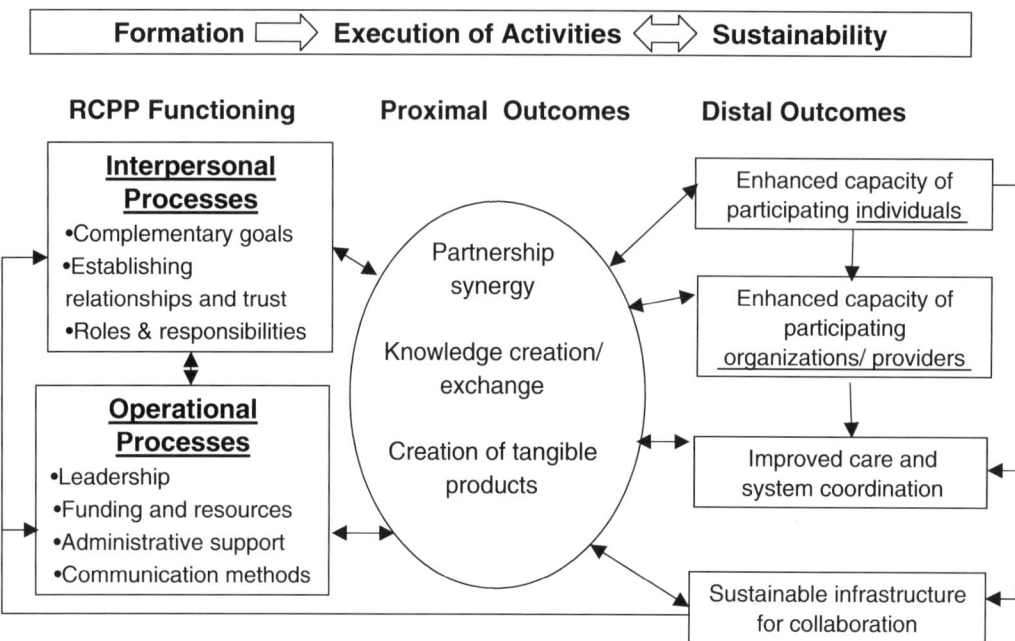

Figure 1. Model of research-community practice partnerships. Adapted from Brookman-Frazee et al. (2012).

funded mental health services in the county and invited agency leaders to identify one well-respected representative from each program (an "opinion leader") to join a partnership group with a team of researchers. Thus, a collaborative group of community-based therapists and researchers was formed and this group met monthly to refine the research questions and methods, and maximize feasibility of the study (including development of participant recruitment procedure strategies to minimize data collection burden). The study design required collecting videotapes of all therapy sessions for therapists and families who consented to participate. This descriptive study offered no training to therapists nor any significant resources beyond video recording equipment for their offices. The study was being initiated in the context of broader national and local tensions in the field regarding pressure to implement evidence-based practices and some criticism of community-based care; thus there were significant potential challenges to achieving high rates of voluntary participation in a study designed to rigorously examine "usual care" practice. Active involvement of key opinion leaders in each of the six participating clinics was thus essential for building the trust necessary to achieve high rates of voluntary participation and for ensuring that study methods fit well within the usual care context. For example, therapist partners' input was essential in refining the methods of characterizing psychotherapy processes to maximize relevance (i.e., ecological validity) to community practice.

As discussed below, trust-building was a critical early step in building this collaborative relationship. A qualitative study of the development of this partnership was conducted and revealed that all participants emphasized the importance of trust-building, as well as the need to develop shared meanings around key concepts (Garland, Plemmons, et al., 2006). These themes are common across partnership efforts (Bradshaw & Haynes, 2012; Sobell, 1996). The partnership was ultimately successful in supporting the completion of the study, including collection of over 3000 videotaped therapy sessions. Upon completion of data collection, the partnership group participated actively in interpretation and dissemination of the findings. This PRAC RCPP has since evolved into a few new RCPPs addressing specific clinical research issues described later. The partnership processes and factors affecting its success are outlined below based on the different components of the conceptual model of research-practice partnership—its developmental phases, processes, and benefits (Figure 1).

Dynamic Phases of Partnerships: Formation, Execution, Sustainability

Formation (Initiation)

Initiation of an RCPP should be based on shared interests or complementary goals. The literature on partnership functioning suggests that forming and

Table I. Case example: Practice and Research: Advancing Collaboration (PRAC)

Funding source(s)	NIMH R01
	University Academic Senate Research Grant
Purpose of research study	Phase 1: To characterize community-based psychotherapy process and outcome
	Phase 2: To develop supervision tools to improve the use of evidence-based strategies in community-based psychotherapy
Applying Model of Research Community Partnership	
Phase of partnership	Sustainability (execution of revised activities and new RCPPs)
RCP functioning: Interpersonal Processes – Role of community partners	Phase 1: To advise the research team on measure development, data collection and interpretation of findings
	Phase 2: Work with the research team to generate supervision tools
	Participate in data collection related to characterizing supervision practice
	Advise on new studies relevant to practice (see AIM Study)
RCP functioning: Operational Processes	Bi-weekly meetings with CASRC/ UCSD researchers and community therapists
	Regular email communication
	Coordinator as "hub" of partnership information and activities
	Meetings held at CASRC
Proximal outcomes	Developed sustained relationships (as evidenced by retention of RCPP members)
	Generated new topic of mutual interest, revised purpose, and identified new members
	Publications reporting observational data of psychotherapy process (e.g., Brookman-Frazee, Garland, Taylor, & Zoffness, 2009; Brookman-Frazee, Haine, Baker-Ericzen, Zoffness, & Garland, 2010; Garland et al., 2010; Garland, Haine-Schlagel, Accurso, Baker-Ericzen, & Brookman-Frazee, 2012; Haine-Schlagel, Brookman-Frazee, Fettes, Baker-Ericzen, & Garland, 2012 & Haine-Schlagel, Fettes, Garcia, Brookman-Frazee, & Garland, 2013)
	Published qualitative study on partnership process (Garland, Plemmons, et al., 2006)
	Coordinated joint research-practice conference to share research findings and discuss topics of mutual interest to researchers and clinicians
Distal outcomes	Developed sustainable infrastructure for revised partnership goals (e.g., Supervision Pilot study)
	Built capacity in CASRC and community clinics new studies using RCPPs (e.g., AIM study)
	Improved capacity in community services
	Improved community-based care for children with disruptive behavior disorders (anticipated)

establishing successful RCPPs requires consideration of the following key issues:

What is the purpose of the RCPP? There are a number of potential reasons why an RCPP might be initiated for mental health services research:

1. To facilitate the efficiency or feasibility of a specific research project when community stakeholders have knowledge or information that is particularly relevant to the research. The PRAC RCPP was initiated to facilitate data collection and maximize relevance of the PRAC research project, including specifically assistance with participant recruitment, refinement of the observational coding system used to characterize observed psychotherapy process, and reinforcement of the focus on "usual care" practice throughout the project.

2. To identify practice-relevant research questions. The purpose of the PRAC RCPP evolved over several years from a supportive mechanism to facilitate the initial PRAC observational study to a more equitable forum to identify new practice-relevant research questions (e.g., clinical supervision methods) to be explored in future research.

3. To increase opportunities for funding. Some partnerships may be initiated specifically for the purpose of qualifying for and/or identifying new funding opportunities. When the initial funding that supported the PRAC RCPP ended, the group volunteered to work together to identify future research and practice funding initiatives.

4. To improve practice. Virtually all research-practice partnerships likely have the implicit, if not explicit goal of ultimately improving the quality of care. Research-practice knowledge exchange and specifically efforts to encourage the integration of research-derived knowledge and practice are designed to improve care and to improve research. The PRAC RCPP sought to "bridge the gap" between research and practice by strengthening working relationships between researchers and therapists, implicitly building more interest in research-based knowledge in the practice community and building improved knowledge and appreciation of practice realities in the research community (Sobell, 1996).

Who will participate?. Setting the foundation for a successful RCPP requires that stakeholders make a commitment to collaborate. This can be particularly challenging on top of already busy professional commitments. Careful attention needs to be paid to with whom and with what organizations one collaborates, including decisions about representation at different levels of an organization (i.e., upper management, front-line staff, etc.). The appropriate partners will largely depend on the purpose of the RCPP. Given that the PRAC study was focused on individual therapist practice, the partners were active therapists, as opposed to administrators or policy-makers.

Literature suggests that members should possess complementary, but non-redundant knowledge and experiences that can be combined and contextualized to facilitate knowledge creation and innovation (Levin & Cross 2004). In our studies, we have found that it is also important that participants demonstrate an openness to and respect for new ideas and perspectives, as well as enthusiasm and optimism about the potential for the collaborative process. In the PRAC RCPP researchers clearly communicated how and why community therapists were critical to driving and refining the most important research questions, facilitating data collection procedures, interpreting findings, and planning next steps. One of the themes that emerged from the qualitative self-study of the PRAC RCPP formation was that initially, some of the therapists felt somewhat skeptical about their role, expressing concern that their participation would be superficial or perfunctory (Garland, Plemmons, et al., 2006). This is a potential risk for research-practice partnerships (Sobell, 1996) and thus it was critical to demonstrate early on that input from all participants would be taken seriously and would drive real changes in the project.

How will the RCPP operate?. Initial considerations for operational processes are discussed below.

Execution of Activities

Once a new RCPP is formed, specific project tasks need to be accomplished but there must also be flexibility to shift priorities based on partnership evolution and knowledge exchange. In the PRAC partnership, there was sometimes a tension between the need to complete specific project tasks (such as revising and pilot-testing the observational coding measurement system used to characterize psychotherapy process), and partners' desire for more open-ended exploratory dialogue about psychotherapy processes and challenges, relevant research, etc. This was particularly true as trust and mutual respect grew and partners recognized the value of sharing ideas. Open dialogue, in and of itself, can foster a stronger integration of science and practice (Sobell, 1996), but, in our experience, it needs to be complemented by task-focused work. The section on "RCPP Functioning" below describes some of the operational supports or processes used to support completion of project tasks.

Sustainability

There has been more research on strategies for initiating collaborative partnerships than there has been on strategies to sustain and grow partnerships. However, public health scholars have highlighted the importance of attention to sustainability, as well as many of the challenges (Lasker & Weiss, 2003; Shortell et al., 2002). Sustainability should be considered a phase in the evolution of partnership and an indicator of partnership success (Cropper, 1996). Sustainability will likely be required to achieve a long-term impact on community practice outcomes as well as research. The following issues are critical to maintenance of collaborative relationships and partnership infrastructure:

What should be sustained?. As RCPPs achieve their initial goals and/or the funding for a specific project ends (if applicable), frank discussions need to occur about whether the partnership will continue and, if so, how it will be supported and what the goals will be. Once the initial aims of the PRAC RCPP were achieved and the research funding that provided infrastructure support ended, the RCPP group debated next steps. The members decided to continue meeting without compensation for their time and without staffing support. Members reported that the collaboration experience and dialogue were intellectually stimulating and professionally valuable. The group then worked to identify new potential funding initiatives and it has served as a forum for broad discussions about research questions of interest to clinicians and researchers. The initial PRAC RCPP has now evolved into a few specific special-interest groups addressing different clinical foci such as mental health treatment for Autism Spectrum Disorders and strategies to improve parents' participatory engagement in psychotherapy.

Resources. For RCPPs like PRACs that are initiated for the purpose of a particular grant or project, the end of funding represents a critical crossroads. In a study of characteristics of successful partnerships, Shortell and colleagues (2002) found that those most successful demonstrated an "ability to patch" (p. 64), referring to efforts to reposition competencies and assets in order to address changing needs and priorities (Shortell et al., 2002). "Patching" resources may require that participating organizations donate resources in the absence of external funding. The necessary process of blending and repositioning resources likely requires planning before the end of funding. As the PRAC RCPP has evolved into multiple special-interest RCPs, there has been significant patching from different funding mechanisms and staffing resources. Flexibility and ongoing negotiation of goals and resources have been identified as essential to effective partnership (Reimer et al., 2012).

RCPP Functioning

In this section we describe the essential interpersonal and operational processes of collaboration, followed by the proximal and distal outcomes that can be achieved.

Managing Interpersonal Processes

Complementary goals. Collaborative partnerships usually need to address multiple mutually rewarding goals, including specific goals of the collaborative partnership, as well as those of the participating individuals and organizations (Bradshaw & Haynes, 2012; Huxham, 2003; Spoth & Greenberg, 2005) We have found that it is not necessary for individual/organizational goals to be the same for all partners; however, these goals should be complementary and combined to form a shared vision and a mutually rewarding purpose for the collaborative activities. For example, when the initial PRAC project was completed, the RCPP members continued to work together and one of the mutual interests (among researchers and therapists) was to learn more about "usual" clinical supervision practices in publicly funded outpatient clinics. The research and therapist representatives had distinct, but complementary goals motivating pursuit of this activity. The researchers were highly motivated to describe usual supervision methods to learn about this mechanism as a potential vehicle for the implementation of evidence-based practices in these clinics. The therapists were interested in learning more about supervision in order to identify resources needed to improve supervision and

to identify useful supervision methods, but implementation of EBP was not the primary focus for them.

Establishing interpersonal relationships, trust and shared language. As noted previously and mentioned across all areas of partnership study, building interpersonal trust and a shared language are essential for successful collaboration. An empirical investigation of strategic alliances found that reciprocal commitment, trust, and mutual influence between collaborative partners were all factors positively associated with successful knowledge exchange (Muthusamy & White, 2005). While not surprising, these findings highlight the importance of explicit attention to the role of interpersonal relationships and interaction in partnership. Given some historical tensions between those who research and those who practice mental health care, mutual trust is not a given and needs to be fostered over time (Garland, Plemmons, et al., 2006; Sobell, 1996). Overall, there needs to be some level of basic trust between both individuals and organizations to initiate the relationship; ideally, trust grows as the collaborative group engages in mutually rewarding activities (Huxham, 2003; Vangen & Huxham, 2003). As in other relationships, trust between collaborative partners grows when members demonstrate responsiveness to each party's needs and willingness to go above and beyond an agreed scope of work (Becker, Israel, & Allen, 2005; Pan et al., 2006).

Qualitative research on behaviors that build interpersonal trust suggests that common language and terminology is important in social exchanges (Abrams, Cross, Lesser, & Levin, 2003). Like others, (e.g., Bradshaw & Haynes, 2012), we have found that developing a common language is a critical communication need to advance partnership between researchers and therapists. It has been particularly helpful to avoid using jargon that may be unknown or may hold different meanings for different stakeholders. It is also important to be aware that certain words/terms can be interpreted differently. For example, the term "directive" (in reference to psychotherapeutic techniques) has evoked discussions of varied interpretations and affective reactions between researchers and therapists in our partnership group.

Roles and responsibilities. Individual participants in an RCP enter the partnership with a conferred "status" reflecting their specific professional identity (e.g., Counselor, Psychologist, Professor, Intern, Graduate Student). Power differentials will likely impact the process of collaboration and knowledge exchange and therefore there needs to be explicit attention given to how power is distributed among members of the collaborative for decision-making. Overall, it may be important to address members' expected roles and unique contributions, and the distribution of power at the outset, as well as explicitly establishing norms for working together (Becker et al., 2005). Then, any changes in power or responsibilities can be discussed with more ease.

Managing Partnership Operations

Unlike formal organizations, or even organized community groups, RCPPs develop their own operational procedures in order to execute the collaborative activities. Although this can be challenging due to limited resources, it also provides great flexibility in how the partnership is managed. The following are practical considerations to address as operational procedures are developed:

Leadership and power. Leader(s) of RCPPs may be in unique positions in that they may be facilitating the collaborative process without any real resources or power over the individual partners (Alexander et al., 2001). Therefore, effective RCPP leaders may differ from effective leaders of traditional organizations. In a qualitative study of leadership in public-private health partnerships, Alexander and colleagues (2001) found that effective leaders of collaborative partnerships find an optimal balance between power sharing and control, process and results, continuity and change, and interpersonal trust and formalized procedures (Alexander et al., 2001). These themes are consistent with other observations of successful partnerships in mental health contexts (e.g., Reimer et al., 2012).

In the PRAC RCPP, the balance of power between partners depended on the nature of the task. While the goals of CBPR, for example, include egalitarian leadership, we have found that it is important to acknowledge differences in skills for certain tasks, and match leadership responsibilities to skill sets. For example, while preparing a grant application, the research members of the partnership in PRAC led the agenda and had more influence than community therapists. Alternatively, when the task was to engage therapist colleagues in an experiential workshop regarding application of research findings to community practice, therapist partners led given their credibility among community therapists. Overall, we have found that the balance of influence between partners and stakeholders shifts naturally given the nature of the task and the respective skills of different partners.

Administrative support. If possible, it may be beneficial to have someone who is employed by the collaborative rather than by one of the partnering organizations to provide administrative coordination. Further, it is potentially helpful to hire staff members who represent community stakeholder groups, especially if they will be interfacing with the broader community (Pan et al., 2006). In the PRAC RCPP, however, the administrative support has primarily been linked to our research center given that the original funding came from a research grant to center investigators. While this approach facilitates central coordination, it also has the relative disadvantage of being largely managed by researcher stakeholders. In other collaborative projects at our center, we have shared staff with community-based organizations, which has resulted in increased communication and mutual understanding of each organization's contexts and priorities.

Communication methods. Just like for any group, effective and efficient communication is critical for a collaborative partnership. It is important to consider how RCPP activities will be recorded and shared within the group and externally to broader constituencies. This is particularly important, as there may be turnover in individual participants and members of participating organizations. While web-based communications methods such as Google Groups can greatly facilitate communication, we have found that face-to-face meetings are essential for partnership development, particularly early in the groups' development as trust is building. Reimer and colleagues (2012) similarly emphasize the importance of face-to-face meetings to build collaboration and explicitly to acknowledge ongoing cultural differences. Although efficient, one of the challenges to using alternative web-based communication methods is the variability in familiarity with these applications across all potential partnership groups.

Proximal (Process) Outcomes

Demonstrating positive impacts of partnerships can be challenging (Butterfoss & Francisco, 2004) and there are few established methods to empirically examine RCPP outcomes. The most obvious proximal outcome of an RCPP is establishing the collaborative relationships. In fact, some suggest that the greatest value of collaboration may be the development of the relationships, rather than achieving specific goals (Huxham & Vangen, 2003).

"*Partnership synergy*" refers to a process whereby the knowledge and skills of diverse partners are combined to (a) foster new and better ways to achieve goals, (b) plan innovative, comprehensive programs, and (c) strengthen the relationship with the broader community (Lasker et al., 2001; Weiss, Anderson, & Lasker, 2002). Scholars are working on operationalizing the important construct of partnership synergy and developing measures to assess the extent to which collaborative groups are achieving it (Daley et al., 1999; Weiss et al., 2002).

Knowledge creation and exchange. Knowledge exchange and creation are a reflection of successful partnership synergy. In the business management context, one of the primary goals of a strategic alliance collaboration is for each of the partners to learn from the other. Organizational scholars have therefore adapted measures of collaboration to assess knowledge exchange (Muthusamy & White, 2005). Knowledge exchange was a primary goal of the PRAC RCPP. Our qualitative investigation of the partnership process found ample evidence of such exchange. Researchers reported shifts in their understanding of "real world" practice challenges and greater respect for the immediate and often risky clinical challenges therapists faced. They reported greater respect for therapists' skills based on the partnership experience. Likewise, therapists reported significant shifts in their attitudes about research, with greater appreciation for the rigor of the research process and the ultimate aim of improving care (Garland, Plemmons, et al., 2006). One of the benefits of research-practice collaboration is improved understanding and mutual respect across roles (Sobell, 1996).

Creation of tangible products. Typically, the most concrete and measurable outcome of a collaborative partnership is the extent to which the stated goals and objectives are achieved. These outcomes will likely be tied to grant funding and/or service provision, either of which requires regular monitoring of progress in activities. On this basis, the PRAC RCPP met its proximal outcome goals. Participation in the research study was strong (approximately 80% of therapists who were randomly selected for recruitment agreed to participate) and data collection was completed successfully. We attribute this success to the PRAC RCPP members (opinion leaders) serving as study champions within each of the clinics throughout the study.

Distal Outcomes

There are many potential distal outcomes of RCPPs. Some are more direct, and easier to quantify than others, and they can occur at individual, organizational and community levels.

Positive impacts of participating members. The most direct distal outcomes include the new skills that individuals develop to apply in their respective settings, and their ability to collaborate and communicate with others from different backgrounds and perspectives. In the PRAC RCPP, one of the best examples of this type of a desirable distal outcome was the fact that one of the therapist partners began leading presentations about evidence-based practices for therapist colleagues and trainees based largely on his partnership experience. Other therapist members are now serving as expert consultants on a variety of federally funded research projects. In addition, recognizing the value of therapist partnerships, the original research participants have forged new collaborative relationships with an expanded network of therapist participants in our community and beyond, and have extended some partnerships to include parents, administrators and other key stakeholders (Brookman-Frazee, Drahota, & Stadnick, 2012; Brookman-Frazee et al., 2012).

Across a few RCPPs in our research center, we have found that community members' (therapists, administrators, and family members) interpretation of research findings have been particularly valuable and have guided how we discuss our findings in publications and presentations. Participants have told us that the partnership experience has been very intellectually stimulating—at times challenging—but overall very enriching, personally and professionally. Participants come away with new perspectives that reportedly enhance their abilities to succeed within their own organizations, participate in new collaborative ventures, and communicate more effectively with other stakeholder groups to strengthen the integration of research and practice.

Positive impacts on participating organizations. The potential positive organizational impacts include organizational learning, improved culture, and capacity-building for innovative new partnerships. Research confirms that organizations learn from collaborative experiences and develop improved collaborative skills (Simonin, 1997). This collaborative "know how" can build an organization's capacity to participate in future collaborative efforts. As the PRAC RCP has evolved into different collaborative pursuits, the lessons learned from each iteration inform the next. For example, we have learned to acknowledge that the goals of researchers and community members may not always be aligned and need to be continually negotiated. Additionally, we have learned the importance of including opinion leaders in RCPPs to maximize the impact of the RCPP on partnering organizations. Partnering community organizations have benefited from developing relationships with our research center which facilitate future collaborative efforts. They have learned the value of research to their organizations, and the benefits of having their clinicians participate in research studies.

Sustainability of partnership infrastructure. As discussed above, it takes time and resources to develop an infrastructure for RCPs. This infrastructure, which includes willing participants and effective communication mechanisms, is an important product of the RCPP. An established infrastructure improves efficiency and potential effectiveness of future collaborations because relationships are already built and operational processes are already established. We've experienced this as new RCPPS have capitalized on the initial infrastructure developed by the PRAC RCPP, including the trust built between researchers and community practitioners.

Improved community-based care or system capacity. The ultimate distal goals of research-community partnership are to improve care and to improve the utility of research toward that end. Indicators of improved care would include reduced disparities in access to care and improved clinical effectiveness of care. Unfortunately, we do not yet have data to test the extent to which the PRAC RCPP and its subsequent evolutions have improved care in the system overall. The baseline clinical effectiveness of usual care is limited, and many different interventions are needed to improve care (Garland et al., 2013), but our belief, based on experience, is that fostering collaborative partnership between researchers and therapists provides a fertile environment for improvement efforts.

Challenges to Collaboration

Despite the multiple potential benefits of RCPPs, there are many challenges to collaboration that potentially limit achievement of desired outcomes. Collaborative groups can experience "collaborative inertia" resulting in slow progress and minimal productivity (Huxham, 2003). Although a comprehensive discussion of challenges is beyond the scope of this paper, it is important to acknowledge that there are several key potential obstacles to successful collaboration that are particularly relevant for RCPPs in mental health. For the sake of brevity, some of these key challenges and potential solutions are outlined in Table II. Many of these challenges were encountered in our case example and are mentioned above. For example, communication challenges related to different interpretations of key

terms (e.g., "evidence," and "directive" approaches to psychotherapy) were encountered early on in our partnership process. The broad challenge of building trust and the time required to do so is also a consistent theme in our experience. We offer brief suggestions for potential solutions to the array of key partnership challenges to reinforce the fact that despite some challenges, partnerships can be sustained and the potential benefits outweigh the challenges.

Conclusions

Given increased national attention to the gap between research and community practice and encouragement of stronger collaboration between researchers and community stakeholders, more scholarly attention to the complexities of collaborative processes and potential outcomes is warranted. The RCPP framework presented here is based on the conceptual literature, case studies and emerging empirical research on collaboration from multiple disciplines, as well as our own practical experience. It highlights the dynamic phases of RCPPs, the complex processes that make up their functioning, and the potential proximal and distal outcomes. We illustrated the framework constructs using practical examples from our multi-year RCPP experience. Not only has collaboration between researchers and other stakeholders in our work been particularly enriching for the individuals and organizations involved, we have directly experienced how these partnerships facilitate bridging the ubiquitous gap between research and practice, ultimately enhancing both enterprises.

Our field is poised to advance beyond strong rhetoric about the value of interdisciplinary research-practice partnerships to increased operational support and study of such partnerships. This shift requires greater explicit attention to partnership development in graduate training, grant funding, academic review and promotion priorities, and scientific publication avenues. We need to move beyond valuing the ideal of partnership to producing empirical evidence of the impact of partnerships on mental health care effectiveness to reinforce the cost-benefit of investment in partnership development and maintenance. Psychotherapy researchers and practitioners are poised to lead these efforts given their expertise in the interpersonal processes essential to such collaborative endeavors.

Acknowledgements

The contents of this work are solely the responsibility of the authors and do not necessarily represent the

Table II. RCP challenges and potential solutions

Challenge	Description/ examples	Potential solutions
Lack of consensual aims	Researchers and practitioners may have differing goals that reflect the tension between relevance and rigor.	Get started on some mutually agreed upon action that can be decided upon without full consensus on overall goals (Huxham, 2003; Huxham & Vangen, 2003)
Communication	Stakeholders may use different language inhibiting clear communication with other stakeholders (Garland, Plemmons, et al., 2006; Huxham & Vangen, 2003)	Identify terms that evoke strong reactions from partners that may have different meaning to different stakeholder groups. Provide specific definitions how terminology is used.
Time	Trusting relationships take time to develop. Stakeholders may operate on different time tables.	Researchers build time into their proposed funding periods and research plans to develop relationships with partners (Frazier, Formoso, Birman, & Atkins, 2008).
Managing interpersonal relationships	People make up RCPs, and have idiosyncrasies and personal agendas. (Sink, 1996) Personality issues are not insignificant in their impact on process and outcome. This may include personalities of individual participants or of those in member organizations (Daley et al., 1999).	Develop roles, expectations and processes, and norms to deal with inevitable conflicts that will arise (Becker et al., 2005).
Lack of understanding of partnering organizations	Stakeholders may not understand context (demands, expectations, culture) or others' organizations.	Individuals invest effort into understanding the world as perceived by the other participant (Huxham & Vangen, 2003).
Lack of organizational support	Stakeholders may have competing demands and expectations from their organizations (e.g., academic institutions may have few incentives for participating in community work) (Reznik, Hahn, Morris, & Daley, 2000).	Communication with organizations about the value and potential benefit of collaboration, emphasizing the products of the RCPP.
Balancing methodological rigor and relevance	Some may be concerned that conducting research in collaboration with the community may somehow reduce the methodological rigor of the science due to "compromises" that need to be made to satisfy all partners (e.g., choosing designs that do not include random assignment or selecting outcome measures that are less reliable).	Reframe rigor and relevance as overlapping concepts that reinforce each other (Pasmore, Stymne, Shani, Mohrman, & Adler, 2008) Conduct scientifically rigorous and clinically relevant research through the use of mixed qualitative and quantitative data and a combination of descriptive and experimental research.

official views of the National Institutes of Health. The authors thank Drs. Sandra Daley, Sheila Broyles, Barry Hill and Robin Taylor.

Funding

This work was supported by the National Institutes of Health [grant numbers R01MH66070, K23MH-077584 and P30 MH074778].

References

Abrams, L. C., Cross, R., Lesser, E., & Levin, D. Z. (2003). Nurturing interpersonal trust in knowledge-sharing networks. *The Academy of Management Executive (1993)*, 17, 64–77. doi:10.5465/AME.2003.11851845

Addis, M. E. (2002). Methods for disseminating research products and increasing evidence-based practice: Promises, obstacles, and future directions. *Clinical Psychology: Science and Practice*, 9, 367–378. doi:10.1093/clipsy.9.4.367

Alexander, J. A., Comfort, M. E., Weiner, B. J., & Bogue, R. (2001). Leadership in collaborative community health partnerships. *Nonprofit Management and Leadership*, 12, 159–175. doi:10.1002/nml.12203

Alexander, J. A., Weiner, B. J., Metzger, M. E., Shortell, S. M., Bazzoli, G. J., Hasnain-Wynia, R., ... Conrad, D. A. (2003). Sustainability of collaborative capacity in community health partnerships. *Medical Care Research and Review*, 60, 130S–160S. doi:10.1177/1077558703259069

Becker, A. B., Israel, B. A., & Allen, A. J. (2005). *Strategies and techniques for effective group process in CBPR partnerships*. San Francisco, CA: Jossey-Bass.

Beutler, L. E., Williams, R. E., Wakefield, P. J., & Entwistle, S. R. (1995). Bridging scientist and practitioner perspectives in clinical psychology. *American Psychologist*, 50, 984–994. doi:10.1037/0003-066X.50.12.984

Blumenthal, R. N., Jones, L., Fackler-Lowrie,Ellison, M., Booker, T., Jones, F., ... Wells, K. B. (2006). Witness for wellness: Preliminary findings from a community-academic participatory mental health initiative. *Ethnicity & Disease*, 16, supplement 1, 18–34.

Bradbury, H. (2008). Quality and "actionability": What action researchers offer from the tradition of pragmatism. In A. B. Shani, S. A. Mohrman, W. A. Pasmore, B. Stymne, & N. Adler (Eds.), *Handbook of collaborative management research* (1st ed., pp. 583–600). Thousand Oaks, CA: Sage.

Bradshaw, C. P., & Haynes, K. T. (2012). Building a scince of partnership-focused research: Forging and sustaining partnerships to support child mental health prevention and services research. *Administration and Policy in Mental Health*, 39, 221–224. doi:10.1007/s10488-012-0427-7

Brookman-Frazee, L. I., Drahota, A., & Stadnick, N. (2012). Training community mental health therapists to deliver a package of evidence-based practice strategies for school-age children with autism spectrum disorders: A pilot study. *Journal* of Autism and Developmental Disorders, 42, 1651–1661. doi:10.1007/s10803-011-1406-7

Brookman-Frazee, L., Garland, A. F., Taylor, R., & Zoffness, R. (2009). Therapists' attitudes towards psychotherapeutic strategies in community-based psychotherapy with children with disruptive behavior problems. Administration and Policy in Mental Health, 36, 1–12. doi:10.1007/s10488-008-0195-6

Brookman-Frazee, L., Haine, R. A., Baker-Ericzen, M., Zoffness, R., & Garland, A. F. (2010). Factors associated with use of evidence-based practice strategies in usual care youth psychotherapy. Administration and Policy in Mental Health and Mental Health Services Research, 37, 254–269. doi:10.1007/s10488-009-0244-9

Brookman-Frazee, L., Stahmer, A. C., Lewis, K., Feder, J. D., & Reed, S. (2012). Building a research-community collaborative to improve community care for infants and toddlers at-risk for autism spectrum disorders. Journal of Community Psychology, 40, 715–734. doi:10.1002/jcop.21501

Butterfoss, F. D., & Francisco, V. T. (2004). Evaluating community partnerships and coalitions with practitioners in mind. Health Promotion Practice, 5, 108–114. doi:10.1177/1524839903260844

Chorpita, B. F., & Mueller, C. W. (2008). Toward new models for research, community, and consumer partnerships: Some guiding principles and an illustration. Clinical Psychology: Science and Practice, 15, 144–148. doi:10.1111/j.1468-2850.2008.00123.x

Chorpita, B. F., Yim, L. M., Donkervoet, J. C., Arensdorf, A., Amundsen, M. J., McGee, C., Morelli, P. (2002). Toward large-scale implementation of empirically supported treatments for children: A review and observations by the Hawaii Empirical Basis to Services Task Force. Clinical Psychology: Science and Practice, 9, 165–190. doi:10.1111/j.1468-2850.2002.tb00504.x

Cropper, S. (1996). Collaborative working and the issue of sustainability. In C. Huxham (Ed.), Creating collaborative advantage (pp. 80–100). London: Sage.

Cropper, S., Huxham, C., Ebers, M., & Ring, P. S. (2008). Oxford handbook of inter-organizational relations. Oxford: Oxford University Press.

Daley, S. P., Roberts, C., Hahn, H., O'Flaherty, V., & Reznik, V. (1999). The San Diego New Beginnings Collaborative: Principles and assessment of a community-government-university partnership. NHSA Dialog: A Research-to-Practice Journal for the Early Intervention Field, 3, 98–127.

Frazier, S. L., Formoso, D., Birman, D., & Atkins, M. S. (2008). Closing the research to practice gap: Redefining feasibility. Clinical Psychology: Science and Practice, 15, 125–129. doi:10.1111/j.1468-2850.2008.00120.x

Garland, A. F., Brookman-Frazee, L., Hurlburt, M. S., Accurso, E. C., Zoffness, R., Haine, R. A., & Ganger, W. (2010). Mental health care for children with disruptive behavior problems: A view inside therapists' offices. Psychiatric Services, 61, 788–795. doi:10.1176/appi.ps.61.8.788

Garland, A. F., Haine-Schlagel, R., Accurso, E. C., Baker-Ericzen, M. J., & Brookman-Frazee, L. (2012). Exploring the effect of therapists' treatment practices on client attendance in community-based care for children. Psychological Services, 9, 74–88. doi:10.1037/a0027098

Garland, A. F., Haine-Schlagel, R., Brookman-Frazee, L., Baker-Ericzen, M. J., Trask, E. V., & Fawley-King, K. (2013). Improving community-based mental health care for children: Translating knowledge into action. Administration and Policy in Mental Health and Mental Health Services, 40, 6–22. doi:10.1007/s10488-012-0450-8

Garland, A. F., Hurlburt, M. S., & Hawley, K. M. (2006). Examining psychotherapy processes in a services research

context. Clinical Psychology: Science and Practice, 13, 30–46. doi:10.1111/j.1468-2850.2006.00004.x

Garland, A. F., Plemmons, D., & Koontz, L. (2006). Research-practice partnership in mental health: Lessons from participants. Administration and Policy in Mental Health, 33, 517–528. doi:10.1007/s10488-006-0062-2

Haine-Schlagel, R., Brookman-Frazee, L., Fettes, D. L., Baker-Ericzén, M. J., & Garland, A. F. (2012). Therapist focus on parent involvement in community-based youth psychotherapy. Journal of Child & Family Studies, 21, 646–656. doi:10.1007/s10826-011-9517-5

Haine-Schlagel, R., Fettes, D. L., Garcia, A. R., Brookman-Frazee, L., & Garland, A. F. (2013). Consistency with evidence-based treatments and perceived effectiveness of children's community-based care. Community Mental Health Journal. doi: doi:10.1007/s10597-012-9583-1

Hardy, C., Phillips, E., & Lawrence, T. B. (2003). Resources, knowledge and influence: The organizational effects of inter-organizational collaboration. Journal of Management Studies, 40, 321–347. doi:10.1111/1467-6486.00342

Huxham, C. (2003). Theorizing collaboration practice. Public Management Review, 5. doi:10.1080/1471903032000146964

Huxham, C., & Hibbert, P. (2008). Manifested attitudes: Intricacies of inter-partner learning in collaboration. Journal of Management Studies, 45, 502–529. doi:10.1111/j.1467-6486.2007.00754.x

Huxham, C., & Vangen, S. (2003). Researching organizational practice through action research: Case studies and design choices. Organizational Research Methods, 6, 383–403. doi:10.1177/1094428103254454

Huxham, C., & Vangen, S. (2005). Managing to collaborate: The theory and practice of collaborative advantage. London: Routledge.

Israel, B. A., Schulz, A. J., Parker, E. A., & Becker, A. B. (1998). Review of community-based research: Assessing partnership approaches to improve public health. Annual Review of Public Health, 19, 173–202. doi:10.1146/annurev.publhealth.19.1.173

Kellam, S. G. (2012). Developing and maintaining partnerships as the foundation of implemenation and implementation science: Reflections over a half century. Administration and Policy in Mental Health, 39, 317–320. doi:10.1007/s10488-011-0402-8

Lasker, R. D., & Weiss, E. S. (2003). Broadening participation in community problem solving: A multidisciplinary model to support collaborative practice and research. Journal of Urban Health-Bulletin of the New York Academy of Medicine, 80, 14–47.

Lasker, R. D., Weiss, E. S., & Miller, R. (2001). Partnership synergy: A practical framework for studying and strengthening the collaborative advantage. Milbank Quarterly, 79, 179–205. doi:10.1111/1468-0009.00203

Levin, D. Z., & Cross, R. (2004). The strength of weak ties you can trust: The mediating role of trust in effective knowledge transfer. Management Science, 50, 1477–1490. doi:10.1287/mnsc.1030.0136

Lindamer, L. A., Lebowitz, B. D., Hough, R. L., Garcia, P., Aquirre, A., Halpain, M. C., & Jeste, D. V. (2008). Improving care for older persons with schizophrenia through an academic-community partnership. Psychiatric Services, 59, 236–239. doi:10.1176/appi.ps.59.3.236

Lindamer, L., Lebowitz, B., Hough, R., Garcia, P., Aguirre, A., Halpain, M., & Jeste, D. (2009). Establishing an implementation network: Lessons learned from community-based participatory research. Implementation Science, 4, 17–27. doi:10.1186/1748-5908-4-17

McMillen, C. J., Lenze, S. L., Hawley, K. M., & Osborne, V. A. (2009). Revisiting practice-based research networks as a platform for mental health services research. *Administration and Policy in Mental Health, 36,* 308–321. doi:10.1007/s10488-009-0222-2

Minkler, M. (2004). Ethical challenges for the "outside" researcher in community-based participatory research. *Health Education & Behavior, 31,* 684–697. doi:10.1177/10901981 04269566

Minkler, M., & Wallerstein, N. (Ed.). (2003). *Community based participatory research in health.* San Francisco, CA: Jossey-Bass.

Muthusamy, S. K., & White, M. A. (2005). Learning and knowledge transfer in strategic alliances: A social exchange view. *Organization Studies, 26,* 415–441. doi:10.1177/0170840605050874

Pan, A., Daley, S., Rivera, L., Williams, K., Lingle, D., & Reznik, V. (2006). Understanding the role of culture in domestic violence: The Ahimsa project for safe families. *Journal of Immigrant and Minority Health, 8,* 35–43. doi:10.1007/s10903-006-6340-y

Pasmore, W. A., Stymne, B., Shani, A. B., Mohrman, S. A., & Adler, N. (2008). The promise of collaborative management research. In A. B. Shani, S. A. Mohrman, W. A. Pasmore, B. Stymne, & N. Adler (Eds.), *Handbook of collaborative management research* (1st ed., pp. 7–32). Thousand Oaks, CA: Sage.

Pasmore, W. A., Woodman, R. W., & Simmons, A. L. (2008). Toward a more rigorous, reflective, and relevant science of collaborative management research. In A. B. Shani, S. A. Mohrman, W. A. Pasmore, B. Stymne, & N. Adler (Eds.), *Handbook of collaborative management research* (1st ed., pp. 567–582). Thousand Oaks, CA: Sage.

Reimer, M., Kelley, S. D., Casey, S., & Haynes, K. T. (2012). Developing effective research-practice partnerships for creating a culture of evidence-based decision making. *Administration and Policy in Mental Health, 39,* 248–257. doi:10.1007/s10488-011-0368-6

Reznik, V. M., Hahn, H., Morris, E., & Daley, S. (2000). Community-university partnerships: Policy and legacy. *California Western Law Review, 36,* 403–416.

Shortell, S. M., Zukoski, A. P., Alexander, J. A., Bazzoli, G. J., Conrad, D. A., Hasnain-Wynia, R., … Margolin, F. S. (2002). Evaluating partnerships for community health improvement: Tracking the footprints. *Journal of Health Politics Policy and Law, 27,* 49–92. doi:10.1215/03616878-27-1-49

Simonin, B. L. (1997). The importance of collaborative know-how: An empirical test of the learning organization. *The Academy of Management Journal, 40,* 1150–1174. doi:10.2307/256930

Sink, D. (1996). Five obstacles to community-based collaboration and some thoughts on overcoming them. In C. Huxham (Ed.), *Creating collaborative advantage* (pp. 101–109). Thousand Oaks, CA: Sage.

Sobell, L. C. (1996). Bridging the gap between scientists and practitioners: The challenge before us. *Behavior Therapy, 27,* 297–320. doi:10.1016/S0005-7894(96)80019-0

Southam-Gerow, M. A., Hourigan, S. E., & Allin, R. B., Jr (2009). Adapting evidence-based mental health treatments in community settings: Preliminary results from a partnership approach. *Behavior Modification, 33,* 82–103. doi:10.1177/0145445508322624

Spoth, R. L., & Greenberg, M. T. (2005). Toward a comprehensive strategy for effective practitioner-scientist partnerships and larger-scale community health and well-being. *American Journal of Community Psychology, 35,* 107–126. doi:10.1007/s10464-005-3388-0

Suarez-Balcazar, Y., Harper, G. W., & Lewis, R. (2005). An interactive and contextual model of community-university collaborations for research and action. *Health Education & Behavior, 32,* 84–101. doi:10.1177/1090198104269512

Vangen, S., & Huxham, C. (2003). Enacting leadership for collaborative advantage: Dilemmas of ideology and pragmatism in the activities of partnership managers. *British Journal of Management, 14,* S61–S76. doi:10.1111/j.1467-8551.2003.00393.x

Weiss, E. S., Anderson, R. M., & Lasker, R. D. (2002). Making the most of collaboration: exploring the relationship between partnership synergy and partnership functioning. *Health Education & Behavior, 29,* 683–698. doi:10.1177/109019802237938

Wells, K. B., & Miranda, J. (2006). Promise of interventions and services research: Can it transform practice? *Clinical Psychology: Science and Practice, 13,* 99–104. doi:10.1111/j.1468-2850.2006.00011.x

Wells, K. B., Miranda, J., Bruce, M. L., Alegria, M., & Wallerstein, N. (2004). Bridging community intervention and mental health services research. *American Journal of Psychiatry, 161,* 955–963. doi:10.1176/appi.ajp.161.6.955

METHOD PAPER

Conducting research and collaborating with researchers: The experience of clinicians in a residential treatment center

ROBERT W. ADELMAN, LOUIS G. CASTONGUAY, DAVID R. KRAUS, & SANNO E. ZACK

Department of Psychology, Pennsylvania State University, State College, PA 16802, USA

Abstract

This paper describes the experience of clinicians in conducting research and collaborating with academic researchers. As part of clinical routine of a residential program for adolescent substance abusers, empirical data have been collected to assess client's needs before and after treatment, improve clinical practice, and identify barriers to change. Some of the challenges faced and the benefits learned in conducting these studies are presented. In addition to highlighting the convergence of research interests between clinicians and academicians, the conclusion offers general recommendations to foster these partnerships and solidify the scientific-practitioner model.

Empirical data published in peer-review journals are largely viewed as irrelevant by clinicians (e.g., Morrow-Bradley & Elliott, 1986). In contrast, we would argue that data collected and owned by practitioners can be both informative and empowering. When integrated within clinical routine, such data can indeed provide them with tools to deliver better care and resources to face pressures for accountability. The goal of this paper is to present the efforts of practitioners in monitoring outcome, increasing treatment impact, and collaborating with researchers in order to better understand and address clients' needs. Although this work has taken place in a specific clinical setting, a residential treatment center for adolescents with substance abuse problems, it is hoped that it will provide helpful guidance to other clinicians interested in better understanding therapy and improving their practice via empirical data. Additionally, while this paper was primarily written for practitioners (which we hope will be conveyed, in particular, in our description of our research efforts and results), it is also hoped that it will offer useful recommendations for researchers and for administrators interested in

collaboration aimed at enhancing mental health services.

As a starting point, we present the clinical context that led to these research efforts and partnership. We then describe the data collected and studies conducted so far. Next, we highlight some of the challenges faced, the strategies implemented to deal with these obstacles, and the benefits earned by these efforts. In discussing these challenges and benefits, we try to be as candid and comprehensive as possible. We believe that shedding light on issues that are usually kept under the table (such as frustration that members of our team have experienced with one another) might be the best way for others to learn from our experience. We end this paper by presenting some future directions of research, as well as by offering general recommendations to foster the accumulation and implementation of empirical evidence in naturalistic settings.

Clinical Needs for Empirical Data

As the first author of this paper experiences on a daily basis, the professional life of clinicians working in a private adolescent residential treatment center can be highly stressful. They work with clients who are difficult to treat, interact with distressed and highly concerned families, and operate within the financial constraints of a strained health care system. Within this context, an emphasis on clinical outcomes is key. At an organizational level, the ability to successfully market and demonstrate (to parents, insurance companies, or funding agencies) favorable outcomes is an essential ingredient to the survival and success of a treatment program. At the level of an individual treatment, it is important for clinicians to consistently promote hope and show their commitment to the treatment progress. To this end, the careful formulation of client problems in solvable terms, the description of treatment goals and methods, and the demonstration of short to mid-range treatment effects are crucial. Clinicians who cannot deliver on such important tasks may struggle to maintain a therapeutic alliance with the client and their families, though they may be prone to interpret the struggle somewhat egocentrically as stemming from client resistance to treatment.

It should also be kept in mind that although clinicians may draw on treatment effects shown in large-scale studies to conjure confidence in common methods of intervention, the families with teens in residential treatment are thinking in terms of an N of 1. Families want to know whether all our research, experience, and knowledge are likely to significantly impact *their* child's chances for success, over and above their own efforts, or above the efforts of previous treatment providers. It thus behooves clinicians to marshal evidence at the inception of treatment, and during the course of therapy, that *this* loved one can benefit from their services. By the time parents arrive at a residential treatment center with their child, they may be experiencing much burnout, desperation, or flagging hope regarding the chances for treatment to succeed. As such, they may exhibit frustration and doubts toward clinicians. We have found that these frustrations and doubts are best understood as desires for accountability for the outcomes of treatment methods applied in addressing their child's issues and behaviors. Thus, the question becomes: What is the method or process of change that would give us reason to expect that this client will maintain sobriety from chemicals of abuse, improve his/her level of psychological functioning, and return and be able to cope in a developmentally appropriate educational or vocational setting? Needless to say, while we as clinicians cannot make absolute guarantees that would oversell our methods, we should not undersell our methods either, by shying away from asserting the strength and viability of therapeutic interventions. At our treatment center, we have decided that the best way to provide a fair and most accurate answer to such questions is to collect and review data internally about the impact of our own clinical routine and share our observations about the process of change with parents.

Within this context, it is fair to say that parents' concerns of accountability have facilitated a systematic implementation of the scientific-practitioner philosophy by posing questions that converge with clinical process and outcome researchers' core interests: How can we define and measure improvement? Do our clinicians have the most efficient and effective treatment methods at their disposal? If not, can we train clinicians to use and improve upon their current methods to produce change? As we have seen many times in our setting, parents are asking clinicians to be behavioral scientists as well as providers of effective care. Before personally committing and investing in the treatment process, they are frequently asking for an understanding of what has been shown to work in treatment, as well as a demonstration of how the therapists can foster a process of change that leads to positive results. Thus, even if they have chosen to define themselves primarily as providers of services, clinicians are routinely being asked by the health care consumer to bring scientific knowledge and procedures to the clinical encounter.

In contrast, the provision of services without accountability appears to be resting on implicit assumptions that may be both erroneous and costly. First, it implies that we as practitioners already have all the answers to problems of human behavior and emotional distress, which is a dubious assumption at best. It also implies that we will be able to apply our knowledge uniformly across the client population without individualizing care and still be able to achieve the same results. As clinicians, we are frequently reminded that these assumptions are false. In treatment centers such as the one described in this paper (and no doubt in other settings as well), many practitioners experience shame or fear to admit to the purchasers of our services (in the present case, the administrators who employ us) that our expertise has its limits and is in a state of evolution. Rather than educate (fairly and accurately) administration about the inherent difficulty of our professional reality and then work together to learn or to develop more effective means to produce change, we may simply hope for the best and keep our nose to the grindstone in trying to effect change in our clients. The result may be professional burnout and stagnation or diminishing returns in the achievement of clinical outcomes. In addition, working without the feedback or the guidelines of a research program places the clinical team at the jeopardy of relying on the preferences of the more socially dominant members of the team, regardless of the clinical efficacy of the preferred models or methods. Considering these issues as a whole, the integration of a scientific attitude and empirical knowledge in clinical practice is perhaps best justified by the complexity, clinical and social, of mental health care.

Studies

Sundown Ranch is a dual diagnosis program for adolescents and young adults with chemical dependency and mental health disorders. It is a 60-bed facility located in rural East Texas. A primary diagnosis of chemical dependency is required for admission, but there are often one or more comorbid mental health diagnoses, either present at the time of admission, or which surface in the course of ongoing treatment and evaluation.

The counseling staff of Sundown Ranch consists of 15 clinicians, five with master's degrees in counseling or Social Work and 10 with licenses in chemical dependency counseling. In addition, there is one licensed psychologist on staff that provides psychological testing services, as well as counselor training and supervision. Medication support is also provided as needed by a licensed psychiatrist.

The average length of client stay was recently estimated as 43.44 days, ranging from 10 to 96 days. Length of stay is based foremost on clinical need, but it is constrained in many cases by the determinations of insurance reviews and family financial considerations.

Within the clinical routine of this professional setting, three avenues of research have been pursued. Although each study has its unique aim, the overarching goals have been to gain insight into the workings of the treatment process, improve treatment outcomes, and provide a foundation for the assurance of quality care to consumers. As clinical research does not come naturally to the day-to-day functioning of a treatment center, it was not until the first author was asked to write this article, and after retrospective discussion with administration, that he realized that what he developed with his colleagues is what university professors might refer to as a "program of research." At this point in time, this program of research has entailed three phases: (i) the incorporation of a database of clinical outcomes, (ii) the incorporation and monitoring of the effectiveness of a cognitive-behavioral program of treatment, and (iii) an investigation into factors affecting client treatment engagement and potentially predictive of treatment outcomes. The first two phases were conducted independently by the members of our center. The third one involved a collaboration with academic researchers at Penn State University.

Assessing, Monitoring, and Becoming More Attuned to Client's Problems

In our clinical setting prior to 1999, we based our assessment of treatment success on subjective clinician reports and surveys of client satisfaction with treatment services. These approaches had some obvious limitations. For example, reports of treating clinicians can be biased, are based on a wide range of criteria, and tend to lack specificity in terms of what aspects of the client's functioning changed or failed to improve. Client satisfaction reports, in turn, while often encouraging, lack objective criteria of markers of success related to the treatment process. In 1999, all of this changed. The Joint Commission Association of Hospital Organizations (JCAHO) came out with its mandate for all hospital and treatment programs within its orbit to begin to collect data for standard and approved markers of treatment outcome. This data were to be collected on an ongoing basis so as to provide indicators of treatment proficiency over time. In a sense, these new procedures provided hospital organizations with a report card of their success in impacting key areas of client functioning.

As the psychometrician of the treatment center, the first author of this paper was asked by the program director to help review the pros and cons of different performance measurement systems approved by the Joint Commission. The program director appeared to be nervous about the implication of this requirement in terms of the prospects of diminished autonomy and increased oversight by a third party. However, the first author made the case that data, if collected via valid and relevant measures, could give the facility a window into important clinical processes and create opportunities for improving meaningful outcomes. Once a measurement system was selected, a partnership was begun in which our data collected onsite were aggregated and processed by an external system, and then returned both to us and to the Joint Commission for review and strategic planning.

In examining the available performance measures, we specifically considered instruments that we felt would help us to chart and to address the emerging dual diagnosis aspect of chemical dependency treatment. We reasoned that if present but left untreated these other clinical problems could be interfering with clinical outcomes. In the end, we chose the Treatment Outcome Package (TOP) because of its psychometric qualities, suitability for naturalistic settings, and multidimensional measurement of a wide range symptoms and functioning. Furthermore, the TOP assesses case-mix variables (such as life-stress and comorbid medical conditions) to provide risk adjustment and benchmarking against a large warehouse of other providers outcomes. These risk-adjusted assessments provided us a means to identify the relative strength and weakness of our treatment center. In a sense, we looked upon it as comparable to a mini-MMPI, but requiring less time and effort, and thus capable of providing repeatable measures for the assessment of the progression of outcome. In addition, the TOP has different versions based on age, allowing us to use a developmentally appropriate measure (adolescent or adult versions) for our individual clients (for more information about the TOP, see Boswell, Kraus, Miller, & Lambert, 2014).

Within the TOP scales, we specifically examined client temper/violence, impulsivity, and depression. We intuitively believed that temper/violence could be a significant problem area in our population because of the frustration of clients with prior failed treatment attempts, their difficulty accepting structure and authority from adults, and increasing reports over time from our staff of incidents of client's aggressive behavior. However, we, nonetheless, assumed that depression and anxiety would be the most prevalent problem areas in our population, as it is the case in general mental health treatment. The data surprised us when we found that temper/violence and impulsivity were the most significant problem areas for our clientele at admission. As depicted in Figure 1, over a period of 19 months of assessment (from 1 July 1999 to 31 January 2001), these TOP scales show the highest elevation at admission. As indicated by the follow-up scores (which reflect the last TOP filled up by clients before discharge) on Figure 1, these were also the problem areas that were still more in need of intervention

after treatment (for more details see Adelman, 2006; Adelman, McGee, Power, & Hanson, 2005).

Thus, this data collection and analysis allowed us to come to know our target population with greater accuracy and guided us in applying our clinical resources to the key variables that might be most liable to interfere with client's treatment success. If not for this initial clinical research effort, we would likely have redoubled our efforts in trying to address client anxiety and depression, instead of identifying the sources of client anger and the means of resolving the anger. The research effort also enabled us to identify cognitive attributions fueling anger as potential triggers for relapse on chemical substances. In summary, the deepening assessment and monitoring of clients' difficulties in this first phase of research, allowed us to be more attuned to our client clinical needs.

Improving Clinical Performance

By revealing a clinical picture that was inconsistent with both our expectations and primary focus of intervention, the initial data collection project also opened up new directions to improve our effectiveness (and, hopefully, reduce treatment failures). To make use of this window of opportunity, however, required a cultural change in the way that clinicians at our center were practicing. At that point in time, clinicians were accustomed to following principles of chemical dependency counseling that had been developed originally with the treatment of adult offenders and without consideration of comorbid conditions. The notion was that if clients were not progressing in treatment, then the denial of their condition of dependency needed to be broken down before they could become more fully cooperative with treatment. In our case, there was a minority view (or hypothesis) among staff that the old style treatment tactics might be fueling client's anger and resistance rather than helping. As the finding of elevated temper/violence scores on the TOP was consistent with this hypothesis, our lead clinicians began to look for an intervention to add to our treatment program that might address anger in its own right and avoid these confrontations with clients over their "denial." By adding a new intervention to the treatment mix, we were also transforming what had been primarily a data collection process, Study No. 1, into a clinical performance improvement project, Study No. 2.

The staff on our Performance Improvement Committee selected Rational Emotive Behavior Therapy (REBT) as our new, adjunctive therapy modality. In choosing REBT, we were adding a cognitive-behavioral approach to what had been predominantly

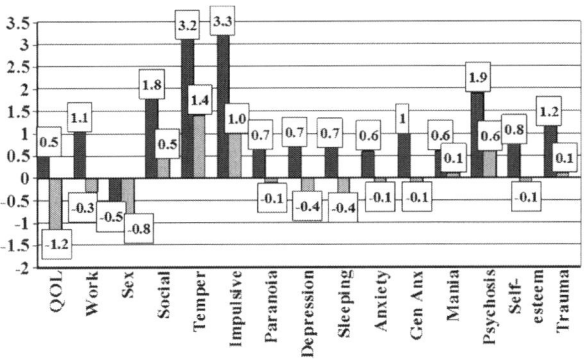

Figure 1. TOP outcome graph: Initial and follow-up data, from July 1999 to January 2001. Y axis represents *Z* score comparison to general population; lower scores are healthier.
Source: Reprinted from Adelman (2006, p. 102). Copyright 2006 by John Wiley & Sons, Ltd.

a 12 Step Recovery Program. The hope was that this more comprehensive, combined, approach would ultimately prove to be more successful for reducing client's anger and achieving positive treatment outcomes.

REBT was chosen for a number of empirical, theoretical, and practical reasons. The committee reviewed the research literature on REBT and found that there was evidence of successful application to a wide range of clinical problems including anger. On a theoretical basis, REBT seemed particularly well suited for helping young people to develop or to acquire increased self-responsibility for one's emotions and actions and for increasing healthy control of one's own life. The "ABC" problem-solving method (which emphasize the relationship between events, beliefs, and experience) appeared to provide a clarity and precision that could give our adolescents the structure they needed to become more effective at mapping the sequence of psychological cause and effect within their personal worlds. And the collaborative model of the helping relationship seemed, at least in theory, well-positioned to promote healthier interpersonal boundaries between staff and clients.

From a pragmatic standpoint, the REBT model has well-traveled over the years from its original development in the 1950s by Dr. Albert Ellis and was therefore well known. Several of our staff members had at least attempted to practice it with varying degrees of success. One staff member had gone to a training workshop and come back and given a presentation on REBT to the rest of the staff. But as is the case with much single-event workshop training, the method had not really taken seed with the rest of the staff, and this staff member had since moved on to another facility.

As a final approach to our evaluation of REBT, we decided to investigate what the training programs of the Albert Ellis Institute had to offer. We were surprised to learn through an Institute brochure that Albert Ellis was still professionally active and was available for telephone consultation. We set up a consultation hour with Dr. Ellis in which our clinical staff described our clinical problem with adolescent anger and negative behavior. He responded in his typical adroit and incisive fashion to delineate for us some of the key elements of REBT and how they would likely apply well to our clinical population. He even addressed a critical issue related to the integration of REBT within our facility. This issue was raised by the 12 Steps practitioners who insisted that any successful recovery program must be a God-based program that advocates turning one's self-will over to a higher power. Ellis responded with his characteristic verve and aplomb, "Tell your clients to not have to make their higher power work so

God-damned hard!" (personal communication, September 17, 2001). Needless to say, this really got our minds humming and made us eager and anxious to test out some of the connections he had drawn between REBT principles, adolescent dysfunction, and healthy empowerment of the adolescent self.

Starting in May 2001, our lead clinicians went on to train formally in REBT at the Albert Ellis Institute with Dr. Ellis and his colleagues and have then trained the rest of the direct care staff. This training includes introductory workshops, separate annual training sessions to counseling and support staff, as well as regular supervision sessions with individual counselors to reach and maintain a criterion set of competency. REBT is applied on a daily basis within our milieu as a problem-solving approach for increasing clients' emotional and behavior self-control and is used as a frontline technique in individual and group counseling sessions (see Adelman [2007] for a detailed description of the REBT curriculum guide that we developed for our population). Our integrated treatment program also includes 12-step study groups, a number of training modules (e.g., vocational planning and life skills), as well as monthly family-based activities (chemical education, family systems and multi-family therapy).

After we introduced and began to integrate REBT into the treatment program, we continued to collect data regarding client outcomes, as part of our obligation to the JCAHO. As depicted in Figure 2, the follow-up score (again reflecting the last TOP before client's discharge) on the temper/violence scale showed a descending curve during the 18-month period when REBT was progressively implemented into the treatment program and general milieu from May 2001 to December 2002.[1] Interestingly, the TOP data that has been since collected monthly shows that (with the exception of a few isolated months) we have been able to maintain the gains we made in resolving anger problems in the client population.

Treatment staff also corroborated these results with their own personal accounts of the positive change in the treatment population. Generally speaking, staff found to their surprise that the clients and their behaviors had become more manageable. They also found the clients were more willing to process their maladaptive actions and behaviors, as opposed to defending or escalating those actions. As further evidence of a change within the client population, clients created and began to perpetuate the phrase, "REBTing it," for describing their use of the REBT model to handle emotional upset when affected by a triggering event. Interestingly, this jargon has withstood the test of time, being passed

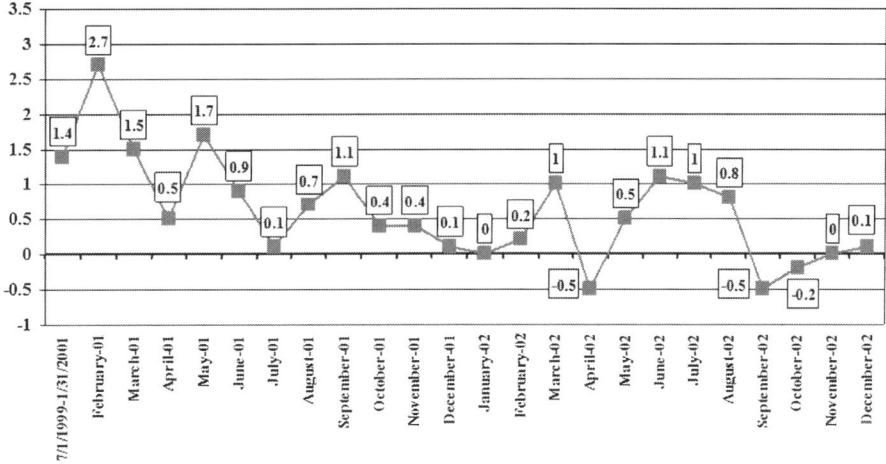

Figure 2. TOP Temper/violence scale: Follow-up data from July 1999 to December 2002. Y axis represents *Z* score comparison to general population; lower scores are healthier.
Source: Reprinted from Adelman (2006, p. 110). Copyright 2006 by John Wiley & Sons, Ltd.

on from one successive client group to another over the course of the intervening 13 years since the introduction of REBT.

Identifying Barriers to Therapeutic Change

The success of our center-wide intervention led to some new questions. How do we consistently facilitate engagement with this difficult population? How do we get our clients to be active consumers of psychological and chemical dependency services, as opposed to being passive toward treatment at best, or otherwise disgruntled, angry, and noncompliant? Is the positive engagement that we observed in some of our clients simply due to the skillful implementation of interventions unique to REBT, or could it be in part fostered by general principles of change that cut across different forms of psychotherapy?

We began addressing some of these questions with our third study, which we developed through collaboration with academic psychologists at Penn State, as well as with the president of the company operating the TOP (now named Outcome Referrals). How did this collaboration arise, and how did it affect or advance our research and clinical efforts?

In 2005, after hearing the results of our previous studies and our use of outcome data to improve our clinical practice, David Kraus (the third author of this paper and the developer of the TOP) introduced the first author to Louis Castonguay (the second author of this paper), who was involved in the development of several types of partnerships between researchers and clinicians. Via this connection, the first author became acquainted with the work of many other researchers associated with the Society for Psychotherapy Research (SPR). Through this community, he began to discover a new language

that provided another lens for viewing clinical work. This language consisted of terms like "evidence-based practice," "process of change," "process-outcome events," "mechanisms of change," and "therapeutic alliance." These terms seemed helpful in lending clinicians a way to talk about how to improve the effectiveness of psychotherapy without blaming the clients for the difficulty and complexity of clinical practice.

In line with the historical philosophy of chemical dependency counseling previously mentioned, many clinicians in our center used to put the burden of responsibility on the clients' shoulders when discussing lack of progress. Why is he/she not improving? Is it due to the severity of the psychopathology? Is it because he/she is unmotivated, noncompliant, resistant, or disrespectful? Is he/she just too impulsive to comply with the rules of the program or the steps of treatment? Or is he/she currently too unstable to benefit from treatment? Should we turn him/her over to the psychiatrist for medication?

Notice that none of these questions encourage a focus on improving the effectiveness of psychological treatment. We hoped to learn to shift the focus back on clinician actions that facilitate or interfere with the therapeutic process, as well as onto other (less blaming) client factors that might be predictive of clinical outcome. In particular, the concept of therapeutic alliance appeared to place the issue of engagement (including the client anger, which has been at the center of our clinical and research focus) within a broader context of therapeutic process. Our conversations with our colleagues at Penn State quickly revealed convergence of interests that would set the foundation for an exciting partnership. Not only was the alliance a core focus of Castonguay's writing and research (going back to his dissertation), but a student in his lab, Sanno Zack (the fourth author of this paper) had just completed a review of the current status of research on alliance in the treatment of adolescents (Zack, Castonguay, & Boswell, 2007). And based on the directions that she delineated for future research, she was looking for a setting to develop and then test ideas regarding the role of attachment relationships and the therapeutic alliance in effecting change—research she was planning as part of a dissertation project. These exchanges led to our third study. Designed and implemented with the expertise, perspective, and resources of various stakeholders (full-time academics, full-time clinicians, and the developer of an outcome instrument), the study was aimed to examine three hypotheses: (i) The strength of the therapeutic alliance predicts outcome; (ii) The quality of attachment history predicts the ability of clients to form a strong therapeutic alliance and to benefit from treatment; (iii) The client's attachment history will moderate the relationship between alliance and outcome, where this relationship would be stronger for client with poor attachment history than for clients with better attachment history. For the practitioners at Sundown, the primary interest in this study was to determine if knowledge of these relational and client factors could be of use to improve the handling of clients' treatment and enhance their therapeutic change.

The first hypothesis, if upheld, would lend more empirical support to the therapeutic alliance as an organizing concept to understand and guide the treatment process in our specific treatment program. From a clinical management perspective, this would suggest the benefit of further training of therapists, this time focused on skills for the development and maintenance of a strong therapeutic alliance within the practice of REBT. Support for the second and third hypotheses could help us identify the clients that might need additional care or intervention in establishing a treatment connection. Logically, this could also help us to avert some potential treatment failures, affirming our commitment to the parental N of 1 that was described earlier.

For a period of six months, all new clients at our facility were invited to participate in the study. If they accepted (and signed informed consent), they were asked to complete additional measures that had not been part of our previous clinical routine. These involved questionnaires at admission measuring client's attachment with caregivers and peers and a brief measure of working alliance filled out after the first week of treatment and every two weeks subsequently in addition to ongoing administration of the TOP. The completed paperwork was faxed to the research team at Penn State University for data entry, scoring,

and analysis. Thus the process of data collection required coordination by three teams of stakeholders: measure administration by primary clinicians and administrative staff at Sundown Ranch, scoring by Outcome Referrals, and entry and analysis by academicians at Penn State. Several main findings emerged from the data: (i) Our clinicians were forming overall strong alliances with their adolescent patients, with alliance scores comparable to those found in treatment provided in academic research settings; (ii) There was a trend for the alliance to improve over time during treatment which is also in keeping with findings from controlled trials in academic settings; (iii) Related to the first hypothesis, the alliance was significantly related to positive outcome; (iv) Supporting the second hypothesis, poor attachment was negatively associated with both the alliance and the treatment outcome; (v) Supporting the third hypothesis, and of particular interest, the clients who benefited the most from the therapeutic alliance were those who had the most severe problems in attachment to their parents or their caregivers (Zack et al., in press).

Thus it seemed the practical take home message for our clinicians was that clients who have the potential to be the most difficult for our counselors, those with poor relationship history and a predisposition toward a poorer alliance, may actually be the clients most in need of therapeutic attachment – as the therapeutic attachment formed was more strongly associated with symptom reduction for these patients who initially show poor attachment histories. Accordingly, one of the lessons that our staff learned from our study is how critical it is that we not give up on these clients, or engage in an adversarial manner with them, but instead find creative, innovative ways to reach them. This can serve as a strong motivator for clinicians if they keep in mind in the midst of challenging client interactions that far from being a hopeless situation, their perseverance in these therapeutic relationships might make the biggest outcome impact. In the process of forming this connection, clinicians may well be repairing clients' attachment wounds as well. As the study findings were presented to members of the clinical staff, a discussion developed about ways in which alliance-building may be inherent in some of the REBT principles, as well as about strategies by which the alliance can be further promoted within the practice of REBT. Afterwards, one of the staff commented, "This is REBT sounding more Rogerian than Rogers!"

Challenges

Despite the exciting findings from our three studies and the joys and enrichment of collaboration between clinicians, researchers, and assessment developers, a number of challenges have emerged during the evolving phases of our research program. In this section, we highlight some of these obstacles and suggest strategies to deal with a number of them, as they related to our initial collection of outcome data, subsequent efforts to improve practice based on outcome findings, and our collaboration with academic researchers in our attempt to identify barriers for therapeutic change.

Obstacles to Measuring Outcome

As the primary focus of our treatment center is to intervene in the lives of adolescents and families in crisis and prevent further harm or distress, time is of the utmost importance. Any work activities that take away from the delivery and delivery of direct services (which may be already limited by the constraints of managed care) can be viewed with skepticism or as an unnecessary luxury by clients, families, and clinicians. Rather than an opportunity to take the time to find out how to be more effective in the client contacts that they have, some of our clinicians seemed to have interpreted the use of clinical outcome as a way to get more work out of them. For many program administrators, devoting resources to clinical research may not be regarded as an acceptable use of time. Setting up and maintaining outcome measurement also requires structural change in the organization, and thus financial costs. From an administrative perspective, the collection of outcome data represents a risk of negative findings, which can have an impact on the accreditation of a program and credibility in the eyes of current and future clients.

Another obstacle toward the assimilation of "psychological science" within clinical routine is that mental health providers have all come through training programs to which they have a professional allegiance and perceive a debt of gratitude. Such attachment and loyalty can make it very difficult for some clinicians to maintain a scientific attitude and keep exploring research questions with a willingness to revise their opinions in areas that might conflict with earlier knowledge and learning. In this sense, clinicians are not unlike their clients who become frustrated when faced with change, or who may have difficulty changing even when they wish to. For example, one staff member when presented with new data or a new perspective about a clinical problem responded angrily, "why should I have to learn this or use this? I already have a degree and am treating the problem by the book." Parallel to one of the risks faced by the administration, the collection of data can also produce anxiety for many clinicians: "What if our (or my) outcomes are poor or wanting?"

"What if the measurement indicators are unstable and there is no clear pattern to the data?" Given these realities, it is fair to say that outcome monitoring raised two questions in our center, both individually among staff and across the organization: "Why should we do this extra work?", and "Do the potential benefits of this risk outweigh the potential costs of this risk?"

As previously mentioned, this data collection was initially driven as a reluctant response to external pressures for accountability. However, several factors seemed to help tip the scale toward the process of "Continuous Quality Improvement," enabling us to move forward in an incremental fashion. Some of these factors may well encourage other treatment centers to begin to pursue and maintain outcome collection. These were the following: (i) The initial data from the measures did show that treatment was working well in respect to many areas of client's functioning; (ii) Treatment effects were relatively stable from month to month; (iii) The outcome measure had unexpected clinical value: by pointing to our failure to define client anger as a problem and to effectively treat it, the TOP revealed how one specific characteristic of our clientele was hijacking the overall treatment effort; (iv) JCAHO's ongoing monitoring of our performance data made it essential to keep pace by continuing to look at our data; and (v) the desire to take control and see if we could find the means for positively impacting our data/clinical performance emerged as a major incentive.

Along with additional incentives described in a later section of this paper, these factors led Sundown Ranch to fully commit to the monitoring of clinical outcomes and, as such, cross over into the territory of clinical research.

Obstacles to Changing Practice

Although staff members were desirous of experiencing improvements in working with our clinical population, they sometimes displayed ambivalence and even resentment, when it came to having to put aside or accommodate some of their prior theoretical affiliations, or personal beliefs and biases, in order to work with the REBT model. In order to sustain the effects of our performance improvement project, we asked ourselves: How do we facilitate staff of varying levels of training and various affiliations toward treatment modalities to reconstruct their attitudes and behavioral tendencies toward angry and offensive adolescents in a manner that avoids conflict and encourages clients to work toward change?

In Personal Communications with Albert Ellis (March 18, 2003 and May 28, 2003), he described this phase of the process as akin to negotiating a paradigm shift with the staff. When the first author of this paper asked Dr. Ellis how to best facilitate this shift, he suggested informing the staff of the effectiveness of REBT and encouraging them to experiment with using the model with clients and seeing what kind of results they got. Taking this advice to heart, it seemed that the effectiveness of REBT with our population might be more strongly conveyed by directly facilitating clinician's progression through the process of cognitive-behavioral change with actual clients. We reasoned that we could provide additional intensive treatment with our clients while providing hand-on supervision to staff simultaneously. A staff member participating in our annual training would request a client to join with him in the training session. The client would be informed that the session could be mutually beneficial to each. The client might be able to gain more resolution on his issues and the staff member might be able to learn through the supervision how to get deeper into his or her use of the model. The sessions typically lasted 2 hr, including time for debriefing the client and time for debriefing the supervisor.

The testimony of the clients in this debriefing phase became an inspiration in our clinical practice and researching of the REBT model. The first author of this paper will likely never forget the spontaneous comments of one client early in our introduction of REBT into the treatment milieu. He was uncertain of our direction with the client and as to how productive the REBT work could be. With other staff members in the room, he was interviewing the client as to her irrational beliefs and hypothesizing about their relationship to one another and the implications for personal choice, dysfunction, and change, when the client moved forward abruptly in her chair and cried out, "What are you doing?" He froze in his tracks, fearful that he had induced some calamity or crisis in the client, or had triggered unresolved issues or affects that were overwhelming her. The client resumed speaking into the empty space of the confused silence in the room, and exclaimed, "What are you doing?! ... you should do more of this ... this really gets to the root of the problem ... this is help that really helps!" This is the kind of exposure to live clinical process that is extremely persuasive to clinicians despite their professional preferences and biases, as the clinical process actually had spurred the client to become an advocate for REBT among our professional group!

Obstacles to Collaborating with Researchers

Although the study of alliance and its potential moderators represented an exciting level of convergence between our clinical needs of Sundown Ranch and the academic interest of Penn State researchers,

there was anxiety on both sides as to the correct and accurate handling of the data, as well as with respect to working time frames that did not neatly overlap between the two working environments. Clearly, both sides were unused to not having complete control over their work product.

Some of the obstacles faced by the project emerged from external factors and were thus experienced as shared challenges. In particular, substantial time and energy were required to address issues raised by the Penn State Office of Research Protection (ORP). At the core of these issues was the concern that the study would be conducted by and for Penn State students and faculty, which could have negative consequences for the needs and rights of both clients and clinicians at Sundown Ranch. It took several meetings and revisions of the Institutional Review Board (IRB) application for the members of ORP to be convinced that the project was based on a collaborative initiative, and that rather than being used as a convenient research site, Sundown Ranch had equal ownership of the research idea, as well as full partnership in the implementation of the study procedure and data collection. In retrospect, the idea that full-time clinicians were building a collaboration with researchers to help them conduct a study that would be seamlessly integrated within their daily professional routine was rather unusual. To a large extent, because the data was collected as part of the clinical services and for the sake of improving treatment, the research protocol posed no conflict of interest on the part of the researchers (at Penn State and Sundown) and did not infringe on the needs and rights of clients.

There were, however, realities specific to one side of the collaborative team that were creating difficulties for the other side of the collaboration. For example, it took some time for Sundown Ranch to set up a system to collect, as part of routine assessment and treatment, additional pretreatment and process measures. Additionally, a relatively large number of clients were required to provide sufficient statistical power to conduct the planned analyses. And since the recruitment of participants was based on natural flow of clients (as opposed to advertisement related to the research project), it took more than six months to complete the data collection. These are not unusual circumstances in psychotherapy research, but they became problematic in the context of our collaboration, since we originally planned for the project to lead to a dissertation. Fortunately, Zack was able to conduct another study using archival data already available in her lab, allowing the collaborative project to progress at a pace more natural for the clinical setting of Sundown Ranch.

Once the data was collected and transferred to Penn State, it was the members of the Sundown team who experienced frustration due to delay. Entering and managing the data began as soon as the complete data were available, but because the student who was leading the project left for internship, the study became a lab project shared by many. With limited time available from several graduate and undergraduate students, it took more than four years for a full report of the findings to be shared with Sundown Ranch. This, again, is hardly an exception in psychotherapy research, but it led to complication and disappointment for clinicians and for administrators at Sundown Ranch.

As a result, this project made both clinicians and researchers fully realize not only that their collaboration entailed a loss of control over processes that they are typically in charge of, but that they live in different worlds: Researchers are continually involved in an array of studies and projects, which may or may not lead to timely and actionable answers; clinicians need to find helpful answers to address immediate and constantly arising questions for current patients. In the context of such different needs and pressures, the development and maintenance of a mutually benefiting partnership is likely to involve alliance ruptures along the way.

In addition to making sure that students who are involved in such collaborative studies have a "Plan B" for their training requirement (and that other students are able to pick up oversight of the project when Plan B is activated), we have learned at least two major lessons from these collaborative challenges: Researchers should not wait for the final analyses of data before sharing results with their colleagues, and clinicians should not wait for completion of a collaborative project to answer clinical questions before continuing doing research (as we described later, the first author of this paper has been successful in avoiding falling into such a passive mode!)

Benefits

While the conduct of research in our clinical setting has been met with several challenges, it has also led to numerous benefits. Some of these have already been referred to, including the identification of two key facts: (i) The most prevalent client problems at intake, and (ii) Which of these highly prevalent problems were not responding to our standard treatment. Moreover, the same data collection provided the opportunity for our providers to receive on-site professional development (training in REBT). Rather than the feared "punishment" from administration for poor outcomes, the collection of data led to the acquisition of new skills (via, for some, meetings with a luminary of the field). This experience demonstrates that although the monitoring of outcome can

understandably be viewed as a threat to the professional self-esteem and livelihood of providers, it can (and should) also be used in the mental health system (private and public agencies), as a way to foster continuing professional development as well as improve care (see Boswell et al., 2014), and to advance knowledge about psychotherapy.

The implementation and investigation of REBT within our clinical routine also had a beneficial impact on the interactions between the clinicians and the clients' parents. A favorite and valuable moment in the first author's casework with families is when after presenting a clinical formulation of the problem in REBT language, or a review of the problematic dynamics of a family dysfunctional interaction that ensues from the internal dysfunction of the client, the parent becomes a convert to the treatment process. Parents commonly make the statement under these circumstances: "Now I understand what has been happening and why my son (or daughter) is acting this way!" This statement is usually followed by a sigh and wistful expression accompanied by the question: "And what is it I can do that would help?" This is often the turning point in what had been an embattled struggle with diminishing returns, to a collaboration and understanding that leads to more targeted and successful cooperation in the treatment process, and the possibility of repairing bonds between the parents and the client.

Clinicians also developed a new understanding of difficult clients (those with problematic attachment history), as well as the importance of working with them in ways that avoid abandonment and possibly create corrective relational experiences. At a more general level, while the clinicians were learning how to apply REBT (in their own work environment and as part of their regular paying job), they were simultaneously participating in a study measuring its outcome. This is a good example of a seamless integration, or confound, of practice and research (Castonguay, 2011). Such an integration allows for the benefit of increasing knowledge (for the sake of the therapists themselves, their clients, their workplace, and the field) without the cost of having to be engaged in separate (nonclinical) tasks. For some clinicians, and especially the first author of this paper, the establishment and development of a research program have allowed them to reconnect with the interest of research that brought them to graduate school, the chance to present and publish data, and the opportunity to join the SPR community.

The academic members (students and faculty) involved in our partnership also benefited from the third study described above. Opportunities to test conceptually interesting and clinically relevant ideas in the real world (and with a large enough sample) are rare, especially in graduate school. And while this study did not materialize into a dissertation thesis, its completion earned a publication in the early careers of three graduate students in the lab.

The collaboration of the first and second authors, in particular, has provided mutually beneficial opportunities to look at the phenomenon at the core of their professional life from different vantage points. Discussions through the planning, implementation and dissemination of the third study (including the writing of the present paper) allowed both of them to gain perspectives about what works in psychotherapy and how best to measure it; perspectives that they do not tend to have access to when working within their respective clinical and academic environment.

It should also be mentioned that the administration of our center also gained substantial returns on their investment. Not only were the administrators proud and excited by our increase in effectiveness, they were particularly pleased when our clinical performance and research study on REBT became the recipient of the Ernest A. Codman Award for Clinical Performance Improvement for a Behavioral Health Facility (given by the Joint Commission in 2004). Our group attended an awards ceremony in Chicago with representatives from ownership, administration, and clinical staff. As the expression goes, "nothing succeeds like success"; suffice it to say we had little trouble from this point on in alerting administration to the value of clinical research in improving treatment efforts and in raising the level of accountability for our treatment approach!

Conclusion

Guided by a quest to improve our understanding and the quality of clinical care, the staff and administration of our treatment center have been involved in three studies, respectively, aimed at better defining clients' needs, implementing and testing techniques to deal with a new target of interventions, and identifying client variables that predict who will benefit more from good therapeutic process. Interestingly, these studies focused on three domains of psychotherapy that have received considerable attention in academic circles, both in terms of research and training: Client characteristics, relationship variables, and technical variables (e.g., Beck et al., in press; Castonguay & Beutler, 2006). These efforts, hopefully, are just the beginning of our attempt to assimilate research projects within our clinical practice. As a way to end this paper, we briefly discuss projects that we are in the process of conducting and offer a few general suggestions that might be helpful to other clinicians/researchers partnerships.

Future Research

Our interest for future studies is on understanding specifically how REBT treatment impacts our population. Rather than addressing the general issue of whether or not REBT works in our setting, we now want to investigate questions, such as: Where do clients become stuck in the process? What are some of the ways to advance the process of change? For which clients is REBT contraindicated? How can we train clinicians to overcome the most common barriers to effective implementation of the model? Our observations of varying levels of skill development in the repertoire of clients (as they learned and practiced REBT) have set the stage for a study that will be addressing the second question above. Specifically, we plan to assess the therapeutic community as a whole in regards to their progress in the learning of REBT. Our general hypothesis is that effective training is best fostered by a series of successive stages in the acquisition of complex therapeutic skills. This process allows clinicians to experiment and practice in between the successive stages. Under the guiding assumption that gradual mastery of the model will lead to better clinical outcomes, the longer-range goal of the study is to identify predictable barriers within the learning process and establish the means to further advance learning and training.

The issue of training has special relevance in clinical settings like our own because it pertains to the questions frequently asked by program reviewers as to whether we can provide assurance of providing consistent, quality care for our clients. Questions remained in our clinical setting as to how we rapidly, reliably, and sustainably increase the skill level of staff, including staff newcomers, in a given therapy modality like REBT. After discussing these questions internally, we consulted with a number of members of SPR through the SPR mail-list regarding the most efficacious methods for training therapists. The consensus opinion was that there was no clear evidence-base for identifying the most efficacious training methods. Reflecting convergence of interests between researchers and clinicians, this exchange took place at about the same time as members of SPR were beginning to form a special interest group to foster research into the training of therapists. Additionally, members of the administration at Sundown Ranch demonstrated a shared interest in this question when asking the first author of this paper, "So, how long before, and by what means, will these counselors be able to practice REBT at your level of competence?" This reflects the administration desire to provide high-quality and reliable (across staff members) services to its consumers, as well as the overlapping interest of a diversity of stakeholders in the field of mental health.

One hypothesis that has emerged from our internal discussion is that therapists are likely to be more efficient in mastering these problem-solving skills, and thus in applying REBT, if they apply REBT to themselves when becoming frustrated with clients and with client behaviors. This clinically driven question, interestingly, directly focuses on a prominent paradox in the field of psychotherapy research: We know that some therapists are better than others, but we do not have a clear understanding of why this is so (Castonguay, 2011). Reflecting further convergence between clinical and academic pursuits, it is interesting to note that while the first author of this paper has been working on developing this line of research with his colleagues at Sundown Ranch, the second author (and his colleague Clara Hill) has been independently grouping internationally well-known scholars and researchers to stimulate new ideas and future research to better understand such therapist effects.

General Recommendations

As a final step, we offer a few general recommendations related to future partnerships between researchers and clinicians that may hopefully solidify the scientific-practitioner model. First, we would like to suggest that there is no reason to believe that clinicians should wait for researchers to approach them before collecting data and conducting studies in their daily clinical routine. They can do this on their own and/or take initiatives, like we and others have done (see Fernández-Álvarez, Gómez, & García, 2014) in contacting researchers to help them address some of the questions they have about therapeutic change. Such a "bottom-up" approach to research, both in terms of process and content, is likely to avoid the problem of researchers using clinical settings merely as a convenient site to pursue their own research interests, which may or may not be relevant to the concerns of day-to-day practice (thus perpetuating empirical imperialism prevalent in the field, Castonguay, 2011).

Second, we believe that one way to optimize collaboration between academic and clinical sites is to focus, at least in part, on the interest and needs of students, as well as to rely on their unique expertise and resources. It may well be, based on our experience, that the first step of such a partnership may not be the optimal context in which to conduct a project that is as important and time sensitive, career wise, as a dissertation thesis. However, there would be tremendous advantages for clinicians and for administrators to set up a system (in terms of IRB approval

and research infrastructure within clinical routine) where masters and dissertation theses can be generated based on prospective and archival data. This is because students have two resources that most clinicians (and experienced researchers) do not have: updated knowledge in scientific (methodological and statistical) advances and time. Creating a "pipeline" for graduate (and undergraduate) projects would be beneficial for many stakeholders, in terms of publications, presentations, and professional networking. For many students, this would provide unique opportunities to simultaneously address their clinical and research interests, as well as training requirements. As noted elsewhere (Castonguay, 2011), this seamless integration of important needs may lay the foundations for an early and, hopefully, secure attachment to the Boulder model.

Our third recommendation is that research by and with clinicians should be encouraged as part of daily practice in the public and private mental health system. Providing conditions to help practitioners design and implement studies within their clinical routine would foster the accumulation of empirical data that are externally valid knowledge, actionable, and relevant to the immediate concerns of clinicians. In turn, such practice-oriented studies could widen the scope of current psychotherapy research and help built a more comprehensive and robust basis for knowledge (Barkham & Margison, 2007; Barkham, Stiles, Lambert, & Mellor-Clark, 2010; Castonguay, Barkham, Lutz, & McAleavey, 2013). In addition to contributing to general knowledge, POR can also have a local impact. As our own experience suggests, studies conducted within one center can address questions that are the most relevant to the needs of clients and practitioners of this particular site. For clinicians and researchers involved, such studies offer a number of advantages in comparison with investigations across multiple sites (including large practice research networks, e.g., McAleavey, Lockard, Castonguay, Hayes, & Locke, 2014): They allow for a higher level of control in terms of what to study and how to study it, impose lesser organizational and communication burdens, and they drastically decrease concerns about the generalization of the findings to their work environment. Since these studies come from and are about their practice, they can directly be use to better understand and potentially improve their provision of care. Considering their potency for broad and local impact, we strongly believe that practice-oriented studies should be recognized and rewarded by scholars, legislators, third-party payers, and administrators.

Note

[1] Revisions of the TOP based on large factor analytic work led to the deletion of the impulsive scale mentioned in the description of the first study.

References

Adelman, R. W. (2006). The angry adolescent and constructivist REBT. In P. Cummins (Ed.), *Working with anger: A constructivist approach* (pp. 99–113). London: Wiley & Sons.

Adelman, R. W. (2007). *Reducing anger in adolescents: An REBT approach.* Center city, MN: Hazelden.

Adelman, R. W., McGee, P., Power, R., & Hanson, C. (2005). Reducing adolescent clients' anger in a residential substance abuse treatment facility. *Journal on Quality and Patient Safety, 31,* 325–327.

Barkham, M., & Margison, F. (2007). Practice-based evidence as a complement to evidence-based practice: From dichotomy to chiasmus. In C. Freeman & M. Power (Eds.), *Handbook of evidence-based psychotherapies: A guide for research and practice* (pp. 443–476). Chichester: Wiley.

Barkham, M., Stiles, W. B., Lambert, M. J., & Mellor-Clark, J. (2010). Building a rigorous and relevant knowledge-base for the psychological therapies. In M. Barkham, G. E. Hardy, & J. Mellor-Clark (Eds.), *Developing and delivering practice-based evidence: A guide for the psychological therapies* (pp. 21–61). Chichester: Wiley.

Beck, J. G., Castonguay, L. G., Chronis-Tuscano, A., Klonsky, E. D., McGinn, L. K., & Youngstrom, E. A. (in press). Principles for training in evidence based psychology: Recommendations for the graduate curricula in clinical psychology. *Clinical Psychology: Science and Practice.*

Boswell, J. F., Kraus, D. R., Miller, S. D., & Lambert, M. J. (2014). Implementing routine outcome monitoring in clinical practice: Benefits, challenges, and solutions. *Psychotherapy Research.* doi:10.1080/10503307.2013.817696

Castonguay, L. G. (2011). Psychotherapy, psychopathology, research and practice: Pathways of connections and integration. *Psychotherapy Research, 21,* 125–140. doi:10.1080/10503307.2011.563250

Castonguay, L. G., Barkham, M., Lutz, W., & McAleavey, A. A. (2013). Practice-oriented research: Approaches and application. In M. J. Lambert (Eds.), *Bergin and Garfield's Handbook of psychotherapy and behavior change* (6th ed., pp. 85–133). New York, NY: Wiley.

Castonguay, L. G., & Beutler, L. E. (Eds.). (2006). *Principles of therapeutic change that work.* New York, NY: Oxford University Press.

Fernández-Álvarez, H., Gómez, B., & García, F. (2014). Bridging the gap between research and practice in a clinical and training network: Aigle's Program, 1977–2012. *Psychotherapy Research.* doi:10.1080/10503307.2013.856047

McAleavey, A. A., Lockard, A. J., Castonguay, L. G., Hayes, J. A., & Locke, B. D. (2014). Building a practice research network: Obstacles faced and lessons learned at the center for collegiate mental health. *Psychotherapy Research.* doi:10.1080/10503307.2014.883652

Morrow-Bradley, C., & Elliott, R. (1986). The utilization of psychotherapy research by practicing psychotherapist. *American Psychologist, 41,* 188–197. doi:10.1037/0003-066X.41.2.188

Zack, S. E., Castonguay, L. G., & Boswell, J. F. (2007). Youth working alliance: A core clinical construct in need of empirical maturity. *Harvard Review of Psychiatry, 15,* 278–288. doi:10.1080/10673220701803867

Zack, S. E., Castonguay, L. G., Boswell, J. F., McAleavey, A. A., Adelman, R., Kraus, D., Pate, G. A. (in press). Attachment history as a moderator of the alliance outcome relationship in adolescents. *Psychotherapy.*

EMPIRICAL PAPER

Brief Strategic Family Therapy: Implementing evidence-based models in community settings

JOSÉ SZAPOCZNIK[1], JOAN A. MUIR[1], JOHNATHAN H. DUFF[2], SETH J. SCHWARTZ[1], & C. HENDRICKS BROWN[3]

[1]*Public Health Sciences, University of Miami, Miami, FL, USA;* [2]*Educational and Psychological Studies, University of Miami, Miami, FL, USA &* [3]*Psychiatry and Behavioral Sciences, Northwestern University, Chicago, IL, USA*

Abstract
Objective: To review a 40-year collaborative partnership between clinical researchers and clinicians, in developing, investigating and implementing Brief Strategic Family Therapy (BSFT). **Method:** First, to review theory, practice and studies related to this evidenced-based therapy intervention targeting adolescent drug abuse and delinquency. Second, to present the BSFT Implementation Model created for the BSFT intervention—a model that parallels many of the recommendations from the implementation science literature. **Results:** Specific challenges encountered during the BSFT implementation process are reviewed, along with ways of conceptualizing and addressing these challenges from a systemic perspective. **Conclusion:** The BSFT implementation uses the same systemic principles and intervention techniques as those that underlie the BSFT clinical model. Building on our on-the-ground experiences, recommendations are proposed for advancing the field of implementation science.

An increasing number of preventive and treatment interventions have been found to be efficacious in tightly controlled trials, and many of these have been found to be effective in randomized controlled trials in real world settings (Faggiano et al., 2010; Watkins et al., 2011). However, current community practice in medicine and behavioral health does not fully incorporate evidence-based interventions (Institute of Medicine, 2007). The present article grew out of our experience with one behavioral intervention, Brief Strategic Family Therapy® (BSFT®), which has undergone nearly 40 years of clinical development and research, and the challenges we encountered in bringing this evidence-based intervention to practice settings. The current article is organized into two major sections: (i) Brief Strategic Family Therapy: Theory, Research and Practice; and (ii) Transporting and Implementing the BSFT Model in Community Based Settings: Challenge and

Solutions. Put together, these two sections trace the evolution of the BSFT approach from initial model development through efficacy, effectiveness, process research, and the recent development of the BSFT Implementation Model.

Brief Strategic Family Therapy®: Theory, Research and Practice

The Brief Strategic Family Therapy® (BSFT®) approach is a short-term family treatment model developed for youth with behavior problems. Developed by a team of clinicians and clinician-scientists over nearly 40 years of research at the University of Miami's Center for Family Studies, the BSFT approach is based on the premise that families are the strongest and most enduring force in the development of children and adolescents (Gorman-Smith, Tolan, & Henry, 2000; Steinberg, 2001;

Szapocznik & Coatsworth, 1999). Families of youth with behavior problems such as drug and alcohol use, delinquency, affiliation with antisocial peers, and unsafe sexual activity tend to interact in ways that permit or promote these problems (Vérroneau & Dishion, 2010). The goal of the BSFT approach, therefore, is to change the patterns of family interactions that allow or encourage problematic adolescent behavior. By working with families, the BSFT intervention not only decreases youth problems, but also creates better functioning families (Santisteban et al., 2003). Because therapists bring about changes in family patterns of interactions, these changes in family functioning are more likely to last after treatment has ended because multiple family members have changed the way they behave with each other.

The BSFT approach is based on an integration of structural (Minuchin & Fishman, 1981) and strategic (Haley, 1976; Madanes, 1981) approaches to family therapy. We proposed such an integration of structural and strategic principles given our early clinical experiences, where (i) adolescent behavior problems were clearly linked to structural problems (i.e., maladaptive patterns of interactions) within the family and (ii) a time-limited, strategic approach, targeting only those family processes that are directly associated with the adolescent's symptoms, appeared to be the most efficacious way to engage and retain families in treatment. Indeed, our own clinical experiences have continued to guide the refinement of the BSFT model. We have used a collaborative, bidirectional approach between clinicians and clinician-scientists in developing the BSFT model and its various modules (e.g., BSFT Engagement).

Based on our early experience with Cuban families, within the BSFT approach, the family is conceptualized as a system that is "greater than the sum of its parts" (Bowen, 1978)—that is, a system in which the behavior and development of each family member are interdependent with the behavior and development of other family members. Changing the adolescent's behavior, then, requires changing the family system as a whole. Specifically, the BSFT approach aims to modify the repetitive patterns of family interactions that support the adolescent's drug use and associated negative behavior, and to strengthen adaptive family interactional patterns that promote healthy development.

Specific Techniques Used in the BSFT Model

The BSFT intervention employs four specific theoretically and empirically supported techniques delivered in phases to achieve specific goals at different times during treatment. These techniques were built from the work of master clinicians such as Minuchin, Haley, and Madanes, and from the clinical experience of our clinicians and clinician-scientists in working with our minority families. As will be noted, this work is intended to make the family fully participatory—a full partner—in the change process. Early sessions are characterized by *joining* interventions that aim to establish a therapeutic alliance with each family member as well as with the family as a whole. The therapist here demonstrates acceptance of and respect toward each individual family member as well as the way in which the family operates as a whole. Early sessions within treatment also include *tracking and diagnostic enactment* interventions designed to systematically identify family strengths and weaknesses and develop an overall treatment plan. A core feature of tracking and diagnostic enactment interventions includes strategies that encourage the family to behave as they would usually behave if the therapist were not present. Family members are encouraged to speak with each other about the concerns that bring them to therapy, rather than have them direct comments to the therapist. From these observations, the therapist is able to diagnose both family strengths and problematic relations. *Reframing* techniques are then used to reduce family conflict and create a motivational context (i.e., hope) for change.

Throughout the entirety of treatment, therapists are expected to maintain an effective working relationship with family members (joining), facilitate within-family interactions (tracking and diagnostic enactment), and directly address negative affect/beliefs and family interactions. The focus of treatment, however, shifts to implementing *restructuring* strategies to transform family relations from problematic to mutually supportive and effective. These interventions include (i) directing, redirecting, or blocking communication; (ii) shifting family alliances; (iii) helping families develop conflict resolution skills; (iv) developing effective behavior management skills; and (v) fostering parenting and parental leadership skills.

BSFT Engagement. Often, the same interactional problems that are linked with the adolescent's symptoms are also associated with the family's inability to come to treatment. Within the BSFT model, specialized engagement techniques have been developed in collaboration with our senior therapists and evaluated by a team of clinical researchers (Coatsworth, Santisteban, McBride, & Szapocznik, 2001; Santisteban et al., 1996; Szapocznik et al., 1988). In this context, engagement refers to a set of strategies designed to bring all the relevant family members into treatment. The same intervention domains used in BSFT treatment—joining, tracking and diagnostic enactment, and reframing—are also used to engage families into therapy. The therapist begins to explore the family interactions in a first call by giving the caller a task such as bringing all the members of the family into the first session. Through the caller's response (e.g., "my husband won't come to treatment") the BSFT therapist can begin diagnosing family interactions. In these cases, and with the caller's approval, the therapist will insert herself into the family's process by reaching out directly to the family member who either does not want to come to treatment or whom the caller is not eager to bring to treatment, as a way of getting around the interactional patterns that interfere with bringing all family members into treatment.

BSFT Research

BSFT research has occurred in four primary domains: (i) studies evaluating BSFT efficacy in reducing adolescent behavior problems and drug use and in improving family functioning; (ii) studies evaluating the efficacy of BSFT Engagement procedures in bringing and retaining families in treatment; (i) studies evaluating the effectiveness of the BSFT intervention in community settings; and (iv) studies examining the effects of BSFT therapist prescribed behaviors on adolescent and family outcomes. These studies have led the US Department of Health and Human Services to label the BSFT approach as one of its "model programs" and to be included in the National Registry of Evidence-based Programs and Practices (NREPP; http://nrepp.samhsa.gov/ViewIntervention.aspx?id=151). We discuss research in each of these four areas in this section.

Led by a team of clinical researchers, the majority of the earlier studies on the BSFT intervention were conducted with Hispanic families in Miami (Coatsworth et al., 2001; Santisteban et al., 1996, 2003; Szapocznik et al., 1988, 1989). The model was originally developed to address acculturation discrepancies between Cuban adolescents and their parents (Szapocznik, Scopetta, & King, 1978a, 1978b). At the time when the BSFT model was developed, Szapocznik et al. (1978a, 1978b) observed that the vast majority of the drug-abusing and delinquent adolescents referred for treatment evidenced cultural, as well as normative developmental, conflicts with their parents. The researchers drew upon their own clinical experience, as well as on the experiences and observations of the therapists working with these adolescents and their families, in developing a model that would decrease the culturally related conflicts within client families. However, in addition to the efficacy research on the BSFT model with Hispanics, effectiveness research has suggested that the

model is equally applicable to African American and White American families as well (Robbins, Feaster, Horigian, Rohrbaugh, et al., 2011). The model is currently being used broadly with a variety of populations in the United States and Europe.

BSFT Efficacy. The efficacy of the BSFT model in reducing behavior problems and drug abuse has been tested in two randomized, controlled clinical trials. In the first trial, Szapocznik and colleagues (1989), including several very experienced clinicians, randomized behavior-problem and emotional-problem 6–11-year-old Cuban boys to BSFT, individual psychodynamic child therapy, or a recreational placebo control condition. The two treatment conditions, implemented by highly experienced therapists, were found to be equally efficacious, and more efficacious than recreational control, in reducing children's behavioral and emotional problems and in maintaining these reductions at 1-year post-termination. However, at 1-year follow-up, the BSFT condition was associated with a significant improvement in independently rated family functioning, whereas individual psychodynamic child therapy was associated with a significant deterioration in family functioning. To reflect the participation of the therapists in the design and conduct of the study, all four therapists were authors on the major outcome paper (Szapocznik et al., 1989).

In a second study, Santisteban and colleagues (2003) randomly assigned Hispanic (half Cuban and half from other Hispanic countries) behavior-problem and drug-abusing adolescents to receive either the BSFT intervention or adolescent group counseling modeled after a widely used program in the community. Three therapists delivered the BSFT condition. One was a highly experienced clinician who was proficient as a BSFT therapist. Reflecting his broad and thoughtful contribution to the intervention delivery as well as to other aspects of the study, he was an author on the outcome article. The other two, more junior therapists were supervised by the experienced BSFT therapist. Within the control condition, group counseling, a very experienced school counselor conducted the sessions in line with the way group counseling was being conducted in the community, without receiving any guidance or interference from the study team.

The BSFT condition was significantly more efficacious than group counseling in reducing conduct problems, associations with antisocial peers, and marijuana use, and in improving independent ratings of family functioning (Szapocznik et al., 1991). Interestingly, baseline family functioning emerged as a moderator of treatment effects. For families entering the study with comparatively good family functioning, family functioning remained high in the BSFT condition, whereas it deteriorated in the families of adolescents in group therapy. For families entering the study with comparatively poor family functioning, the BSFT condition significantly improved family functioning, whereas family functioning did not improve in families assigned to adolescent group therapy.

The BSFT model has also been tested with African American as well as Hispanic adolescents with behavior problems. In fact, Santisteban and colleagues (1997) found that BSFT treatment significantly reduced associations with antisocial peers and improved family functioning for both Hispanics and African Americans. However, BSFT treatment was significantly more efficacious in reducing association with antisocial peers among African Americans than among Hispanics, whereas it was significantly more efficacious in improving family functioning among Hispanics than among African Americans.

BSFT Engagement. The efficacy of BSFT Engagement was tested in three separate studies with Hispanic adolescents with behavior problems and their families. Clinicians played key roles on the research teams for all three of these studies. In the first study (Szapocznik et al., 1988), Hispanic (mostly Cuban) families with drug-abusing adolescents were randomly assigned to BSFT + Engagement as Usual or to BSFT + BSFT Engagement. Results indicated that 93% of the families in the BSFT Engagement condition, compared with only 42% of the families in the Engagement as Usual condition, engaged in treatment. Further, 75% of families in the BSFT Engagement condition completed treatment, compared with 25% of families in the Engagement as Usual group. Two clinicians were authors on the major outcome paper (Szapocznik et al., 1988).

A second study (Santisteban et al., 1996), which included the senior clinician in the study as an author, found similar results, with 81% of families randomly assigned to BSFT Engagement successfully engaging in treatment compared to 60% of the families in an Engagement Control condition. A third study (Coatsworth et al., 2001) tested the ability of BSFT + BSFT Engagement to engage and retain adolescents and their families in comparison to a *community* control condition implemented by a community treatment agency. Findings in this study indicated that BSFT Engagement successfully engaged 81% of families in treatment—significantly higher than the 61% rate in the community control condition. Likewise, among families who were successfully engaged, 71% of BSFT cases, compared to 42% in

the community control condition, were retained to treatment completion.

BSFT Effectiveness. A BSFT effectiveness study was conducted within NIDA's National Drug Abuse Treatment Clinical Trials Network (Tai et al., 2010). The Network is composed of 13 nodes, each led by a university research team (the lead author is PI of one of these nodes) in collaboration with community providers, community-based substance abuse treatment centers, and medical programs. The Network was established to increase the rate at which evidence-based practices were being translated into the frontlines of practice. Providers had argued that many research studies had not been designed with provider settings in mind, making it challenging to translate evidence-based practices tested under laboratory conditions into clinical practice. To achieve increased translation, it was essential to involve both researchers and practitioners in designing the effectiveness studies that would be implemented in the Network's community settings (Tai, Sparenborg, Liu, & Straus, 2011). The concept was to conduct rigorous randomized clinical trials of evidence-based practices in real-world, community-based settings. To help ensure that studies were designed to maximize adoption by providers, interventions would be delivered by real-world providers. To achieve this kind of synergy between researchers and practitioners, teams of providers and researchers selected the studies to be conducted and were intimately involved in their design. In this spirit, the BSFT study design, implementation, and manuscript writing team included clinician-scientists and provider-investigators, the latter from participating study sites. For example, denoting this kind of collaboration, the major outcome paper (Robbins, Feaster, Horigian, Rohrbaugh, et al., 2011) was authored by seven clinicians in leadership roles in community-based adolescent drug abuse treatment programs, six university-based clinician-scientists, and one biostatistician. In the BSFT effectiveness trial, we recruited 480 families of adolescents (213 Hispanic, 148 White, 110 Black and 9 Other; 377 male, 103 female) who had been referred to drug abuse treatment at eight community treatment agencies located around the United States. Adolescents and their families were randomized to either BSFT or Treatment as Usual (TAU, which was allowed to vary based on whatever treatment the agency typically provided for drug-using adolescents). Participating therapists were employees of the participating community agencies. They had a broad range of educational backgrounds (ranging from bachelor's to doctoral degrees) and prior experience (from minimal to extensive; from having worked with teens and families to never having done so).

Both families and therapists were randomized within each agency to either the BSFT or TAU modalities. Regarding engagement and retention, families in TAU were 2.33 times (11.4% BSFT; 26.8% TAU) more likely to fail to engage and 1.41 times (40.0% BSFT; 56.6% TAU) more likely to fail to retain compared to families in the BSFT condition. These significant differences were consistent across racial/ethnic groups.

Median drug use at 12 months, the final follow-up, was significantly lower in the BSFT condition (Mdn = 2 days) than TAU (Mdn = 3.5 days), although the actual number of drug use days remained low from baseline through follow-up in both conditions. These low levels of drug use may have been, at least in part, a function of the majority of adolescents having come from residential treatment or having been referred (and monitored) by the juvenile justice system.

Family functioning in this study differed between adolescent and parent reports, with the BSFT condition producing significantly greater improvements in parent-reported family functioning compared to the treatment as usual condition. Adolescents in both conditions, however, reported significant improvements in family functioning, with no statistically significant differences by treatment condition. Post-hoc analyses also demonstrated that the BSFT intervention was more effective than Treatment as Usual in improving parental functioning, and that this effect was mediated by parental reports of family functioning.

BSFT Therapist Behaviors, Therapy Process, and their Relationship to Outcomes

Research has demonstrated that negativity in family interactions in the first session leads to failure to retain families in treatment past the first session (Fernandez & Eyberg, 2009); that families are more likely to engage in treatment if negativity is reduced (Robbins, Alexander, & Turner, 2000); that reframing is an effective method of reducing negativity (Moran, Diamond, & Diamond, 2005); and that reframing is the technique that is least likely to damage therapists' rapport (alliance, bond) with family members (Robbins et al., 2006). Research on BSFT engagement has indicated that if, in the first session, the therapist does not develop a balanced set of bonds with the parent and the youth, this imbalance leads to early dropout from treatment (Robbins et al., 2000). The empirical evidence derived from the work of these clinicians has brought about findings

that have been incorporated into BSFT treatment as conducted today.

Therapist collaboration in delivering evidence-based interventions is essential to achieve high adherence rates and, consequently, better outcomes. Using data from the effectiveness study, Robbins, Feaster, Horigian, Puccinelli, et al. (2011) examined the extent to which BSFT therapists implemented the treatment protocol properly. Adherence (prescribed) items were rated in terms of the four theoretically and clinically relevant expected/prescribed therapist behaviors: joining, tracking and eliciting enactments, reframing, and restructuring. Therapist adherence to the BSFT model was associated with:

(1) *Engagement*: Higher levels of restructuring and reframing (creating a motivational context for change) significantly increased the likelihood of families being engaged in treatment. Because joining, tracking, and diagnosis were high across most cases, what distinguished cases that came to a second session from those that did not were reframing and restructuring, the technique domains that therapists found most challenging.

(2) *Retention*: The impact of adherence on retention was evaluated using adherence ratings for sessions 2–7, with retention defined as a family attending at least eight sessions. Higher levels of all four technique domains—therapist joining, tracking and enactment, reframing, and restructuring—predicted significantly higher rates of retention. A one standard-deviation increase in reframing predicted a 19% increase in the likelihood of retention; a one standard-deviation increase in joining predicted a 22% increase in the likelihood of retention; a one standard-deviation increase in restructuring predicted a 59% increase in the likelihood of retention; and a one standard-deviation increase in tracking and eliciting enactment predicted a 62% increase in the likelihood of retention.

(3) *Family functioning*: Overall joining levels predicted improvements in observer-reported family functioning.

(4) *Adolescent drug use*: Therapists who were high in joining in early sessions and remained so throughout treatment were associated with "better" adolescent drug use outcomes. Therapists whose attempts to restructure maladaptive family interactions increased most during the course of treatment were also associated with "better" adolescent drug use outcomes. Thus, therapists who failed to implement sufficient numbers of restructuring interventions were less able to affect the youths' drug use.

These results indicate that, within a sample of therapists from community agencies, therapists' clinical interventions follow a pattern that is consistent with the theory behind the BSFT model. Indeed, the specific therapist behaviors prescribed by the BSFT approach are needed to engage families in treatment, retain them, improve family functioning, and reduce adolescent drug use. However, when therapists did not engage sufficiently in these behaviors, adolescent outcomes tended to suffer. On the basis of considerable input from the participating therapists as well as the authors' own observations, the authors concluded that adherence ratings were affected by a number of systemic factors, including over-burdened therapists and therapists' lack of embeddedness within dedicated BSFT units. That an effectiveness study, conducted with community providers as therapists, revealed such impactful effects of therapist adherence suggests strongly that implementing the model with fidelity in community agencies is necessary for adolescents and families to achieve the maximum benefits from the BSFT treatment model.

Transporting and Implementing the BSFT Model in Community Settings: Challenges and Solutions

What is involved in transporting an evidence-based intervention into community agencies? The literature suggests that the combination of a detailed treatment manual, well-developed training programs, and an organization (sometimes called a purveyor) that promotes the intervention and provides therapists with training and ongoing monitoring, coaching, and feedback is needed (Fixsen, Blase, Naoom, & Wallace, 2009). These resources were all available for the BSFT model a decade ago. However, implementation brings a number of challenges in terms of transforming agency practices to ensure that the model is implemented with fidelity (Fixsen, Blase, & Van Dyke, 2011) and sustained (Henggeler, 2011). Community agencies and clinicians may not be accustomed to the rigors of evidence-based treatments, and there are a number of important challenges that arise during the process of working with an agency that has expressed interest in delivering an evidence-based treatment.

Our experiences in implementing the BSFT model within community agencies have been consistent with the challenges reported in the emerging literature on implementation (Fixsen, Blase, et al., 2011). The solutions that we have utilized were not directly informed by the implementation literature—but our solutions have dovetailed with recommendations from leaders in the implementation science field (Addiction Technology Transfer Center Network Technology Transfer Workgroup, 2011). Similar to the implementation science literature (see Fixsen et al., 2009; Fixsen, Blase, et al., 2011), we view successful implementation in terms of adoption, fidelity, and sustainability. *Adoption* refers to an agency's decision to deliver an evidence-based treatment model and to reconfigure itself so that the model can be delivered as intended; *fidelity* represents delivery of the model in accordance with the treatment manual; and *sustainability* represents a lasting commitment and ability to continue delivering the model on a long-term basis. Broadly, we have developed a systems approach to working with agencies, where some of the same principles that we use with families around the presenting symptom of "adolescent problem behaviors" are utilized with funders, agency leaders, supervisors, and therapists around the challenges of implementation. We describe these challenges and approaches in more detail in this section.

Our early implementation experience. Our first attempts to disseminate the BSFT clinical intervention into the community involved simply training therapists from community agencies in the BSFT approach and supervising them to achieve a specified level of fidelity in their delivery of the BSFT approach. These therapists would attend our training sessions, and would then apply the BSFT model, receiving monitoring, coaching, and feedback for fidelity. Many therapists would reach fidelity levels for "BSFT Therapist Certification." In most cases, however, these therapists encountered a number of obstacles to using the BSFT approach, and initial attempts to infuse the BSFT model into practical settings were largely unsuccessful in terms of attaining *enduring* fidelity and sustainability. We received considerable input from therapists that helped us to identify the challenges they were encountering. Agency supervisors, for instance, often place additional demands on therapists' time, such as additional caseloads using other therapy models that distracted therapists from their BSFT caseloads. For example, the BSFT approach mandates that families be seen wherever and whenever necessary—meaning that therapists must be available during evening and weekend hours. However, when therapists have large additional daytime caseloads, they may not be available when families are available—evenings and weekends. Indeed, we experienced these challenges in our effectiveness study when therapists who were assigned to deliver the BSFT model almost always had large caseloads using various treatment approaches. A dedicated BSFT team is necessary to deliver the model, given all of the requirements involved, and given the need for therapists to maintain conceptual focus on the model.

In our early implementation experience, although the agency had expressed interest in delivering the BSFT model, the agency leadership did not understand all that this entailed. When we followed up with therapists and agencies after training, we found that many therapists had not been able to continue to conduct the BSFT model without agency support, and had consequently reverted to previous, less demanding treatment models. Moreover, without ongoing monitoring, coaching, and feedback, therapists were unable to maintain acceptable levels of adherence or fidelity.

As our experience attempting to solely train (with monitoring, coaching, and feedback throughout training) therapists using the BSFT model demonstrates, an evidence-based model cannot simply be "picked up" from the research setting and "put down" into a community agency. The members of the BSFT research team, most of whom are clinically trained, recognized that a second layer of intervention at the organizational level was needed to facilitate successful implementation. From a family systems theory perspective, we understand that it is difficult to change one family member's behavior without changing the family system. Similarly, we learned that the same principles applied to agencies and their therapists: It is difficult to implement an evidence-based intervention in a community agency without creating a participatory process with agency and therapist personnel that establishes the context that will support the adoption, fidelity, and sustainability of the model. Based on this experience, and on our unsuccessful attempts to train therapists without working directly with the agency leadership, we developed a BSFT Implementation model, based on the systemic principles in which BSFT is grounded.

The feedback that we received from therapists and their local supervisors helped to shape the kind of implementation intervention that was needed. For example, it was clear that therapists were being pulled in many directions and did not have the time to dedicate to providing services to each family with the persistence required by the BSFT model. Therapists felt pulled in many directions not only by their heavy caseloads, but also because of the need to provide services using other approaches that are incompatible with the theoretical perspective underlying the BSFT approach. As a consequence, it became clear that a dedicated BSFT team with an agency advocate was needed to deliver the model, given all of the requirements involved, and given the need for the therapist to maintain conceptual focus on the model. This made sense because the efficacy of the BSFT model (and other family-based models) had always been tested with dedicated teams. Moreover, when we looked at other family-based models with successful sustainability, such as Functional Family Therapy (Breuk et al., 2006) and Multisystemic Therapy (Henggeler, 2011), we observed that these models had dedicated implementation teams.

How the BSFT model informs "adoption" in our implementation model. The BSFT Implementation model now extends the concept of systems to apply to therapists, the agencies with which they work, and these agencies' social ecology. Similar to our work in BSFT intervention, our experience in BSFT Implementation has taught us that *a participatory approach* to organizational work—at all levels of the agency—is essential to establish the context for adoption, fidelity, and sustainability.

Just as families require support from their social ecologies—such as adequate financial resources and freedom from excessive stress on the parent figures—treatment agencies must become partners in the implementation process to ensure that they, for example, seek and receive sufficient support from their funders, referral sources, and other stakeholders. Such support is essential to ensure that agencies have the flexibility to adopt (e.g., funding by case rather than by session), reach acceptable levels of fidelity (e.g., have time set aside for therapists and supervisors to train, be supervised, and review their own work), and achieve sustainability (e.g., long-term funding based on clinical outcomes rather than hours of services delivered; demonstrated cost savings to the funder and/or society; trained and certified BSFT on-site supervisor to ensure ongoing supervision to fidelity over time who can also function as an advocate for the model within the agency). Therefore, successful BSFT implementation requires full collaboration between the BSFT Institute, the agency (e.g., BSFT therapists and supervisors, agency middle and upper management), and its context (e.g., funders and other stakeholders such as judges who are often a major referral source). Such collaborations help to create a broadly participatory process in which all of the levels of the organization and its context, from therapists to agency middle-management, agency leadership, and funders, are actively involved in the implementation process.

To provide a BSFT Implementation intervention, we created the *BSFT Institute*, an example of an implementation "purveyor" whose goal is to facilitate adoption of, fidelity to, and sustainability of the evidence-based treatment model (Fixsen et al., 2009). The BSFT Institute is run by clinicians who are highly experienced and proficient in the BSFT therapy and/or implementation models. The BSFT Implementation approach borrows from the BSFT clinical intervention by engaging all members of an organization to create a participatory process. For example, the BSFT consultant *joins* with each of the individuals, inside and outside the agency, who has, or will have, a critical impact on the functioning of the BSFT unit. This joining requires identifying the "key" members of the system—therapists, administrative supervisors, agency director, clinical director, community referral sources, funders, and other stakeholders. Joining also often includes identifying the goals of agency personnel at all levels and ensuring that the BSFT model can help to achieve these goals. For example, an agency director may cite pressure from funders to treat as many adolescents as possible, for the least possible cost, within a given period of time. We would then present evidence indicating that the BSFT approach is more effective in reducing adolescent drug use and behavior problems compared to other approaches commonly used by community agencies (Robbins, Feaster, Horigian, Puccinelli, et al., 2011; Santisteban et al., 2003), and present evidence from Florida's Redirection program demonstrating reduced cost to the state (http://www. evidencebasedassociates.com/featured_projects/flori da.html). Presenting such evidence helps promote buy-in on every level, making it more likely that the BSFT model will be adopted and supported by funders. Similarly, therapists are interested in outcomes in the sense that they want to help their client families. When therapists see their ability to engage and retain families increase, they quickly become supporters of the BSFT approach.

Fidelity. Research on the BSFT clinical intervention (Robbins, Feaster, Horigian, Puccinelli, et al., 2011) and other family-based models (e.g., multisystemic therapy; Schoenwald, Sheidow, & Letorneau, 2004) has demonstrated that fidelity is essential to achieve desired outcomes. Our research has demonstrated that independently rated adherence to prescribed BSFT behaviors predicts engaging and retaining families in treatment, improving family functioning, and reducing adolescent drug use. As a result, ensuring fidelity to the model is a core principle of moving intervention research into practice. As with other similar models (e.g., Functional Family Therapy, Multisystemic Family Therapy), BSFT Implementation experience indicated that, to attain and maintain fidelity over time, administrative units need to be established and dedicated to the BSFT model. These units have therapists devoted solely to delivering the evidence-based intervention. In the BSFT model, typically four or five therapists are selected to form a BSFT team within the agency, and weekly supervision occurs after initial training to ensure the therapists are adherent to the model.

Additionally, an agency person outside the BSFT therapy team is appointed by the agency as the BSFT program administrative coordinator to manage the BSFT program within the organization and the community, and to serve as a liaison between the BSFT Institute and the agency. The organizational component of the BSFT Implementation model is consistent with our BSFT intervention theory, in which agency-supported leaders are identified who can motivate and support therapists in such a way that the agency's desired outcomes of adoption, fidelity, and sustainability can be achieved—that is, that will better adolescent outcomes and sustained funding for the program.

Interfacing with therapists. In addition to addressing relevant organizational factors important for successful implementation, it is also essential to listen carefully to therapists' objections and feedback regarding their experiences with the BSFT model. In our experiences, along with those reported by others in the field of family therapy research (e.g., Henggeler, 2011), therapists, like professionals in other service fields, often understand the importance of fidelity to the evidence-based model, but they dislike the scrutiny that accompanies intensive supervision and regularly scheduled feedback sessions (Fixsen, Scott, Blase, Naoom, & Wagar, 2011). Some of the therapists in the agencies with whom we have worked have commented that the intensive supervision involved in delivering the BSFT approach "feels like graduate school all over again."

BSFT Implementation maintains an essential commitment to the clinicians who, at the front line of practice, make or break successful implementation. Although joining with agency clinicians and selecting and training the BSFT team of therapists enhances successful adoption and faithful utilization of the BSFT approach, obstacles nonetheless arise. Many therapists, for example, are often reluctant to adopt a manualized treatment (Henggeler, 2011), with the most experienced therapists often expressing the greatest doubts. Often therapists earlier in the careers are more willing to explore new clinical models, particularly when they feel that they are struggling with their current caseloads. Another challenge arises out of the BSFT supervision approach, which involves monitoring through videotaping *all* sessions. Therapists are often initially uncomfortable with the perceived scrutiny involved in this process. Given the systemic approach underlying the BSFT clinical and intervention models, the BSFT model manager views her/himself as maintaining a systemic relationship with each therapist, and as such the model manager shares responsibility for therapists' behavior in therapy sessions. Thus, the BSFT model manager assumes a leadership role in helping therapists develop comfort with the manualized intervention and behaving with families in ways that are consistent with the model. BSFT clinical techniques such as reframing, which are useful in creating a motivational context for change with families, are also useful in creating a motivational context for change for therapists: "I can see that you struggle with videotaping. Yet your commitment to providing the best treatment for your clients is exemplary. Even when videotaping feels so awkward, you are willing to do it for the benefit of your clients."

Selecting therapists. One way to maximize the likelihood that therapists will deliver the BSFT model properly is to select therapists who are best matched with the model's assumptions and requirements. The BSFT approach requires a strong commitment to systemic work, conceptual ability, the ability and willingness to take on challenging cases, and the willingness to work in rough neighborhoods. Moreover, bringing whole families to treatment is often quite difficult—and many therapists are wary of the work and potential frustration involved. Indeed, specialized BSFT engagement strategies would not be necessary if drug-abusing or delinquent adolescents' families were able to come to treatment together easily. When considering whether to accept therapists, the BSFT Institute uses these and other criteria, as assessed through interviews. In addition, a therapist's family therapy audition tape is used in the selection process. We do not expect therapists to know the BSFT model or to have experience in family therapy. However, because we work with all family members, candidates must be able to support all family members and not to take sides for personal reasons. An example of an unsuitable therapist candidate would be someone who is unable to be supportive of male or female parents, who is likely to staunchly support one parent to the detriment of her/his relationship with another parent, or who takes generational sides (e.g., youth vs. parent). Although some of these abilities can be taught such as having balanced alliances, others such as the ability to relate to all family members may be more difficult to teach. The therapist must be the leader who will help the parent and the child change their behaviors—which the therapist cannot achieve if she/he is unable to establish a strong bond with all of the people who need to change. Thus, therapists must be able to adopt a nonjudgmental stance toward family members who behave in ways that appear maladaptive. Therapists must also possess the maturity to "own" their negative reactions to family members, to set aside their own views of family members whom they dislike, and to avoid permitting their frustration concerning a family's lack of progress to derail the course of therapy. We all may have negative reactions to particular people, but, when conducting therapy, we must be aware of these feelings so that we can manage them effectively. Accordingly, during the therapist selection phase, therapists are rated on a number of systems-based criteria, including the ability to communicate with *all* family members without judgment, the ability to recognize family strengths and to validate family members, and speaking to each family member in ways with which that family member can resonate.

Further, as noted by Phares, Lopez, Fields, Kamboukos, and Duhig (2005), fathers are seldom involved in family-based treatment, even if they are present in the home and/or in the child's life. In our experiences with BSFT therapist trainees, individuals in fathering roles—those who play responsible roles in their children's lives—are left out of treatment because therapists may not fully understand the critical role that every family member (especially father figures) plays in the family system. Fathers who have mental health, substance abuse, or criminal problems, and/or who appear not to be involved in their children's lives, are often left out of treatment because of the difficulties involved in engaging them in therapy. For example, a frequent family pattern of interaction has mothers and behavior-problem sons in a close relationship, whereas fathers are alienated from both mother and son. This pattern of interactions often gives rise to triangulations that can only be addressed when all members of the triangle are present. Hence, restructuring the father's (and the mother's) relationship with other family members—including the target adolescent—is vital to improving family functioning and to ameliorating the adolescent's symptoms. Fathers, like mothers, are essential members of the family and must be included in the treatment process. In our experience, when a critical family member is missing from the therapy session, it is impossible for the therapist to observe the family's repetitive patterns of interactions as they would occur at home (i.e., to diagnose the repetitive patterns of interactions that may be linked to the adolescent's problem behaviors) because a critical individual is missing who, when present, changes the family's patterns of interactions dramatically. What is essential in the selection process is to identify therapists who have the ability to relate to *all* family members, including fathers. Many people may be intimidated by father figures, more so than by mother figures.

Involving fathers may require conducting sessions at times when both parents are available; interfacing with substance-abuse, mental health, or criminal justice systems for fathers involved with these systems; or reaching out to a father who has remarried or lives with a new family. Therapists may initially be reluctant to take on the additional work that is required to include fathers in treatment. Just as joining with a family member requires convincing that person that she or he has something to gain from coming to therapy, overcoming a therapist's objection to working with whole families (including fathers) may require presenting research evidence demonstrating the importance of fathers (and all relevant family members) in adolescents' lives—and in their success in helping the target adolescent. The parental system must always participate in BSFT treatment, and fathers are very often part of the parental system.

A broad organizational perspective. As we suggested earlier, consistent with the systemic approach on which the BSFT intervention is based, challenges in implementing the BSFT model and working with clinicians are also viewed from a broader, organizational perspective. Examples of such obstacles include cases where BSFT therapists are located in administrative units that are not dedicated to delivering the BSFT model. In such situations, therapists may be given a caseload of 30–60 patients. Such caseloads can be managed through individual and group interventions, but are not possible to manage when whole families need to be engaged in treatment, when sessions often must be conducted in families' homes during evening and weekend hours, and when retaining family members requires frequent out-of-session contacts. The usual caseload for BSFT therapy is 10 families. For another example, if a community agency is not fully involved in the delivery of the BSFT model, therapists will often fail to submit videotapes required for supervision. Without these videotapes, we are unable to provide adequate monitoring, coaching, and feedback on BSFT adherence. Hence, supervisors cannot be successful unless the agency leadership is actively involved in ensuring that therapists have a caseload that allows them to deliver the BSFT intervention properly, are provided with adequate time to review their own videotapes, and are required to submit videotapes for supervision.

Rather than faulting therapists or other agency members for implementation challenges, such as clinicians' reluctance to quickly adopt the BSFT model, BSFT Implementation focuses on exploring the interactional patterns that support and maintain these obstacles. Using this systemic thinking, the BSFT Implementation team focuses on transforming interactional patterns that represent obstacles to change toward BSFT adoption and fidelity. BSFT

Implementation applies BSFT intervention techniques such as joining, tracking and eliciting, diagnosing, reframing, and restructuring to transform organizational interactional patterns that are obstacles to implementation. Because the BSFT intervention is a problem focused model, BSFT Implementation focuses only on those interactional patterns within the agency that must be reconfigured for the BSFT model to be delivered successfully. This principle is parallel to the focus of the BSFT clinical intervention—only those family interactions that are directly associated with the adolescent's symptoms are targeted in therapy. Other organizational issues are unlikely to be addressed if they are peripheral to BSFT Implementation.

Sustainability. Much of the work already mentioned has found that engaging multiple levels of an agency is essential to sustainability. In addition, we collaborate with agency leadership to facilitate support from funders and referral agents, often giving presentations on the BSFT model to educate these stakeholders on evidence-based practices generally and the BSFT approach specifically. In terms of promoting sustainability, nothing is more important than an engaged funder. In addition, to ensure sustainable fidelity to the BSFT manual within the agency, as part of the training, monitoring, coaching, and feedback related to the BSFT approach, an "on-site" supervisor is selected in collaboration with agency leadership. The on-site supervisor is one of the therapists in training who distinguishes him/herself in their BSFT abilities, demonstrates leadership skills by helping his/her co-workers in providing guidance with their BSFT work, and has the support of his/her co-workers and the agency leadership. In addition to providing ongoing on-site supervision, this person becomes the BSFT advocate or champion within the agency, ensuring that agency functioning continues to support BSFT fidelity and sustainability.

Benefits for Clinicians

Despite their initial hesitations, clinicians often enjoy the parallel process in which they observe the BSFT Implementation consultant applying BSFT principles at an organizational level that are parallel to the BSFT principles clinicians are learning to apply at a family level. Often to a fault, clinicians are dedicated to their clients. BSFT clinicians develop a broader and more thorough skill set, which enhances their ability to work effectively with families and often improves their clients' outcomes. Consequently, when clinicians first realize that they are able to engage and retain families in treatment, they become excited by their new skill set, but more importantly by their newly acquired abilities to help their client families. Ultimately, clinicians realize that they no longer experience the frustration of so many family drop-outs, and that they can bring more families to treatment completion—which is highly rewarding both because families are being helped and because of the feeling of success that comes with helping families.

The supervision that BSFT therapists receive promotes a consistently high-quality level of therapy and provides sustained support for their professional and often times their personal growth. Additionally, BSFT-trained therapists tend to be well regarded by others within the organization and are afforded the potential for enhanced career growth as they often become leaders within their respective organizations. After all, developing skills to manage complex systems, such as families, provides therapists with skills that can be used at the organizational level as well. BSFT therapists also find that they are more marketable, which increases their chances for career development; and as they learn to become leaders of the family-therapeutic system, they develop leadership skills that serve them well inside and outside therapy.

Implementing the BSFT approach into a community setting also confers broader benefits on the organization and community. Like any evidence-based treatment, the BSFT model provides a structured framework for an organization, with demonstrated evidence for effectiveness and support for strong clinical outcomes. The BSFT Institute provides support throughout the process of adoption as well, providing guidance and recommendations that often improve the agency's functioning. For example, communication between segments of an agency may be improved as a result of the BSFT Implementation process—such as reducing the number of people required to approve administrative decisions related to the BSFT unit. Communities are likely to benefit as well when the prevalence and severity of adolescent drug abuse, delinquency, and other forms of risk-taking are reduced. The BSFT model may serve as a secondary or tertiary prevention strategy. Secondary and tertiary prevention efforts may help to decrease costs involved with incarceration, hospitalization, and residential drug treatment (McCollister, French, & Fang, 2010).

Future Research

The field of implementation science is quite new, and much of what has been written is theoretical or anecdotal. The implementation science field within substance abuse prevention and treatment emerged out of a collective recognition within the research, practice, and policy communities that evidence-based treatments cannot simply be "installed" into treatment agencies, and that systemic barriers within the agency (or said more systemically, "developers' naiveté about integrating new services into existing organizations") often interfered with the successful delivery of the intervention (Fixsen et al., 2009). We have much to learn about how to achieve successful implementation, including designing appropriate measures to index and quantify "buy-in" from various members of the treatment agency, to examine the efficacy of the training program, and to evaluate the systemic strategies used to transform the agency in the service of facilitating adoption, fidelity, and sustainability (Landsverk et al., 2007).

One of the first steps that should be taken in the implementation science field, and that we plan to take with the BSFT approach, is to conduct a randomized clinical trial—the gold standard for evaluating the efficacy of an intervention approach (where the systemic implementation strategy is an intervention)—to evaluate the BSFT Implementation program. As is typical in the implementation science field (Fixsen et al., 2009) and of BSFT Implementation (Szapocznik, Muir, & Schwartz, 2013), community providers would be full partners in all aspects of the design, conduct, and analysis of the study. Treatment agencies might be randomly assigned to "intervention" and "control" conditions. The intervention agencies would receive the full BSFT Implementation intervention, whereas the control agencies would receive only standard BSFT training, including therapist monitoring, coaching, and feedback on BSFT fidelity. An alternative trial would be to compare the full BSFT Implementation intervention to an implementation model derived from organizational theory, such as the models now being used to deliver other evidence-based interventions (Glisson & Schoenwald, 2005). Outcomes would be assessed at multiple levels, including (i) changes in family functioning and adolescent problem behavior for individual client families; (ii) therapists' BSFT adherence and fidelity; (iii) cost-effectiveness of the implementation intervention; (iv) therapists' satisfaction with their work and with the outcomes of their cases; (v) agency, stakeholder, and referral source support for the BSFT approach; and (vi) sustainability of the BSFT model over time.

Because the field of implementation science is so new, mixed-methods research—including qualitative as well as quantitative components—should be conducted (Palinkas & Soydan, 2012). Such research will provide first-person perspectives from therapists and agency leadership regarding the experience of participating in a structured implementation process versus an alternative condition. What specific challenges does BSFT Implementation address? Are therapists' initial concerns—such as concerns about manualized intervention strategies, discomfort with intensive supervision, and reluctance to engage whole families into treatment—diminished by the end of the implementation intervention? What aspects of the BSFT Implementation system are most beneficial for therapists, and are there interactions between the implementation approach and specific therapist and agency characteristics? And perhaps most importantly, do decreases in therapists' objections and concerns predict increased fidelity to the BSFT model and improved client outcomes? Answering these questions will help to advance not only BSFT Implementation, but also the field of implementation science as a whole.

Funding

Preparation of this article was supported by Clinical Translational Science Institute Grant 1UL1TR000460 from the National Center for Clinical and Translational Science and the National Institute on Minority Health and Health Disparities, and U10 DA013720 and RC2 DA028864 from the National Institute on Drug Abuse to José Szapocznik, by Grant DA026595 from the National Institute on Drug Abuse to Seth J. Schwartz, and by Grant AA021888 from the National Institute on Alcohol Abuse and Alcoholism to Jonathan G. Tubman and Seth J. Schwartz, and Grant P30 DA027828 from the National Institute on Drug Abuse to C. Hendricks Brown. The information presented in this article is the sole responsibility of the authors and does not necessarily reflect the views of the funding agencies involved.

References

Addiction Technology Transfer Center (ATTC) Network Technology Transfer, W. (2011). Research to practice in addiction treatment: Key terms and a field-driven model of technology transfer. *Journal of Substance Abuse Treatment, 41*, 169–178. doi:10.1016/j.jsat.2011.02.006

Bowen, M. (1978). *Family therapy in clinical practice*. New York: Jason Aronson.

Breuk, R. E., Sexton, T. L., van Dam, A., Disse, C., Doreleijers, T. A. H., Slot, W. N., & Rowland, M. K. (2006). The implementation and the cultural adjustment of functional family therapy in a Dutch psychiatric day-treatment center. *Journal of Marriage and Family Therapy, 32*, 515–529. doi:10.1111/j.1752-0606.2006.tb01625.x

Coatsworth, J. D., Santisteban, D. A., McBride, C. K., & Szapocznik, J. (2001). Brief strategic family therapy versus community control: Engagement, retention, and an exploration of the moderating role of adolescent symptom severity. *Family Process, 40*, 313–332. doi:10.1111/j.1545-5300.2001.4030100313.x

Faggiano, F., Vigna-Taglianti, F., Burkhart, G., Bohrn, K., Cuomo, L., Gregori, D., ... the EU-Dap Study Group. (2010). The effectiveness of a school-based substance abuse prevention program: 18-month follow-up of the eu-dap cluster randomized controlled trial. *Drug and Alcohol Dependence, 108*, 56–64. doi:10.1016/j.drugalcdep.2009.11.018

Fernandez, M. A., & Eyberg, S. M. (2009). Predicting treatment and follow-up attrition in parent-child interaction therapy. *Journal of Abnormal Child Psychology, 37*, 431–441. doi:10.1007/s10802-008-9281-1

Fixsen, D. L., Blase, K. A., Naoom, S. F., & Wallace, F. (2009). Core implementation components. *Research on Social Work Practice, 19*, 531–540. doi:10.1177/1049731509335549

Fixsen, D. L., Blase, K. A., & Van Dyke, M. K. (2011). Mobilizing communities for implementing evidence-based youth violence prevention programming: A commentary. *American Journal of Community Psychology, 48*, 133–137. doi:10.1007/s10464-010-9410-1

Fixsen, D., Scott, V., Blase, K., Naoom, S., & Wagar, L. (2011). When evidence is not enough: The challenge of implementing fall prevention strategies. *Journal of Safety Research, 42*, 419–422. doi:10.1016/j.jsr.2011.10.002

Glisson, C., & Schoenwald, S. K. (2005). The ARC organizational and community intervention strategy for implementing evidence-based children's mental health treatments. *Mental Health Services Research, 7*(4), 243–259. doi:10.1007/s11020-005-7456-1

Gorman-Smith, D., Tolan, P. H., & Henry, D. B. (2000). A developmental-ecological model of the relation of family functioning to patterns of delinquency. *Journal of Quantitative Criminology, 16*, 169–198. doi:10.1023/A:1007564505850

Haley, J. (1976). *Problem-solving therapy*. San Francisco, CA: Jossey-Bass.

Henggeler, S. W. (2011). Efficacy studies to large-scale transport: The development and validation of multisystemic therapy programs. *Annual Review of Clinical Psychology, 7*, 351–381. doi:10.1146/annurev-clinpsy-032210-104615

Institute of Medicine (IOM). (2007). *The state of quality improvement and implementation research: Expert views and workshop summary*. Washington, DC: Author.

Landsverk, J., Brown, C. H., Chamberlain, P., Palinkas, L., Horwitz, S. M., & Ogihara, M. (2012). Design and analysis in dissemination and implementation research. In R. Brownson, G. Colditz, & E. Proctor (Eds.), *Dissemination and implementation research in health: Translating science to practice*. Oxford: Oxford University Press.

Madanes, C. (1981). *Strategic family therapy*. San Francisco, CA: Jossey-Bass.

McCollister, K. E., French, M. T., & Fang, H. The cost of crime to society: new crime-specific estimates for policy and program evaluation. *Drug and Alcohol Dependence, 108*, 98–109. doi:10.1016/j.drugalcdep.2009.12.002

Minuchin, S., & Fishman, C. (1981). *Family therapy techniques*. Cambridge, MA: Harvard University Press.

Moran, G., Diamond, G. M., & Diamond, G. S. (2005). The relational reframe and parents' problem constructions in attachment-based family therapy. *Psychotherapy Research, 15*, 226–235. doi:10.1080/10503300512331387780

National Registry of Evidence-based Programs and Practices. (2012). Brief Strategic Family Therapy. Retrieved from http://nrepp.samhsa.gov/ViewIntervention.aspx?id=151.

Palinkas, L. A., & Soydan, H. (2012). *Translation and implementation of evidence based practice*. New York: Oxford University Press.

Phares, V., Lopez, E., Fields, S., Kamboukos, D., & Duhig, A. M. (2005). Are fathers involved in pediatric psychology research and treatment? *Journal of Pediatric Psychology, 30*, 631–643. doi:10.1093/jpepsy/jsi050

Robbins, M. S., Alexander, J. F., & Turner, C. W. (2000). Disrupting defensive family interactions in family therapy with delinquent adolescents. *Journal of Family Psychology, 14,* 688–701. doi:10.1037/0893-3200.14.4.688

Robbins, M. S., Feaster, D. J., Horigian, V. E., Puccinelli, M. J., Henderson, C., & Szapocznik, J. (2011). Therapist adherence in brief strategic family therapy for adolescent drug abusers. *Journal of Consulting and Clinical Psychology, 79,* 43–53. doi:10.1037/a0022146

Robbins, M. S., Feaster, D. J., Horigian, V. E., Rohrbaugh, M., Shoham, V., Bachrach, K., ... Szapocznik, J. (2011). Brief strategic family therapy versus treatment as usual: Results of a multisite randomized trial for substance using adolescents. *Journal of Consulting and Clinical Psychology, 79,* 713–727. doi:10.1037/a0025477

Robbins, M. S., Liddle, H. A., Turner, C. W., Dakof, G. A., Alexander, J. F., & Kogan, S. M. (2006). Adolescent and parent therapeutic alliances as predictors of dropout in multidimensional family therapy. *Journal of Family Psychology, 20,* 108–116. doi:10.1037/0893-3200.20.1.108

Santisteban, D. A., Szapocznik, J., Perez-Vidal, A., Kurtines, W. M., Murray, E. J., & LaPerriere, A. (1996). Efficacy of an intervention for engaging youth and families into treatment and some variables that may contribute to differential effectiveness. *Journal of Family Psychology, 10,* 35–44. doi:10.1037/0893-3200.10.1.35

Santisteban, D. A., Coatsworth, J. D., Perez-Vidal, A., Mitrani, V., Jean-Gilles, M., & Szapocznik, J. (1997). Brief structural strategic family therapy with African American and Hispanic high-risk youth. *Journal of Community Psychology, 25,* 453–471. doi:10.1002/(SICI)1520-6629(199709)25:5%3C453::AID-JCOP6%3E3.0.CO;2-T

Santisteban, D. A., Coatsworth, J. D., Perez-Vidal, A., Kurtines, W. M., Schwartz, S. J., LaPerriere, A., & Szapocznik, J. (2003). Efficacy of brief strategic family therapy in modifying Hispanic adolescent behavior problems and substance use. *Journal of Family Psychology, 17,* 121–133. doi:10.1037/0893-3200.17.1.121

Schoenwald, S. K., Sheidow, A. J., & Letourneau, E. J. (2004). Toward effective quality assurance in evidence-based practice: Links between expert consultation, therapist fidelity, and child outcomes. *Journal of Clinical Child and Adolescent Psychology, 33,* 94–104. doi:10.1207/S15374424JCCP3301_10

Steinberg, L. (2001). We know some things: Parent-adolescent relationships in retrospect and prospect. *Journal of Research on Adolescence, 11,* 1–19. doi:10.1111/1532-7795.00001

Szapocznik, J., & Coatsworth, J. (1999). An ecodevelopmental framework for organizing the influences on drug abuse: A developmental model of risk and protection. In M. Glantz & C. Hartel (Eds.), *Drug abuse: Origins and interventions* (pp. 331–366). Washington, DC: American Psychological Association.

Szapocznik, J., Hervis, O., Rio, A. T., Mitrani, V. B., Kurtines, W., & Faraci, A. (1991). Assessing change in family functioning as a result of treatment: The Structural Family Systems Rating scale (SFSR). *Journal of Marital and Family Therapy, 17,* 295–310. doi:10.1111/j.1752-0606.1991.tb00897.x

Szapocznik, J., Muir, J. A., & Schwartz, S. J. (2013). Brief Strategic Family Therapy for adolescent drug abuse: Treatment and implementation. In P. M. Miller (Ed.), *Encyclopedia of addictive behaviors* (Vol. 3, pp. 97–108). New York: Elsevier.

Szapocznik, J., Perez-Vidal, A., Brickman, A., Foote, F., Santisteban, D., Hervis, O., & Kurtines, W. (1988). Engaging adolescent drug abusers and their families in treatment: A strategic structural systems approach. *Journal of Consulting and Clinical Psychology, 56,* 552–557. doi:10.1037/0022-006X.56.4.552

Szapocznik, J., Rio, A. T., Murray, E., Cohen, R., Scopetta, M. A., Rivas-Vazquez, A., ... Kurtines, W. (1989). Family versus child therapy for problematic Hispanic boys. *Journal of Consulting and Clinical Psychology, 57,* 571–578. doi:10.1037/0022-006X.57.5.571

Szapocznik, J., Scopetta, M. A., & King, O. E. (1978b). Theory and practice in matching treatment to the special characteristics and problems of Cuban immigrants. *Journal of Community Psychology, 6,* 112–122. doi:10.1002/1520-6629(197804)6:2%3C112::AID-JCOP2290060203%3E3.0.CO;2-R

Szapocznik, J., Scopetta, M. A., & King, O. E., (1978a). The effect and degree of treatment comprehensiveness with a Latino drug abusing population. In D. Smith, S. Anderson, M. Burton, N. Gotlieb, W. Harvey, & T. Chung (Eds.), *A multicultural view of drug abuse* (pp. 563–573). Cambridge, MA: G. K. Hall.

Tai, B., Sparenborg, S., Liu, D. S., & Straus, M. M. (2011). The National Drug Abuse Treatment Clinical Trials Network: Forging a partnership between research knowledge and community practice. *Substance Abuse and Rehabilitation, 2,* 21–28. doi:10.2147/SAR.S16756

Tai, B., Straus, M., Liu, D., Sparenborg, S., Jackson, R., & McCarthy, D. (2010). The first decade of the national drug abuse treatment clinical trials network: Bridging the gap between research and practice to improve drug abuse treatment. *Journal of Substance Abuse Treatment, 38,* S4–S13. doi:10.1016/j.jsat.2010.01.011

Véronneau, M.-H., & Dishion, T. J. (2010). Predicting change in early adolescent problem behavior in the middle school years: A mesosystemic perspective on parenting and peer experiences. *Journal of Abnormal Child Psychology, 38,* 1125–1137. doi:10.1007/s10802-010-9431-0

Watkins, K. E., Hunter, S. B., Hepner, K. A., Paddock, S. M., de la Cruz, E., Zhou, A. J., & Gilmore, J. (2011). An effectiveness trial of group cognitive behavioral therapy for patients with persistent depressive symptoms in substance abuse treatment. *Archives of General Psychiatry, 68,* 577–584. doi:10.1001/archgenpsychiatry.2011.53

EMPIRICAL PAPER

Building a practice research network: Obstacles faced and lessons learned at the Center for Collegiate Mental Health

ANDREW A. MCALEAVEY[1], ALLISON J. LOCKARD[2], LOUIS G. CASTONGUAY[1], JEFFREY A. HAYES[2], & BENJAMIN D. LOCKE[3]

[1]*Department of Psychology, Pennsylvania State University, University Park, PA, USA;* [2]*Department of Counselor Education, Counseling Psychology, and Rehabilitation Services, Pennsylvania State University, University Park, PA, USA &* [3]*Center for Counseling and Psychological Services, Pennsylvania State University, University Park, PA, USA*

Abstract
Objective: The Center for Collegiate Mental Health (CCMH) was created through a grass-roots initiative among university and college counseling centers to standardize assessment procedures, conduct empirical studies, and advocate clinical services. **Method:** At present, CCMH has over 240 college counseling center members and oversees a research infrastructure based on these centers' routine services, describing approximately 90,000 individual clients annually. These data are used to provide clinical tools, which can be useful for ongoing clinical services as well as program evaluation, quality assurance, and advocacy on behalf of the counseling centers and clients. **Results:** There have been substantial obstacles to overcome, and there remain numerous challenges in day-to-day operations. This article provides a brief overview of the challenges and current solutions. **Conclusions:** Large-scale collaborations between researchers and practitioners are possible, and some recommendations can be made based on the experience of CCMH.

University and college counseling centers (UCCs) are often the first-line treatment setting for mental health difficulties on college campuses, especially at residential colleges and universities. Like other outpatient clinical settings, UCCs have faced increasing pressure in recent years: pressure to provide evidence of their own efficacy, and pressure to justify their continued value within a college or university setting (Sharkin, 2004; Varlotta, 2012). The movements to identify empirically-supported treatments (ESTs; Chambless & Hollon, 1998) and toward evidence-based practice in psychology (EBPP; APA, 2006) demand that psychotherapists base their clinical practice on sound empirical footing. Another pressure is the clinical needs of the clients seen in

UCCs (Benton, Robertson, Tseng, Newton, & Benton, 2003). Studies of college student mental health have revealed that college students suffer from mental illness at similar rates to the national population. For instance, Eisenberg, Hunt, and Speer (2013) conducted a representative survey of 26 colleges and universities, and found an estimated 9.0% prevalence of positive screen for current Major Depression, not dissimilar from the Kessler, Chiu, Demler, Merikangas, and Walters (2005) estimate for 12-month prevalence of any mood disorder in the general population (9.5%). Since 2000, the rate of students being diagnosed with depression has increased 10–15% (Hunt & Eisenberg, 2010). Given the pressures to demonstrate value, and simultaneously respond to rapidly escalating demand, UCCs would benefit from a mechanism that provides for self-evaluation and outcome monitoring without unduly interfering with clinical services.

The Center for Collegiate Mental Health (CCMH) was developed in order to fill this role. Over nearly 9 years, it has matured into a large-scale practice research network (PRN), with numerous interrelated goals and a diverse group of stakeholders. Similar to the National Institute on Drug Abuse's Clinical Trials Network (see Szapocznik, Muir, Duff, & Schwartz, in press), CCMH is composed of a network of separate centers, each with its own clinical needs and procedures, and an administrative/leadership core.

In this paper we first describe the CCMH infrastructure with an emphasis on the goals and work that led to the current organization. We then summarize a few studies that have been conducted using data generated within CCMH. Following this is a review of several major obstacles encountered during the establishment of CCMH and current day-to-day operations, along with some of the solutions. A description of the benefits achieved through CCMH follows, emphasizing the benefits to different stakeholders in the system. And finally, we conclude with some of the lessons learned during the process of developing and maintaining this large practice-oriented infrastructure.

CCMH Development, Goals, and Operations

Origin and Early Development

CCMH is a grass-roots effort among counseling centers aimed at meeting the changing needs and demands of UCCs discussed above. As a result of these demands and the emphasis on clinical service, UCCs have generally lacked the time and resources to accurately describe, through research and dissemination, the students they serve, their resource needs, and the efficacy of their services. Given the high demand for services, lack of funding, and time constraints, conducting research has necessarily been a lower priority than providing direct services at UCCs. In the past, UCCs have often have relied on statistics from treatment-seeking college students that were retrospective and hard to generalize (Castonguay, Locke, & Hayes, 2011). As such, UCCs have been left in a vulnerable state: Unable to fully describe the nature of students seeking services or the value of the treatments offered, while struggling to meet an escalating demand.

CCMH was formally established in 2005 as a multidisciplinary research center at Penn State University. Since this time, it has grown to become a collaborative effort of many mental health stakeholders including clinicians, researchers, university administrators, and funders with shared goals including accurately describing clinical college student mental health at a national level, supporting self-advocacy for centers, conducting large-scale psychotherapy research, and improving the range of clinical tools available to clinicians in the college setting. The overarching goal of CCMH is to facilitate these mutually beneficial and interdependent relationships between the collaborators for the purpose of enhancing the clinical resources available to UCCs while also improving the mental health services provided to college students (Castonguay et al., 2011; Locke, Bieschke, Castonguay, & Hayes, 2012).

CCMH initially operated on a shoestring budget, and focused on developing grassroots support and buy-in from UCCs, researchers, and funders. It officially became a center after obtaining the support of invested colleagues, reaching a critical mass of UCC members (about 35), and receiving a small amount of seed funding, along with an endorsement, from the leadership organization of UCCs, the Association of University and Counseling Center Directors (AUCCCD). Critical to the establishment of CCMH was administrative support at Penn State University from Counseling and Psychological Services and Student Affairs, which provided support for the project's goals by providing the staff member who founded CCMH with time to coordinate the project during its infancy (Castonguay et al., 2011; Locke, Bieschke, et al., 2012).

Data Standardization

In order to achieve the necessary collaboration between clinicians and researchers, it was imperative for CCMH to establish a sense of community, "including shared ownership of the kinds of data gathered and the research conducted" (Locke, Bieschke, et al., 2012, p. 238). To address this goal, while avoiding the pitfall of creating more work for already strained UCCs, CCMH began by standardizing the data gathered during routine clinical practice (Locke, Bieschke, et al., 2012).

As a first step, CCMH gathered and synthesized intake materials from more than 50 counseling centers, which led to the development of a proposed Standardized Data Set (SDS). The proposed SDS then served as the base for an inaugural working conference in 2006 that consisted of more than 70 counseling staff members from 55 colleges and universities. Together they reviewed the proposed data standards and worked towards consensus, question by question, via small groups and plenary reporting/discussion. Over a period of 2 days, conference attendees made critical progress on the SDS and agreed to the creation of a 12-member Advisory Board composed of staff from member centers. The Advisory Board ensures that the activities and decisions of CCMH are reflective of the UCC field and consistent with the founding mission of CCMH. After extensive discussions and further debate, the CCMH Advisory Board finalized the SDS in the summer of 2007. The SDS, which measures client demographics and mental health history, serves as the foundation of the data collection for CCMH (Castonguay et al., 2011; Locke, Bieschke, et al., 2012). Refined each subsequent year, the SDS underwent a major revision in 2012 aimed at improving the accuracy of the information collected. After 2 years of work, the advisory board approved a new set of response options focused on both recency and frequency of past mental health concerns, drug use, and past traumatic events. In response to feedback from member centers, additional questions were added to more accurately assess gender identity and sexual orientation. To ensure that counseling centers continue to guide the work of the SDS, and therefore maintain a sense of shared ownership, feedback from members is gathered and reviewed annually. The advisory board is tasked with reviewing feedback from member centers in the context of current research and making final decisions about the iterative development of the SDS.

Included within the intake paperwork from 50 counseling centers used to create the SDS, there were also more than 35 self-report assessment instruments in use. Counseling centers have historically used several different instruments that are common in psychotherapy settings for initial assessment and treatment outcome monitoring, including the Outcome Questionnaire-45.2 (Lambert, 2004), Symptom Checklist-90-R (Derogatis, 1992), and the Behavioral Health Monitor-20 (Kopta & Lowry, 2002). After reviewing each of these instruments, the executive director of CCMH (Benjamin D. Locke) chose four to be considered by the CCMH membership/advisory board for selection as a common instrument for assessing clinical college student mental health. Each instrument was discussed at the 2006 conference and the CCMH Advisory Board reviewed additional feedback from over 100 centers. From this conference and discussion, it was clear that a free or low-cost instrument, designed for the college population, which assesses multiple areas of concern, was preferred by the CCMH membership. The Advisory Board, after much discussion and debate, selected the Counseling Center Assessment of Psychological Symptoms (CCAPS; see Locke et al., 2011; Locke, McAleavey, et al., 2012;

McAleavey et al., 2012) because it was (a) multidimensional, (b) psychometrically sound, (c) developed by counseling center staff specifically for college students, (d) open for refinement to meet the needs of participating centers, and (e) it could be provided at no charge to counseling centers for their use (Castonguay et al., 2011; Locke, Bieschke, et al., 2012). After the CCAPS was chosen, it was donated to CCMH for continued development on behalf of the field (as discussed below).

Technological Partnership

With the initial instruments selected, CCMH partnered with Titanium Software to integrate the CCAPS and SDS into their electronic medical records (EMR) software (Titanium Schedule is a commonly used EMR software by counseling centers). This step of technological partnership and data integration guaranteed that standardized questions and answers would not be edited over time, thus ensuring that only high-quality, reliable data would be generated. A potential problem with data standardization is a lack of flexibility or customization, which can result in reduced participation by many member centers. To avoid this pitfall, the SDS was integrated into Titanium Schedule in a manner that permits centers to add custom items, change the order in which items are presented, and turn individual items on or off (Locke, Bieschke, et al., 2012). This solution balances the needs of researchers (e.g., high-quality, standardized data) with the needs of practitioners (e.g., flexibility; center-specific data needs) and contributes to the mutually beneficial nature of the PRN. CCMH was fortunate to be able to partner with a business partner interested in a mutually beneficial partnership. Starting in 2006, Titanium Software supported CCMH through large in-kind donations of technical work/time and financial support for conferences in 2006 and 2009. In-kind support for CCMH has included the integration of standardized data materials into Titanium Schedule, refinements of these materials over time, and helping to design and build our data pooling infrastructure. While CCMH has been able to pay for some work over the years, much of the work has been completed for no charge. In turn, CCMH has benefitted Titanium by pooling feedback from members to guide new feature prioritization, helping to design and publicize a unique feature set that attracts new customers, and providing an attractive mechanism for counseling centers to contribute to national research. Over time, counseling centers began to use the linkage between Titanium and the ability to contribute to CCMH research as a primary factor when deciding which software to purchase.

This unique partnership has been mutually beneficial for CCMH and Titanium over time, as well as counseling centers in general, and underscores the value of a multi-disciplinary PRN and the role of technology.

The SDS and CCAPS became available within Titanium Schedule in January 2008, which allowed participating centers to gradually convert their intake materials to the CCMH standardized materials by September 2008 (Castonguay et al., 2011; Locke et al., 2012). Since then, CCMH has continued to grow and UCCs that do not use Titanium Schedule have expressed interest in accessing the CCAPS instruments. CCMH is working to address this need by distributing the CCAPS via additional authorized EMR vendors that pay a fee to make the instruments available to their customers. This approach enables CCMH to grow, meet the needs of more UCCs, and generate income by leveraging the influence of our membership within the EMR marketplace. CCMH now comprises over 240 counseling centers as members, many of which regularly submit data from approximately 80,000 counseling center clients per year. The centers vary widely in geographic location across the country, student body size (from fewer than 1000 to over 50,000 students), location (urban, rural), and services offered (see http://ccmh.squarespace.com/participating-centers/ for a complete list). The SDS and CCAPS, which serve as the data foundation of CCMH, have made it possible for UCCs to collaboratively gather large sets of high-quality data which can then be used to describe services, demonstrate value, advocate resources, and develop beneficial clinical tools.

Current Organization and Data Collection

As mentioned earlier, CCMH is best considered a network of individual UCCs. Within each center, the administrative staff (e.g., counseling center directors) oversee the many decisions necessary for the UCC's aims, along with the counselors who regularly provide assessment and treatment to clients (depending on the size of the center, these roles may be completely fused or completely separated). The 12-member CCMH Advisory Board provides broad oversight and final decision-making authority for CCMH. Board members are selected from a pool of applicants from member centers. The CCMH central organization, which is currently located at the Counseling and Psychological Services of The Pennsylvania State University, coordinates the creation and maintenance of data standards across participating centers, receives and stores incoming data, and provides the participating counseling centers with "refined data products": tools that assist in clinical

practice, reporting, and self-advocacy. In addition, the CCMH central organization is host to numerous collaborations between researchers and practitioners, with a primary goal of conducting practice-relevant research through the CCMH infrastructure. The CCMH research team is composed of faculty and graduate students in Counseling and Clinical Psychology, as well as clinical staff members from the UCC at Penn State. Through regular meetings, this group discusses ongoing and prospective research projects, and aims to conduct clinically relevant studies. A smaller group of faculty, staff, and graduate students also work on CCMH organizational projects, such as maintaining Institutional Review Board approval across all member sites, recruiting new centers, and other necessary functions. Thus, at every level of CCMH organization, there is an inherent collaboration between clinicians, researchers, and students.

The main source of data generated in CCMH is ongoing, real-world data collection that is conducted at each member center on each of their (participating) clients, and includes SDS, CCAPS, and appointment information. That is, in many cases (depending on the local IRB agreement), CCMH receives a nearly complete electronic record for many if not all clients at a counseling center. These data are completely de-identified once they are uploaded, so that not only are the clients' identities protected, but also the counseling centers are not identifiable. This data flow is the primary data output of CCMH centers, and apart from monthly data uploads, requires almost no time from individual counseling centers. So far, four major data sets have been defined. The first, called the CCMH Pilot data set, is data collected during the Fall 2008 academic semester, from 66 institutions. Following that pilot, data sets have been created for the 2010–2011, 2011–2012, and 2012–2013 academic years. The most recent annual data set includes data on over 90,000 individual clients, and over 3000 counselors. These data comprise almost one million lines of data each year, since each client may appear in any number of observations: Each CCAPS, SDS, and appointment is recorded when appropriate consent is obtained. These data are available for outside researchers for the benefit of the counseling field, through the data sharing mechanism discussed below.

Other data collection mechanisms have been established by CCMH and its partners for specific purposes. For example, a large national nonclinical data collection mechanism has been created with CampusLabs (described below) in order to conduct a national survey of college students who are not necessarily in counseling. This nonclinical data collection has grown to survey over 10,000 students per year, and uses measures developed by CCMH (the SDS and CCAPS-62). In addition, comparison data have been collected through a university subject pool, composed of nonclinical, non-treatment-seeking individuals. And for certain projects, ad hoc data collection has been conducted in counseling centers, with the consent and participation of several member centers and their clients.

Studies Conducted in CCMH

A number of scientific papers and conference presentations have stemmed from the CCMH data sets. Many of these studies have either been led by or included graduate students, demonstrating the feasibility of integrating research and clinical interest early in the career of mental health professionals, as in the scientist-practitioner model (see Castonguay, 2011; Castonguay, Pincus, & McAleavey, in press). All of these studies, however, also involve the collaboration of research mentors, and rely on CCMH clinical staff and administrators, including, for several studies, full-time clinicians as authors on publications and consultants during study development and manuscript preparation. Studies from CCMH have focused on topics of assessment, impacts of minority identity, UCC service utilization, and outcomes of counseling. Here, we summarize some of the key papers that have been or will soon be published across the wide areas of interest represented by CCMH researchers and clinicians.

Assessment. As described above, one of the first major tasks completed by CCMH was the selection of a self-report instrument for use in member centers. After selecting the CCAPS for this purpose, it was important to ensure that the measurements provided were valid and reliable estimates of distress. So far, three development and validation papers related to the CCAPS instruments have been produced. The first paper (Locke et al., 2011) documented the development of the CCAPS-62 from the initial pool of potential items, to the 70-item version used by the counseling center at the University of Michigan. It also included results from an exploratory factor analysis (EFA) and confirmatory factor analysis (CFA) of the CCAPS-70, which was used in CCMH's Pilot Study, and which was trimmed to the 62-item CCAPS-62 based on the empirical findings of this paper. The CCAPS-62 has 8 factor-analytically derived subscales covering a broad range of Axis I symptoms: Depression, Generalized Anxiety, Social Anxiety, Eating Concerns, Substance Use, Family Distress, Academic Distress, and Hostility. This paper also included analyses of data collected specifically to test the validity of the subscale scores of the CCAPS-62, providing some evidence for convergent and divergent validity of the CCAPS-62 subscales.

A second paper (Locke, McAleavey, et al., 2012) described the development and validation of a short form of the CCAPS-62, for the clinical and research purposes of obtaining repeated measurement of outcomes in counseling. This instrument was developed in direct response to feedback from CCMH members. Using the Pilot data set, collected in 2008, the authors used classical test theory and item-response theory methods along with input from practicing counselors to determine which items from the CCAPS-62 were most valuable. The result of this process was the 34-item CCAPS-34, which has seven subscales (Family Distress was removed from the CCAPS-62, and the Substance Use subscale was changed to only assess Alcohol Use on the CCAPS-34). Though these subscales are shorter, the results of validation studies suggested that they had nearly equivalent construct validity to the CCAPS-62 subscales (though less construct coverage overall).

A third study, McAleavey et al. (2012), focused on the clinical uses of the CCAPS-62. Specifically, the subscales' convergent and divergent validity was tested in a multi-site sample of counseling center clients, which CCMH collected at over 10 volunteer member centers. This data collection reflects a benefit of establishing CCMH as a PRN: By diffusing the burden of data collection across multiple sites, each center only administered one additional measure at a time, but 16 measures were collected in total. This study also used item-response theory analyses to show that the subscales of the CCAPS-62 are especially sensitive around the mean of counseling center clients, making them good screening measures in UCCs. The relationships among subscale scores were also explored using a second-order factor analysis, suggesting that some subscales may be closely related to one another—a finding that eventually led to the development of the Distress Index for the CCAPS instruments, which is a measure of general distress derived from items across several subscales. Finally, this study also provided empirical evidence for the development of clinical cut scores for the CCAPS-62, showing that some CCAPS-62 subscales were quite effective at discriminating diagnostic groups from clients who had not been diagnosed with specific disorders (e.g., an optimal cut point was derived for the Social Anxiety subscale to predict diagnoses of Social Phobia). As a whole, these three CCAPS development papers represent a significant effort to address one of the foundational needs of CCMH: To provide a low-cost, multi-dimensional, reliable, and valid instrument to counseling centers with direct clinical utility. A large part of this process required direct collaboration among counseling center staff, administrators, and researchers in data collection and interpretation. Future studies will continue to examine the validity and utility of the CCAPS instruments as well as other potentially useful instruments in counseling.

Minority and underserved populations. Culture and diversity play an important role in most clinical settings because minorities are subject to additional stressors and prejudice, and may experience increased levels of mental health difficulties and thus require particular clinical care. Not surprisingly, therefore, several studies from CCMH have examined correlates and effects of minority status in counseling centers. For instance, Nelson, Castonguay, and Locke (2011) examined the prevalence of high scores on the CCAPS-62 Eating Concerns subscale across sexual orientation and race/ethnicity categories at the first administration of the CCAPS at counseling centers. This study found that though there were different effects associated with each demographic category, these differences were not large. The authors interpreted these findings to challenge the stereotype of eating disorders as a "white women's disease." In addition, they compared scores on individual CCAPS items that assess dissatisfaction with body shape and body weight and found that males—including heterosexual males—evidence high rates of dissatisfaction with body shape. Though somewhat lower than women, over half of the males in the sample endorsed this item at least at a moderate level. This suggests that assessing for male clients' body image issues may be important.

Another study, conducted by McAleavey, Castonguay, and Locke (2011), investigated sexual orientation minority students and heterosexual students across the subscales of the CCAPS-62, investigating both in-treatment and not-in-treatment students. One of the findings indicated that sexual minority groups (individuals who identified as gay, lesbian, bisexual, and questioning) reported differences in the types of symptoms experienced, on average, when seeking treatment. For instance, bisexual students reported more Hostility than other groups, while Questioning students reported more Social Anxiety. This study suggests that treating sexual minorities as one group (e.g., heterosexual or not heterosexual) may not accurately reflect real differences in the experiences of these groups.

Another study, conducted by Hayes, Chun-Kennedy, Edens, and Locke (2011), examined whether students of different minority groups report different levels of distress and, in particular, whether students who identify with two minority groups (i.e., race/ethnicity and sexual orientation minorities) report especially high distress. In general, they found that race/ethnicity minority students experienced more distress than did White students, and that sexual minority students experienced more distress than did heterosexual students. In addition, though "double minority" status did not universally predict increased distress over single minority status, sexual orientation minority students who were also racial/ethnic minorities did experience more distress than heterosexual racial/ethnic minority students. Building on this study, Kawamoto, Youn, Castonguay, and Locke (manuscript submitted for publication) examined international students in particular compared with minority domestic students. They found that while Asian-American and international students reported higher levels of clinical difficulties on several CCAPS domains, White students reported higher level of substance abuse concerns than other students. Further, they compared international students of different continents of origin and found that both Asian and African students had higher levels of symptomatology than other international students, with the exception of substance abuse.

Utilization of counseling services. Several projects conducted through CCMH have examined predictors and correlates of service utilization at UCCs, hoping to address the question of what determines whether a student seeks help at a counseling center or not. This type of study can address both clinical and administrative purposes, such as how to direct outreach efforts and how to manage counseling centers' resources to best address the needs of their clientele. For instance, Hayes, Youn, et al. (2011) compared the racial/ethnic composition of 45 institutions' general student bodies to the race/ethnicity of counseling center clients at those institutions. They found little to no evidence of underutilization of counseling center services by racial and ethnic minority students, suggesting that, at least on average, these students make initial contact with UCCs at similar rates to White students. Note that this study did not examine dropout rates during treatment, nor does this suggest that a pattern of underutilization does not exist at some particular centers. However, these authors did find that UCC staff racial/ethnic composition was a significant predictor of utilization rates by ethnic minority students (e.g., a higher percentage of African-American students used UCC services at centers with greater proportions of African-American staff). In addition, among students of color, being a first-generation college student significantly predicted an increased likelihood of seeking treatment at a UCC, as did current and past financial difficulty.

Interestingly, using two large samples of students of various ethnic backgrounds, Nordberg, Hayes, McAleavey, Castonguay, and Locke (2013) found that being the first person in one's family to go to college differentiated treatment seekers from non-treatment seekers: Even after controlling for other factors, first-generation students were more likely to attend counseling than people who were not the first in their family. Also predictive of seeking treatment in this study were high levels of Depression, Generalized Anxiety, Family Distress, and Academic Distress.

Studies of change and outcome. One of the primary goals of CCMH is to study the process and outcome of counseling. As such, one focus of research has been on predictors of improvement as well as characterizing "typical" improvement during counseling. For instance, Boswell, McAleavey, Castonguay, Hayes, and Locke (2012) examined whether clients who had previously been in treatment would show more rapid or slower response in a new course of counseling than clients without a treatment history. They found that clients who had previously had counseling for psychological or emotional reasons showed slower progress and less change overall than clients without it, but this was not the case for previous medication use. This was somewhat surprising, since it suggests that a history of mental health problems in and of itself was not the primary contributing factor (else all previous treatments might be expected to predict slower change), but that previous counseling in particular seems to predict slower response to treatment in UCCs, perhaps due to lowered outcome expectations.

Also addressing therapeutic change, Lockard, Hayes, McAleavey, and Locke (2012) conducted a study focused on the Academic Distress subscale of the CCAPS-34. Since most clients in UCCs are students, especially undergraduate students, Academic Distress is an important marker of functional competency—somewhat like self-efficacy for job performance. However, it is rarely the case that counseling focuses solely on academic concerns instead of emotional and psychological symptoms and/or interpersonal problems. In this paper, Lockard et al. found that academic distress significantly decreases in counseling. Further, the change observed during counseling is greater than the change observed in students who are not in counseling. In this study, the authors were able to collaborate with the counseling center at one university to collect clinical data and directly compare them to nonclinical data collected from the same university during the same semester.

The studies briefly discussed above represent only a portion of the research that has been conducted so far through CCMH, covering a range of college student mental health concerns. Even more exciting is the potential for future studies that will benefit from this unique clinical and data generation collaboration, some of which are briefly mentioned in the conclusion of this paper.

Obstacles and Working Solutions

In developing and running CCMH, a number of difficulties have emerged, along with some successful (and less successful) strategies for solving these problems. Here, we have organized some of these challenges into broad categories: Organizational and operational challenges, challenges for researchers, challenges for counselors, and challenges of funding.

Organizational and Operational Challenges

Implementation of standardized materials. Since one of the primary goals of CCMH has always been to standardize some aspects of UCC data collection (particularly questionnaires given to clients at first contact to allow for cross-center comparisons), implementing these standardized materials has been a tremendously important task. However, the challenges inherent in this task include ensuring that the materials reach clients in the same format every time; that the measures are easily administered by and meet the needs of each UCC; that the data from clients are efficiently and accurately recorded, scored, reported to the counselor and transmitted to CCMH; and that any future updates to the standardized materials can be accommodated.

In order to meet these challenges, CCMH partnered with a popular electronic medical records (EMR) and scheduling company, Titanium Software. Through Titanium Schedule (EMR software), CCMH has been able to provide the Standardized Data Set (SDS), CCAPS instruments, and other standardized questionnaires using electronic data entry methods. Clients complete these measures, often directly on a computer kiosk or iPad, and the appropriate data are stored in their clinical record. This system not only allows for the accurate recording of data directly as a part of clinical routine, but also allows CCMH to update the standardized materials as necessary (for instance by changing the wording of items related to gender and sexual orientation on the SDS). Without this EMR integration, it would be very difficult, or impossible, to maintain up-to-date data across hundreds of institutions.

Communication. With the number of centers currently involved in CCMH, managing the communications between counselors, UCC directors, and CCMH central organization is a major challenge. This is important, because good communication allows CCMH to provide updates and trainings, and allows member centers to ask questions and offer input of CCMH and other member centers.

Given the size of CCMH, the tools used to communicate are often large-scale mass communication utilities. These include email lists for communication between centers, which are often useful when one UCC has run into some clinical difficulty or question that other member centers may have encountered and resolved previously (such as: "How can we implement the CCAPS and SDS on iPads?"). For direct communications with CCMH, web-based form submissions and direct email have been most efficient, generally when a particular issue unlikely to be replicated by another member center is at hand. Though these are the most common forms of communication, less frequent communications have also been invaluable, including annual meetings of the Advisory Board, meetings at conferences (including some conferences organized entirely by CCMH), webinars to disseminate information and train counseling center staff on using CCMH-related clinical tools, and multiple print publications to summarize findings and progress, such as an annual report.

Recruitment of centers and ongoing collaboration. Though CCMH is now quite large and covers a broad swath of the UCCs in the US and a few in Canada, it started as just an idea stemming from conversations among counseling center staff. One goal of CCMH is to include member centers from institutions representing diverse populations and geographic regions, in order to accurately reflect the mental health needs and services at UCCs. To continue recruitment, CCMH reaches out to centers via email over the summer (a time when centers tend to see less student traffic) to inform them about the purpose and goals of CCMH and inviting them to become a member center. Often, all that is necessary is providing centers with information on the purpose and benefits of CCMH, to make them see the advantages of contributing data for their own center and the field of college counseling. Over the last few years, awareness of CCMH in the college mental health field has grown and UCCs have started to reach out to CCMH to become members. However, there are still barriers to entry and reasons that

member centers may choose not to renew membership in any given year.

One such barrier, which has emerged from a solution to another problem, is that centers not using Titanium Software were reluctant to join CCMH because electronic data entry and scoring for CCAPS instruments were not initially available outside Titanium. Recently, several other EMR providers expressed interest in meeting their customers' requests for these instruments. Anticipating that CCAPS scoring and reports will evolve over time, CCMH was reluctant to invest time in facilitating complicated custom integrations across multiple software platforms. To address this, CCMH sought to build a web-service that vendors could contract to access for scoring services. In 2010, CCMH received a $70,000 grant to design such a service capable of receiving raw data from approved vendors and returning a scored CCAPS report which can be stored in the EMR software. As a result, non-Titanium EMR providers (Point and Click, PyraMED, and Medicat) have implemented this service, helping to meet the needs of new member centers while also supporting CCMH financially. These relationships illustrate how clinical needs, when coordinated nationally, can influence research, technology, and corporate practices: By advocating their clinical practice through membership with CCMH, UCCs were able to indirectly create a change in the type and quality of service provided by multiple EMR vendors to meet their needs.

Schools without an EMR have the more difficult task of administering the SDS and scoring the CCAPS instruments by hand, which is more time-consuming and cumbersome. While CCMH will continue to explore options for making the CCAPS and SDS available to all UCCs (e.g., Excel-based scoring programs), EMR integration remains one of the most promising.

Data management. One challenge relevant to any data collected in a clinical setting is ensuring that the data are accurate and comprehensive. This challenge is multiplied in multisite studies due to the need for data uniformity and merging process. This is, therefore, a central challenge in the enterprise of operating CCMH: Managing the incoming data from clients and counselors, at each center, and then the transfer to CCMH's data repository. At each stage in this process, different people and computer systems assume responsibility for data integrity and confidentiality. One major boon to CCMH in this endeavor has been the partnership with Titanium Software, which has provided critical technical expertise during the data transfer process including security, server management, and data export and variable creation.

Titanium Schedule, installed at many UCCs, is a confidential electronic medical record system, which provides an excellent foundation for securely collecting data from clients, entering those data into client files (generally with the approval of an administrator), and storing the data once it is accepted. CCMH asks member centers using Titanium to upload de-identified data once per month, which allows for a nearly continuous flow of data into CCMH's data repository. This repository houses data from all participating centers. As described earlier, this continuous data flow is ultimately divided by data "seams" according to the American academic years. These have the effect of creating discrete data sets that can be analyzed separately. Not only does this partition the data into more useful packets, but it also helps ensure that the data reflects typical practices in UCCs. That is, UCCs are often heavily impacted by the academic calendar: Not only do many of their clients (undergraduate students) leave campus during summer months, staff numbers may be considerably lower during summer, new counselors may be hired to start the school year, and trainee therapists mostly begin and end their training at UCCs with the academic calendar. By keeping academic years separate, CCMH is able to minimize (though perhaps not eliminate) the noise inherent in these data. Four data sets have been defined to date: The Pilot Study, which occurred in the Fall of 2008 across 66 UCCs administering the CCAPS-70 and SDS; the 2010–2011 data set which comprised over 60,000 clients from 97 UCCs; the 2011–2012 data set consisting of over 80,000 clients from 120 UCCs; and the 2012–2013 data set, which includes data on over 95,000 clients and 130 UCCs.

Translating empirical findings to clinicians and administrators. Another element of communication that has proven to be vital to the continued success of CCMH has been translating research findings into meaningful and understandable information for two audiences: Clinicians who use the CCAPS and other instruments in their regular practice, and the UCC and college administrators who control the budget of each UCC. Translating empirical findings for clinicians should be a familiar task to anyone involved in collaborations between researchers and clinicians. In general, we have found that the counselors working within CCMH are eager to learn what is being done with the data that they and their clients contribute. We have worked to share our findings by providing webinars designed to disseminate findings and publications such as the annual report (Center for Collegiate Mental Health

2013a) and CCAPS Clinician's Guide (Center for Collegiate Mental Health, 2013b) that provide nontechnical descriptions of research efforts.

A larger, and perhaps more unique, challenge has been translating empirical findings to administrators. Often, this challenge is greater because the questions that seem both critically important and very simple to administrators are among the most complex empirical tasks available. For example, a college vice president may wish to know, "How effective are the services offered at our counseling center?" This question, though vitally important, requires both extensive clarification (e.g., "Compared to what: Controlled trials, other counseling centers or something different?" or, "On what measurement: Client satisfaction, academic retention, symptomatic improvement?") and may lead to complex and specialized quantitative methods (e.g., the benchmarking methods described by Minami et al., 2009; linear mixed-effects modeling), which themselves may be difficult to explain. However, CCMH has tried to provide support for member centers that want to address some of these questions. For instance, CCMH created a report that centers can run with minimal input to determine how much change on the CCAPS instruments clients show, given a certain number of sessions, a date range, type of sessions, or for any particular therapy group or staff member(s). Ideally, this relatively simple calculation can then be taken as some (albeit limited) evidence of the efficacy of counseling, or may more appropriately be used to direct areas in need of future training.

Some other relevant questions, however, are easier to translate accurately. For instance, many clinic directors are interested to find out if the clients in their center differ meaningfully from clients at other centers in terms of the severity of concerns. CCMH, again with Titanium, has developed a report that allows centers to compare the scores of incoming clients' CCAPS subscale scores against the national average. So, if a particular counseling center sees clients who, on average, report more difficulty with eating concerns than clients at other centers, the counselors may benefit from focused training on that issue. In addition, through collaborations with CampusLabs, a company that offers web-based benchmarking services for higher education, CCMH provides schools with the opportunity to compare their clients' CCAPS and SDS reports to other institutions as well as a nonclinical sample of college students from a nationwide study. Member centers are able to limit comparisons to similar schools (e.g., size, location) and/or compare only their clients' responses to responses from the nonclinical survey respondents from their own school. The reports from CampusLabs can be used to present administrators with data in a clear, concise way allowing UCCs to advocate their needs and the needs of the students based on these comparisons.

Intellectual property and other legal issues. A particular challenge encountered in CCMH has been managing the various legal contracts and intellectual property rights involved. While more could be said about this challenge than space permits, we will mention some of the issues that have arisen. One is that CCMH has a shared copyright over the CCAPS instruments along with its initial developers, and provides the CCAPS instruments to counseling centers free of charge. Despite that, other uses of the CCAPS instruments are not necessarily free to all users, requiring various contracts and licenses. Each collaboration (for instance with Titanium Software and CampusLabs) requires careful review, and some collaborations have required approval from a team of legal experts at PSU. Large-scale PRNs are very likely to include the use of intellectual property or the development of corporate partnerships, and our experience suggests planning for risk-management and legal resources is necessary for success.

Challenges for Researchers

Heterogeneity in the data. In attempting to make use of the data available from CCMH, probably the biggest single challenge (and simultaneously a potential strength) is that there are tremendous differences across different UCCs, therapists, and clients. Each counseling center has a unique set of clinical practices, from the size of the center (number of clients and therapists seen), to the frequency of regular sessions, to the services offered (individual counseling, group therapies, skills-based treatments, career counseling and various assessment-only services are offered at some but not necessarily all UCCs), to the available external mental health resources near each institution (which may draw students away from counseling centers or provide referral sources); no two UCCs in CCMH are quite the same. In addition, the therapists are heterogeneous themselves, ranging from first-year trainees to expert therapists and coming from a variety of training backgrounds. Finally, though the clients are generally more constrained by age than many mental health services (most clients at counseling centers are undergraduate students), the reasons for seeking counseling are diverse. This is particularly important when using the CCAPS instruments, which assess several different concerns that are each relevant to college student populations, but not every

client would be expected to endorse elevated distress across all subscales. Without knowing additional information, such as the reason for seeking counseling and/or diagnosis of individual clients, it is difficult to know which clients should be expected to improve in any given domain of the CCAPS (see McAleavey et al., 2012, for more information).

Much of the heterogeneity present in CCMH data is essential, in that it is a real and integral part of describing practice across these settings and individuals. Thus, though it does pose challenges to researchers, it must also be considered a necessary difficulty—not an evil. There are also a few benefits of this heterogeneity: It allows for examinations of complex questions that are not possible when data are homogeneous. Differences between clients, for example, can be examined in more nuanced ways than is possible in less varied and smaller data sets. Research must instead search for ways to use and understand this heterogeneity, rather than eliminate it.

IRB approval. Each step in CCMH's process is monitored and approved by relevant Institutional Review Boards (IRBs)—each center has to receive approval from their own IRB. This approval process allows CCMH and its member centers to collect, store, and distribute de-identified data. While this is often seen as a difficult and time-intensive task (generally speaking, each IRB approval needs to be renewed annually, and, since each center has their own approval, this is a large task in total), CCMH has found some ways to ease the process for member centers. Generally, CCMH has tried to provide examples of successful IRB applications from other UCCs and even reviewing or editing applications prior to submission. Providing this assistance has been an essential aid to member centers (many of which are not experienced in seeking IRB approval for research purposes) and makes the process of contributing data much less cumbersome for these centers.

Field setting. The fact that each member center of CCMH is primarily a clinical service provider rather than a research laboratory has its own challenges when conducting research. Every UCC is bound by the clinical needs of their clients and only able to take on tasks that do not interfere with these needs, and that are achievable within their limitations. As such, CCMH does not, and cannot, dictate, for instance, the schedule at which CCAPS instruments are administered at each center—they choose whether and when to do this themselves. And of course, working in this naturalistic setting can make randomization of treatment conditions and interventions difficult—not impossible, as in Castonguay, Boswell, et al. (2010)—but would likely require additional funding to provide the necessary infrastructure. This challenge makes traditional experimentation and strong causal inference difficult—limiting many studies to correlational methods.

Volume of data. Counter to many research endeavors, a challenge facing CCMH is not usually a lack of data: Instead, the challenge is that there can be too much data at times, for both technological and scientific reasons. Technologically, even simple computational tasks become demanding in data sets approaching 1,000,000 lines of data: they can take several minutes on current computers, if they are even possible (some tasks require more computer memory than can be allocated without specialized computer resources). Storing large data files also requires large capacity, since data files can exceed 10 gigabytes.

The volume of data also has an effect on statistical analyses that must be considered: Large numbers of clients and therapists, generally speaking, allow even very small effects to be detectable in the data. Though this is a strength it can certainly lead to misleading interpretations, especially because the certainty that there is an effect is not the same thing as the magnitude of the effect: If an effect is so small as to be trivial in meaning and clinical significance, the statistical significance can be misleading. To help with this CCMH has developed formal policies regarding best practices when working with large samples, for instance, by asking researchers to divide samples into training and cross-validation samples, using appropriate methods of Type I error control (e.g., Bonferroni correction for family-wise error rates), and providing and interpreting effect size estimates when possible. However, this is not the most familiar form of statistical thinking for many psychologists, nor is it the most common form of research interpretation.

What instruments to use? One of the main tasks of CCMH from conception through current practice has been determining what instruments to include in a standardized battery. This has centered on self-report symptomatic and distress measures and treatment outcome monitoring, though other measures (like the SDS) have also been part of these ongoing discussions. As previously mentioned, CCMH convened a conference of counseling center representatives, in part, to help select a standardized multi-dimensional instrument to be used by CCMH member centers. The CCAPS (now the CCAPS-62 and CCAPS-34) was originally donated to CCMH

with the understanding that it would be made available to counseling centers free or for a very low cost, and could be further developed based on psychometric data and clinical need. One goal of CCMH is to make the CCAPS-62, CCAPS-34, and any other measures developed in CCMH useful resources for all counseling centers. Other instruments, for instance assessing resiliency, client strengths, and presenting concerns, may be developed and disseminated in the future.

Prioritizing clinically valuable research. Since CCMH is a fairly large organization, and the vast majority of participating counselors do not have regular contact with CCMH research personnel, CCMH needs to make extra efforts to understand and incorporate the needs and desires of counseling center staff into research priorities. To these ends, many of the regular research meetings of CCMH researchers (full-time academics and graduate students) are also attended by several interested counseling center staff (full-time clinicians). Some of these counselors have done or are currently engaged in conducting their own research with CCMH (at all stages, from conceptualization to authoring research papers), and others simply attend out of interest. Their views are sought to provide clinical interpretations and suggestions for further studies that CCMH could conduct. In addition, CCMH has conducted a survey of counselors and clinic directors to gauge interests in various topics of research. Since we cannot know exactly what the most important projects are without receiving feedback from clinicians, these efforts help to prevent "empirical imperialism" (Castonguay, 2011): Researchers telling clinicians what is important without inquiring what practitioners want to know.

Challenges for Counselors

Time for training. As we have already stated, UCCs are very busy clinical environments. The demand for services is often high, resulting in long waits for service. Within this context, the additional time constraints required of counselors to receive training, even when the training is consistent with their clinical practices, are not a trivial concern. Perhaps the chief training requirement is that counselors understand the meaning of the standardized assessment materials (e.g., the SDS and CCAPS instruments) given to their clients. With quantitative, multi-dimensional instruments such as the CCAPS-62 and CCAPS-34, which provide both raw item responses and at least eight summary scores for each administration, this can be a time-consuming task. To help assist with this, CCMH has provided explicit training materials in the form of in-person trainings, web-based instructional videos, and print materials targeting the clinical audience. However, more trainings like this are likely to be in perennial demand. In addition, this requires recognition on the part of UCC administrators that training in these domains will provide a clinical return-on-investment that benefits clients, even though it initially detracts from direct-service hours. This type of perception (e.g., that participation will decrease clinical hours) may be one reason why some UCCs do not join CCMH.

Time for ongoing tasks. In addition, counselors and counseling centers must be willing to devote some time, otherwise usable for other clinical practice, to the various ongoing tasks of participation in CCMH. For example, coordinating the administration of standardized questionnaires along with data-entry to Titanium may be a substantial hurdle for some UCCs whereas others already do this as part of routine practice. In addition, though it only takes a few minutes, the monthly upload of data requires someone with appropriate security clearance in Titanium to login and process the upload steps. Coordinating related tasks, such as reports on UCC effectiveness or comparisons to national data sets, requires further time-commitment from these individuals. Counselors at many UCCs find it helpful to regularly review the CCAPS-62 and CCAPS-34 reports prior to meeting with their clients, even though this requires changing the way they prepare for sessions. Thus, there is a slight but noticeable effect on everyday activities (clinical and administrative) inherent in participating in CCMH; it is hoped that this investment of time and effort by each counseling center results in increased knowledge, clinical efficiency, and effectiveness.

Confidentiality of data. Counselors, it should be noted, are sometimes also confronted with the challenges associated with data confidentiality. They may field questions to this effect from their clients, who of course may wish to know what data will be shared with whom, but the counselors themselves have every right and reason to know what of their own data is being collected and shared. At some member centers, some basic information regarding counselors—age, training background, demographics, and so on—is collected by the UCC for the purpose of sharing with the CCMH data repository. This is a voluntary procedure on the part of the counselors, and they are consented like any other research participant. And despite all of the precautions in place, concerns regarding therapist identification and loss of confidentiality are sometimes quite significant.

In some cases, the concern is related to the possibility that therapists may be compared to one another in terms of effectiveness on CCAPS subscales. This is a concern emerging from the empirical identification of differences between therapists, which suggests that there may be ways to identify the most effective (and most ineffective) therapists (e.g., Brown, Lambert, Jones, & Minami, 2005; Kraus, Castonguay, Boswell, Nordberg, & Hayes, 2011), and that with this identification, therapists who appear to produce less change than their peers may suffer some negative consequences. This is not an unreasonable concern. In part because of this, CCMH has attempted to retain therapist confidentiality as a primary issue. Even though CCMH has no plans to impose contingencies on therapists based on effectiveness, such plans may emerge from other parties in the future. Our belief is that therapists should be able to opt-in to any such program entirely voluntarily, especially while the long-term benefits of any program like this are unknown.

Challenges of Funding

Cart before the horse. In many ways, the organization and operational responsibilities of CCMH have far exceeded initial expectations—and have done so on a shoestring budget. From 2008 to 2012, the annual budget for CCMH has ranged from $30,000 to $70,000. The expenses of starting the network were met primarily through modest membership fees, donations, and small foundation grants—funding levels that will not meet the burden of maintaining and expanding the functions of CCMH over time. Effectively, the unexpected success of CCMH has put the cart before the horse, and we are now working to establish a stable financial plan to support ongoing operations.

More specifically, CCMH exists as a non-profit research center, legally affiliated with the Pennsylvania State University (PSU). Penn State's Center for Counseling and Psychological Services provided key support (in the form of staff time) during the original formation of CCMH and this support has been critical to the ongoing operation and growth. The primary funding for CCMH comes from annual membership fees of $200 per school. Despite the fact that this is a very low annual fee (especially in comparison to fees for many psychometric instruments) it is waived for about 10–15% of members due to lack of funding. Additional resources have been given by individuals and departments affiliated with PSU, such as volunteer time from students and faculty along with shared support for funded graduate assistants (e.g., CCMH covers the stipend and the department covers tuition).

In addition, CCMH has cultivated a wide variety of relationships to support its work including corporate partners, association partners, and even customers interested in our intellectual property. Titanium Software, a founding partner, has provided direct financial contributions through conference-support grants and in-kind donations related to technical development. Another corporate partner, CampusLabs, provides benchmarking services free to our member centers in exchange for marketplace exposure for their tools. Association partners include the Association for University and College Counseling Center Directors (AUCCCD), the American College Counseling Association (ACCA), Student Affairs Administrators in Higher Education (NASPA), and American College Personnel Association (ACPA). AUCCCD has provided funding to CCMH since it was officially established in 2005. ACCA provides financial support to CCMH as well as acting as a dissemination partner by publishing CCMH research in a peer review format. NASPA, which oversees the NASPA Assessment Consortium, maintains a profit-sharing arrangement with CCMH related to a national mental health benchmarking survey, and ACPA provides financial support by hosting CCMH webinars. EMR vendors, such as Point and Click, PyraMED, and Medicat, became customers of CCMH in order to distribute the CCAPS to their counseling center customers. Finally, CCMH has received funding through traditional grant mechanisms including grants from the Ittleson Foundation, the van Amerigen Foundation, and American Psychological Association.

Despite this range of partners and revenue streams and unprecedented success in data collection, CCMH has yet to fully fund all of its operations and remains heavily dependent on volunteer time, partnerships, and contributions from within Penn State University.

Funding options. Looking forward, CCMH must now focus significant energy on the creation of a long-term sustainable business plan that funds the "mission-critical" operations. This business plan will ideally draw from an optimal set of funding sources that will allow CCMH to stay true to its original mission, membership, and source of data: University and college counseling centers.

The potential ingredients of a sustainable business plan are many, but each has pros and cons that must be weighed against the mission of the project. For example, small grants (in the range of $5000 to $150,000) can cover key expenses and specific roles/tasks, but many foundations explicitly forbid grants

to support ongoing operations while still requiring frequent, work-intensive, applications. Alternatively, CCMH could also continue to pursue large research-oriented grants from government agencies (e.g., NIH, NIMH, PCORI, NSF, etc.). In theory, a large research grant would cover all operational expenses and provide a measure of stability for the project while also supporting research. On the other hand, CCMH has already invested hundreds of hours in this domain (for more than $7 million in grant applications) without success. While the promise of such a grant is immense, so is the work required. This genre of funding amplifies the tension between research and practice—pulling the project towards currently endorsed research methodologies that may or may not be in the best interest of the membership and founding mission. Similarly, large grants of this nature do expire and could force large research efforts to shutter due to a lack of ongoing funding. Clearly, each funding source must be carefully evaluated in order to maintain operations, stay true to the mission of the project, and accomplish a wide variety of goals at the intersection of science and practice.

Benefits

Although there have been many challenges in the establishment and maintenance of such a large PRN of UCCs, member centers, clinicians, and researchers have already begun to experience some of the benefits that result from contributing standardized data to a collaborative national data warehouse.

Counselors and Clients

One of the main goals of CCMH is to provide counseling centers with clinical tools that are helpful to clinicians. The CCAPS-62, which was designed as an intake assessment tool, can be viewed by clinicians prior to their initial session with a client through Titanium Schedule. Clinicians can use the CCAPS to inform their work by examining scores on the CCAPS Profile Report and identifying clinical problems that might have gone previously unnoticed. They can then gear their intake interview to incorporate questions targeted at elevated item responses and subscales. Using the CCAPS as a talking point in session then gives clients the opportunity to clarify and/or expand on why they endorsed a question in a certain way, resulting in the clinician gathering more pertinent information on the client.

In addition, the CCAPS-34, which was designed for repeated assessment, provides clinicians with an opportunity to track trends over time for individual clients. The CCAPS Profile Report displays the client's last 10 administrations, showing how sub-scale scores have changed over time. Clinicians are then able to discuss with the client any improvement or deterioration that has occurred since a previous session and discuss with clients potential reasons for change. Further, the profile report tracks student suicidal/homicidal responses, alerting the clinician to changes that have occurred, which is particularly important if there has been an increase in harmful thinking. Centers have reported using the CCAPS to show progressive deterioration and to support the decision to hospitalize a student.

As centers continue to see an increase in client traffic, repeated measures of the CCAPS can serve as a tool in making ongoing treatment decisions. Many centers refer students to community providers given that the limited resources on campus do not meet the growing demands of students. Tracking CCAPS subscale scores over time can provide support for terminating a client, referring a client out, or requesting extended sessions. For example, a clinician may refer a student to a community provider when the CCAPS subscale scores for the student are elevated yet stable and long-term therapy is thought to be beneficial to the client. As an administrator from a CCMH member center stated, "The CCAPS helps us measure change across sessions, or lack thereof, which is helpful in documenting improvement and a logical basis for termination of care, or document that treatment has not been helpful and the student needs to be referred out."

Counseling Centers

The ability to track changes and trends within the client population. In the past, counseling centers have not had the tools needed to detect and track trends within the overall clinical college student population. Often, "trends" that have been reported were based on anecdotal accounts instead of sound research. Within Titanium Schedule, there is a center-wide change report, which counseling center administrators can run to determine how clients as a whole are changing within their center. This report shows how many clients, over a specified timeframe, made reliable changes in symptom levels based on each subscale of the CCAPS. This provides feedback to centers regarding the effectiveness of their treatments for different symptom/problem types, including the areas in which clients make the most improvement and what areas are most problematic. In addition, administrators can run reports on which subscales are the highest endorsed at intake, which can inform their outreach efforts to staff and students on campus as well as be used to

help UCC administrators advocate services and resources within their center.

Benchmarking. In the past, counseling centers have had trouble communicating their needs to student affair administrators in ways that were easy to understand and concise. They have not had the necessary data to provide to increasingly data-driven institutions. Bishop (2006) highlighted that administrators (student affairs) are more likely to be influenced by data rather than affective arguments—and without data to support their perspectives, UCCs have struggled to influence decisions. As a way to give back to centers that contribute data to the national data set, the CCMH-CampusLabs partnership described above provides UCCs with a tool to collect and compare important data points. This comparison, or benchmarking, allows UCCs to create reports for themselves comparing the subscale scores and item responses on the CCAPS and SDS for clients in their center to those from other member centers. The comparison schools can be based on criteria such as size or location and the report can be tailored to compare specific groups of students, such as first-year students or students who identified as being involved in extra-curricular activities. One administrator from a CCMH member school stated, "The CCAPS provides our center with better data to 'tell our story' to the schools/colleges and in our annual reports, especially to be able to make national comparisons. Having this national data (that is 'hard' and not 'soft') improves our credibility as counseling centers … we can speak with greater authority as to the 'story' of college student mental health." Benchmarking provides centers with an additional tool that helps them advocate their needs.

Contributing to a national data set. The 2011–2012 CCMH data set, the second full year of data collected by CCMH, consists of approximately 80,000 counseling center clients from 120 colleges and universities. These data exist because centers have come together and agreed to contribute data to CCMH using the CCAPS and SDS. It has been noted that in the past, research has not always been a priority at UCCs given the time constraints and priority on clinical work (Castonguay et al., 2011). However, many CCMH members feel a sense of pride contributing data to a national data set that is advancing the field of college mental health. One administrator noted, "We believe that use of the CCAPS and involvement with CCMH will help research take off because CCMH makes available the data sets to people all over the country." As described above, studies have already been conducted on topics ranging from diverse populations, counseling outcomes, and utilization of services. The size and scope of this national data set provide a very real benefit: Belief that findings from CCMH will be generalizable and valid research observations.

Ultimately, by presenting these findings to university decision makers, administrators of counseling centers might well be able to help shape mental health practice by using studies conducted in actual clinical settings. This type of study, referred to as practice-oriented research (Castonguay, Barkham, Lutz, & McAleavey, 2013), deserves to be recognized as a crucial component of an empirical knowledge base regarding clinical services—a component that should be viewed as complementary and equipoise to studies conducted in controlled settings (Barkham & Margison, 2007; Barkham, Stiles, Lambert, & Mellor-Clark, 2010).

Researchers

A data set as large as the CCMH data sets allows researchers to examine questions about college student mental health that have not previously been explored due to small data sets and complications with the data collection that come from working at a UCC. Needless to say, such data sets have allowed researchers that are part of CCMH to expand their research programs in many clinically meaningful directions. And, as mentioned above, this has been particularly beneficial for researchers at an early phase of their career (by allowing graduate students to conduct not only their masters and doctoral research but additional projects that can bolster their academic potential). To optimally make use of these data, however, CCMH has also developed a data sharing policy: Researchers outside the CCMH research team have access to the large database after a set period of time has elapsed. Researchers interested in examining questions that will benefit and add to the knowledge base of college mental health can request the CCMH data sets to use for their research projects. Given that one goal of CCMH is to produce research that informs the field, CCMH encourages research using its data conducted by outside researchers. Non-CCMH researchers can access national data sets through CCMH by following the procedures outlined on CCMH's website (http://ccmh.squarespace.com/data/). Further, there have already been collaborations between CCMH and other researchers. For example, the CCMH team is currently working with outside researchers at various institutions to have the CCAPS translated into four different languages. These projects were initiated by outside researchers to make the CCAPS

more accessible. It is the hope of CCMH that many more research projects and collaborations will be initiated with the goal of advancing the field of college mental health.

Lessons Learned

From the challenges that CCMH has faced since 2005, as well as the accomplishments realized, several general lessons about multidisciplinary partnership have been learned. Interestingly, many of these lessons are repetitions and variations of a single theme: Understand the needs of all stakeholders and proactively work to balance these such that all stakeholders realize a benefit. Below is a brief description of some of the lessons learned.

Look for common ground. Actively seek out shared interests and goals for all the stakeholders in the project. For CCMH, this includes UCCs, researchers, and funding organizations, along with counselors, clients, and administrative staff at numerous colleges and universities. Though all stakeholders share in the effort to improve mental health on campuses, each stakeholder is dealing with their own needs and demands, so the common ground can get lost. Specifically, while all stakeholders can benefit from more standardized data collection in UCCs, vigilance is required to maintain this focus and shared engagement.

Focus on clinical services. Though maintaining common ground is very important, we have found it essential to prioritize the needs of counseling centers and clinical processes in general. Simply put, there is no common ground if the PRN's work does not meet clinical needs or provide a clinical benefit. Though much work is required of researchers, the need to continuously understand and respond to clinical needs is paramount.

Reduce barriers to entry. We have found that membership in CCMH has grown rapidly, often because the requirements for entry are quite low, the ease of joining is apparent, and the attractiveness of contributing to a larger shared goal is high. CCMH does not mandate clinical practices, and generally prefers to offer clinical tools that can be taken up by UCCs on their own schedule. In addition, the cost of membership in CCMH is often minimal in terms of both money and time. If CCMH were to have switched to a higher bar of entry—say, requiring a particular data collection paradigm without receiving clinical input—it is likely that there would not have been as rapid an acceptance among UCCs.

Give back (to everyone). Focusing on all of the stakeholders involved is important, but it is especially important to ensure that the organization is providing clear, obvious, and valuable benefits to as many people involved as possible. This means that there have to be clinical tools provided to the counseling centers (both for therapists working with clients and for UCC administrators who need to advocate their budgets), but there also has to be a benefit to the researchers involved. No one can simply volunteer time without the promise of a reasonable return-on-investment.

Clinicians will help with research—if the research helps them clinically. This lesson is surprisingly important. We have found that many counselors at CCMH member centers are enthusiastic about participating in certain research-oriented activities. Notably, many counselors have worked to increase the frequency and intensity of the standardized assessments at their centers, and several times when CCMH has asked for assistance with a research project counselors and counseling center directors have nominated themselves to do additional work. This enthusiasm is more than simply prioritizing research: It reflects the belief that some counselors have that conducting these research projects actually improves their clinical work, directly or indirectly. That is, many counselors want to conduct or participate in research projects, but especially if those projects are important to them clinically.

Create a sustainable funding plan. This lesson is much easier said than done, yet it is extremely important. While goodwill and volunteer efforts may be necessary to create a PRN, they are not sufficient to maintain it over time. CCMH has been fortunate to receive financial support from partners, associations, and foundation sponsors, but the burden of running a large PRN now demands a sustainable financial plan. In addition to the non-profit and foundation sponsors, researchers at CCMH have also targeted other funding sources—notably governmental and health services-related organizations. In other PRNs, university or other clinical entities may be available and interested in providing some funds; such funding sources should be aggressively pursued.

It takes vision, time, and a village. Those who might consider building a large PRN infrastructure need to dream big. The vision of CCMH came out of the mind of one dreamer (Benjamin Locke), who was working full time in a counseling center (at Penn State). But to get to where CCMH is now has necessitated two fundamental resources: Time (and a lot of it) and people (and a lot of them). In addition to many unpaid hours for Dr. Locke, building CCMH has required (1) early support from the director of Penn State's counseling center (Dennis Heitzmann) to provide dedicated time, (2) connection between faculty members in different departments (who first enjoyed occasional breakfast meetings and then decided to make CCMH the major focus of their respective research programs), (3) a large number of graduate students from several research labs volunteering time and energy to the project, (4) financial support from different departments and colleges to cover some graduate student assistantships, and (5) the commitment of members of the Advisory Board (who contribute to the development and implementation of every major initiative emerging from CCMH). Even with such extensive and committed collaborations, however, the "village" that has raised CCMH constantly needs new "citizens" (e.g., project managers, post-doctoral fellows), which, as mentioned above, may require further external funding.

Conclusion

The Center for Collegiate Mental Health is a large practice-research network encompassing nearly 200 university and college counseling centers. This PRN is focused on balancing the needs of counselors, administrators, and researchers, primarily by standardizing the data collection process in counseling centers, and returning clinical tools and data to the field in return. The data generated by CCMH have led to a number of studies covering a wide range of issues, but the majority of these studies have been based on data collected as part of the assessment procedures adopted by counseling centers.

Reflecting a new phase in the development of our PRN, some of the next studies that we envision would involve the collection of data that are not part of clinical routine. For example, using a plurality of research methods (including process-outcome, experimental, and qualitative designs) we hope to conduct investigations addressing various mechanisms of change, therapist effects, client variables, effectiveness of specific interventions, and the interaction between participant characteristics, relational, and technical variables. In planning these studies, however, we are aware of two major challenges that can jeopardize any type of practice-oriented research. First, as researchers, we need to remain constantly mindful of the risk of being engaged in some form of "empirical imperialism" (Castonguay, 2011). Thus, while we can't refrain from being excited about myriad future studies, we will have to resist imposing them on clinicians. This is the primary reason that guided the previously mentioned survey aimed at "knowing what clinicians want to know," and what questions they are interested in enough to devote time and energy to address as part of their clinical work. Once we will have identified a potential new wave of projects that show high convergence between clinicians' and researchers' respective interests, we also plan to create an active collaboration in all aspects of the studies to be conducted, such as the design and implementation of the study protocols and the analyses and dissemination of the findings. This is possible because, within CCMH, not every center or every counselor need be involved in a research study—only those clinicians or centers who volunteer will be included. As noted elsewhere (Castonguay, Nelson, et al., 2010), asking clinicians to only fill out questionnaires (unilaterally chosen by researchers) is a likely recipe to confirm the frequently held bias that clinicians are "resistant" to participate in research.

A second challenge will be to create studies that are not only clinically relevant, but "clinically syntonic" (Castonguay, Nelson, et al., 2010). Considering how busy clinicians are, an optimal way to integrate science and practice is by designing study protocols in which the collection of data is fully confounded with the delivery of clinical services. In other words, clinicians are not likely to conduct studies if the research tasks require a substantial amount of additional time to their workload and if those tasks are not clinically informative or actionable.

It should be recognized that because CCMH focuses on a specific population and operates within a distinct clinical setting, it is a unique infrastructure. Nevertheless, it is likely that the obstacles, benefits, and lessons learned in building this infrastructure could be helpful to the creation and development of partnerships in other settings. In particular, we believe that our experience would be relevant to large infrastructures that involve the connection of many groups of researchers and clinicians, such as the development of "networks of PRNs" (Castonguay, 2011) that have been discussed as a future step of practice-oriented research in training clinics and private practice (see Castonguay et al., in press; Koerner & Castonguay, in press). The creation of a repository of data, coordination of multiple IRB agreements, connection with academic settings (including statistical expertise, resources, and help from graduate students), and the operation of an Advisory Board are just a few examples of the challenges and successes experienced by CCMH that could be relevant to other large connective PRNs. It is also likely that many of the studies

conducted in CCMH will be relevant to clinicians operating in settings outside college mental health. Optimally, the convergence of interest and the aggregation of findings across diverse practice services may bolster the influence of practice-oriented research in the scientific knowledge base about psychotherapy, and thus make research conduct by clinicians influential in planning and delivery of mental health care (Castonguay et al., 2013).

References

APA Presidential Task Force on Evidence-Based Practice. (2006). Evidence-based practice in psychology. *American Psychologist*, *61*, 271–285. doi:10.1037/0003-066X.61.4.271

Barkham, M., & Margison, F. (2007). Practice-based evidence as a complement to evidence-based practice: From dichotomy to chiasmus. In C. Freeman & M. Power (Eds.), *Handbook of evidence-based psychotherapies: A guide for research and practice* (pp. 443–476). Chichester: Wiley.

Barkham, M., Stiles, W. B., Lambert, M. J., & Mellor-Clark, J. (2010). Building a rigorous and relevant knowledge-base for the psychological therapies. In M. Barkham, G. E. Hardy, & J. Mellor-Clark (Eds.), *Developing and delivering practice-based evidence: A guide for the psychological therapies* (pp. 21–61). Chichester: Wiley.

Benton, S. A., Robertson, J. M., Tseng, W.-C., Newton, F. B., & Benton, S. L. (2003). Changes in counseling center client problems across 13 years. *Professional Psychology: Research and Practice*, *34*, 66–72. doi:10.1037/0735-7028.34.1.66

Bishop, J. B. (2006). College and university counseling centers: Questions in search of answers. *Journal of College Counseling*, *9*, 6–19. doi:10.1002/j.2161-1882.2006.tb00088.x

Boswell, J. F., McAleavey, A. A., Castonguay, L. G., Hayes, J. A., & Locke, B. D. (2012). Previous mental health service utilization and change in counseling clients' depressive symptoms. *Journal of Counseling Psychology*, *59*, 368–378. doi:10.1037/a0028078

Brown, G. S. J., Lambert, M. J., Jones, E. R., & Minami, T. (2005). Identifying highly effective psychotherapists in a managed care environment. *American Journal of Managed Care*, *11*, 513–520.

Castonguay, L. G. (2011). Psychotherapy, psychopathology, research and practice: Pathways of connections and integration. *Psychotherapy Research*, *21*, 125–140. doi:10.1080/10503307.2011.563250

Castonguay, L. G., Barkham, M., Lutz, W., & McAleavey, A. A. (2013). Practice-oriented research: Approaches and application. In M. J. Lambert (Ed.). *Bergin and Garfield's handbook of psychotherapy and behavior change* (6th ed., pp. 85–133). New York: Wiley.

Castonguay, L. G., Boswell, J. F., Zack, S. E., Baker, S., Boutselis, M. A., Chiswick, N. R., ... Holtforth, M. G. (2010). Helpful and hindering events in psychotherapy: A practice research network study. *Psychotherapy: Theory, Research, Practice, Training*, *47*, 327–344. doi:10.1037/a0021164

Castonguay, L. G., Locke, B. D., & Hayes, J. A. (2011). The Center for Collegiate Mental Health: An example of a practice-research network in university counseling centers. *Journal of College Student Psychotherapy*, *25*(2), 105–119. doi:10.1080/87568225.2011.556929

Castonguay, L. G., Nelson, Boutselis, M., Chiswick, N., Damer, D., Hemmelstein, N., ... Borkovec, T. B. (2010). Clinicians and/or researchers? A qualitative analysis of therapists' experiences in a practice research network. *Psychotherapy: Theory, Research, Practice, Training, 47*, 345–354. doi:10.1037/a0021165

Castonguay, L. G., Pincus, A. L., & McAleavey, A. A. (in press). Practice-research network in a psychology training clinic: Building an infrastructure to foster early attachment to the scientific-practitioner model. *Psychotherapy Research, 24.* doi:10.1080/10503307.2013.856045

Center for Collegiate Mental Health. (2013a, January). *2012 Annual Report* (Publication No. STA 13-68).

Center for Collegiate Mental Health (2013 b). *Clinician's Guide to the Counseling Center Assessment of Psychological Symptoms.* University Park, PA.

Chambless, D. L., & Hollon, S. D. (1998). Defining empirically supported therapies. *Journal of Consulting and Clinical Psychology, 66*(1), 7–18. doi:10.1037/0022-006X.66.1.7

Derogatis, L. R. (1992). *SCL-90-R administration, scoring, and procedures manual II.* Towson, MD: Clinical Psychometric Research.

Eisenberg, D., Hunt, J., & Speer, N. (2013). Mental health in American colleges and universities: Variation across student subgroups and across campuses. *The Journal of Nervous and Mental Disease, 201*(1), 60–67.

Hayes, J. A., Chun-Kennedy, C., Edens, A., & Locke, B. D. (2011). Do double minority students face double jeopardy? Testing minority stress theory. *Journal of College Counseling, 14*, 117–126. doi:10.1002/j.2161-1882.2011.tb00267.x

Hayes, J. A., Youn, S. Y., Castonguay, L. G., Locke, B. D., McAleavey, A. A., & Nordberg, S. (2011). Rates and predictors of counseling center utilization among college students of color. *Journal of College Counseling, 14*, 105–116. doi:10.1002/j.2161-1882.2011.tb00266.x

Hunt, J., & Eisenberg, D. (2010). Mental health problems and help-seeking behavior among college students. *Journal of Adolescent Health, 46*(1), 3–10. doi:10.1016/j.jadohealth.2009.08.008

Kawamoto, A., Youn, S. J., Castonguay, L. G., & Locke, B. D. *Utilization of counseling among international students: Between- and- within culture differences in symptomatology.* Manuscript submitted for publication.

Kessler, R. C., Chiu, W. T., Demler, O., Merikangas, K. R. & Walters, E. E. (2005). Prevalence, severity, and comorbidity of 12-month DSM-IV disorders in the National Comorbidity Survey Replication. *Archives of General Psychiatry, 62*, 617–627. doi:10.1001/archpsyc.62.6.617

Kopta, S. M., & Lowry, J. L. (2002). Psychometric evaluation of the Behavioral Health Questionnaire-20: A brief instrument for assessing global mental health and the three phases of psychotherapy outcome. *Psychotherapy Research, 12*, 413–426. doi:10.1093/ptr/12.4.413

Koerner, K., & Castonguay, L. G. (in press). Conducting psychotherapy research in private practice. *Psychotherapy Research, 24.*

Kraus, D. R., Castonguay, L., Boswell, J. F., Nordberg, S. S., & Hayes, J. A. (2011). Therapist effectiveness: Implications for accountability and patient care. *Psychotherapy Research, 21*, 267–276. doi:10.1080/10503307.2011.563249

Lambert, M. J. (2004). *Administration and scoring manual for the OQ-45.2 (Outcome Questionnaire).* Salt Lake City, UT: OQ Measures, LLC.

Lockard, A. J., Hayes, J. A., McAleavey, A. A., & Locke, B. D. (2012). Change in academic distress: Examining differences between a clinical and non-clinical college sample. *Journal of College Counseling, 15*, 233–246. doi:10.1002/j.2161-1882.2012.00018.x

Locke, B. D., Bieschke, K. J., Castonguay, L. G., & Hayes, J. A. (2012). The Center for Collegiate Mental Health (CCMH): Studying college student mental health through an innovative research infrastructure that brings science and practice together. *Harvard Review of Psychiatry, 20*, 233–245. doi:10.3109/10673229.2012.712837

Locke, B. D., Buzolitz, J. S., Lei, P.-W., Boswell, J. F., McAleavey, A. A., Sevig, T. D., ... Hayes, J. A. (2011). Development of the Counseling Center Assessment of Psychological Symptoms-62 (CCAPS-62). *Journal of Counseling Psychology, 58*, 97–109. doi:10.1037/a0021282

Locke, B. D., McAleavey, A. A., Zhao, Y., Lei, P.-W., Hayes, J. A., Castonguay, L. G., ... Lin, Y.-C. (2012). Development and initial validation of the Counseling Center Assessment of Psychological Symptoms-34 (CCAPS-34). *Measurement and Evaluation in Counseling and Development, 45*, 151–169. doi:10.1177/0748175611432642

McAleavey, A. A., Castonguay, L. G., & Locke, B. D. (2011). Sexual orientation minorities in college counseling: Prevalence, distress, and symptom profiles. *Journal of College Counseling, 14*, 127–142. doi:10.1002/j.2161-1882.2011.tb00268.x

McAleavey, A. A., Nordberg, S. S., Hayes, J. A., Castonguay, L. G., Locke, B. D., & Lockard, A. J. (2012). Clinical validity of the Counseling Center Assessment of Psychological Symptoms-62 (CCAPS-62): Further evaluation and clinical applications. *Journal of Counseling Psychology, 59*, 575–590. doi:10.1037/a0029855

Minami, T., Davies, D. R., Tierney, S. C., Bettmann, J. E., McAward, S. M., Averill, L. A., ... Wampold, B. E. (2009). Preliminary evidence on the effectiveness of psychological treatments delivered at a university counseling center. *Journal of Counseling Psychology, 56*, 309–320. doi:10.1037/a0015398

Nelson, D. L., Castonguay, L. G., & Locke, B. D. (2011). Challenging stereotypes of eating and body image concerns among college students: Implications for diagnosis and treatment of diverse populations. *Journal of College Counseling, 14*, 158–172. doi:10.1002/j.2161-1882.2011.tb00270.x

Nordberg, S. S., Hayes, J. A., McAleavey, A. A., Castonguay, L. G., & Locke, B. D. (2013). Treatment utilization on college campuses: Who seeks help for what? *Journal of College Counseling, 16*, 258–274.

Sharkin, B. (2004). College counseling and student retention: Research findings and implications for counseling centers. *Journal of College Counseling, 7*, 99–108. doi:10.1002/j.2161-1882.2004.tb00241.x

Szapocznik, J., Muir, J. A., Duff, J., & Schwartz, S. J. (in press). Brief strategic family therapy: Implementing evidence-based models in community settings. *Psychotherapy Research, 24.* doi:10.1080/10503307.2013.856044

Varlotta, L. E. (2012). Toward a more data-driven supervision of collegiate counseling centers. *Journal of American College Health, 60*, 336–339. doi:10.1080/07448481.2012.663843

METHOD PAPER

APIRE Practice Research Network: Accomplishments, challenges, and lessons learned

JOYCE C. WEST[1], EVE K. MOŚCICKI[1], FARIFTEH F. DUFFY[1], JOSHUA E. WILK[2], LISA COUNTIS[1], WILLIAM E. NARROW[1], & DARREL A. REGIER[1]

[1]*American Psychiatric Institute for Research and Education, Arlington, VA, USA &* [2]*Division of Psychiatry and Neuroscience, Walter Reed Army Institute of Research, Silver Spring, MD, USA*

Abstract

The Practice Research Network (PRN) was established in 1993 to bridge the gap between the science base and the clinical practice of psychiatry by expanding the generalizability of findings and involving clinicians in the development and conduct of research. It began as a nationwide network of psychiatrists and has evolved to conduct large-scale, clinical and policy research studies using randomly selected samples of psychiatrists from the AMA Physician Masterfile. This paper provides an overview of major PRN initiatives and the impact of these studies. It describes the benefits to clinicians of participating in PRN research, as well as strategies developed to address key challenges.

I. Background and Introduction

The American Psychiatric Institute for Research and Education's (APIRE) Practice Research Network (PRN) was established in 1993 by the American Psychiatric Association (APA) in recognition of the need for more practice-relevant research in the field of psychiatry. The PRN was envisioned as a way to bridge the gap between the science base and the clinical practice of psychiatry by expanding the generalizability of findings and involving clinicians in the development and conduct of research studies (Zarin, Pincus, West, & McIntyre, 1997). It was designed to complement traditional research methods by generating information across patients, treatments, and treatment settings so that a wide range of clinical and policy issues could be studied.

Two major impetuses drove the development of the PRN. The first was the need to generate systematic data on the clinical practices of psychiatrists to help inform the development of the APA's evidence-based practice guidelines. The second was the need for empirical data to assess the impact of dramatic changes in the organization, delivery, and financing of mental health care, and rapidly evolving models of "managed care." The PRN was also seen as a promising vehicle to systematically collect longitudinal data on the patterns and outcomes of psychiatric care, facilitating studies to assess the effectiveness of treatments (Zarin, West, & Pincus, 1995).[1]

APIRE's PRN began as a research initiative composed of a nationwide network of nearly 800 APA members who cooperated to collect data and conduct research studies on a variety of clinical and health services delivery issues. The PRN has evolved to conduct large-scale, national clinical and policy research studies using randomly selected samples of psychiatrists from the AMA Physician Masterfile, which includes both APA members and non-members, and the APA Membership database. As a result, PRN research findings are relevant to a broad array of day-to-day policy and clinical decision-making issues.

The research goals and strategic priorities of the PRN have changed over time to reflect APIRE's mission. With the recent reorganization of the APA, APIRE is now a division of the American Psychiatric Foundation, a 501(c)(3) subsidiary of the American Psychiatric Association (APA). APIRE's mission is to contribute to psychiatry's science base and to improve the quality of psychiatric care through research, education, health policy analysis, and dissemination. The PRN and its research infrastructure have provided a unique resource and played a vital role in conducting quality of care research and gathering policy-relevant data through its five general, integrated priority areas of research: health policy and services research, quality improvement and evidence-based care, psychiatry workforce, diagnostic research, and psychiatric epidemiology.

APIRE and its Practice Research Network routinely collaborate with leading academic and government investigators as well as clinician collaborators, with over 200 peer-reviewed publications and other scientific communications developed by APIRE PRN staff and their collaborators. Our experience in developing the PRN and conducting practice-based research has demonstrated that involving clinicians in the research enterprise significantly enhances the quality of the research. In addition to their primary contribution of participating in and implementing the actual studies which are fielded, our clinician collaborators have helped us to strengthen our research enterprise and efforts by: (i) Identifying and selecting topics that are clinically relevant and important; (ii) ensuring that studies are designed to optimize feasibility and success; and (iii) facilitating dissemination of findings. The input and participation of our clinician collaborators have proven to be particularly valuable in improving the quality, feasibility, and strength of our studies through their generous contributions of time, expertise, and valuable insights to strengthen our research.

This paper provides an overview of the PRN's major research initiatives, along with selected examples of the impact of some PRN studies. It also provides an overview of the infrastructure of the PRN with regard to staffing and the roles of our physician collaborators, along with key challenges that have faced the network and strategies which have been developed for addressing these challenges and obstacles. We conclude by providing some recommendations to enhance the success of future studies involving partnerships with clinicians.

II. Overview of Major Research Initiatives

Initially, most of the PRN's studies utilized data from two primary PRN datasets which were developed as a platform for a wide range of descriptive and analytic studies and secondary data analyses: (i) The *National Survey of Psychiatric Practice* (NSPP), conducted in 1993, 1996, 1998 and 2002; and (ii) the *National Study of Psychiatric Patients and Treatments* (NSPPT), conducted in 1993, 1997, and 1999. The data were collected from the original network of APA members, which included practicing clinicians who work in the full range of public and private treatment settings in the United States. Approximately half (48%) of the PRN psychiatrists were randomly selected and recruited from the APA membership; the remainder were self-selected volunteers recruited nationally by APA and local district branches. These datasets are described in more detail below.

In the past decade, the PRN has focused on fielding large national studies on priority topics of special interest, primarily conducted among randomly selected samples of psychiatrists in the USA that include both APA members and non-members to enhance representativeness. While these studies have been on more focused research issues, many have also facilitated secondary analyses of a broader range of clinical and policy issues. Clinicians have provided valuable input at every stage in these studies, including identifying study topics and developing and refining study aims. Clinician input has been especially helpful in developing and refining study protocols and data collection instruments to enhance implementation and facilitate participation among practicing clinicians by ensuring that study questions are clear and response burden associated with studies is reasonable.

While most of the initial PRN research used mail survey research methods, we have increasingly turned to internet-based survey research methods to implement studies in recent years. Details of these studies and methods can be found in our published papers (please see bibliography for selected publications and http://www.psychiatry.org/PRN-Bibliography.pdf for a complete listing of PRN publications). In the section below, we describe some of the major studies conducted by our research group, beginning with the earlier studies and concluding with our most recent research initiative, the DSM–5 Field Trials in Routine Clinical Practice.

The National Survey of Psychiatric Practice (NSPP)

This is a practice-level survey used to collect periodic information about the practice and patient caseload characteristics of a representative sample of psychiatrists in the United States, and to track changes in the psychiatric workforce over time

(Zarin, Pincus, et al., 1998). The NSPP gathers information on routine practice from psychiatrists in the USA, collecting information on professional work activities (e.g., practice settings, hours per week spent on direct patient care, consultation, administrative activities, etc.); sociodemographics and diagnostic characteristics of patient caseload; services provided (e.g., proportion of patients receiving psychotherapy, pharmacotherapy, or both); and financial factors such as sources of payment for services and patients' enrollment in managed health insurance plans. After an initial pilot study in 1993, in which clinician collaborators provided important input on the study aims and measures, the NSPP was conducted in 1996, and again in 1998, using random samples of 1500 members of the American Psychiatric Association. Response rates of over 70% were achieved for both surveys. In 2002, the NSPP was conducted using a random sample of 2000 psychiatrists drawn from the American Medical Association's Physician Masterfile, a listing of all physicians in the USA self-identified by their specialty, including psychiatry. This list included all PRN members; the response rate was 57%.

National Study of Psychiatric Patients and Treatment (NSPPT)

This study, conducted in 1993, 1997, and 1999, provided an invaluable resource to assess and document a range of important clinical, policy, and workforce-related issues in psychiatry. This series of studies provided a clinically detailed, national database on patient characteristics and psychiatric treatments in a large national sample of psychiatric patients across the full range of public and private treatment settings (Pincus et al., 1999; West, Zarin, Pincus, & McIntyre, 1996a, 1996b). As illustrated below in the descriptions of specific PRN studies, this database generated numerous peer-reviewed publications and other scientific communications. It has been particularly valuable in studying clinical quality of care (and factors affecting quality of care) as measured by evidence-based practice guideline recommendations. Because our study investigators and our clinician advisors for this study had direct experience in the initial development of the APA's evidence-based practice guidelines, the basic clinical and treatment measures included in this study were designed to help understand and assess the extent to which routine clinical care was consistent with many key practice guideline treatment recommendations.

Other available claims and national survey databases generally do not provide the level of clinical detail needed for these assessments. For example,

the SPPT collected information on up to seven Axis I and II DSM IV mental and personality disorders; Axis III general medical conditions; Axis IV psychosocial and environmental problems; current health and disability status; severity of depressive, anxiety, and psychotic symptoms; presence of various substance use, sleeping, medication side effect, and treatment compliance problems; and detailed data on specific mental health psychosocial and pharmacologic treatments provided by the psychiatrist and other providers. At the time, this was the largest, clinically detailed, national database characterizing psychiatric patients and has been indispensable in studying access and disparities in psychosocial and psychopharmacologic treatments.

Studies of Quality of Care and Evidence-Based Treatment Guideline Adherence

The PRN has completed several studies assessing conformance with evidence-based treatment recommendations for severe mental illness, including studies focusing on the treatment of schizophrenia (West, Wilk, et al., 2005) and major depressive disorder (West, Duffy, et al., 2005; West, Leaf, & Zarin, 2000), which were conducted using the NSPPT. We have also included similar measures in more recently fielded studies. These studies have been informative in highlighting gaps in evidence-based best practices, particularly with respect to access to evidence-based psychosocial treatments. For example, despite the existence of an extensive and robust research base for the treatment of patients with schizophrenia, PRN data revealed that fewer than half (0 to 43%) of patients with schizophrenia treated by psychiatrists received evidence-based psychosocial treatments (i.e., psychotherapy, illness education, assertive community treatment, vocational rehabilitation/supported employment, social skill straining, or substance use treatment) recommended by APA and the Patient Outcomes Research Team (PORT) practice guidelines (West, Wilk, et al., 2005). Although physician adherence to the evidence base for psychopharmacologic treatments was generally higher, with 99% of patients with schizophrenia receiving antipsychotic medications, only 30 to 51% of patients were prescribed other specifically recommended pharmacological treatments.

Additional efforts in promoting improvement in quality of care and guideline adherence involved development of quality indicators and performance measures, derived from key assessment and treatment recommendations of major published guidelines for select psychiatric disorders. Examples include the assessment of nicotine, alcohol or other substance use problems as a part of a comprehensive psychiatric evaluation, or use of an appropriately dosed selective serotonin reuptake inhibitor (SSRI) and/or evidence-based psychotherapeutic intervention (e.g., cognitive behavior therapy) as a first-line treatment for major depressive disorders. To date, quality indicators and performance measures for bipolar disorder (Duffy et al., 2005), depression (Fochtmann, Duffy, West, Kunkle, & Plovnick, 2008), posttraumatic stress disorder (Duffy, Craig, Mościcki, West, & Fochtmann, 2009; Duffy, Fochtmann, Craig, West, & Mościcki, 2013), substance use disorder (Duffy, West, et al., 2011), suicidality (Duffy, Mościcki, et al., 2011), and schizophrenia (Duffy et al., 2012) have been published. Wherever possible, we have sought to embed these quality indicators in our studies to facilitate assessments of quality of care in routine clinical practice.

Child and Adolescent Treatment Study of Attention Deficit Hyperactivity Disorder

This study was implemented in the fall of 1996 to gather detailed information on treatments provided by psychiatrists to children and adolescents with Attention Deficit Hyperactivity Disorder (ADHD), in order to understand the variation of these treatments across psychiatrists and patients. At the time, our clinician collaborators and advisors were concerned about potential quality of care issues associated with the over-use of medications among children and adolescents. Our clinician collaborators were highly supportive of this project and helped to develop, test, and revise the study data collection instruments to ensure that relevant items were being appropriately assessed. An important finding was that psychopharmacologic medications other than psychostimulants were prescribed for the majority of children and adolescents receiving treatment for ADHD (55%) (Zarin, Suarez, et al., 1998).

Study of Outpatient Referral Patterns

The aim of this study was to understand and characterize the interface between primary care and psychiatry with regard to mental health referrals. This study, conducted in 1997–1998 in collaboration with the Ambulatory Sentinel Practice Network (ASPN) and other primary care researchers, gathered psychiatrist-level and patient-level data on the referral process for new outpatients referred to psychiatrists by non-psychiatric physicians. Results indicated that primary care physicians were a significant source of referrals for psychiatrists, and that psychiatrists were generally satisfied with the communication interface with the referring physicians.

However, 69% of psychiatrists reported that communications with primary care physicians regarding follow-up to care were poor or fair. The level of satisfaction was lowest for adequacy and sufficiency of patient data provided by primary care physicians (Tanielian et al., 2000).

Race/Ethnicity and Variations in Psychiatric Diagnosis and Treatment

Using data from the 1999 NSPPT, these studies examined variation in psychiatric diagnosis and treatments observed among racial/ethnic minority and non-minority patients, adjusting for sociodemographic, diagnostic, and clinical factors, including psychiatric symptom severity, previous psychiatric hospitalization, and global assessment of functioning score (Herbeck et al., 2004; West, Herbeck, et al., 2006). Results indicated statistically significant differences by race/ethnicity with respect to diagnosis, symptom severity, and level of impairment. African American patients were twice as likely as white patients to be diagnosed as having a psychotic disorder and 40% less likely to be diagnosed as having a mood disorder. Compared to white patients, African American patients were 48% less likely to receive an antidepressant, more likely to receive conventional antipsychotics, and less likely to receive second-generation antipsychotics. The findings from this study were analyzed and reported in close collaboration with physicians who had extensive clinical experience working with racially and ethnically diverse populations. The findings highlighted striking differences in diagnosis and treatment associated with race and ethnicity. Psychometric validation of the diagnostic data is, however, needed to assess whether there are actual differences in the diagnostic case mix associated with race/ethnicity or whether these findings reflect racial/ethnic differences in patterns of detection, treatment seeking, or referral.

Psychiatric Management of Non-adherent and Treatment-Resistant Patients with Schizophrenia

In 2003–2004, The PRN collaborated with Columbia University (Mark Olfson, MD, MPH, Principal Investigator) in completing the nation's largest study of the management and outcomes of treatment for patients with schizophrenia treated in routine practice settings. A sample of 2300 psychiatrists was randomly selected from the AMA Physician Masterfile; over 1000 psychiatrists who met eligibility criteria responded, representing a response rate of

66%. For this study, we used a more aggressive approach to involving clinicians in the development and refinement of the study data collection instruments. We conducted telephone interviews with the clinicians who pre-tested the study data collection instruments to obtain more in-depth feedback. Incorporating an honorarium not only facilitated a high response to these telephone interviews, but also generated extensive qualitative information on the study protocol and survey items, which, in turn, helped to strengthen the study. Key findings indicated that many patients were not receiving evidence-based treatments the psychiatrists reported to be most effective. For example, although approximately two-thirds of psychiatrists considered depot or long-acting injectable medications to be somewhat or extremely effective in treating non-adherent patients with schizophrenia, less than 20% of non-adherent patients were prescribed these medications (West et al., 2008). Similarly, although about one-third of psychiatrists reported clozapine to be the most effective treatment for patients with treatment-resistant psychotic symptoms, less than 10% of patients were receiving these medications in response to their treatment-resistant symptoms (Olfson, Marcus, Wilk, & West, 2006). This study highlighted opportunities to improve evidence-based care for patients with schizophrenia.

Federal Employees Health Benefits Program (FEHBP) Parity Evaluation

This study assessed how the management, financing, and pricing of mental health services affected treatment provision and access to mental health care in the FEHBP program and in other privately and publicly funded programs in the Washington DC metropolitan area. The study was fielded in 2005 in collaboration with the American Psychological Association and the National Association of Social Workers to broaden the generalizability of the study findings. We worked closely with practicing clinicians affiliated with the APA's Washington DC District Branch to help facilitate a high response, as we were targeting all practicing clinicians in the area. They also worked closely with us to ensure that the study measures and instrumentation reflected their experiences with the FEHBP program. Key findings from the study highlighted potential barriers to parity-level benefits due to the limited number of clinicians enrolled in FEHBP provider networks as well as the limited number of FEHBP network clinicians accepting new patients (Regier et al., 2008). In addition, many patients receiving treatment from FEHBP network clinicians were reported to have experienced problems accessing clinically indicated treatment, with treatment access problems most commonly reported for substance abuse services, partial hospitalization for mental illnesses, psychological or neurological testing, psychosocial or vocational rehabilitation, and case management services. Findings from this study provided critical and timely information to advocates who were successful in having parity applied to both "in" and "out" of network care under the landmark federal Parity legislation.

Patterns of Adult Psychotherapy in Psychiatric Practice

This study used data from the 1999 NSPPT to examine patterns and predictors of psychotherapy services received by patients of psychiatrists. Data were collected from 587 psychiatrists who generated national data for 1589 adult patients. Findings indicated that more than 66% of patients received some form of psychotherapy in the past 30 days—56% from their psychiatrist and 10% from another clinician. Although 72% of patients with depression received psychotherapy, more than half of those with schizophrenia did not. Patients whose care was subject to utilization review by their insurance company, who used Medicaid or Medicare to pay for their services, or who were older than 65 were less likely to receive psychotherapy (Wilk, West, Rae, et al., 2006), highlighting opportunities to improve psychotherapy treatment access.

Comorbidity Patterns in Routine Psychiatric Practice

This study examined data on the rates of diagnosis and patterns of DSM-IV Axis I comorbidity in patients treated by psychiatrists in routine psychiatric practice. Data were analyzed on 2117 psychiatric patients gathered by 754 psychiatrists who participated in the 1997 and 1999 National Study of Psychiatric Patients and Treatments (NSPPT). These data were compared to a clinical subset of patients in the National Comorbidity Survey (NCS) (Kessler et al., 1994) who had been treated in the specialty mental health sector. Rates of comorbidity were higher in the NCS (53.9%) than in the SPPT (31.5%). Schizophrenia diagnoses were more than twice as prevalent in the SPPT as in the NCS sample; anxiety disorders were 2 to 22 times more prevalent in the NCS sample. Results of these analyses suggest greater differences in the patterns and rates of comorbidity than one might expect between these two samples. In particular, anxiety disorders appeared to be under-detected and underdiagnosed in routine psychiatric practice (Wilk, West, Narrow, et al., 2006).

National Depression Management Leadership Initiative: Improving Depression Care

The National Depression Management Leadership Initiative was a joint undertaking of the APIRE's PRN, the American Academy of Family Physicians (AAFP), and the American College of Physicians (ACP), implemented in 2005–2006. The specific aims of this collaboration were to: (i) assess the clinical utility of a simple quantitative instrument (the nine-item Patient Health Questionnaire – PHQ – 9) to measure the severity of depression, and (ii) test office systems and management strategies that optimize monitoring of depression in routine clinical practice.

"Leadership Teams," which consisted of a physician and a non-physician co-leader from 16 primary care and 17 psychiatric practices, participated in three "Learning Sessions" during the 12-month project period. The sessions were modeled after the *Institute for Healthcare Improvement Breakthrough Series* and engaged participants in a collaborative learning environment to identify, refine, and implement effective depression management strategies as a routine part of depression care.

Key findings indicated that PHQ – 9 scores influenced clinical decisions during 93% of patient visits (Duffy et al., 2008). For 40% of patient contacts, the overall PHQ – 9 score or item review led to a change in treatment (for example, the use of a different medication, or change in dosage); for 60%, the score affirmed the benefits of continuing a course of treatment. In a follow-up study conducted 1 year later, 15 of the 17 psychiatric practices reported sustained use of the PHQ – 9 for screening, diagnosis, or severity monitoring purposes, demonstrating that measurement-based care approach to disease management is feasible and sustainable in psychiatry (Chung et al., 2013). Many of these practices and clinical leaders also reported that, as a result of their participation in this study and the demonstrated clinical utility of this approach, they have led efforts to disseminate use of the PHQ – 9 to other practices and services delivery systems to facilitate measurement-based care for depression.

National Studies of Medicaid and Medicare Medication Access and Continuity

The overall goal of these studies was to monitor psychiatrists' practices with respect to the medication management of Medicaid and "dual eligible" Medicaid and Medicare patients with mental and addictive illnesses, including: (i) Assessing medication access issues and the extent of any disruptions in medication continuity; (ii) characterizing adverse events which may be associated with medication access problems; and (iii) examining the functioning of specific prescription drug utilization management features and policies to inform prescription drug policies and practices. Nearly 5000 psychiatrists from the AMA Physician Masterfile were randomly selected to participate in the Dual Eligible study (West, Wilk, et al., 2010). For the Medicaid study, we sampled an additional 500 psychiatrists per state in ten states of particular policy interest (West et al., 2009). Both studies were conducted in 2006. Key findings indicated that medication access problems were commonly experienced among both Medicaid patients and Medicare dual eligible psychiatric patients. These access problems were highly associated with increased hospital days, emergency department visits, homelessness, incarceration, and suicidal ideation or behavior (Mościcki et al., 2010; West, Rae, et al., 2010; West, Wilk, et al., 2010; West et al., 2012). Data from this study have been used by mental health advocates, including a number of our clinical advisors and collaborators, to ensure pharmacologic treatment continuity and access for psychiatric patients under Medicare Part D plans and state Medicaid programs.

Psychotherapy Treatment Access Study

Trends in the delivery of psychiatric care have documented a move away from psychotherapy to pharmacotherapy (West, Wilk, Rae, Narrow, & Regier, 2003). While APA Practice Guidelines indicate psychotherapy is a best practice in improving patient outcomes for a range of diagnoses, psychiatrist visits involving psychotherapy have decreased significantly (Mojtabai & Olfson, 2008). The specific aims of this study, which was conducted in collaboration with practicing clinicians from the APA's Committee on Psychotherapy by Psychiatrists and the Canadian Psychiatric Association in 2010, were to: (i) Generate current data to document trends in the provision of psychotherapy and medication management; (ii) identify factors associated with the provision of psychotherapy by psychiatrists; and (iii) quantify the major barriers to providing or facilitating access to psychotherapy among patients of psychiatrists. Data were collected through an electronic survey of 3000 APA members. Members of the Committee on Psychotherapy by Psychiatrists played a leadership role in developing this study and identifying the key study aims and measures. They then worked closely with PRN staff in refining the data collection instrument, developing and fielding this study, and analyzing and reporting the key findings.

Selected findings indicated that, despite significant financial, administrative, and other barriers to providing psychotherapy, psychiatrists reported a high level of satisfaction and interest in providing more psychotherapy if reimbursed at levels comparable to medication management. However, nearly half of the psychiatrists reported having no psychotherapy referral sources for new patients they wanted to refer for clinically indicated psychotherapy, highlighting the need to enhance the nation's psychotherapy provider workforce to address the significant unmet needs for psychotherapy services.

Improving Treatment for Combat and Operational Mental Health Problems

In order to generate more systematic, quantifiable data on the routine practice of the Army's specialty mental health workforce, APIRE collaborated with the Walter Reed Army Institute of Research (WRAIR) to develop and field an internet-based survey of the universe of the Army's mental health providers across disciplines in 2010. The primary aims of this study were to: (i) Characterize routine practice in Army behavioral health treatment settings, including clinician, setting, and patient characteristics; (ii) assess the degree to which clinical practice in Army mental health treatment settings conforms to treatment guideline recommendations; and (iii) test methods to regularly collect basic practice- and clinical-level data to facilitate tracking practice patterns in Army mental health treatment settings. APIRE is currently working with WRAIR to analyze and report the key findings of this study, which provide an analytically rich resource for the Department of Defense to examine workforce issues as well as clinical issues related to treatment access and quality. Based in part on initial findings from this study, the Army has implemented a new policy in April 2012 for the assessment and treatment of PTSD.

This study was also notable in including basic measures of fidelity to three trauma-focused psychotherapies for PTSD, including prolonged exposure (Foa, Rothbaum, Riggs, & Murdock, 1991), cognitive processing therapy (Resick & Schnicke, 1992), and eye movement desensitization retraining (Shapiro, 1989). We worked with the clinician developers of each intervention to assure that we captured the essential elements of each therapeutic approach. Analyses of the fidelity data identified significant variation in the use of the basic techniques underlying these psychotherapies, highlighting

opportunities to enhance psychotherapy treatment fidelity.

PTSD Care Dissemination Project

This pilot study was initiated in 2008 and developed a multipronged approach to practice improvement for the management of PTSD in military behavioral health treatment settings. The project expanded to also target depression and alcohol use problems, which have been shown to be highly comorbid with PTSD. To this end, key evidence-based assessment and treatment recommendations for management of PTSD and substance use disorders were extracted from the US Departments of Veterans Affairs and Defense (VA/DoD) Clinical Practice Guideline and other major practice guidelines. Based on this work, Performance in Practice (PIP) Clinical Tools for PTSD (Duffy et al., 2009, 2013) and substance use disorders were developed (Duffy, West, et al., 2011), which provided evidence-based resources to facilitate practice evaluation and identification of potential gaps in patient care. Next, the PTSD Checklist-Civilian Version (PCL-C), the nine-item Patient Health Questionnaire (PHQ–9), and AUDIT-C were selected as evidence-based tools for screening, severity monitoring, and management of PTSD, depression, and alcohol use problems, respectively.

Lastly, APIRE collaborated with the Workflow Division, Office of the Chief Information Officer, Air Force Medical Support Agency, and Army clinical staff to arrive at a practical clinical workflow that is responsive to the needs of behavioral health clinicians in military health care settings. The principal goals of the Workflow Division's initiative were to improve usability of the military's electronic health record, AHLTA, and arrive at a standardized clinical workflow for the assessment and treatment of PTSD, depression, and alcohol use problems at the pilot site. The PCL-C, PHQ–9, and AUDIT-C were incorporated into AHLTA to support routine screening and severity monitoring for these conditions. The pilot site was able to successfully implement use of this enhanced AHLTA system and standardize clinical workflow approaches. An additional site within the military behavioral health care system also adopted this approach, following the successful pilot implementation.

DSM – 5 Field Trials in Routine Clinical Practice Settings

The PRN research infrastructure was harnessed during the landmark DSM – 5 development process to implement one arm of the DSM – 5 Field Trials, the DSM – 5 Field Trials in Routine Clinical Practice

Settings (RCP). This arm of the field trials examined the feasibility, clinical utility, and responsiveness to symptom change of the proposed DSM–5 diagnostic criteria and dimensional assessment measures as implemented by individual clinicians in routine clinical practice settings. An important contribution in the pilot stages of this effort came from clinicians who had participated as network members in previous PRN studies, who reviewed our data collection instruments and provided important feedback before the main study went into the field. The DSM–5 RCP Field Trials were conducted in a wide range of practice settings in the United States and in settings in Canada, Australia, and the United Kingdom. Data collection took place over a 6-month period from the fall of 2011 through early 2012. Study participants included mental health professionals from six disciplines and their patients. Clinicians included psychiatrists, advanced practice psychiatric-mental health nurses, clinical psychologists, clinical social workers, licensed counselors, and marriage and family therapists. Six hundred and twenty-one clinicians completed a rigorous online training program and at least one patient study visit and provided diagnostic data for 1269 patients (Mościcki et al., 2013). This study broke new ground by working with large numbers of mental health clinicians from a wide range of clinical disciplines and settings to test the proposed diagnostic criteria. Findings demonstrated that the DSM–5 approach was feasible and clinically useful in a wide range of practice settings, and acceptable to both clinicians and their patients.

III. PRN Staffing and Physician Collaborators

This section provides an overview of some of the key pragmatic aspects of the PRN's research infrastructure. This includes a description of the PRN's core staff as well as physician and academic collaborators and their respective roles.

A. Staff

At full staffing capacity, the immediate PRN staff include four doctoral-level, professional staff with strong scientific backgrounds in psychiatric epidemiology, mental health services research, survey research, and biostatistics. A fifth staff member has extensive experience in multiple technical aspects of survey implementation, including both mail and electronic surveys. Four staff are full-time; one is part-time. In addition to the immediate PRN staff, frequent internal collaborators who bring an essential clinical perspective to PRN studies include two APIRE psychiatrists and other clinicians in APA, a research statistician with clinical experience, and other APIRE and APA professional staff. PRN also

provides limited research training experience by taking on graduate-level temporary staff, and hosting graduate and undergraduate interns. During the implementation of field work, several temporary staff may be hired to assist with mass mailings.

B. Physician Collaborators

The clinician participants in most PRN research studies have generally been recruited through mail or email contacts, particularly as we have moved towards primarily conducting research using randomly selected samples of psychiatrists from the AMA Physician Masterfile. We have identified physician research collaborators and clinical advisors through several mechanisms. The leadership and organizational governance infrastructure of the APA was instrumental in initially identifying clinicians interested in collaborating with the PRN, who provided key advice on the development of the PRN's research agenda, study development and implementation, and the recruiting of clinician study participants. This was accomplished with the support and involvement from the highest levels of the APA, including past President John S. McIntyre, MD. PRN Area and District Branch Liaisons regularly provided feedback on PRN initiatives via conference calls, in-person working meetings, and social events scheduled in conjunction with APA meetings. Their feedback on proposed studies and advice on study communications, research protocols, and data collection instruments, which was also solicited via mail and email, has been invaluable in ensuring the feasibility and success of our studies. Although we no longer have the resources to convene these advisors in person, they continue to be invited to provide feedback on pilot studies and participate in research initiatives where generalizability is not a goal.

A PRN Scientific Advisory Committee was also formed when the PRN was first developed. It primarily consisted of psychiatrists recognized in the fields of health services, policy, and clinical research, along with several statistical and methodological experts. The Committee advised on the development of a strategic research agenda and helped to identify potential sources of external funding. These experts met primarily via conference calls and were also available to provide technical and substantive advice on specific PRN studies, and generously contributed their time and expertise in this capacity. To enhance organizational efficiency, this general oversight role is currently provided by the APF Board of Directors. Our cadre of accomplished academic collaborators continues to advise on various scientific and technical issues.

PRN physician collaborators with substantive and technical expertise in specific research areas have also been routinely identified through the APA's various councils and committees, including those related to psychotherapy, addiction, military mental health, quality of care, health care financing, advocacy, and child and geriatric psychiatry. Other physician collaborators have been identified through the professional contacts of PRN staff as well as contacts made at scientific meetings and within other advocacy and professional organizations. In addition, PRN staff participate in the APA's annual health services research breakfast at the APA's Annual Meetings. These events provide opportunities for physicians conducting health services research or interested in participating in health services research to network and learn more about APA and APF research programs, including the PRN. This informal breakfast meeting has proven to be an effective way to facilitate PRN research collaborations among clinicians and clinician investigators, including young investigators.

IV. Benefits of Study Participation

In theory, we hope that participating in studies and receiving preliminary as well as published findings may help facilitate changes in clinical practices to improve patient care. With the exception of our studies where quality improvement and practice change were the primary goals however, it is not clear whether this is generally true for most of our studies. In studies of quality improvement and practice change, the collaborating clinicians were generally integrally involved in all phases of these studies, and we have empirical evidence that participation in these studies has led to sustained changes in clinical practices. We have anecdotal evidence from other studies suggesting that study participation and sharing of findings may have provided some additional insight to physician participants and motivated them to modify their clinical practices to improve patient care and treatment outcomes. Examples of comments we have received include, e.g., "I am one of those doctors. I realize I really should be providing more psychotherapy or spend more time to find a more consistent referral source for psychotherapy for more of my patients." Or "Yes, I would also say Clozapine is definitely the most effective med we have for treatment-resistant schizophrenia, but with the potential for agranulocytosis and the blood monitoring issues, I haven't really used it since residency."

Some of our physician collaborators have used PRN study findings to help advocate policy and services delivery changes as we have described.

A number of our physician collaborators have served as Principal Investigators on the studies we have conducted, obtaining funding to implement these studies using the PRN infrastructure. In other instances, subsequent to collaborating on a PRN research project, physician participants and collaborators have applied for and obtained research funding to conduct their own studies.

We have informally observed that many of our physician study participants and advisors have enjoyed and taken pride in the opportunity to contribute to the research enterprise, without an excessive burden in terms of time and effort. In addition, our physician study participants have often received CME credit for their contributions, which appears to be an appreciated benefit of participating in research.

V. Key Challenges and Strategies for Addressing Obstacles Encountered

Although our practice-based research group has been highly productive, there have been several challenges we have faced. The primary challenges have included: (i) Ensuring the generalizability of practice-based research; (ii) maintaining high participation and response rates; (iii) utilizing electronic data collection systems; (iv) implementing longitudinal studies and collecting data from patients; (v) obtaining external funding; (vi) involving clinician collaborators; and (vii) disseminating findings and using findings to improve care for patients. In this section, we briefly highlight these issues and some of the strategies which we have employed to address these challenges.

Ensuring the Generalizability of Practice-Based Research

Because an initial aim of many of our studies was to generate national estimates regarding the practice of psychiatry, generalizability was especially important and continues to be important as a major goal of practice-based research. While generalizability is not always a primary focus of our studies (e.g., pilot studies of the feasibility of quality improvement interventions or studies where internal validity is the primary focus), it is typically a major consideration. Consequently, when the PRN was initially developed, rather than relying exclusively on self-selected volunteers, approximately half of the network members were randomly selected and recruited from the American Psychiatric Association membership (West, Zarin, Peterson, & Pincus, 1998), allowing us to generalize our study findings to APA members. However, over time there was an aging of the network cohort, and network clinicians became an important source of information during the pilot phases of APIRE's new initiatives. Since 2002, PRN studies have primarily drawn randomly selected samples of psychiatrists from the AMA Physician Masterfile to enhance representativeness and generalizability to all psychiatrists practicing in the USA.

Maintaining High Participation and Response Rates

The relatively high response rates to our studies have largely been a result of sophisticated implementation and tracking techniques refined by our staff, with the studies generally fielded in three phases: An initial mailing and two follow-up mailings to non-respondents. Reminders are sent following each main study mailing via postcard, e-mail, and fax to encourage participation. This approach was primarily used for studies implemented in the late 1990s and early 2000s. For some of our earlier or smaller studies, telephone contacts were also made with non-responders to the third mailing. To further enhance study participation and response, our mailings have frequently been delivered using priority mailing. Because incentives have been shown to be effective (Thorpe et al., 2009), when resources have permitted, we have included tangible incentives (such as an engraved clock or an Amazon.com gift certificate) or monetary incentives to increase study participation. Over time, we have found it increasingly difficult to obtain consistently high participation rates to our studies. However, financial incentives appear to be most effective for encouraging participation. We have typically found incentives of about $75 for 15 minutes of study participation to be most cost-efficient to increase response.

Utilizing Electronic Data Collection Systems

Our efforts to use electronic data collection for practice-based research have met with mixed results. In a number of PRN studies where data collection was solely accomplished via web-based surveys or other electronic means, the resulting response rates (15% to 30%) were generally much lower than when paper-based methods were used (response rates: 21% to 79%), either solely or as an alternative to electronic data collection. Moreover, when using electronic data collection methods, we have found that contacting clinicians via email to provide a direct survey link is a more effective approach than paper-based methods requiring clinicians to type in the link to the survey once it is mailed to them.

The variability in response rates generally is influenced by a number of factors, including the length and complexity of the survey (i.e., response burden); the accompanying incentives for participation; time of the year when fielding the survey (with summer months, August in particular, and November and December holiday seasons generally yielding lower responses); the relative importance of the topic to its audience; and adequacy and effectiveness of follow-up reminders for completion of the survey. For web-based or electronically based surveys, operability of the electronic data collection system also plays a role: The more difficult the navigation through the system, the lower the response rate.

Electronic surveys have generally proven to be more cost-efficient since costs associated with data entry and cleaning are minimized; we have not, however, obtained consistently high response rates to electronic surveys. As we continue to collaborate with organized delivery systems which use electronic health records and clinical information systems, this will be an important approach we hope to continue to build upon to more efficiently collect data for clinical studies in particular.

Implementing Longitudinal Studies and Collecting Data from Patients

While one of the original aims for the PRN was to conduct longitudinal clinical effectiveness research, this goal has proven to be one of the most challenging. Although we have had success in conducting longitudinal studies and collecting longitudinal data from clinicians, patients, and patient informants (Compton, Olfson, & West, 2006), these efforts are generally costly and staff- and resource-intensive. The primary obstacles to implementing longitudinal studies and collecting data from patients include challenges in obtaining informed consent from patients and enrolling patients and caregivers in studies; identifying simple, streamlined methods for busy clinicians to consistently track, follow up, and report on patients over time; devising efficient, effective methods of collecting data from patients and caregivers; and implementing follow-up communications required for high response rates. Currently we are exploring the use of electronic health records, registries, and clinical information systems as a promising cost-effective approach for conducting longitudinal practice-based research. Clinician involvement in these efforts will be important to ensuring feasibility and sustainability.

Obtaining External Funding

An important and continuing challenge our research group faces is the identification and pursuit of stable sources of support. PRN receives support from internal funds from the American Psychiatric Foundation (APF) and the American Psychiatric Association, and external funds from a variety of sources. The combined internal and external sources support staff salaries, operating expenses, and project costs.

The relative proportions of internal and external support can fluctuate a great deal from one year to the next, from approximately 50% internal support to much less, with unwelcome consequences that can include delays in research initiatives and reductions in staffing. The PRN achieved early success in obtaining development and start-up funding from the National Institute of Mental Health and the MacArthur Foundation, which also supported infrastructure. Federal grants from the Center for Mental Health Services (CMHS), the Center for Substance Abuse Treatment (CSAT), and the private van Ameringen Foundation supported early work on the mental health workforce, quality of care, and substance abuse treatment. Support also came from contracts and subcontracts with university-based collaborators to study specific health services research issues. Some of our more recent practice-based research studies have relied on the APF as the primary source of funding for specific research initiatives, through support from coalitions of pharmaceutical industry sponsors. Studies supported by this source generated multiple publications in important areas of health policy, health services research, and quality improvement, and were also used as a foundation for new initiatives that enabled us to secure research support from other outside sources, but the main source of funding remained APF.

Recent research reflects our broader pursuit of external funding and new collaborations. In partnership with both external and internal clinician and patient collaborators, we have begun to actively pursue and receive Federal research support from external sources that include the Department of Defense, Agency for Healthcare Research and Quality (AHRQ), and the National Institutes of Health (NIH). A new opportunity for potential health services research support has emerged with the establishment of the Federal Patient-Centered Outcomes Research Institute (PCORI), and we have submitted grant applications in priority research areas identified by PCORI. We continue to monitor potential sources of funding in both the public and private sectors for appropriate grant application opportunities that address our priority research areas.

Divergence of Research Priorities

Related to the general challenges associated with the process of obtaining stable funding for studies are existing inconsistencies between our research priorities and those of potential external funders. Our primary research areas—health policy and services research, quality improvement and evidence-based care, psychiatry workforce, diagnostic research, and psychiatric epidemiology—may not necessarily reflect the research priorities of potential external funders. Incongruity between priority areas can delay or preclude obtaining necessary support for specific research initiatives. This tension limits our ability to strategically address important areas of research in a timely fashion and can limit the potential impact and benefits of our study findings for psychiatrists and patients. We have remained flexible in the face of this important challenge and have continued to identify new potential collaborations and broaden the field of potential funding sources. The PRN has also obtained funding from the APA and the APF to support targeted research in line with organizational educational and research objectives.

Involving Clinician Collaborators

While the input and participation of clinician collaborators have proven to be highly valuable in improving the quality and feasibility of our studies, this is an area we find more challenging than one might expect. The clinicians we have collaborated with have been incredibly generous and helpful in contributing their time, expertise, and valuable insights to strengthen our research; however, obtaining sufficient numbers of practicing clinicians to volunteer their time to advise and participate in pilot studies is nearly as challenging and staff-intensive as implementing the main study. Despite our affiliation with a professional association, which has proven very helpful in identifying potential clinician collaborators through the association's organizational infrastructure, involving sufficient numbers of clinician collaborators remains a challenge: developing these contacts often requires significant networking as well as time and effort.

Ensuring that funded studies include resources to support the sustained and significant involvement of clinician advisors and collaborators could facilitate the integral involvement of clinicians. To date, we have generally been more successful in involving clinicians at the data-gathering stage of studies (i.e., participating in studies and reporting data based on their clinical experience or patients), rather than more intensively involving them in ongoing study development, implementation, and reporting and dissemination of findings. Integral clinician involvement and collaboration on studies requires considerable time and effort, which is difficult to elicit on a voluntary basis. For some of our studies, we have engaged clinicians as paid consultants. Committing more study resources to more intensively engage and involve clinicians could greatly strengthen practice-based research initiatives. The advent of PCORI, which requires that patient and clinician stakeholders be true partners and participate in all aspects of the research process, holds considerable promise for strengthening collaborations with practicing clinicians.

We have been very fortunate in having been able to readily establish productive research collaborations with exceptional clinician investigators from leading academic institutions as well as other institutional and organized delivery settings. These collaborations have significantly strengthened and expanded our research portfolio. In addition, having in-house professional research staff who are practicing clinicians has also strengthened our research. In the future, seeking to develop more collaborations with organized services delivery systems may help facilitate the integral involvement of clinician collaborators in our studies, as has been the case with our collaborations with the Department of Defense's military health systems and the Depression Management Leadership Initiative described above.

Disseminating Findings and Using Findings to Improve Care For Patients

In our experience, studies in which the resulting findings have been actively used to improve care for patients, either through clinical or policy changes, have had the following attributes: (i) Decision-makers and clinical or policy leaders have been involved in the development, implementation, and dissemination of findings; (ii) the findings have been timely and we have been able to get the findings into the right hands at the right time, as was the case with the findings from our FEHBP Parity Evaluation and the Medicare and Medicaid medication access studies; or (iii) study participants have experienced the direct benefits or effects of the study first-hand, as was the case with the National Depression Management Leadership Initiative and the DoD PTSD Care Dissemination project.

As investigators, it is generally highly challenging to find time to facilitate dissemination of study findings beyond publication of results, as we are

typically also working on writing the next grant proposal, fielding the next study, presenting the latest study findings at scientific meetings, and developing the next round of manuscripts. Consequently, it is important to facilitate collaboration or interest in a study from decision-makers, advocacy organizations, and other key stakeholders at the outset of the study. Developing partnerships with researchers, clinicians, and clinical and policy decision-makers at the outset is vitally important in strengthening a proposed study and in generating valued research findings that may be more likely to have an impact on clinical practices or policy.

VI. Recommendations for Future Studies Involving Partnerships with Clinicians

Based on our experience in developing and fielding practice-based research studies over the past 20 years, we offer the following recommendations for future studies involving partnerships with clinicians:

1. Strengthen clinician partnerships and integrally involve practicing clinicians in the conduct of research. This is increasingly challenging in a world with competing demands and limited funding as well as time constraints and pressures to field studies as soon as possible, making it even more difficult to find the resources and time required to integrally involve practicing clinician collaborators in the design, implementation, and analysis of findings. However, to ensure research is optimally relevant and ultimately used by clinicians and policymakers, this is essential, and, as research increasingly focuses on patient-centered outcomes, is becoming more feasible.

2. Utilize clinical informatics platforms, such as electronic health records or clinical information or decision support systems, to facilitate more cost-efficient data collection or implementation of clinical studies.

3. Engender collaboration and participation in studies by framing or marketing studies so they are compelling and appealing to clinicians. How studies are presented to clinicians makes a notable difference in participation. Significant time, effort, and resources should be allocated to this, including involving target clinicians in the development and implementation of the most effective, time-efficient, and compelling communications and messages to solicit participation.

4. Appeal to altruism and the importance of contributing to and participating in research to strengthen the science base and improve care for patients. Involving leaders in the field in training programs, professional organizations, and organized practice settings to cultivate a culture emphasizing the importance and need for participation and leadership in research is important to the future success of these initiatives.

5. Minimize response burden and ensure that study procedures are as simple and streamlined as possible whenever primary data collection is needed. Take advantage of lessons already learned by becoming familiar with practice based research methods (Thorpe et al., 2009) and involving or consulting practice-based research experts.

6. Where generalizability is a goal, identify the best available sampling frame and sampling methods and consider tangible incentives such as using an honorarium to increase participation and response rates.

VII. Conclusion

APIRE has been highly productive over the past 20 years in developing and disseminating practice-based research conducted in close collaboration with clinicians, despite a number of challenges. Challenges have included enhancing the generalizability of research; utilizing electronic data collection methods; implementing longitudinal studies; collecting data from patients; obtaining external funding; and facilitating consistently effective dissemination of findings. A research culture focusing on continuous innovation and adaptation of research methods and approaches has been critical to our continued success in addressing these challenges, particularly as our target physician study participants face increasing competing demands and requests to participate in various studies and surveys. Future PRN studies will likely seek to strengthen partnerships with services delivery systems, make use of clinical informatics platforms, and continue to involve clinician collaborators and clinical and policy leaders in the development and implementation of studies to ensure studies are optimally relevant and feasible and to facilitate more effective dissemination of findings.

Note

[1] The Practice Research Network was one of the key presidential priorities of former APA president and APA Chair of the Steering Committee on Practice Guidelines, John S. McIntyre, MD. His leadership, along with the vision and direction of Harold Alan Pincus, MD, former Director, APA Office of Research, and Deborah A. Zarin, MD, former Associate Director, APA Office of Research and Director, APA Office of Quality Improvement and Psychiatric Services, were instrumental in facilitating the successful development of the PRN.

References

Chung, H., Duffy, F. F., Katzelnick, D. J., Williams, M. D., Rae, D. S., Regier, D. A., & Trivedi, M. H. (2013). Sustaining practice change one year after completion of the national depression management leadership initiative. *Psychiatric Services, 64*, 703–706. doi:10.1176/appi.ps.201200227

Compton, M. T., Olfson, M., & West, J. C. (2006). Prolonged duration of untreated psychosis in nonaffective first-episode psychotic disorders compared to other psychoses. *International Journal of Psychiatry in Clinical Practice, 10*, 264–268. doi:10.1080/13651500600736684

Duffy, F. F., Chung, H., Trivedi, M., Rae, D. S., Regier, D. A., & Katzelnick, D. J. (2008). Systematic use of patient-rated depression severity monitoring: Is it helpful and feasible in clinical psychiatry? *Psychiatric Services, 59*, 1148–1154. doi:10.1176/appi.ps.59.10.1148

Duffy, F. F., Craig, T., Mościcki, E. K., West, J. C., & Fochtmann, L. J. (2009). Performance in practice: Sample tools for the care of posttraumatic stress disorder. *Focus, 7*, 186–203.

Duffy, F. F., Fochtmann, L. J., Craig, T., West, J. C., & Mościcki, E. K. (2013). Performance in practice: Clinical module for the care of patients with posttraumatic stress disorder. *Focus, 11*, 341–349. doi:10.1176/appi.focus.11.3.341

Duffy, F. F., Mościcki, E. K., Fochtmann, L. J., Jacobs, D. G., Clarke, D. E., Plovnick, R., & Kunkle, R. (2011). Performance in practice: Physician practice assessment tool for the assessment and treatment of adults at risk for suicide and suicide-related behaviors. *Focus, 9*, 171–182.

Duffy, F. F., Narrow, W. E., West, J. C., Fochtmann, L. J., Kahn, D. A., Suppes, T., ... Regier, D. A. (2005). Quality of care measures for the treatment of bipolar disorder. *Psychiatric Quarterly, 76*, 213–230. doi:10.1007/s11126-005-2975-4

Duffy, F. F., West, J. C., Fochtmann, L. J., Dixon, L., Kreyenbuhl, J., Mościcki, E. K., & Kunkle, R. (2012). Performance in practice: Physician practice assessment tool for the care of adults with schizophrenia. *FOCUS, 10*, 157–171.

Duffy, F. F., West, J. C., Fochtmann, L. F., Willenbring, M. L., Plovnick, R., Kunkle, R., & Eld, B. (2011). Performance in practice: Physician practice assessment tools for the screening, assessment, and treatment of adults with substance use disorder. *Focus, 9*, 31–41.

Foa, E. B., Rothbaum, B. O., Riggs, D. S., & Murdock, T. B. (1991). Treatment of posttraumatic stress disorder in rape victims: A comparison between cognitive-behavioral procedures and counseling. *Journal of Consulting and Clinical Psychology, 59*, 715–723. doi:10.1037/0022-006X.59.5.715

Fochtmann, L. J., Duffy, F. F., West, J. C., Kunkle, R., & Plovnick, R. M. (2008). Performance in practice: Sample tools for the care of patients with major depressive disorder. *Focus, 6*, 22–35.

Herbeck, D. M., West, J. C., Ruditis, I., Duffy, F. F., Fitek, D. J., Bell, C. C., & Snowden, L. R. (2004). Variations in use of second generation antipsychotic medication by race and ethnicity among adult psychiatric patients. *Psychiatric Services, 55*, 677–684. doi:10.1176/appi.ps.55.6.677

Kessler, R. C., McGonagle, K. A., Zhao, S., Nelson, C. B., Hughes, M., Eshleman, S., & Kendler, K. S. (1994). Lifetime and 12-month prevalence of DSM-III-R psychiatric disorders among persons age 15–54 in the United States: Results from the National Comorbidity Survey. *Archives of General Psychiatry, 51*, 8–19.

Mojtabai, R., & Olfson, M. (2008). National trends in psychotherapy by office-based psychiatrists. *Archives of General Psychiatry, 65*, 962–970. doi:10.1001/archpsyc.65.8.962

Mościcki, E. K., Clarke, D. E., Kuramoto, S. J., Kraemer, H. C., Narrow, W. E., Kupfer, D. J., & Regier, D. A. (2013). Testing DSM–5 in routine clinical practice settings: Feasibility and clinical utility. *Psychiatric Services, 64*, 952–960. doi:10.1176/appi.ps.201300098

Mościcki, E. K., West, J. C., Wilk, J. E., Rae, D. S., Rubio-Stipec, M., & Regier, D. A. (2010). Medication access/continuity problems and suicidal ideation and behavior. *Journal of Clinical Psychiatry*, 71, 1657–1663. doi:10.4088/JCP.10m06177gre

Olfson, M., Marcus, S. C., Wilk, J., & West, J. C. (2006). Illness awareness and management of medication non-adherence in schizophrenia. *Psychiatric Services*, 57, 205–211. doi:10.1176/appi.ps.57.2.205

Pincus, H. A., Zarin, D. A., Tanielian, T. L., Johnson, J. L., West, J. C., Pettit, A. R., Marcus, S. C., & McIntyre, J. M. (1999). Psychiatric patients and treatments in 1997. *Archives of General Psychiatry*, 56, 441–449. doi:10.1001/archpsyc.56.5.441

Regier, D. A., Bufka, L. F., Whitaker, T., Duffy, F. F., Narrow, W. E., Rae, D. S., ... West, J. C. (2008). Parity and the use of out-of-network mental health benefits in the FEHB program. *Health Affairs*, 27, w70–w83. doi:10.1377/hlthaff.27.1.w70

Resick, P. A., & Schnicke, M. K. (1992). Cognitive processing therapy for sexual assault victims. *Journal of Consulting and Clinical Psychology*, 60, 748–756. doi:10.1037/0022-006X.60.5.748

Shapiro, F. (1989). Eye movement desensitization: A new treatment for post-traumatic stress disorder. *Journal of Behavior Therapy and Experimental Psychiatry*, 20, 211–217. doi:10.1016/0005-7916(89)90025-6

Tanielian, T., Pincus, H. A., Dietrich, A. J., Williams, J. W., Oxman, T. E., Nutting, P., & Marcus, S. C. (2000). Referrals to psychiatrists: Assessing the communication interface between psychiatry and primary care. *Psychosomatics*, 41, 245–252. doi:10.1176/appi.psy.41.3.245

Thorpe, C., Ryan, B., McLean, S. L., Burt, A., Stewart, M., Brown, J. B., Reid, G. J., & Harris, S. (2009). How to obtain excellent response rates when surveying physicians. *Family Practice*, 26, 65–68. doi:10.1093/fampra/cmn097

West, J. C., Duffy, F. F., Wilk, J. E., Rae, D. S., Narrow, W. E., Pincus, H. A., & Regier, D. A. (2005). Patterns and quality of treatment for patients with major depressive disorder in routine psychiatric practice. *Focus*, 3, 43–50.

West, J. C., Herbeck, D. M., Bell, C. C., Colquitt, W. L., Duffy, F. F., Fitek, D. J., ... Narrow, W. E. (2006). Race/ethnicity among psychiatric patients: Variations in diagnostic and clinical characteristics reported by practicing clinicians. *Focus*, 4, 48–56.

West, J. C., Leaf, P. L., & Zarin, D. A. (2000). Health plan characteristics and conformance with key practice guideline psychopharmacologic treatment recommendations for major depression. *Mental Health Services Research*, 2, 223–237. doi:10.1023/A:1010164520469

West, J. C., Marcus, S. C., Wilk, J., Countis, L. M., Regier, D. A., & Olfson, M. (2008). Use of depot antipsychotic medications for medication nonadherence in schizophrenia. *Schizophrenia Bulletin*, 34, 995–1001. doi:10.1093/schbul/sbm137

West, J. C., Rae, D. S., Huskamp, H. A., Rubio-Stipec, M., & Regier, D. A. (2010). Medicaid medication access problems and increased psychiatric hospital and emergency care. *General Hospital Psychiatry*, 32, 615–622. doi:10.1016/j.genhosppsych.2010.07.005

West, J. C., Rae, D. S., Mojtabai, R., Rubio-Stipec, M., Kreyenbuhl, J. A., Alter, C. L., & Crystal, S. (2012). Clinically unintended medication switches and inability to prescribe preferred medications under Medicare Part D. *Journal of Psychopharmacology*, 26, 784–793. doi:10.1177/0269881111406304

West, J. C., Wilk, J. E., Olfson, M., Rae, D. S., Marcus, S., Narrow, W. E., Pincus, H. A., & Regier, D. A. (2005). Patterns and quality of treatment for patients with schizophrenia in routine psychiatric practice. *Psychiatric Services*, 56, 283–291. doi:10.1176/appi.ps.56.3.283

West, J. C., Wilk, J. E., Rae, D. S., Muszynski, I. L., Rubio-Stipec, M. R., Alter, C. L., ... Regier, D. A. (2010). First-year Medicare Part D prescription drug benefits: Medication access and continuity among dual eligible psychiatric patients. *Journal of Clinical Psychiatry*, 71, 400–410. doi:10.4088/JCP.08m04608whi

West, J. C., Wilk, J. E., Rae, D. S., Muszynski, I. L., Stipec, M. R., Alter, C. L., ... Regier, D. A. (2009). Medicaid prescription drug policies and psychopharmacologic treatment access and continuity: Findings from ten states. *Psychiatric Services*, 60, 601–610. doi:10.1176/appi.ps.60.5.601

West, J. C., Wilk, J. E., Rae, D. S., Narrow, W. E., & Regier, D. A. (2003). Economic grand rounds: Financial disincentives for the provision of psychotherapy. *Psychiatric Services*, 54, 1582–1583, 1588. doi:10.1176/appi.ps.54.12.1582

West, J. C., Zarin, D. A., Peterson, B. D., & Pincus, H. A. (1998). Assessing the feasibility of recruiting a randomly selected sample of psychiatrists to participate in a national practice-based research network. *Journal of Social Psychiatry and Psychiatric Epidemiology*, 33, 620–623. doi:10.1007/s001270050102

West, J. C., Zarin, D. A., Pincus, H. A., & McIntyre, J. S. (1996a). Characteristics of psychiatric patients. *Psychiatric Services*, 47, 693.

West, J. C., Zarin, D. A., Pincus, H. A., & McIntyre, J. S. (1996b). Treatments provided to psychiatric patients. *Psychiatric Services*, 47, 577.

Wilk, J. E., West, J. C., Narrow, W. E., Regier, D. A., Marcus, S. C., Rubio-Stipec, M., & Rae, D. S. (2006). Comorbidity patterns in routine psychiatric practice: Is there evidence of under-detection and under-diagnosis? *Comprehensive Psychiatry*, 47, 258–264. doi:10.1016/j.comppsych.2005.08.007

Wilk, J. E., West, J. C., Rae, D. S., & Regier, D. A. (2006). Patterns of adult psychotherapy in psychiatric practice. *Psychiatric Services*, 57, 472–476. doi:10.1176/appi.ps.57.4.472

Zarin, D. A., Pincus, H. A., Peterson, B. D., West, J. C., Suarez, A. P., Marcus, S. C., & McIntyre, J. S. (1998). Characterizing psychiatry with findings from the 1996 National Survey of Psychiatric Practice. *American Journal of Psychiatry*, 155, 397–404.

Zarin, D. A., Pincus, H. A., West, J. C., & McIntyre, J. S. (1997). Practice-based research in psychiatry. *American Journal of Psychiatry*, 154, 1199–1208.

Zarin, D. A., Suarez, A. P., Pincus, H. A., Kupersanin, E., & Zito, J. M. (1998). Clinical and treatment characteristics of children with attention-deficit/hyperactivity disorder in psychiatric practice. *Journal of the American Academy of Child and Adolescent Psychiatry*, 37, 1262–1270. doi:10.1097/00004583-199812000-00009

Zarin, D. A., West, J. C., & Pincus, H. A. (1995). APA Psychiatric Research Network. In L. Sederer & B. Dickey (Eds.), *Outcomes assessment in clinical practice*. Baltimore, MD: Williams and Wilkins.

METHOD PAPER

Building clinicians-researchers partnerships: Lessons from diverse natural settings and practice-oriented initiatives

LOUIS G. CASTONGUAY[1], SOO JEONG YOUN[1], HENRY XIAO[1],
J. CHRISTOPHER MURAN[2,3], & JACQUES P. BARBER[2]

[1]Department of Psychology, Penn State University, University Park, PA, USA; [2]Derner Institute for Advanced Psychological Studies, Adelphi University, New York, NY, USA & [3]Department of Psychiatry, Beth Israel Medical Center, New York, NY, USA

Abstract

In this concluding paper, we identify the type of studies conducted by 11 teams of contributors to a special issue on building clinicians-researchers partnerships. Those studies were conducted across a variety of clinical settings. We also integrate the lessons that have emerged from their collaborative initiatives in terms of obstacles faced, strategies adopted to address these challenges, benefits gained, and general recommendations offered to facilitate studies conducted with or by clinicians. The paper ends with the authors' thoughts about the future success of practice-oriented research in general.

The wide gap between science and practice is due in part to the one-way direction that has mostly defined the connection between researchers and clinicians (Goldfried et al., 2014); researchers are generating empirical knowledge with the hope that practitioners will implement it in their working environment (Kazdin, 2008). This predominant, top-down approach to the generation and implementation of empirical knowledge has no doubt led to major contributions to our understanding and the efficacy of psychotherapy (Castonguay, 2013). However, since it is primarily guided by the theoretical interest of academicians and frequently conducted in highly controlled settings, this traditional approach to research has not been an optimal strategy to address day-to-day concerns of clinicians or to provide easily generalizable (applicable, actionable, and retainable) practice guidelines in clinical routine.

In contrast to what may be labeled "evidence-based research" (EBR) stands a bottom-up approach that has been referred to as Practice-Oriented Research (POR; Castonguay, Barkham, Lutz, & McAleavey,

2013). POR is characterized by studies that are (1) conducted as part of clinical routine, (2) foster the participation of clinicians in different aspects of the decision, design, implementation, and dissemination of research, and (3) allow for the use of collected data in day-to-day practice. POR thus offers opportunities for clinicians to not only contribute to the advancement of scientific knowledge but to also be involved in setting up the agenda of future research (Zarin, Pincus, West, & McIntyre, 1997). By relying on the unique expertise and resources of practitioners, it represents an antidote to the current state of empirical imperialism in psychotherapy within which full-time researchers have a dominant voice in terms of what should be studied and how it should be studied (Castonguay, 2011). Simultaneously, it offers a remedy for the colander effect that reflects our inattention to clinical knowledge and experience (Kazdin, 2008). Rather than being mutually exclusive, EBR and POR can be viewed as complementary paradigms, whereby the strengths and limitations (in terms of internal and external validity, for instance) of each approach can lead to a more comprehensive and robust base of knowledge (Barkham & Margison, 2007; Barkham, Stiles, Lambert, & Mellor-Clark, 2010).

A variety of POR studies have already been conducted (see Castonguay et al., 2013 for a review), but this type of research is still at an early phase of development. In order to generate more interest in and to facilitate future collaboration in studies, 11 groups of contributors who have been involved in POR in different naturalistic settings around the world were invited to share their experience in a special series of papers (Castonguay & Muran, 2014). As a concluding piece, the goal of the current paper is to identify convergences between the clinicians-researchers partnerships featured in this special series in terms of studies conducted, obstacles faced, and strategies used to deal with problems encountered, benefits earned, and general recommendations offered, as well as to highlight some aspects that are only found in particular research programs. We hope that these common and distinct experiences will provide useful lessons and guidelines that could be helpful to all clinicians and researchers interested in conducting future POR, as well as offer new perspectives to current POR investigators working in their own respective naturalistic settings.

Studies

A variety of topics have been investigated in the POR initiatives described in this series. A common focus is the assessment of change using standardized outcome monitoring. This involves tracking or predicting the progress of individual, large groups, or specific types of clients (Adelman, Castonguay, Kraus, & Zack, 2014; Boswell, Kraus, Miller, & Lambert, 2014; Castonguay, Pincus, & McAleavey, 2014; Fernández-Álvarez, Gómez, & García, 2014; Holmqvist, Philips, & Barkham, 2014; Koerner & Castonguay, 2014; McAleavey, Lockard, Castonguay, Hayes, & Locke, 2014; Strauss et al., 2014; West et al., 2014). The use of outcome monitoring in day-to-day practice has allowed some of these programs to investigate a number of issues related to specific patterns of change (such as dose–effect and good enough models, predictors of differential response patterns, sudden changes, deterioration, and therapist–client responsiveness), as well as the impact of providing feedback and clinical tools to therapists based on client change.

Several other types of research have been conducted by a smaller number of partnerships. For example, the effectiveness of psychotherapy has been assessed, whether conducted in psychological services or in private practice (Holmqvist et al., 2014; Koerner & Castonguay, 2014). The outcome of

specific types of treatments or interventions for a wide range of clinical problems (e.g., children bed-wetting and adolescents with behavior and drug problems) has also been investigated or compared (Adelman et al., 2014; Fernández-Álvarez et al., 2014; Holmqvist et al., 2014; Szapocznik, Muir, Duff, Schwart, & Brown, 2014). Using different research methodologies (including randomized trials and single-case experimental designs), studies have assessed the impact of specific training programs aimed at fostering relationship skills, behavioral activation techniques, and two-chair techniques associated with emotion focused therapy (Koerner & Castonguay, 2014). The differential effectiveness of therapists has also been a core focus of POR studies (Holmqvist et al., 2014).

Also investigated are a number of characteristics related to the client, such as sociodemographic factors, treatment history, diagnostic variables, pre-treatment severity and family functioning, and attachment (Adelman et al., 2014; Castonguay et al., 2014; Holmqvist et al., 2014; McAleavey et al., 2014; Szapocznik et al, 2014; West et al., 2014); therapist, such as hours per week of direct care and personal style (see Fernández-Álvarez et al., 2014; West et al., 2014); treatment, such as practice settings, referral process, access to, utilization and provision of different types of services (psychotherapy and/or pharmacotherapy), sources of payment and management of care, as well as societal beliefs toward psychotherapy (Fernández-Álvarez et al., 2014; McAleavey et al., 2014; West et al., 2014); and the relationship between some of these variables, such as the congruence between client and therapist's perceptions of symptoms, as well as differences in diagnosis and treatment provided across patients' race and ethnicity (Holmqvist et al., 2014; West et al., 2014).

In addition, diverse POR programs have conducted process studies, focusing on topics such as the use of (or adherence/fidelity to) interventions associated with empirically supported treatments, consistency of routine care with evidence-based practice guidelines, helpful events, therapeutic alliance, and principles of change (Adelman et al., 2014; Castonguay et al., 2014; Fernández-Álvarez et al., 2014; Garland & Brookman-Frazee, 2014; Holmqvist et al., 2014; Koerner & Castonguay, 2014; Strauss et al., 2014; Szapocznik et al., 2014; West et al., 2014). POR studies have also involved the evaluation of assessment measures and DSM-5 diagnostic criteria (McAleavey et al., 2014; West et al., 2014). The development of tools for supervision of evidence-based interventions has also been a focus of a collaborative initiative (Garland & Brookman-Frazee, 2014). Perhaps reflecting, from an epistemological perspective, an ultimate form of integration of science and practice, efforts have begun to train therapists from different parts of the world in designing feasible and highly rigorous research (single-case experimental studies) to test hypotheses tied to their clinical practice (Koerner & Castonguay, 2014).

Obstacles

A number of obstacles and difficulties are to be expected when building clinicians–researchers partnerships, as well as conducting POR within them. In the following text are some of the problems that the authors in this series have encountered in their collaborative work.

Clinical Concerns: Is it Worthwhile? Is it Dangerous? Is it Feasible?

One of the most serious challenges faced by POR is the fact that the tasks involved can be perceived by therapists as being irrelevant or even detrimental to their clinical work. This is a major issue confronted by the implementation of outcome monitoring systems (Boswell et al., 2014; Fernández-Álvarez et al., 2014; Holmqvist et al., 2014; Strauss et al., 2014). Practitioners are not likely to be fully engaged in data collection if they are concerned that it might generate negative reactions from clients, create difficulties in the therapeutic relationship, or simply fail to provide clinically helpful information. Above and beyond outcome monitoring, Fernández-Álvarez et al. (2014) argued that any research task can force clinicians to shift their attention away from an exclusive focus on the immediate clinical situations, to a consideration of the more distal research implications of the data collected. As they noted, weighting the long-term value of research data can be "a challenge to participants' patience" (p. 8).

Other concerns observed include the fear that outcome data might reveal negative findings or that results could have negative impact on a clinician's practice—or a treatment center—in terms of performance evaluation, referrals, or income (Adelman et al., 2014; Boswell et al., 2014; Strauss et al., 2014). Not knowing who will have access to outcome data and what will be done with it can also be experienced as a major threat to clinicians' autonomy. As evocatively stated by Boswell et al. (2014), clinicians "do not like 'big brother' and perhaps with good reason" (page 7). Rightly so, practitioners have questioned the ability of specific outcome results to accurately capture the clients' change, as well as the appropriateness of interpreting any outcome data without proper context or consideration of other sources of information (e.g.,

how complex the client's problems are, including his/her life circumstances; McAleavey et al., 2014; Strauss et al., 2014).

Anxiety and apprehension experienced by clinicians have not been limited to outcome monitoring. The fear, in the eyes of both therapists and clients, of potential breach of confidentiality can be an obstacle to the conduct of any type of research in naturalistic settings (Boswell et al., 2014; Koerner & Castonguay, 2014). As reported by Szapocznik et al. (2014), anxiety can also be raised by videotape observation of sessions (as a means of monitoring therapy adherence), or by the adoption of a treatment manual—especially with highly experienced practitioners. For the less experienced, the idea of having to ask clients to participate in research can trigger intense feelings of impostor syndrome, as some may feel a lack of competence and justification to ask clients to do anything extra for them or for the clinic (Castonguay et al., 2014).

Aside from matters of relevance, immediate value, potential detriment, and anxiety are the issues of feasibility. Research protocols that require too many tasks or intense supervision have been difficult to implement, let alone adopted as part of routine clinical practice after the completion of the study (Koerner & Castonguay, 2014; Szapocznik et al., 2014).

Collaboration and Communication Problems: Can This Really be a Team?

Not surprisingly, various collaboration and communication problems can jeopardize the design, plan, and implementation of any kind of POR. First and foremost, researchers must be constantly vigilant of potential pitfalls of empirical imperialism. These could manifest by subtle errors of omission, as in having innocuous or unplanned conversations about study design without the presence or previous input of practitioners. Or it can take the form of explicit dismissal and exploitation, as when "the researcher determines all aspects of the study, agrees with the clinical director to take advantage of the practice setting's volume of patients, and then the therapist and client participants are roped into additional work that may not align with their goals" (Koerner & Castonguay, 2014, p. 9).

Even when true collaboration and active participation has been sought, communication problems are to be expected. With many stakeholders involved, orchestrating the exchange of information represents a difficult endeavor (McAleavey et al., 2014). It is also important to recognize that stakeholders frequently "talk different languages": Not only do they have their respective jargon, but they can also have discrepant perspectives on the same words. For example, as pointed out by Garland & Brookman-Frazee (2014), a term such as "evidence" can be interpreted in various ways, evoking very different emotional experiences (threat or approval) in those devoting their professional lives to help clients navigate complex lives, in contrast to those paid to contribute to the advancement of empirical knowledge. Language problems between researchers and administrators have also been observed regarding the translation of research findings. As noted by McAleavey et al. (2014), these problems can be particularly challenging because "questions that seem both critically important and very simple to administrators are among the most complex empirical talks available" (p. 9).

Closely linked to variant languages and perspectives is the fact that the various partners live in different cultures, face different demands and expectations, and pursue different goals (Garland & Brookman-Frazee, 2014; Strauss et al., 2014), all of which may at times reflect or lead to conflictual needs—such as the researchers need to collect publishable data, the clinicians wish to obtain clinically informative data, and the administrators need for actionable data at minimal cost (Boswell et al., 2014). As correctly stated by Garland & Brookman-Frazee (2014), stakeholders can also operate on "different time tables" (p. 11). For example, clinicians who need to figure out quickly how to address issues that emerge on a session-by-session basis can experience frustration by the time that it frequently takes for researchers to present or publish answers to the questions they have investigated together (Castonguay, Nelson et al., 2010). Frustration can also be mutual. As reported by Adelman et al. (2014), the difficulties involved by the implementation of a standardized research protocol within a natural setting can have unfortunate consequences for time-sensitive academic requirements (e.g., dissertation projects).

As in any kind of team enterprise, interpersonal dynamics have been identified as challenges to clinician and researcher partnerships. Garland & Brookman-Frazee (2014) noted that "power differentials" associated with various professional status may influence the way that participants collaborate and communicate. The same authors have also warned against the danger of having a partnership based on a unidirectional exchange of knowledge, as opposed to a reciprocal one. Intentional or not, this power dynamic is akin to or is reflecting the issue of empirical imperialism mentioned earlier. Garland & Brookman-Frazee (2014) have also identified interpersonal problems (personality issues and personal agenda) that, as with any type of group project, can interfere with POR initiatives.

Pragmatics: Being Bugged Down by Reality

The development, implementation, and maintenance of POR also face a number of pragmatic obstacles. For Koerner and Castonguay (2014), practical incompatibilities between research tasks and clinicians' workflow actually represent the primary challenge of POR. Perhaps the most obvious and intractable of these barriers is time, or lack of it. Irrespective of the world that they live in, most POR stakeholders are extremely busy. And although they share an interest in their collaborative endeavor, for many of them such an endeavor represents only a fragment of their professional responsibilities. Put bluntly, POR means extra work. For example, in addition to the training involved in the proper use of a particular measurement system, outcome monitoring requires time to administer and interpret the questionnaire, provide feedback to clients, and keep track of assessment points (Boswell et al., 2014; Holmqvist et al., 2014; McAleavey et al., 2014; Strauss et al., 2014). The more and/or bigger tasks required by a research project, the more its preparation and implementation may compete with the daily demands of all participants involved (Koerner & Castonguay, 2014; Szapocznik et al., 2014; West et al., 2014). As a case in point, the design of a study on helpful and hindering events in therapy required practitioners to meet regularly with researchers for a year. Having to fill out a process measure for each of their private clients after every therapy session over the course of 18-months of implementation also forced therapists to sometimes have to choose between research tasks and bathroom breaks (Koerner & Castonguay, 2014).

Not surprisingly, time for research is particularly difficult to find when participation is on a voluntary basis (West et al., 2014). The lack of financial incentives to clients and therapists has indeed been identified as an obstacle to the successful implementation of POR (Koerner & Castonguay, 2014). When it applies to outcome monitoring in naturalistic settings, the lack of finances, let alone the cost to therapists, reflects an unfair burden. As pointed out by Boswell et al. (2014), whereas physicians do not have to pay for their patient tests, the insurance industry has refused to reimburse the routine collection of behavioral health data. Financial support also represents a major source of challenge and stress for large naturalistic projects and POR infrastructures (Fernández-Álvarez et al., 2014; Garland & Brookman-Frazee, 2014; McAleavey et al., 2014; West et al, 2014). Directly related to the financial needs of these large initiatives are the organizational challenges that come with the collection and management of data across multiple sites, assignment of responsibilities and distribution of resources across partners, as well as training, management, and retention of staff members (Boswell et al., 2014; Fernández-Álvarez et al., 2014; McAleavey et al., 2014; Strauss et al., 2014; West et al., 2014).

Costs: When Research Interferes with Other Needs

Conducting POR can also be costly for many involved in the partnership. For example, having to remember all tasks required by a research protocol, especially in the early phase of a study, may make it difficult for therapists to allot their full attention to the needs of their clients. Moreover, some procedures, such as getting informed consent during the first session of therapy, can infringe on the therapist's time to conduct a full assessment and/or foster therapeutic bond (Koerner & Castonguay, 2014). Any research-related tasks, big or small, can also impact practitioners' (or a treatment center's) capacity to generate income. By possibly interfering with care delivery and earning potential, the time devoted to research can thus be viewed as an unnecessary luxury by clinicians, clients, and administrators (Adelman et al., 2014). In brief, POR is impeded by a double financial challenge (double whammy): Not only there are often no financial incentive for clients or therapists but it also costs them in terms of time and effort. Researchers also have to struggle with negative consequences that can come along with an engagement in POR, such as the frequent lack of fit between nontraditional research and the priorities of funding agencies (West et al., 2014), the lack of incentives from academic institutions for community-based work (Garland & Brookman-Frazee, 2014), or the incompatibility between the publishing pressure of academia and the slow pace and the demanding efforts of practitioners and researchers collaborations (Koerner & Castonguay, 2014). Accordingly, researchers interested in building POR initiatives should consider inviting others living in their world (such as colleagues and students) and seeking administrative assistance—especially if they are not yet tenured (Castonguay, Nelson et al., 2010; Castonguay et al., 2014).

Fostering Strategies

A number of strategies have been identified by the contributors of this series, both to address the obstacles mentioned earlier, as well as to facilitate POR studies and partnerships in general.

Putting Premium on Clinical Relevance and Beyond

It should be of no surprise to anyone that studies that fail to be directly related to clinical practice are not likely to stimulate therapists' engagement. One of the lessons that emerged from POR collaborations, however, is that in order to generate and maintain practitioners' commitment, such studies have to go beyond the threshold of "clinical relevance" and be more than potentially interesting; they have to suggest ways of improving clinical work. "Clinicians will help with research—if the research helps them clinically" (McAleavey et al., 2014, p. 6) is one of the major conclusions derived from a survey that asked busy counselors what kind of research they would be willing to participate in, knowing that this participation would require additional work and time on their part.

One way to increase the helpfulness of research is to integrate it into different aspects of clinical work. For example, Fernández-Álvarez et al. (2014) pointed out that using data within clinical supervision can increase therapists' motivation to collect it. Perhaps the ultimate test of helpfulness is that studies have to be actionable and retainable. To facilitate the clinician's willingness to go along with research tasks and cope with the added stress and anxiety that may come with them, these tasks have to be immediately informative by providing therapists, for example, "here-and-now" guidance about interventions that can be used to best address the clients' needs (Koerner & Castonguay, 2014). Repeating Fernández-Álvarez et al. (2014)'s wise comment, it is testing the therapist's patience to present findings only after completion of a study. As argued elsewhere, research tasks are likely to be performed during the study (and retained in clinical routine after its completion) if they are "clinically syntonic" (Castonguay et al., 2010). Beyond the abstract concept of "clinical relevance," POR investigations will be most successful if they foster a seamless integration of research and practice or, put differently, if the study protocols confound research and practice. As described elsewhere, "clinicians truly integrate science and practice every time they perform a task in their clinical practices and are not able to provide an unambiguous answer to questions such as: 'Right now, am I gathering clinical information or am I collecting data?,' or 'At this moment, am I trying to apply a helpful intervention with my client or am I implementing a research task?'" Frequently, setting up rigorous empirical investigations will lead them to answer these questions by saying, "Perhaps both," may be the most fruitful and exciting pathway to bridge research and practice (Castonguay et al.,

2010, p. 352). Koerner & Castonguay (2014) also use the metaphor of research and practice being woven as a whole cloth to describe POR studies that cause minimal disruption to the clinical workflow and that may "improve clients outcome by meeting therapists' learning needs" (p. 4). It should also be obvious that in many cases confounding research and practice can be a fruitful strategy to protect the limited resource of time. The more infringement on time, the less likely it is to learn empirically from clinical practice.

Also going beyond the concept of relevance, clinicians are more likely to participate in studies and continue to use research procedures in poststudy completion when such procedures do not require drastic changes to their practice (Castonguay, 2013; Koerner & Castonguay, 2014). Most clinicians will be indifferent to or even resentful if they are asked to put aside the way they have been practicing for years and forced to adopt completely new treatment packages (and/or theoretical orientations) in order to test a protocol within their own clinical routine. Rather, they are more likely to join a project and retain what they might learn from it if what they do for research is additive to their clinical repertoires, such as obtaining process and outcome feedback from their clients, using new interventions to address specific clinical issues, or having access to clinical tools that they can use on their own terms and time schedule (see Adelman et al., 2014; Koerner & Castonguay, 2014; McAleavey et al., 2014).

In POR, or any kind of psychotherapy research, clinical relevance is frequently brought up in contrast with scientific rigor—as if clinical utility and internal validity were opposite poles of a continuum, or irreconcilable categories by which one is to judge research quality. It should indeed be recognized that the strengths of POR, such as high external validity, may at times come at a price. As noted in Koerner and Castonguay (2014), some methodological components of psychotherapy research that can increase its internal validity (e.g., multiple observer assessments of pre- and posttreatment outcome) are not likely feasible or desirable in most studies conducted in clinical routine. However, it is also important to avoid false dichotomies. First, naturalistic studies can reach both high levels of clinical helpfulness and validity, internal and external. This has been illustrated by the use of randomized clinical trials and single experimental designs in several studies presented in this series (Boswell et al., 2014; Koerner & Castonguay, 2014; Strauss et al., 2014; Szapocznik et al., 2014). More importantly, rigor and relevance can be seen as complementing and reinforcing of each other (Garland & Brookman-Frazee, 2014). For example, the

more valid an instrument or a finding is, the more confidence we may have that they are truly actionable.

Yet, it is undeniable that a tension frequently exists between making a study both feasible and scientifically rigorous. At least two directions have been suggested in this special series with regard to finding a balance between these crucial issues. The first is to offer some flexibility (or customization) in the way that instruments can be used and data can be collected. For example, in the large practice-research network (PRN) infrastructure of university counseling centers described by McAleavey et al. (2014), specific sites have the ability to change the order and turn on or off individual items of one of the standardized measures used by all participating centers. Another strategy is to explicitly recognize that no study can ever be perfect and that partners have to make an informed choice in terms of level of rigor balanced with the costs entailed (Koerner & Castonguay, 2014).

Addressing Threats and Anxiety

As described earlier, fears of negative impact (e.g., breach of confidentiality, threats of autonomy, risks of negative evaluation, and potential decreases in referrals and revenue) and concerns about the clinical accuracy of empirical data represent major challenges in building up clinicians–researchers partnerships. For many of those involved in POR, a key component to address these understandable apprehensions is transparency (Boswell et al., 2014; Strauss et al., 2014). For example, Boswell et al. (2014) have recommended a full disclosure in writing regarding issues such as confidentiality. Researchers have also found that clinician participation is enhanced not only when they are informed of the complete anonymity of the data collected but also by the explicit reassurance that the data will not be used to control the financing of their practice or to replace clinical judgment (Strauss et al., 2014). POR researchers have clearly voiced that empirical data, even collected in the naturalistic setting where it is used, are not sufficient to guide clinicians about what to do, when to do it, and with whom. In fact, we tend to forget that the philosopher David Hume (1739) had already mentioned a few centuries ago that one cannot get from making descriptive statements ("is") to making prescriptive statements ("ought"). Not only should data be interpreted within the context of the client's life and current situation, but it should also be viewed as complementary to clinicians' judgment and used to point to potential directions for further professional development and training (Castonguay et al., 2013; Holmqvist et al., 2014; McAleavey et al., 2014).

In addition to recognizing the limitations of their instruments, some researchers have also stressed that one way to address clinicians' concerns about the accuracy and adequacy of empirical data is to continually seek to increase the psychometric quality of measures, improve their utility and predictability (e.g., what types of clients are particular therapists predominantly effective with?), and provide clinical tools (Boswell et al., 2014).

Another apprehension experienced by clinicians is whether the research tasks can be of value to their clients. Data can be helpful in decreasing such fear. A case in point is how outcome data were used to address the imposter syndrome experienced by graduate students which, as mentioned earlier, made them anxious to ask anything of their clients, including filling out pre and posttreatment measures or participating in studies conducted by their peers. Showing students that compared to experienced clinicians in private practice, their interventions had higher impact on serious clinical difficulties such as suicide, and psychosis was a turning point in terms of their sense of self-efficacy and motivation to use and conduct POR studies (Castonguay et al., 2014). Szapocznik et al. (2014) have also observed that the presentation of empirical evidence about the efficacy of a treatment to be tested can facilitate various stakeholders' buy-in.

Yet having clinicians share their experiences with other clinicians might be an even stronger strategy to address apprehensions, as it avoids perceptions of bias, self-serving, or controlling motivation from researchers. As Boswell et al. (2014) have learned from their experience:

> researcher's attempts to impart the "wisdom of routine outcome monitoring" are far less effective than the wisdom imparted by fellow clinicians who have used the particular outcome monitoring system of interest. It is through direct clinical experience and by sharing these experiences (e.g., through vignettes) that other clinicians begin to seriously entertain the potential benefits. (p. 8)

It is also important to note that such direct experience is frequently discordant from previous expectations of clinicians who are being asked to use outcome monitoring. As such, perception of the relevance and value of an instrument is sometimes acquired via a corrective experience (Youn, Kraus, & Castonguay, 2012).

While the strategies mentioned above can and should be used to address clinicians' concerns about their participation in POR, it is, nevertheless, crucial to constantly gather feedback and closely attend to therapists' criticisms about the protocols (assessment, treatment, or otherwise) implemented (McAleavey et al., 2014; Szapocznik et al., 2014). This will not only build a stronger sense of collaboration but is likely to also improve the quality of the research conducted.

Pumping Blood in the Partnership: Enhancing Communication and Collaboration

For it to be worthwhile, a partnership should be based on a diversity of expertise and opinions. True advances in complex fields are rarely achieved by the joint work of individuals who think the same way. As cogently stated by Garland and Brookman-Frazee (2014), partnership members "should possess complementary, but non-redundant knowledge and experiences that can be combined and contextualized to facilitate knowledge creation and innovation" (p. 6). Like any kind of teamwork, however, the success of POR also rests on strong communication and collaboration between individuals who typically live in different professional worlds. Metaphorically, communication and collaboration is the blood that maintains the life in professional partnerships. As described earlier, joint research initiatives face serious challenges, including different languages, perspectives, goals, expectations, demands, as well as wishes and fears of various stakeholders involved. These discrepancies are unavoidable and should be faced with transparency, as well as frequent and open dialogues.

Many papers in this series have emphasized the importance of regular meetings to discuss, understand, validate, and optimally incorporate the needs, concerns, and contributions of diverse collaborators, in addition to remind or inform all parties involved of the goals, tasks, and progress of the joint projects (Boswell et al., 2014; Castonguay et al., 2014; Fernández-Álvarez et al., 2014; Garland & Brookman-Frazee, 2014; Koerner & Castonguay, 2014; McAleavey et al., 2014; Strauss et al., 2014). As noted by Garland & Brookman-Frazee (2014), face-to-face meetings are crucial to build trust and develop a shared language. For these authors, such trust and common language are dependent upon a number of interpersonal processes that are common to many successful relationships, including an openness and responsiveness to others' perspectives, a reciprocal enthusiasm about the collaboration and, interestingly, a willingness "to go above and beyond an agreed upon scope of work" (p 7). Yet, Garland & Brookman-Frazee (2014) have also pointed out that partners should be aware of potential pitfalls that can undermine face-to-face meetings, such as the failure to recognize and adequately process invalidating power differentials, unidirectional sharing of knowledge, and monopolization of control. To prevent or deal with these group processes, they argued it is "important to address members' expected roles and unique contributions, and the distribution of power at the outset, as well as explicitly establishing norms for working together" (p. 8). At the same time, they wisely recommend that input from all members should not only be attended to but should also contribute to actual changes in collaborative work. Not surprisingly, members of POR have also indicated that interpersonal problems, in the form of conflict and alliance ruptures, are to be expected and should be addressed to foster the development and optimal functioning of collaborative partnerships (Castonguay et al., 2014; Garland & Brookman-Frazee, 2014)

Fundamentally, successful POR requires two things: A strong level of engagement and commitment from each member to the philosophy and tasks of research (Holmqvist et al., 2014; Strauss et al., 2014), as well as a genuine alliance between them. This state of alliance both reflects and fosters a sense of equality and respect, as well as a recognition of diverse ways of understanding and investigating complex realities (Castonguay et al., 2013). The same state of alliance or collaboration has been referred by Garland & Brookman-Frazee (2014) as "egalitarian leadership." This overarching principle of healthy group process, however, does not negate differential skills and the adaptive strategy of matching leading responsibilities with specific knowledge and expertise. But what egalitarian leadership implies, process and outcome wise, is full rights of all participants. For clinicians, this means that they should have access and control over what is frequently in the researchers' exclusive province. As Holmqvist et al. (2014) noted, "a key process that needs to be achieved in practice-based evidence is to ensure a sense of local ownership by practitioners in the data they collect" (p. 8). This includes providing opportunities for clinicians to be involved in the plan (not only with respect to what to analyze but also what not to analyze; see Strauss et al., 2014) and conduct of statistical analyses of data collected, as well as to request data for the investigation of questions related to their own interest (Koerner & Castonguay, 2014; McAleavey et al., 2014). Increasing a sense of ownership can also be achieved by involving practitioners in the selection of instruments to be used for research purposes (Holmqvist et al., 2014) and by giving them the opportunity to modify the way these measures can be used. An example of this is the decision of therapists in training to improve the clinical utility of outcome monitoring by implementing it, as part of their POR infrastructure, after every session rather than at limited assessment points (Castonguay et al., 2014).

As illustrated in several papers in this series, collaboration in POR studies can involve a broad array of stakeholders (e.g., therapists, supervisors, researchers, graduate students, administrators at different levels of management, funders, parents, judges, and policy decision-makers), each of them deserving to have their voices heard and their expertise recognized in the research partnership (see Adelman et al., 2014; Boswell, et al., 2014; Garland & Brookman-Frazee, 2014; Koerner & Castonguay, 2014; McAleavey et al., 2014; Strauss et al., 2014; Szapocznik et al., 2014; West et al., 2014). Building upon such diversity of partners can not only strengthen a study but also help generate "valued research findings that may be more likely to have an impact on clinical practice and policy" (West et al., 2014, p. 12). And while it should be recognized, as we did before, that all stakeholders have different needs, expectations, and demands, it is also important to keep in mind that these diverse goals can be highly complementary. There is, for example, no a priori counterindication between clinicians' desire to get quick and helpful information about the pattern of change of an individual client, researchers' interest in identifying moderators and mediators of change in groups of clients, and administrators and funders' hope of finding ways to efficiently address the needs of all their clients. These are different levels of investigation that can have synergetic impact on each other, where the answer to each particular question can benefit from and contribute to the clarification of other questions.

As illustrated in several papers in this series, partnerships can also be built upon and enhanced by focusing on convergent goals. Academicians and clinicians can actually be pleasantly surprised at the high level of convergence in their interest and research ideas (Adelman et al., 2014; Castonguay in Lampropoulos et al., 2002). Considering how powerful a motivation such shared interest could be, it is not surprising that many authors of this series have emphasized the value of clinicians' full involvement in the selection of the ideas to be examined, design to investigate them, recruitment of participants, implementation of the study, and efforts to disseminate findings (Koerner & Castonguay, 2014; Szapocznik et al., 2014; West et al., 2014). Stakeholders also share general goals, above and beyond the specific focus of a particular study. At least two major ones can be delineated: Many individuals (including, of course, clinicians) are interested in contributing to the advancement of empirical knowledge and the reduction of the gap between science and practice, and most, if not all, professionals in the mental health field are invested in improving the care of clients. Accordingly, one way to foster partnerships is to lead stakeholders to identify themselves, both at a personal and an organizational level, with research projects that are specifically aimed at these far-reaching goals (Fernández-Álvarez et al., 2014). Put differently, successful POR can be fostered by building a "sense of community" (McAleavey et al., 2014) that is guided by the shared ambition to contribute to the advancement of knowledge and reduction of suffering.

Making it Possible: Resources and Pragmatics

McAleavey et al. (2014) have identified two fundamental resources for the development and maintenance of their large PRN infrastructure, and it is fair to say that these supplies are necessary for any kind of POR initiative: "Time (and a lot of it) and people (and a lot of them)" (p. 16). We have already mentioned the large number and variety of stakeholders involved in these partnerships. What has also been emphasized by several authors in this series is the amount of time that collaborative work can require with respect to the preparation, coordination, and implementation of a study (Garland & Brookman-Frazee, 2014; Koerner & Castonguay, 2014; Strauss et al., 2014; Szapocznik et al., 2014; West et al., 2014). For example, the preparation of one of these studies (which included the development of the research design, planning of the management, analysis and publication of the data, and the allocation of funding) took four years (Strauss et al., 2014).

A particular aspect of preparation that has been highly recommended might best be called the "routinization" of a protocol. Routinization begins with thorough planning. Clinicians and researchers have learned that the more time you spend laying down the details of a protocol and anticipating problems that could emerge when implementing it, the more you save in terms of energy, frustration, and time later (Koerner & Castonguay, 2014). Specific strategies have been developed to help practitioners "automatize" (learn, remember, and recall) the research procedures as part of their clinical routine, such as through the use of web technology (e.g., Krug's (2006) "Don't make me think"), or the construction of multiple scripts, each of them including the same research procedures but with differing levels of details. Additional recommendations that have been made to facilitate "routinization" are the inclusion of email and phone consultations, as well as frequent meetings at the beginning of a study to discuss problems that some participants have faced and ways that other partners have devised to prevent and resolve difficulties. It also seems advisable to have clinicians implement the research protocol, or at least parts of it (e.g., core measures), in their clinical routine before the study is launched (Koerner & Castonguay, 2014; Strauss et al., 2014). Such pilot work not only provides opportunities for practice and consultation but also sets up an optimal test for participants to decide whether or not the benefits of research procedures (e.g., in terms of actionable information they can provide during treatment) outweigh their costs (e.g., in terms of disruption of clinical workflow).

Another concrete key to successful POR is to keep things as simple as possible and to avoid imposing unreasonable burden to clinical routine (Boswell et al., 2014; Koerner & Castonguay, 2014; West et al., 2014). Based on their separate experience, Koerner & Castonguay (2014) concluded that "[t]he best strategy we have found in our practice-oriented research designs is to accept the constraints faced by practitioners and design research procedures that map as directly onto clinical care already provided as possible" (p. 9). The clinicians' contribution in the design of feasible studies is critical—as they know best what is possible and impossible to add to their day-to-day work schedule (West et al., 2014). A good example of such wisdom comes from one of the lessons learned in a PRN study conducted in private practice (see Koerner & Castonguay, 2014). In this study, clinicians and researchers had decided that each therapist would be inviting all of their new clients to participate. Because this study required therapists to fill out measures at the end of every therapy session, it became clear that having their entire client caseload as participants was too burdensome. Based on this experience, the subsequent study conducted in the same PRN involved no more than four participating clients for each of the therapist at any given point in the study.

Feasibility, however, not only refers to how possible it is for clinicians to adopt and adequately implement a research protocol but also how to sustain such implementation. Organizational support has been identified as a critical addition at each of these steps (Koerner & Castonguay, 2014; Szapocznik et al., 2014). For example, Szapocznik et al. (2014) collaborated with treatment agencies to recruit "on-site" supervisors for the training, monitoring, coaching, and provision of feedback to clinicians participating in a psychotherapy effectiveness study. In another study, clinicians greatly benefitted from the help of research assistants (graduate and undergraduate students), who kept a close and timely monitoring of data collected, providing them with rapid feedback about adherence problems observed, and were easily reachable to answer questions regarding the study protocol (Koerner & Castonguay, 2014). Garland & Brookman-Frazee (2014) have argued that, ideally, organizational support should not be tied to one specific stakeholder, and instead, can be shared among various members, such as between administrative staff and university research assistants (Koerner & Castonguay, 2014). In other initiatives, however, the administrative support has been provided primarily by the research stakeholders, via grant funding or university funds (e.g., Garland & Brookman-Frazee, 2014; McAleavey et al., 2014). Irrespective of its source, POR are likely to be particularly burdensome, in terms of time and energy, if administrative help is not provided to both clinicians and researchers.

The provision of concrete incentives has been recommended, including financial rewards (for both clients and therapists), as well as credits toward professional licenses (Boswell et al., 2014; Koerner & Castonguay, 2014; Strauss et al., 2014; West et al., 2014). Successful conduct of POR, small and large, has also benefited from continued refinement of computer and online technology—to train participants, implement protocols, as well as to collect and manage data (Boswell et al., 2014; Castonguay et al., 2014; Koerner & Castonguay, 2014; McAleavey et al., 2014; Strauss et al., 2014; West et al., 2014). The technical challenges involved for the efficient administration of instruments and management of data has at times been met by integrating software companies as part of the POR partnership (Castonguay et al., 2014; Koerner & Castonguay, 2014; McAleavey et al., 2014). Others have built their own technology to collect data in naturalistic settings (see Fernández-Álvarez et al., 2014; Koerner & Castonguay, 2014).

Technology can, of course, be expensive. Needless to say, this is not the only cost entailed by research. And, of course, the larger a study is, the more substantial are the financial needs. But since it has been observed that monetary incentives can facilitate data collection (Koerner & Castonguay, 2014; West et al., 2014), funding is an important pragmatic issue for any type of POR, small or large. Several investigators have been successful in securing substantial financial support (e.g., Garland & Brookman-Frazee, 2014; Holmqvist et al., 2014; Koerner & Castonguay, 2014; Strauss et al., 2014; Szapocznik et al., 2014; West et al., 2014). However, it is also a fact that for mental health investigators, and perhaps for psychotherapy researchers in particular, external funding is extremely difficult to obtain. Some POR programs have benefitted from support outside of much prized funding sources (mostly governmental), including private foundations, professional associations, and university or treatment center internal funds (e.g., Adelman et al., 2014; Castonguay et al., 2014; Koerner & Castonguay, 2014; McAleavey et al., 2014; West et al., 2014). As a nonprofit research infrastructure, the Center for Collegiate Mental Health (CCMH) has also been able to rely on membership fees from its participating counseling centers, as well as from individuals and companies interested in its intellectual properties (McAleavey et al., 2014).

It may well be, however, that the financial foundation of most POR, especially if partners are interested in long-term sustainability, has to rely in part on the concept of "patching." As defined by Garland & Brookman-Frazee (2014), patching refers to the reorganization of partnership and donation of resources when there is no external funding. In fact, several of the POR initiatives described in this series have operated within a "pre-patching" mode, i.e., without having had any or enough external funding to fully support their research activities. Instead, they have received contributions from business partners (e.g., software companies), donation of time (from therapists, students, and researchers), and even funding from their own members (e.g., Fernández-Álvarez et al., 2014; Koerner & Castonguay, 2014; McAleavey et al., 2014). This level of participatory process clearly demonstrates a strong commitment toward two major goals mentioned above (contribution to the advancement of knowledge and the improvement of mental health care), but it also reflects the synergetic and meaningful contribution that can be generated from a milieu that is characterized by mutual trust and a shared pursuit of professional actualization. As stated by Fernández-Álvarez et al. (2014), clinicians set aside personal resources because they know that the conduct of research fits institutional needs, which in turn "are oriented to meet the individual's professional development" (p. 8).

Though there is no doubt that financial support can be extremely beneficial and even crucial for large POR initiatives, it should also be considered that external funding may, in some circumstances, become a curse. In the current context of "get grants or perish," funding might be the principal motivation for some academicians to establish connections with clinicians. At worst, using clinicians' time and milieu only to please a dean or a chair would be committing a faux pas that is beyond empirical imperialism—it may well be nothing less than "empirical invasion." At best, the search for funding for the sake of funding is likely to guarantee that a research program, including the long-term implementation of its findings, will cease to continue once the grant ends and the researcher will look for other "hot" funding areas. Once the research team begins to pay anybody, it is hard to "go back" to a place where collaborators are not paid. If we want to conduct studies that lead to retainable findings, we should therefore strive to avoid becoming dependent on external findings, at least in some contexts.

Handling Organizational Challenges

As mentioned earlier, true and successful partnership is based on transparent and open communication. In the case of large, including multi-sites, collaborations, however, another layer of communication must be addressed: The orchestration and dissemination of information to various partners. Different tools have been used to facilitate this crucial aspect of organizational functioning, including email lists to raise and address problems between sites, web-based methods to facilitate communication (e.g., google groups) or to submit research projects to a centralized research team, in-person and video (webinars) training, annual meetings with representatives of local sites, research conferences to present projects conducted across the collaborative infrastructure, and in-print publications (e.g., annual reports) to describe research findings in friendly (for both clinicians and administrators) ways (Garland & Brookman-Frazee, 2014; McAleavey et al., 2014).

Another organizational challenge that must be met by large POR initiatives is the centralization of data, in order to minimize data sources and reduce resources needed to manage it (Strauss et al., 2014). As noted by Strauss et al. (2014), procedures to ensure quality of data have to be systematically assessed and improved upon. A good example of the complexity required for quality control is provided by the standardization and centralization process developed for the CCMH PRN, which aimed at ensuring that:

> the materials reach clients in the same format every time; that the measures are easily administered by and meet the needs of each UCC; that the data from clients are efficiently and accurately recorded, scored, reported to the counselor and transmitted to CCMH; and that any future updates to the standardized materials can be accommodated. (McAleavey et al., 2014, p. 7)

The goal of centralizing data collection is particularly challenging and requires complex technological skills when data is collected and stored using different software packages, as it is the case for CCMH.

Centralized coordination, however, is not restricted to data management. Recommendations for the successful operation of multisite initiatives have also emphasized the coordination of the various aspects related to a study. For example, one of the most baffling tasks of research, for most clinicians and administrators, is the submission of proposals to get ethical approval for conducting a study. In CCMH, for instance, such time-consuming requirement has been handled by having a team of graduate students (themselves part of the centralized research team) to provide examples of and feedback to the various sites in submitting their respective research ethic proposal.

To facilitate the aforementioned tasks of communication, data management, and project coordination, many large POR initiatives have created advisory boards (e.g., McAleavey et al., 2014; Strauss et al., 2014; West et al., 2014), which bear the broader responsibilities of providing recommendations about research agenda and potential sources of funding, as well as ensure that current and future projects are sensitive to the needs of different stakeholders and consistent with ethical standards.

While a centralization process and administrative board structures might be an efficient way to oversee and manage large projects, the implementation of such projects generally takes place at specific sites. To increase the probability of such implementation, some POR programs have recommended the identification of "local champions" (Boswell et al., 2014), "study champions" (Garland & Brookman-Frazee, 2014), or "model managers" (Szapocznik et al., 2014). These are individuals responsible for building trust with stakeholders' on-site, easing the adoption and implementation of research protocols, helping to adjust the project to be consistent with clinical routine, providing training with regard to tasks, expectations, and anticipated benefits, as well as to monitor and facilitate the data collection.

Whether it is accomplished by one specific individual on-site or a group of representatives of different stakeholders, a key organizational task is to preserve a continuity of information regarding goals, procedures, and problems faced in POR (Boswell et al., 2014; Strauss et al., 2014). This is an especially crucial issue when recruitment of new participants and/or turnover of staff members are anticipated. The principle underlying this recommendation is that "you can never communicate too much" (Castonguay et al., 2014, p. 10). As an example, the first author of this paper and his colleagues observed that while the students who had been involved in the development of the PRN within our training clinic were fully cognizant of the purposes and benefits of combining the research and clinical requirements of the doctoral program, this was not always the case for later cohorts of students. Accordingly, many from this latter group felt that procedures implemented by former students were additional burdens imposed on their already hectic clinical responsibilities. To address this obvious obstacle, annual meetings are organized by faculty, clinical staff, and advanced graduate students to describe the origin and goals of our PRN, as well as to inspire a sense of ownership of the data collected at the clinic. As noted in Castonguay et al. (2014), these meetings are aimed at conveying one message: "This is not for us (faculty members), and not imposed by us. It is mostly for you and it has been driven in part by previous and current students" (p. 11)

Building large and long-standing partnerships can also involve organizational tasks or procedures that are foreign to the daily activities of most clinicians and researchers. As noted by McAleavey et al. (2014), for example, "large-scale PRNs are very likely to include the use of intellectual property or the development of corporate partnerships, and our experience suggests planning for risk-management and legal resources is necessary for success" (p. 10). As another case in point, the transformation of a training clinic into a fully operational PRN required a unique agreement with the office of research protection, which itself involved extensive negotiation with leaders of this office and their attorney (Castonguay et al., 2014).

Researching Research and Processing Process

Two other strategies, or meta-strategies, have been recommended to foster POR. One is to rely on research that has been conducted on research collaborations. For example, Garland & Brookman-Frazee (2014) have derived lessons from management and implementation sciences, as well as from studies on factors of successful research–practice partnerships in public health, to construct a model of research–community practice partnership; a model which has guided the development of their own researchers and clinicians collaboration. Of course, research directly related to the collection and use of psychotherapy data in naturalistic settings should be highly encouraged. As an example, Boswell et al. (2014) argued that research is sorely "needed on the factors (e.g., participant factors, organizational factors, training factors) that facilitate or inhibit the adoption, implementation, and sustainability of routine outcome monitoring" (p. 11).

Just as the research on research implementation might facilitate the conduct and use of POR, so is the use of conceptual models of psychotherapy process to understand and improve the process of research in psychotherapy. This is a conclusion that can be derived from the experience reported by Szapocznik et al. (2014), who have used their family therapy model to guide the testing of the same model in naturalistic settings. Put in other words, they relied on principles underlying their conceptual framework of therapy to anticipate and deal with organizational difficulties faced in their research program. By addressing difficulties encountered during three different phases of research–practice partnership (adoption, fidelity, and sustainability), their work has not only been consistent with major recommendations of implementation sciences, it has also offered an innovative contribution to this literature. Reflecting an intrinsic integration of science and practice, the recognition of the potential benefits of "using a model to test a model" was facilitated by the fact that the researchers involved in their POR were clinically trained. There is no reason to assume that their model (or any other theoretical frameworks of therapy) could not provide insightful recommendations, process and content wise, about research on various aspects of psychotherapy in clinical routine.

Benefits

Successfully resolving major challenges that come when building professional partnerships is, of course, intrinsically gratifying. In addition to such transcending reward, POR can have benefits for each of its stakeholders and beyond.

Improving Clients' Outcome

To be viable, ultimately, POR has to be beneficial to clients. As a paradigm of applied science, its credibility rests in part on its ability to have an effect on treatment outcome. Based on a diversity of methodologies, including randomized clinical trials, there is evidence that research collaboration between clinicians and researchers can impact psychotherapy in clinical routine (e.g., Adelman et al., 2014; Szapocznik et al, 2014). Related to the issue of outcome, this partnership can also lead to an increase of treatment retention compared to usual clinical care (Szapocznik et al., 2014). Moreover, POR findings have demonstrated that feedback on progress (as well as the provision of related clinical tools) can significantly reduce the rate of deterioration in psychotherapy (Boswell et al., 2014; Lambert, 2010). While it remains to be seen if it is beneficial across diagnostic groups and settings (e.g., Johnson, 2014), outcome feedback is providing tools for clinicians to meet their most important ethical responsibility, "first do no harm." Outcome monitoring and feedback can also improve the cost effectiveness of psychotherapy; when therapists are receiving feedback on therapeutic change, patients who show early improvement have shorter treatment durations than those who do not (Strauss et al., 2014).

While more traditional research has focused extensively on the impact of particular forms of therapies, POR studies have shown that client outcome are in part due to the individual therapist they are seeing. Specifically, clients seen by particularly effective therapists have a higher probability of being better off at the end of treatment than those who are seen by particularly ineffective therapists (Castonguay et al., 2013). Evidence emerging from POR also suggests that particular therapists may have specific areas of outcome expertise, fostering some types of change (e. g., reduction of depression) more than others (e.g., reduction of substance-abuse symptoms; Kraus, Castonguay, Boswell, Nordberg, & Hayes, 2011). If appropriately used in clinical routine, such findings on outcome variability (between and within therapists) can be a valuable source of feedback about a practitioner's unique strengths and limitations (Strauss et al., 2014)— which should ultimately be beneficial to their clients.

Enhancing the Therapeutic Process

Empirical data collected by clinicians also has the potential of facilitating the process of therapy. Outcome monitoring, for example, can help case formulation by providing assessment of a range of problems at different phases of treatment (Boswell et al., 2014; McAleavey et al., 2014), at times revealing difficulties that clients are reluctant to share verbally or that therapists may not have thought to ask. Tracking outcome can thus open communication about needs—told or untold, met or unmet. It can also help treatment planning by anticipating patterns of change, with regard to clients who are likely to change, those who are not (Castonguay et al., 2014), and those who are at risk of deterioration (Boswell et al., 2014; Lambert, 2010). Since research indicates that clinicians are generally not good at accurately predicting clients who will deteriorate during treatment, such empirical information can be invaluable to shift the focus of treatment as needed (Boswell et al., 2014; Lambert, 2010). In contrast, as reported by Strauss et al. (2014), clients tend to have a positive view of outcome monitoring, which by itself, can contribute to the quality of the therapeutic relationship, and for those clients who are progressing well, the presentation of data documenting their improvement can reinforce the working alliance (Boswell et al., 2014).

Helpful feedback is not restricted to outcome improvement, or lack of thereof. For example, clients' descriptions of helpful and hindering events during therapy can provide therapists with unique information that might help them adjust their interventions to better address their clients' needs (Koerner & Castonguay, 2014). Interestingly, asking clients to identify such events at the end of every session can provide them with an opportunity to reflect on and process their therapeutic experience. For some of them, writing down positive and negative aspects of treatment is an easier way to provide feedback than verbally expressing them (Koerner & Castonguay, 2014). As described by Fernández-Álvarez et al. (2014), a variety of data collected as part of the clinical routine (e.g., notes, video tapes, and assessment measures) can help detect difficulty in the treatment process and provide guidance for modifications of treatment (e.g., adding family therapy, enhancing involvement of client's social support network, and adjusting frequency of sessions).

At a scientific level, some POR studies have provided findings that contribute to our understanding of the process of change. For example, Szapocznik et al. (2014), found that therapist's adherence to theoretically specific components of their family-based treatment for substance-abuse adolescents was associated with higher retention, greater engagement, as well as better outcome in terms of family functioning and substance use in the adolescent clients. In another study conducted with therapists of different theoretical orientations, interventions intended to increase awareness were perceived, by both clients and therapists, as the most helpful events in therapy sessions (Koerner & Castonguay, 2014). From a clinical standpoint, however, what may be the most important "process" benefit of POR is that it can lead to changes in practice. West et al. (2014) have gathered both empirical and anecdotal evidence indicating that the participation in PRN studies led clinicians to not only modify their clinical practice but also disseminate the use of research findings and procedures.

Professional Development

While motivated by the goal of improving the outcome and process of therapy, POR partners themselves gain from their collaboration. At one basic but important level, such partnership allows for the establishment and growth of connections with others—locally, across different parts of a country, or around the world. Both clinicians and researchers described their exchanges with other stakeholders as stimulating and gratifying, as well as supportive and validating (Adelman et al., 2014; Fernández-Álvarez et al., 2014; Garland & Brookman-Frazee, 2014; Koerner & Castonguay, 2014). As described in Garland & Brookman-Frazee (2014), these exchanges can foster reciprocal learning, as with researchers gaining "greater respect for the immediate and often risky clinical challenges therapists faced" and clinicians having "greater appreciation for the rigor of the research process and the ultimate aim of improving care" (p.9).

Also related to professional development, the participation in POR can provide beneficial training experiences, such as learning strategies to improve the therapeutic relationship and work with particular types of clients (e.g., highly resistant), acquisition of skills prescribed by specific orientations (cognitive-behavioral, psychodynamic, humanistic, and systemic), and increase in awareness of one's own personal style and its impact on clients (Adelman et al., 2014; Castonguay et al., 2014; Fernández-Álvarez et al., 2014; Koerner & Castonguay, 2014; Szapocznik et al., 2014; West et al., 2014). Interestingly, such learning opportunities are not only helpful to trainees but also to experienced clinicians;

as Fernández-Álvarez et al. (2014) learned from their research and practice experience, "[t]eaching and training are the most powerful tools for remaining updated, because they demand contact with new developments and improving training methodology in the communication of knowledge." (p. 2)

Various marks of professional recognition can also result from therapists' (as well as researchers and students) engagement in POR, such as publications, conference presentations, research awards, and requests for consultation (Adelman et al., 2014; Koerner & Castonguay, 2014; Szapocznik et al., 2014). In addition to providing a source of quality control, outcome monitoring can also be used by clinicians to increase reimbursement (Koons, O'Rouke, Carter, & Erhardt, 2013). A less public but perhaps more important form of recognition, some therapists have reported having gained credibility in clients' eyes by their association with scientific projects (Koerner & Castonguay, 2014). Another intangible but, nonetheless, important aspect of professional development reported by therapists through a number of POR partnerships is the sense of purpose and pride gained from contributing to the advancement of science and practice (e.g., Castonguay et al., 2014; McAleavey et al., 2014; West et al., 2014). Interestingly, similar feelings have been reported by clients when agreeing to participate in research conducted by their therapists (Castonguay, Nelson et al., 2010).

Organizational Gains

POR benefits are not restricted to individuals, whether these are clients or therapists. Organizations can also make gains in terms of recognition, quality of care, and climate. For example, studies based on outcome monitoring can provide evidence of effectiveness, which can be used by administrators and clinicians to increase clients' positive expectations, referrals from other professionals, and credibility in the eyes of funding agencies (Adelman et al., 2014; Holmqvist et al., 2014; Szapocznik et al., 2014). Within a particular center or service, collection of data can also be used to better understand the needs of clients, as well as to guide the refinement of interventions to better address these needs (Adelman et al., 2014; Holmqvist et al., 2014; McAleavey et al., 2014). As described in Adelman et al. (2014), for instance, the initial use of outcome monitoring in a residential center for adolescents with substance-use problems revealed high levels of violence, both before and at the end of treatment. These unexpected findings led members of the administration and a psychologist to organize the training of the entire clinical staff in a treatment approach specifically targeting anger. Continued outcome monitoring showed gradual decrease of anger at posttreatment during the training period, as well as the maintenance of this improvement after training.

With the same goal of improving the quality of care, large POR partnerships can also provide means to compare data across sites. For example, in the large PRN infrastructure of university counseling centers described in McAleavey et al. (2014), each site receives benchmarked reports allowing administrators to contrast the pre- and posttreatment scores of the clients they serve with others centers. Both good and bad news revealed by such reports can provide lobbying tools for additional funding and/or policy changes at higher levels of university administration.

In the same way that it can foster interpersonal relationships among individuals that work in different worlds (e.g., private practice and university), POR can also have a positive impact on the culture and climate within an organization (Castonguay et al., 2014; Garland & Brookman-Frazee, 2014). As a case in point, the success that students in a PRN training clinic have had in recruiting their colleagues for their masters or doctoral thesis has both relied on and improved the collaborative attitude that is predominant in many doctoral training programs; an attitude that could be expressed by many statements, including, "Graduate school is hell, but we are in together and we should do what we can to help friends get their degree" (a much more eloquent and well-known statement would be "Un pour tous, tous pour un"! Castonguay et al., 2014, p. 9).

Contributing to Health Care System

POR can, and optimally should, also have an impact at a more global level of mental health services, by providing information about current needs and interventions, as well as by pointing out directions for improvement. For example, outcome data collected within the context of health-care management have been able to predict psychiatric and substance-abuse hospitalizations (Boswell et al., 2014). Considering the costs (for the individuals, their family, and the society) of inpatient treatments, it could be beneficial to use this kind of data to provide targeted, immediate, and more efficient care to those who need them the most. Interestingly, findings obtained in PRN studies have already contributed to important changes at the national level, such as the increase of access and continuity of psychiatric treatment in governmental health programs, and a new policy for assessment and treatment of posttraumatic stress disorder in the US Army (West et al., 2014). Needless to say, PRN could be conducted to study the effectiveness of those social and clinical interventions.

POR findings on the effectiveness and process of psychotherapy in general are also available to inform policy-makers and third-party payers in decisions regarding implementation and reimbursement of mental health services. In the current context of evidence-based practice, the empirical support for the effectiveness of psychotherapy in naturalistic settings (see Castonguay et al., 2013) should give it credence as a high priority form of intervention (Barber, 2009). This recommendation should not be restricted to problems like depression or anxiety. For example, results from a PRN study show that the use of psychotherapy as an evidence-based recommendation has yet to be adequately implemented in the day-to-day treatment of schizophrenia (West et al., 2014). Other large POR studies have reported similar levels of effectiveness between different forms of psychotherapy, including cognitive-behavioral, psychodynamic, and humanistic (see Castonguay et al., 2013). Such data should dissuade decision-makers from emphasizing a limited repertoire of interventions in routine clinical practice (Barber, 2009; Stiles, Barkham, Mellor-Clark, & Connell, 2008). POR findings can also be helpful to assess the actual use of evidence-based interventions in naturalistic settings, as well as to provide directions about how to increase their dissemination, which is one obvious way to facilitate the integration of science and practice in routine care (Garland & Brookman-Frazee, 2014; Koerner & Castonguay, 2014).

Advancing Science

Not only do clinicians (and clients) feel, as we mentioned before, that they are contributing to the advancement of science when they participate in POR, they actually do. Some features of this type of research are rarely found in studies conducted in controlled settings; most noteworthy is the access to extremely large samples of therapists (of various theoretical orientations), clients (with wide range of clinical problems), and varying lengths of therapy. With the use of sophisticated statistical analyses that take into account the nested structure of psychotherapy data, these features offer unique conditions (in terms of statistical power and score variance) to investigate participant and treatment characteristics, as well as process and outcome variables (e.g., Barber, 2009). Because of these distinctive features, and since it has been guided in part by clinicians' interests, POR has led to the much-needed knowledge about underinvestigated treatments (other than cognitive-behavioral), service effects, long-term impact, and cost–benefits of therapy, differential effectiveness of therapists, and training (Castonguay et al., 2014;

Holmqvist et al., 2014; Strauss et al., 2014)— just to name a few of the innovative contributions.

At its most general level, POR can provide two major contributions to the advancement of science. First, because of its particular foci, it can complement more traditional forms of research (e.g., randomized studies in controlled settings) and thus broaden the knowledge base in psychotherapy (Barber, 2009; Barkham & Margison, 2007; Barkham et al., 2010). Second, because some of its findings (with regard to the alliance, for example) are convergent with those obtained in academic settings, POR can increase the strength of this knowledge. As argued elsewhere, when similar effects are cross-validated across different methodologies, each with its own strengths and limitations, we can feel more confident about the veracity and generalizability of these effects (Castonguay, 2013).

In addition to these general contributions to the field, POR can also bring local benefits—benefits that have more to do with the process of science than the content of scientific knowledge. Members of different clinicians–researchers partnerships have reported that their experiences have generated new and better research. Garland and Brookman-Frazee (2014)'s first PRN with disruptive children, for example, has served as the basis for later partnerships on autism. For clinicians in another PRN, one primary benefit of conducting research is learning how to do so (Koerner & Castonguay, 2014).

General Recommendations

The contributors of the present series of papers have also delineated general recommendations to facilitate the collaboration of practitioners and researchers in the conduct and use of research in clinical practice. A number of these have already been integrated in the previous section on fostering strategies. Following are a few others, with some of them, as we will highlight, reflecting overarching guidelines that were previously offered for the future of POR.

Technological Advances

To begin with, technological advances should be relied upon. Electronic health records software, for example, has been found helpful, or at least promising, in the collection of long-term clinical data (McAleavey et al., 2014; West et al., 2014). Electronic technologies can and should be made available by researchers and administrators to provide clinicians with easy and immediate tracking and reporting of outcome monitoring (Boswell et al., 2014; Strauss et al., 2014). Yet, not all aspects of research should mandate the use of sophisticated technology. Boswell et al. (2014), for instance, suggest that alternative methods of data collection (including paper and pencil options) should be available to therapists depending on their preferences.

Instruments Development

In addition to technological developments, instruments related to outcome monitoring could be refined and expanded upon. Boswell et al. (2014) have recommended that feedback based on client's progress should be benchmarked (and if possible risk adjusted) to identify therapists' strengths and limitations across caseloads or with respect to particular types of clients. They also advise that the same feedback be complemented with clinical support tools that can provide guidelines for therapists on how to address difficulties in clients' lives and/or treatment that could interfere with change. Holmqvist et al. (2014) also suggest that service delivery systems and governmental policies provide access to a set of measures from which therapists could choose particular instruments that are best suited to the needs of individual clients. Such a measurement system, they argued, would operate "at a holistic level akin to the practitioner working with the whole person of the patient rather than with fragmented parts determined by diagnosis and dominated by symptom specific measures" (p. 8).

"Just do it!"

While the recommendations above highlight what researchers (as well as administrators and policy-makers) can do to facilitate therapists' engagement in the collection and use of data, several papers in the present series clearly demonstrated that therapists do not have to rely on academic researchers to build their own research programs (Adelman et al., 2014; Fernández-Álvarez et al., 2014; Koerner & Castonguay, 2014). For therapists who have the time and energy to combine clinical and empirical work in their own practice, our suggestion is simple: "Just do it!" Although the complementarity of expertise and resources can be of great value, partnership with academicians is not always feasible—it can unfortunately be difficult and frustrating (see Adelman et al., 2014). Full-time clinicians should thus be aware of both benefits and costs that come along with partnering with people living in the world of academia, and decide for what projects, under what conditions, and to what extent they want or need to collaborate with them. Moreover, past experiences suggest that POR is likely to be successful if it allows flexibility at the level of therapist participation. Time, interest, and expertise of each clinician should dictate whether he/she

wants to be involved in only one, some, or all aspects of a study, from the selection of the idea to be investigated, the design and implementation of the protocol, and/or the dissemination of the findings (Koerner & Castonguay, 2014).

Graduate Students

For both the short- and long-term viability of POR, it has also been recommended to gather the help of graduate students. Among the many contributions they can offer, students have resources that most professionals, clinicians, and academicians, are short of: Up-to-date knowledge of methodological and statistical advances and, most precious of all, time and energy (Adelman et al., 2014). For students, POR can provide unique opportunities to be involved in projects (including publications and scientific presentations) that combine clinical relevance with scientific rigor at an early phase of their career. Their participation might thus be an optimal way to achieve one of several overarching recommendations that were recently offered for the future of POR: Begin early (Castonguay et al., 2013). As stated elsewhere, "simultaneous, seamless, and repeated integration of science and practice activities as early as possible in a psychotherapist's career might create an intellectual and emotional (hopefully secure) attachment to principles and merits of the Boulder model" (Castonguay, 2011, p. 135). A research partnership that involves students, clinicians, and academicians can also lead to the creation of a pipeline for both archival and prospective data that cohorts of trainees within a university program could have access to (Adelman et al., 2014). Such pipeline, needless to say, can have long-term benefits for all stakeholders involved, let alone the field of mental health. To actualize this beneficial collaboration, universities should perhaps accept a sense of responsibility toward preparing trainees to collect and use data from clinical routine. As argued by Boswell et al. (2014):

> training programs should instill the value of collecting routine data, on both process and outcome, and using this information to inform case conceptualization and treatment planning (Castonguay, Boswell, Constantino, Goldfried, & Hill, 2010). In addition, training faculty would do well to encourage an openness to receiving progress feedback (Boswell & Castonguay, 2007), as well as encourage the use of outcomes data to answer clinically relevant research questions early on in training. (p. 11)

Networks of Networks

Seeking the engagement of students is one form of expansion that has been recommended for the growth of some partnerships. Another one is the creation of networks of networks (Castonguay, 2011). Irrespective of the clinical setting, small research-practice infrastructures will be confronted with limitations in terms of expertise, knowledge, and resources. In particular, small partnerships can be restricted in their ability to recruit large samples of clients and therapists (e.g., Adelman et al., 2014; Koerner & Castonguay, 2014), which can slow down the collection of required data and/or raise serious concerns with regard to the generalizability of research findings. One recommendation that has been offered to address these important issues is for members of specific partnerships to connect with other similar groups of partners (Castonguay et al., 2014; Koerner & Castonguay, 2014). The idea is for multiple groups of clinicians and researchers to work together in the development of a study, or for one group of partners to design an investigation and then invite therapists from other networks to join their project by implementing the protocol in their own setting. As yet another overarching recommendation for future PRNs, this has been referred elsewhere as: "work locally and collaborate globally" (Castonguay, 2011; Castonguay et al., 2013).

This network of networks is in line with Borkovec's (2002) dream of a large infrastructure of psychology training clinics, all of them linked by a shared basic assessment protocol. Interestingly, this infrastructure could provide an avenue to address a problem of "extinction" frequently observed in graduate research. As noted by Castonguay et al. (2014), many students complete graduate school without having the time and resources to fully pursue the creative research program that they began with their masters and/or dissertations. Referring to this problem as the "dusty piles in the lab" effect, they suggest that a large network of training clinics could serve as a forum of knowledge exchange and long-term collaboration, during and after graduate school.

Worldwide Collaboration

The concept of global collaboration can also be applied to connections among solo practitioners. Koerner and Castonguay (2014) have described a training initiative where clinicians from around the world are provided with expert feedback about single-case experiments to test a wide range of hypotheses and interventions in their own clinical practice. As they noted, "[t]his line of research begins to build a network of therapists and a library of open enrollment research designs and protocols that make it feasible to scale single-case designs to make meaningful contributions to the scientific literature" (p. 4). In addition to offering a perfect example of local action

and global collaboration, this training infrastructure also has the potential of fostering three other overarching recommendations for future POR (Castonguay et al., 2013). First, to be most valuable and sustainable, this type of research should address clinicians' concerns and should be designed, at least in part, based on their observations and expertise. Nothing comes closer to this recommendation than helping practitioners test interventions that they are implementing, or want to implement with their own clients. Second, it should add minimally to, or be as confounded as possible with clinical work. In this case, clinicians are simultaneously applying, learning, or refining both therapeutic and empirical skills, thereby reflecting not only a seamless clinical and research integration, but an epistemological one. Third, POR has to count. Findings obtained from naturalistic settings have to be made known to scholars and decision-makers so that the results can be taken into account in practice, training, and funding guidelines. The first step in making POR count is in dissemination, as when researchers and clinicians work together to create an open library of scientific contributions. One might also say that when they do so, they go further than building bridges between science and practice—a metaphor that suggests that clinicians and researchers live on different banks of a river and maintain connections by importing or exporting knowledge that was independently secured. Instead, by blending together their expertise and resources to directly investigate questions emerging from clinical routine, they are creating new landscapes of knowledge and action (Castonguay, 2013).

Conclusion

Building POR partnerships is for those who dream big (McAleavey et al., 2014), not only because of the amount of work required but also for the ambitious goals they embrace: Fostering rapprochements of minds, integrating research and clinical work, and improving our understanding and practice of the mental health field. In their respective pursuit of these goals, the contributors of the present series have shared their experience about the studies they have conducted, challenges they have faced, strategies they have adopted to tackle these obstacles, and benefits that they and their collaborators have gained. They have also offered general suggestions about future POR.

Additional lessons can be derived from research programs in the field of mental health that have not been represented in this series, such as the process and outcome studies by Jacqueline Persons (e.g., Persons, Roberts, Zalecki, & Brechwald, 2006) and

David Burns (e.g., Burns & Nolen-Hoeksema, 1992) in specialized cognitive therapy centers, as well the work that has been conducted within the Healthy Families America Research Practice Network (Galano & Schellenbach, 2007) on the prevention of child maltreatment (see Castonguay et al., 2013; McMillen, Lenze, Hawley, & Osbourne, 2009). Moreover, much can be learned from partnerships of practitioners and researchers in a wide range of health care and medical fields, including nursing, primary care, pediatrics, and family medicine. Nevertheless, it is hoped that the breadth of contributions and recommendations captured in the papers of this series will provide both encouragement and guidance to clinicians and researchers to conduct and use psychotherapy research in clinical routine.

As part of our attempt to integrate core features of the diverse partnerships presented in this series, we have identified a number of characteristics of successful POR. Optimally, each study or project conducted within such paradigm should be aimed at providing actionable findings, while imposing minimal level of extra work, negative consequences, and drastic changes to clinical practice. We would like to end this paper by offering our thoughts about what will make the whole enterprise of POR successful. In a most basic way, research partnerships in naturalistic settings will be judged as worthwhile, at least in our opinion, if they contribute in the reduction of the problem that we identified in the introduction of this series: The fact that research does not significantly and substantially influence practice (Castonguay & Muran, 2014). The best and most stringent way to achieve this is perhaps for POR to deliver retainable findings. Some partnership initiatives have reported that participation in research has led to changes in practice (e.g., West et al., 2014). However, more efforts will be needed to systematically ensure a feedback loop between the generation of findings and their implementation in the setting where they have been obtained (see Castonguay et al., 2014). Studies should be conducted to inform not only the field in general but also to quickly and meaningfully transform the clinical practice that has been investigated.

While research findings should, optimally, be retainable, this does not imply that they have to become the only source for clinical guidance. Clinical experience, theories, supervision, and training workshops will, as they should, remain crucial sources of influence. For example, as mentioned above, monitoring of outcome data should not be viewed as a way to replace clinical judgment, but instead, it should be used as one of several complementary tools. Similarly, the success of POR as a whole should not rest on clinicians' continued involvement in empirical studies—even those who are members of researchers–practitioners partnerships. While many therapists do seek extra training during their career, most of these experiences are time limited. And while these experiences can allow them to acquire new and usable skills, it is safe to assume that they do not lead therapists to abandon their traditional ways of practicing. The same expectations should be attached to POR. Ideally, collaborative research should be perceived as opportunities that are available to clinicians who, at different times in their career, may want to be engaged in and, as in all learning experiences, might lead to some (but by no mean complete) changes of practice. If these experiences also lead them to be more interested in research and find ways to improve their practice through the use of empirical literature then, in our eyes, POR will have fulfilled its potential.

References

Adelman, R. W., Castonguay, L. G., Kraus, D. R., & Zack, S. (2014). Conducting research and collaborating with researchers: The experience of clinicians in a residential treatment center. *Psychotherapy Research*. doi:10.1080/10503307.2014.935520

Barber, J. P. (2009). Towards a working through of some core conflicts in psychotherapy research. *Psychotherapy Research*, *19*, 1–12. doi:10.1080/10503300802609680

Barkham, M., & Margison, F. (2007). Practice-based evidence as a complement to evidence-based practice: From dichotomy to chiasmus. In C. Freeman & M. Power (Eds.), *Handbook of evidence-based psychotherapies: A guide for research and practice* (pp. 443–476). Chichester: Wiley.

Barkham, M., Stiles, W. B., Lambert, M. J., & Mellor-Clark, J. (2010). Building a rigorous and relevant knowledge-base for the psychological therapies. In M. Barkham, G. E. Hardy, & J. Mellor-Clark (Eds.), *Developing and delivering practice-based evidence: A guide for the psychological therapies* (pp. 21–61). Chichester: Wiley.

Borkovec, T. D. (2002). Training clinic research and the possibility of a national training clinics practice research network. *The Behavior Therapist*, *25*, 98–103.

Boswell, J. F., & Castonguay, L. G. (2007). Psychotherapy training: Suggestions for core ingredients and future research. *Psychotherapy: Theory, Research, Practice, and Training*, *44*, 378–383.

Boswell, J. F., Kraus, D. R., Miller, S. D., & Lambert, M. J. (2014). Implementing routine outcome monitoring in clinical practice: Benefits, challenges, and solutions. *Psychotherapy Research*. doi:10.1080/10503307.2013.817696

Burns, D. D., & Nolen-Hoeksema, S. (1992). Therapeutic empathy and recovery from depression in cognitive-behavioral therapy. *Journal of Consulting and Clinical Psychology*, *60*, 441–449. doi:10.1037/0022-006X.60.3.441.

Castonguay, L. G., Boswell, J. F., Constantino, M. J., Goldfried, M. R., & Hill, C. E. (2010). Training implications of harmful effects of psychological treatments. *American Psychologist*, *65*(1), 34–49. doi:10.1037/a0017330

Castonguay, L., Nelson, D., Boutselis, M., Chiswick, N., Damer, D., Hemmelstein, N., ... Borkovec, T. (2010). Clinicians and/or researchers? A qualitative analysis of therapists' experiences in a practice research network. *Psychotherapy: Theory, Research, Practice, and Training*, *47*, 345–354.

Castonguay, L. G. (2011). Psychotherapy, psychopathology, research and practice: Pathways of connections and integration.

Psychotherapy Research, 21(2), 125–140. doi:10.1080/10503307.2011.563250

Castonguay, L. G. (2013). Psychotherapy outcome: A problem worth re-revisiting 50 years later. *Psychotherapy: Theory, Research, Practice, and Training, 50*, 52–67.

Castonguay, L. G., Barkham, M., Lutz, W., & McAleavey, A. A. (2013). Practice-oriented research: Approaches and application. In M. J. Lambert (Eds.), *Bergin and Garfield's Handbook of psychotherapy and behavior change* (6th ed., pp. 85–133). New York, NY: Wiley.

Castonguay, L. G., & Muran, J. C. (2014). Fostering collaboration between researchers and clinicians through building practice-oriented research: An introduction. *Psychotherapy Research.*

Castonguay, L. G., Pincus, A. L., & McAleavey, A. A. (2014). Practice research network in a psychology training clinic: Building an infrastructure to foster early attachment to the scientific-practitioner model. *Psychotherapy Research.* doi:10.1080/10503307.2013.856045

Fernández-Álvarez, H., Gómez, B., & García, F. (2014). Bridging the gap between research and practice in a clinical and training network: Aigle's program. *Psychotherapy Research.* doi:10.1080/10503307.2013.856047

Galano, J., & Schellenbach, C. J. (2007). Healthy families America research practice network: A unique partnership to integrate prevention sciences and practice. *Journal of Prevention and Integration in the Community, 34*, 39–66.

Garland, A. F., & Brookman-Frazee, L. (2014). Therapists and researchers: Advancing collaboration. *Psychotherapy Research.* doi:10.1080/10503307.2013.838655

Goldfried, M. R., Newman, M., Castonguay, L. G., Fuertes. J. N., Magnavita, J. J., Sobell, L. C., & Wolf, A. W. (2014). On the dissemination of clinical experiences in using empirically supported treatments. *Behavior Therapy, 45*, 3–6. doi:10.1016/j.beth.2013.09.007

Holmqvist, R., Philips, B., & Barkham, M. (2014). Developing practice-based evidence: Benefits, challenges, and tensions. *Psychotherapy Research.* doi:10.1080/10503307.2013.861093

Hume, D. (1739). *A treatise of human nature.* London: John Noon.

Johnson, J. E. (2014). Integrating psychotherapy research with public health and public policy goals for incarcerated women and other vulnerable populations. *Psychotherapy Research, 24*, 229–239. doi:10.1080/10503307.2013.838656

Kazdin, A. E. (2008). Evidence-based treatment and practice: New opportunities to bridge clinical research and practice, enhance the knowledge base, and improve patient care. *American Psychologist, 63*, 146–159. doi:10.1037/0003-066X.63.3.146

Koerner, K., & Castonguay, L. G. (2014). Practice-oriented research: What it takes to do collaborative research in private practice. *Psychotherapy Research.* doi:10.1080/10503307.2014.939119

Koons, C. R., O'Rouke, B., Carter, B., & Erhardt, E. B. (2013). Negotiating for improved reimbursement for dialectical behavior therapy: A successful project. *Cognitive and Behavioral Practice, 20*, 314–324. doi:10.1016/j.cbpra.2013.01.003

Kraus, D. R., Castonguay, L. G., Boswell, J. F., Nordberg, S. S., & Hayes, J. A. (2011). Therapist effectiveness: Implications for accountability and patient care. *Psychotherapy Research, 21*, 267–276. doi:10.1080/10503307.2011.563249

Krug, S. (2006). *Don't make me think! A common sense approach to web usability* (2nd ed.). Berkeley, CA: New Riders.

McAleavey, A. A., Lockard, A. J., Castonguay, L. G., Hayes, J. A., & Locke, B. D. (2014). Building a practice research network: Obstacles faced and lessons learned at the Center for Collegiate Mental Health. *Psychotherapy Research.*

McMillen, J. C., Lenze, S. L., Hawley, K. M., & Osbourne, V. A. (2009). Revisiting practice based research networks as a platform for mental health services research. *Administration and Policy in Mental Health, 36*, 308–321. doi:10.1007/s10488-009-0222-2

Lambert, M. J. 2010. *Prevention of treatment failure: The use of measuring, monitoring, and feedback in clinical practice.* Washington, DC: American Psychological Association.

Lampropoulos, G. K., Goldfried, M. R., Castonguay, L. G., Lambert, M. J., Stiles, W. B., & Nestoros, J. N. (2002). What kind of research can we realistically expect from the practitioner? *Journal of Clinical Psychology, 58*, 1241–1264. doi:10.1002/jclp.10109

Persons, J. B., Roberts, N. A., Zalecki, C. A., & Brechwald, W. A. G. (2006). Naturalistic outcome of case-formulation-driven cognitive behavioral therapy for anxiety depressed outpatients. *Behaviour Research and Therapy, 44*, 1041–1051. doi:10.1016/j.brat.2005.08.005

Stiles, W. B., Barkham, M., Mellor-Clark, J., & Connell, J. (2008). Effectiveness of cognitive–behavioural, person-centred, and psychodynamic therapies in UK primary care routine practice: Replication in a larger sample. *Psychological Medicine, 38*, 677–688. doi:10.1017/S0033291707001511

Strauss, B., Lutz, W., Steffanowski, A., Wittmann, W., Böhnke, J. R., Rubel, J., …Kirchmann, H. (2014). Benefits and challenges in practice-oriented psychotherapy research in Germany: The TK and the QS-PSY-BAY projects of quality assurance in outpatient psychotherapy. *Psychotherapy Research.*

Szapocznik, J., Muir, J. A., Duff, J., & Schwartz, S. J. (2014). Brief strategic family therapy: Implementing evidence-based models in community settings. *Psychotherapy Research.*

Youn, S., Kraus, D. R., & Castonguay, L. G. (2012). Treatment outcome package: Facilitating practice and clinically relevant research. *Psychotherapy: Theory, Research, Practice, and Training, 49*, 115–122.

West, J. C., Mościcki, E. K., Duffy, F. F., Wilk, J. E., Countis, L., Narrow, W. E., & Regier, D. A. (2014). APIRE practice research network: Accomplishments, challenges, and lessons learned. *Psychotherapy Research.*

Zarin, D. A., Pincus, H. A., West, J. C., & McIntyre, J. S. (1997). Practice-based research in psychiatry. *American Journal of Psychiatry, 154*, 1199–1208.

Index